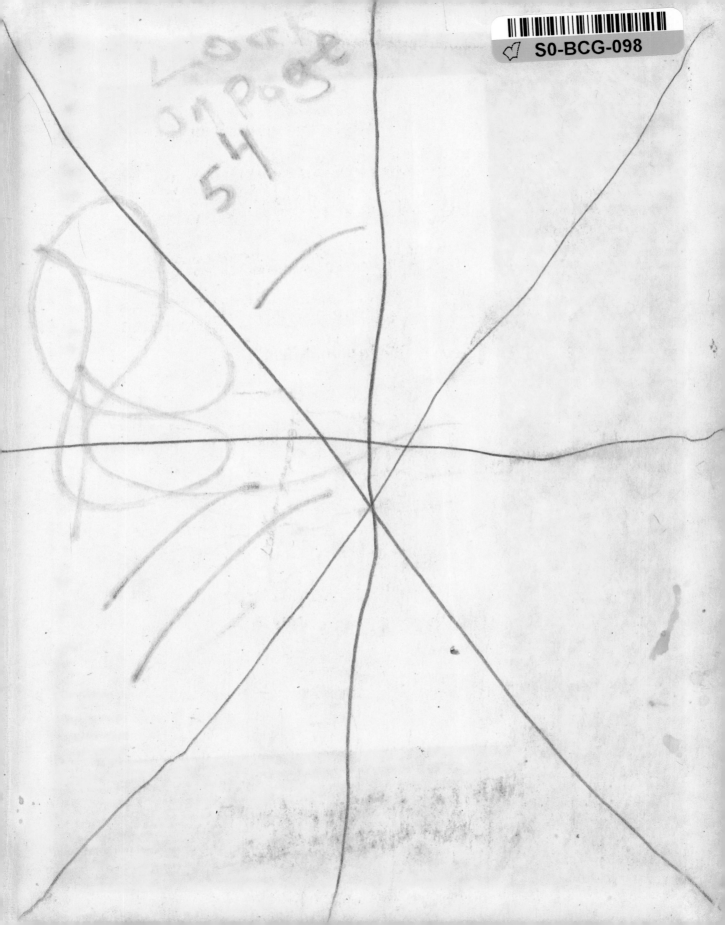

macmillan mathematics

TINA THOBURN
Senior Author

MACMILLAN PUBLISHING COMPANY
New York

COLLIER MACMILLAN PUBLISHERS
London

TEXTART, INC.

Cover Photography: Jeff Smith

Technical Art: Dave Hannum, Phil Jones, Gary Tong

Illustrations: Anthony Accardo 6, 40, 47 / Lynn Uhde Adams 204, 246 / Teresa Anderko 58, 59, 61, 67, 68, 69, 74, 75, 76, 77, 86, 87, 95, 100, 101, 111 / Daniel DelValle 22, 88, 91, 383, 386, 387, 459 / Len Ebert 98, 124 / Meryl Henderson 8, 172 / Anita Luvitt 13 / Anthony Malone 16, 18, 46 / Kim Melnazick 2, 3, 51, 96 / Verlin Miller 70, 72 / Michael O'Reilly 56, 106, 109, 134, 310 / Tom Powers 50, 102, 103, 127, 329, 354, 355 / Jan Pyk 90, 94, 174 / Bob Shein 12, 158, 326, 332 / Arthur Thompson 137 / Deb Troyer 9, 12, 114, 116, 119, 122, 126, 130, 138, 183, 184, 185, 186, 190, 194, 200, 240, 265, 266, 284, 300, 312, 363, 364, 365, 366, 368, 384, 385, 388, 458, 461 / Eva Burg Vagreti 5, 23, 24, 25, 60, 78, 92, 118, 120, 123, 128, 132, 135, 136, 146, 149, 151, 152, 156, 161, 163, 165, 166, 169, 171, 173, 175, 177, 188, 196, 198, 199, 222, 229, 230, 231, 232, 234, 235, 236, 237, 241, 242, 244, 259, 264, 267, 270, 272, 273, 274, 279, 285, 289, 302, 320, 322, 323, 324, 325, 326, 330, 334, 335, 342, 343, 344, 346, 347, 348, 350, 352, 356, 395, 460 / Sally Jo Vitsky 4, 14, 168, 304, 328 / Lane Yerkes 164, 176, 192, 206, 208, 309

Photography: Clara Aich Photography, Craig Aurness / Woodfin Camp & Associates, David Barnes / The Stock Market, Jay Brenner, Ira Block / The Image Bank, Robin Forbes / The Image Bank, Ingbert Gruttner, Craig Hammell / The Stock Market, The Image Bank, George E. Jones, Russ Kinne / Photo Researchers Inc., Paolo Koch / Photo Researchers Inc., Magnum Photo, Roy Morsch, Photo Researchers, Inc., Jim Pickerell / Black Star, Guido Alberto Rossi / The Image Bank, Shostal Associates, Taurus Photos, Tom Walker / Stock Boston, Frank Whitney / The Image Bank, Wide World Photos, Inc., Woodfin Camp.

Parts of this work were published in earlier editions of Macmillan Mathematics.

Macmillan Publishing Company
866 Third Avenue
New York, N.Y. 10022
Collier Macmillan Canada, Inc.

Printed in the United States of America

ISBN: 0-02-105960-8
9 8 7 6 5 4 3 2

Contents

5 DIVIDING BY ONES   113–144

6 TIME, MONEY, MEASUREMENT   145–182

PROBLEM SOLVING SITUATIONS   183–188

7 DIVIDING BY TENS AND ONES   189–214

8 FRACTIONS

9 ADDING AND SUBTRACTING WITH DECIMALS

10 GEOMETRY AND MEASUREMENT

FASTEST SCHEDULED PASSENGER TRAIN RUNS

Country	From	To	Distance miles	Time minutes	Speed mph
France	Macon	Monchanin	39	20	118
Japan	Nagoya	Yokohama	197	105	112
Great Britain	London	Bristol Parkway	112	66	102
Italy	Rome	Chiusi	92	65	85
United States	Rensselaer	Hudson	28	20	84
Sweden	Skvode	Laxa	52	41	77

Addition Facts

A. There are 8 adult dogs and 6 young dogs at the kennel. How many dogs are there in all?

Add to find
how many in all.

$$\begin{array}{r} 8 \\ +6 \\ \hline 14 \end{array}$$

There are 14 dogs at the kennel.

B. You can write an addition in two ways.

The numbers you add are called the **addends.** The answer is called the **sum.**

Vertical Form

$$\begin{array}{r} 9 \\ +7 \\ \hline 16 \end{array}$$ — sum

addends

Horizontal Form

9 + 7 = 16

addends   sum

TRY THESE

Add to find the sums.

1. $\begin{array}{r}9\\+6\\\hline\end{array}$	**2.** $\begin{array}{r}5\\+3\\\hline\end{array}$	**3.** $\begin{array}{r}4\\+3\\\hline\end{array}$	**4.** $\begin{array}{r}7\\+7\\\hline\end{array}$	**5.** $\begin{array}{r}2\\+2\\\hline\end{array}$	**6.** $\begin{array}{r}6\\+9\\\hline\end{array}$	**7.** $\begin{array}{r}7\\+0\\\hline\end{array}$

8. 9 + 3 =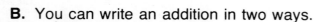

9. 2 + 8 = ■

10. 5 + 7 = ■

11. 5 + 6 = ■

12. 6 + 4 = ■

13. 3 + 3 = ■

Add.

1. 6
   +7

2. 5
   +8

3. 4
   +7

4. 9
   +9

5. 4
   +0

6. 7
   +5

7. 3
   +8

8. 9
   +2

9. 8
   +2

10. 7
    +4

11. 6
    +5

12. 8
    +4

13. 7
    +9

14. 2
    +5

15. 2
    +9

16. 5
    +9

17. 9
    +8

18. 3
    +9

19. 7
    +3

20. 5
    +5

21. 9
    +1

22. 8
    +3

23. 5
    +1

24. 9
    +4

25. 2
    +4

26. 7
    +6

27. 8
    +8

28. 6
    +8

29. 6
    +6

30. 4
    +4

31. 7
    +8

32. 8
    +1

33. 3
    +6

34. 9
    +0

35. 1
    +7

36. 6
    +2

37. 8
    +7

38. 7
    +2

39. 8
    +9

40. 9
    +5

41. 1
    +8

42. 2
    +6

43. $4 + 8 =$ ▨

44. $3 + 9 =$ ▨

45. $0 + 0 =$ ▨

46. $8 + 5 =$ ▨

47. $4 + 6 =$ ▨

48. $3 + 7 =$ ▨

49. Add 5 and 4.

50. Find the sum of 6 and 3.

51. One addend is 7. The other addend is 8. What is the sum?

★52. One addend is 3. The sum is 11. What is the other addend?

★53. One addend is 6. The sum is 13. What is the other addend?

THINK!

Following Instructions

Find the name of the kennel.

1. Write the eleventh letter of the alphabet.

2. Find the sum of $4 + 5$.

K-NINE

Subtraction Facts

A. Julius kept 16 pigeons
on his roof. 7 pigeons
flew away. How many pigeons
does Julius have now?

> **Subtract** to find how many
> are left after 7 pigeons
> flew away.

$$\begin{array}{r} 16 \\ -\ 7 \\ \hline 9 \end{array}$$

Julius has 9 pigeons left.

B. You can write a subtraction in two ways.

The answer to a subtraction is called
the **difference.**

Vertical Form

$$\begin{array}{r} 12 \\ -\ 5 \\ \hline 7 \end{array} \longleftarrow \text{difference}$$

Horizontal Form

$$12 - 5 = 7$$
$$\uparrow$$
difference

TRY THESE

Subtract to find the differences.

1. $\begin{array}{r} 13 \\ -\ 5 \\ \hline \end{array}$
2. $\begin{array}{r} 17 \\ -\ 8 \\ \hline \end{array}$
3. $\begin{array}{r} 6 \\ -6 \\ \hline \end{array}$
4. $\begin{array}{r} 16 \\ -\ 9 \\ \hline \end{array}$
5. $\begin{array}{r} 12 \\ -\ 4 \\ \hline \end{array}$
6. $\begin{array}{r} 16 \\ -\ 8 \\ \hline \end{array}$
7. $\begin{array}{r} 11 \\ -\ 3 \\ \hline \end{array}$

8. $15 - 9 = \blacksquare$ **9.** $11 - 4 = \blacksquare$ **10.** $16 - 7 = \blacksquare$

11. $11 - 7 = \blacksquare$ **12.** $7 - 0 = \blacksquare$ **13.** $12 - 5 = \blacksquare$

SKILLS PRACTICE _____

Subtract.

1. $\begin{array}{r} 11 \\ -\ 3 \\ \hline \end{array}$	**2.** $\begin{array}{r} 7 \\ -4 \\ \hline \end{array}$	**3.** $\begin{array}{r} 12 \\ -\ 6 \\ \hline \end{array}$	**4.** $\begin{array}{r} 8 \\ -0 \\ \hline \end{array}$	**5.** $\begin{array}{r} 11 \\ -\ 9 \\ \hline \end{array}$	**6.** $\begin{array}{r} 14 \\ -\ 8 \\ \hline \end{array}$	**7.** $\begin{array}{r} 8 \\ -1 \\ \hline \end{array}$
8. $\begin{array}{r} 10 \\ -\ 4 \\ \hline \end{array}$	**9.** $\begin{array}{r} 11 \\ -\ 7 \\ \hline \end{array}$	**10.** $\begin{array}{r} 14 \\ -\ 9 \\ \hline \end{array}$	**11.** $\begin{array}{r} 15 \\ -\ 8 \\ \hline \end{array}$	**12.** $\begin{array}{r} 12 \\ -\ 7 \\ \hline \end{array}$	**13.** $\begin{array}{r} 7 \\ -\ 7 \\ \hline \end{array}$	**14.** $\begin{array}{r} 11 \\ -\ 2 \\ \hline \end{array}$
15. $\begin{array}{r} 10 \\ -\ 6 \\ \hline \end{array}$	**16.** $\begin{array}{r} 13 \\ -\ 4 \\ \hline \end{array}$	**17.** $\begin{array}{r} 11 \\ -\ 8 \\ \hline \end{array}$	**18.** $\begin{array}{r} 0 \\ -0 \\ \hline \end{array}$	**19.** $\begin{array}{r} 12 \\ -\ 8 \\ \hline \end{array}$	**20.** $\begin{array}{r} 8 \\ -5 \\ \hline \end{array}$	**21.** $\begin{array}{r} 9 \\ -7 \\ \hline \end{array}$
22. $\begin{array}{r} 17 \\ -\ 9 \\ \hline \end{array}$	**23.** $\begin{array}{r} 6 \\ -5 \\ \hline \end{array}$	**24.** $\begin{array}{r} 10 \\ -\ 5 \\ \hline \end{array}$	**25.** $\begin{array}{r} 8 \\ -7 \\ \hline \end{array}$	**26.** $\begin{array}{r} 7 \\ -5 \\ \hline \end{array}$	**27.** $\begin{array}{r} 12 \\ -\ 9 \\ \hline \end{array}$	**28.** $\begin{array}{r} 7 \\ -3 \\ \hline \end{array}$

29. $11 - 6 = \blacksquare$ **30.** $14 - 5 = \blacksquare$ **31.** $18 - 9 = \blacksquare$

32. $8 - 4 = \blacksquare$ **33.** $13 - 9 = \blacksquare$ **34.** $9 - 0 = \blacksquare$

Add or subtract.

35. $\begin{array}{r} 7 \\ +6 \\ \hline \end{array}$	**36.** $\begin{array}{r} 10 \\ -\ 8 \\ \hline \end{array}$	**37.** $\begin{array}{r} 15 \\ -\ 6 \\ \hline \end{array}$	**38.** $\begin{array}{r} 8 \\ +4 \\ \hline \end{array}$	**39.** $\begin{array}{r} 13 \\ -\ 7 \\ \hline \end{array}$	**40.** $\begin{array}{r} 14 \\ -\ 6 \\ \hline \end{array}$	**41.** $\begin{array}{r} 9 \\ +4 \\ \hline \end{array}$

42. $15 - 7 = \blacksquare$ **43.** $9 + 9 = \blacksquare$ **44.** $12 - 3 = \blacksquare$

45. Subtract 9 from 12. **46.** Find the difference of 15 and 8.

47. What is the difference in this subtraction fact? $10 - 7 = \blacksquare$

★**48.** Subtract a number from itself. What is the difference?

★**49.** One number is 7. The difference is 0. What is the other number?

THINK!

Fact Patterns

These subtraction facts have the same difference.

$15 - 9 = \blacksquare$ $6 - 0 = \blacksquare$

How many other basic subtraction facts have the same difference as the two facts above? Write them.

Addition and Subtraction Properties: Mental Math

Addition properties help you find sums quickly.

Subtraction properties help you find differences quickly.

Order + Property

You can change the order of addends. The sum is the same.

$$7 + 9 = 16$$
$$9 + 7 = 16$$

★Subtraction does not have an order property!

$$12 - 4 = 8,$$

but $4 - 12$ is not 8!

Zero + − Properties

When 0 is an addend, the sum is the other addend.

$$6 + 0 = 6$$
$$0 + 6 = 6$$

Any number minus zero is that same number.

$$6 - 0 = 6$$

Any number minus itself is zero.

$$6 - 6 = 0$$

Grouping + Property

You can group addends different ways. The sum is the same.

$$(6 + 2) + 7 = \blacksquare$$
$$8 \quad + 7 = 15$$

$$6 + (2 + 7) = \blacksquare$$
$$6 + \quad 9 \quad = 15$$

★Subtraction does not have a grouping property!

$$(14 - 8) - 3 = \blacksquare$$
$$6 \quad - 3 = 3$$

$$14 - (8 - 3) = \blacksquare$$
$$14 - \quad 5 \quad = 9$$

Not the same

Inverse + − Property

Subtraction undoes addition.

$$7 + 5 = 12$$
$$12 - 5 = 7$$

Addition undoes subtraction.

$$\begin{array}{r} 17 \\ -\ 8 \\ \hline 9 \end{array} \qquad \begin{array}{r} 9 \\ +\ 8 \\ \hline 17 \end{array} ✔$$

Add to check subtraction.

TRY THESE

Find the sums. Think about properties.

1. $\begin{array}{r} 6 \\ +3 \\ \hline \end{array}$ **2.** $\begin{array}{r} 3 \\ +6 \\ \hline \end{array}$ **3.** $\begin{array}{r} 2 \\ +0 \\ \hline \end{array}$ **4.** $\begin{array}{r} 0 \\ +8 \\ \hline \end{array}$ **5.** $\begin{array}{r} 3 \\ 1 \\ +6 \\ \hline \end{array}$ **6.** $\begin{array}{r} 2 \\ 5 \\ +4 \\ \hline \end{array}$ **7.** $\begin{array}{r} 5 \\ 3 \\ +6 \\ \hline \end{array}$

Find the differences. Check your answers.

8. $\begin{array}{r} 6 \\ -6 \\ \hline \end{array}$ **9.** $\begin{array}{r} 3 \\ -3 \\ \hline \end{array}$ **10.** $\begin{array}{r} 0 \\ -0 \\ \hline \end{array}$ **11.** $\begin{array}{r} 5 \\ -0 \\ \hline \end{array}$ **12.** $\begin{array}{r} 8 \\ -0 \\ \hline \end{array}$ **13.** $\begin{array}{r} 14 \\ -\,6 \\ \hline \end{array}$ **14.** $\begin{array}{r} 16 \\ -\,7 \\ \hline \end{array}$

Complete the number sentences.

15. $6 + 7 = \blacksquare$ **16.** $7 - \blacksquare = 0$ **17.** $3 - \blacksquare = 3$ **18.** $2 + 5 + 3 = \blacksquare$

SKILLS PRACTICE

Add.

1. $\begin{array}{r} 1 \\ +5 \\ \hline \end{array}$ **2.** $\begin{array}{r} 0 \\ +4 \\ \hline \end{array}$ **3.** $\begin{array}{r} 7 \\ +3 \\ \hline \end{array}$ **4.** $\begin{array}{r} 9 \\ +0 \\ \hline \end{array}$ **5.** $\begin{array}{r} 6 \\ +6 \\ \hline \end{array}$ **6.** $\begin{array}{r} 8 \\ +9 \\ \hline \end{array}$ **7.** $\begin{array}{r} 3 \\ +7 \\ \hline \end{array}$

Subtract.

8. $\begin{array}{r} 14 \\ -\,8 \\ \hline \end{array}$ **9.** $\begin{array}{r} 12 \\ -\,3 \\ \hline \end{array}$ **10.** $\begin{array}{r} 5 \\ -0 \\ \hline \end{array}$ **11.** $\begin{array}{r} 11 \\ -\,4 \\ \hline \end{array}$ **12.** $\begin{array}{r} 16 \\ -\,8 \\ \hline \end{array}$ **13.** $\begin{array}{r} 7 \\ -7 \\ \hline \end{array}$ **14.** $\begin{array}{r} 14 \\ -\,9 \\ \hline \end{array}$

Complete the number sentences.

15. $0 + 7 = \blacksquare$ **16.** $8 + \blacksquare = 15$ **17.** $6 + 2 + 5 = \blacksquare$ **18.** $5 - \blacksquare = 5$

19. $9 - \blacksquare = 0$ ★**20.** $72 + 0 = \blacksquare$ ★**21.** $137 - 137 = \blacksquare$ ★**22.** $85 - 0 = \blacksquare$

MIXED REVIEW

Add or subtract.

1. $\begin{array}{r} 5 \\ +4 \\ \hline \end{array}$ **2.** $\begin{array}{r} 13 \\ -\,4 \\ \hline \end{array}$ **3.** $\begin{array}{r} 9 \\ +5 \\ \hline \end{array}$ **4.** $\begin{array}{r} 7 \\ +8 \\ \hline \end{array}$ **5.** $\begin{array}{r} 17 \\ -\,9 \\ \hline \end{array}$ **6.** $\begin{array}{r} 2 \\ +9 \\ \hline \end{array}$ **7.** $\begin{array}{r} 7 \\ -0 \\ \hline \end{array}$

8. $\begin{array}{r} 8 \\ -8 \\ \hline \end{array}$ **9.** $\begin{array}{r} 9 \\ +6 \\ \hline \end{array}$ **10.** $\begin{array}{r} 13 \\ -\,4 \\ \hline \end{array}$ **11.** $\begin{array}{r} 18 \\ -\,9 \\ \hline \end{array}$ **12.** $\begin{array}{r} 5 \\ +6 \\ \hline \end{array}$ **13.** $\begin{array}{r} 14 \\ -\,7 \\ \hline \end{array}$ **14.** $\begin{array}{r} 8 \\ +5 \\ \hline \end{array}$

Problem Solving

A 5-Step Plan

Use these five steps to help
you solve problems.

1 Read the problem.

Lisa found 7 orange tennis balls.
Then she found 5 yellow tennis balls.
How many tennis balls does
Lisa have now?

2 Plan what to do.

I need to
find how many
tennis balls
in all.

7 Orange:

5 Yellow:

} in all

ADD to find how many in all.

7 + 5 = ▪

3 Do the arithmetic.

$$7 + 5 = 12$$

4 Give the answer.

Lisa has 12 tennis balls now.

5 Check your answer.

Use the Order Property.

$$5 + 7 = 12$$

TRY THESE

1. Jana had 15 tennis balls. She lost 6
of them. How many tennis balls did
she have left?

2. Luis has 4 wood golf clubs and 4
iron clubs. He plans to buy 3 more
wood clubs. How many clubs will
he have in all?

PROBLEM SOLVING PRACTICE

Use the five steps to solve each problem.

1. The track coach bought 5 medium uniforms and 8 small uniforms. How many uniforms did he buy?

2. The sport shop had 17 hats in stock. It sold 9 hats today. How many hats are left?

3. The tennis club had 15 rackets. It sent 6 rackets away for new strings. How many rackets are left?

4. Orrin had $14. After buying a pair of bowling shoes, he had $6 left. How much did the shoes cost?

5. Pete kicked 3 goals in the first half of the soccer game. He kicked 4 goals in the second half. How many goals did he kick in all?

6. The cafeteria cooked 12 kilograms of chicken. At lunch, 7 kilograms of chicken were eaten. How many kilograms were left?

7. Darlene paid $2 for a can of tennis balls at the discount store and $3 for a can at the sport shop. How much money did she spend in all?

8. A group of campers caught 2 trout on Monday, 5 trout on Tuesday, and 4 trout on Wednesday. How many trout did they catch in all?

9. Wilma rented a rowboat for $5. The next day she rented a sailboat for $7. How much money did she spend to rent the two boats?

10. Tony rode his bike 4 kilometers in the morning and 6 kilometers after school. How many kilometers did he ride in all?

★11. Seven members of the track team drank orange juice and eight members drank grapefruit juice. The rest drank milk. How many drank juice?

★12. Cathy ran a total of 10 kilometers in three days. She ran 3 kilometers the first day and 4 kilometers the second day. How far did she run the third day?

ON YOUR OWN

Make up a word problem for each number sentence.

1. $3 + 8 = $ ■   **2.** $13 - 7 = $ ■   **3.** $5 + 4 + 3 = $ ■

Problem Solving

Uses of Subtraction

Subtraction can be used to answer many questions.

A. A ship has 15 crew members.
This morning, 7 crew members
have gone ashore. How many
members remain on the ship?

	Check.
15	8
−7	+7
8	15

There are 8 members remaining.

B. A sailing ship has 13 sails.
8 sails are already up.
How many sails are not up?

	Check.
13	5
−8	+8
5	13 ✔

There are 5 sails not up.

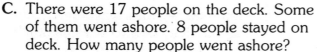

C. There were 17 people on the deck. Some
of them went ashore. 8 people stayed on
deck. How many people went ashore?

$$\begin{array}{r} 17 \\ -\ 8 \\ \hline 9 \end{array}$$

There were 9 people
who went ashore.

D. It costs $12 to dock the ship. The captain
has $6. How much more does he need?

$$\begin{array}{r} \$12 \\ -\ 6 \\ \hline \$\ 6 \end{array}$$

He needs $6.

E. The line for one anchor is 13 meters long.
The line for another is 9 meters long. How
much shorter is the second line?

$$\begin{array}{r} 13 \\ -9 \\ \hline 4 \end{array}$$

The second line is 4
meters shorter.

Solve the problems. Would you add or subtract?

1. A sailboat had 9 flags. 3 of the flags were lost. How many flags were left?

2. A store had 8 motorboats on sale yesterday. Today there are 3 left. How many were sold?

3. One sailor has 18 meters of rope. Another sailor has 9 meters of rope. How much more rope does the first sailor have?

4. Juan spent $6 at the dock. Susan spent $9 at the dock. How much money did they both spend at the dock?

PROBLEM SOLVING PRACTICE

Add or subtract. Use the five steps to solve each problem.

1. A store has 18 boating T-shirts. The boating club members buy 9 T-shirts. How many T-shirts are left?

2. The boating club has 15 members. The club owns 7 life jackets. How many more life jackets are needed?

3. The club rented 10 boats on Saturday and 8 boats on Sunday. How many more boats did the club rent on Saturday?

4. There were 9 portholes on the left side of the boat and 8 portholes on the right. How many portholes were there in all?

5. One sailor used 3 meters of rope to make knots. Another sailor used 9 meters of rope. How much more rope did the second sailor use?

6. Saturday morning there were 5 sailboats at dock B. At noon 3 of them sailed. How many were left at the dock?

7. There were 4 sailboats at dock A and 5 sailboats at dock B. How many sailboats in all were at dock A and dock B?

8. A speedboat ride costs $8. A sailboat ride costs $11. How much more does the sailboat ride cost?

9. The members of the sailing club collected $8 in dues last week. They need $17 to rent a large boat. How much more money do they need?

★10. There were 18 boats at the starting line at 3 o'clock. 9 of them had their sails up. How many boats did not have their sails up?

ON YOUR OWN

Make up a word problem for each number sentence.

1. $14 - 8 = $ ■

2. $17 - 9 = $ ■

3. $\$15 - \$8 = $ ■

Problem Solving Strategy

Draw a Picture

Sometimes drawing a picture will help you to solve a problem.

Four boys got to a concert at different times. They stood in line to buy tickets. Ben was ahead of Jim in line. Jim was 2 places behind Tom. Al was ahead of Jim but not ahead of Tom. Who bought the first ticket? In what order were the rest of the boys standing in line?

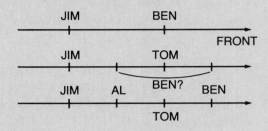

Ben was first, followed by Tom, Al, and Jim.

Solve these problems. Draw a picture to help you.

1. In an art display, a Van Gogh is two places to the left of a Corot and next to a Degas. A Monet is next to the Corot. A Toulouse-Lautrec is in the middle. List the art from left to right. **Degas, Van Gogh, Toulouse-Lautrec, Corot, Monet**

2. Four girls also attended the concert. Ann is taller than Lynn. Vicki is also taller than Lynn, but not as tall as Jane. Jane is almost as tall as Ann. Arrange the girls in order from tallest to shortest. **Ann, Jane, Vicki, Lynn**

3. At the concert a Mozart symphony was played before a Brahms concerto. A Beethoven suite was played after the Mozart symphony. There was an intermission before the Brahms. Ravel's *Bolero* concluded the concert. The same number of compositions were played before and after the intermission. In what order were the compositions played? **Mozart, Beethoven, Brahms, Ravel**

4. In the foyer of the concert hall there is a display of jewels used in costumes. The ruby is two places after the sapphire. A pearl is two places before the sapphire. An emerald is three spaces after the pearl. There is a garnet between the pearl and the sapphire. A diamond is four spaces after the garnet. Show the order of the jewels on display. **pearl, garnet, sapphire, emerald, ruby, diamond**

Challenge Problems page 457

Problem Solving Project

Collecting and Organizing Data

Hal asked the students in his class what they like to do after school. They chose jogging, computer club, swimming, drama club, or crafts. Hal recorded each student's answer in a table with a **tally mark** (/). Tallies are written in groups of 5 (////).

ACTIVITY	TALLY	NUMBER
Jogging	//// /	6
Computer Club	///	3
Swimming	//// ////	9
Drama Club	////	5
Crafts	//// ///	8

To complete the table, Hal wrote the number of students who chose each activity. He also made a **bar graph** from his data.

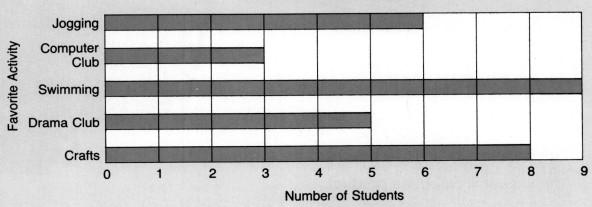

AFTER-SCHOOL ACTIVITIES

1. How many students liked swimming?

2. How many students liked crafts?

3. Did more students like computer club or crafts?

4. Did more students like jogging or drama club?

5. Which activity was chosen by the greatest number of students?

6. Which activity was chosen by 3 students?

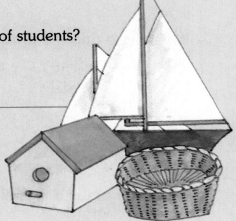

ON YOUR OWN

Data Search

Think of 5 or 6 after-school activities.
Ask your classmates which activity they prefer.
Make a tally table and a bar graph from your data.

13

Multiplication Facts

A. Adam has 4 rolls of film. He can take 8 photographs with each roll. How many photographs can he take in all?

Multiply to find how many in all when each set has the same number.

$$\begin{array}{r} 8 \\ \times 4 \\ \hline 32 \end{array}$$

Adam can take 32 photographs in all.

B. You can write a multiplication in two ways.

Vertical Form	Horizontal Form

$$\begin{array}{r} 3 \\ \times 9 \\ \hline 27 \end{array}$$ —— factors ... product

$9 \times 3 = 27$

factors product

The numbers you multiply are called the **factors.**

The answer is called the **product.**

C. A product is a **multiple** of each of its factors.
27 is a multiple of 9 and of 3.
Some other multiples of 9 are 0, 9, and 18.

TRY THESE

Multiply to find the products.

1. $\begin{array}{r} 7 \\ \times 7 \end{array}$
2. $\begin{array}{r} 8 \\ \times 0 \end{array}$
3. $\begin{array}{r} 2 \\ \times 5 \end{array}$
4. $\begin{array}{r} 9 \\ \times 6 \end{array}$
5. $\begin{array}{r} 2 \\ \times 8 \end{array}$
6. $\begin{array}{r} 8 \\ \times 7 \end{array}$
7. $\begin{array}{r} 9 \\ \times 9 \end{array}$

8. $7 \times 9 =$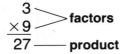
9. $6 \times 6 =$ ■
10. $9 \times 1 =$ ■

11. $5 \times 4 =$ ■
12. $0 \times 7 =$ ■
13. $4 \times 8 =$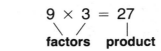

14. Name five multiples of 2.
15. Name five multiples of 7.

Multiply

1. 7
×5

2. 5
×9

3. 4
×7

4. 3
×6

5. 0
×0

6. 8
×3

7. 5
×5

8. 3
×7

9. 5
×0

10. 6
×5

11. 7
×4

12. 8
×5

13. 4
×9

14. 7
×8

15. 6
×2

16. 7
×3

17. 2
×8

18. 8
×6

19. 2
×9

20. 5
×8

21. 4
×0

22. 1
×8

23. 5
×4

24. 7
×9

25. 6
×7

26. 2
×3

27. 4
×6

28. 4
×8

29. $5 \times 7 = $ ■

30. $9 \times 4 = $ ■

31. $4 \times 6 = $ ■

32. $7 \times 9 = $ ■

33. $7 \times 6 = $ ■

34. $3 \times 5 = $ ■

35. $6 \times 8 = $ ■

36. $9 \times 8 = $ ■

37. $8 \times 8 = $ ■

38. Multiply 6 times 7.

39. Find the product of 3 and 8.

40. One factor is 9. The other factor is 7. What is the product?

41. Name five multiples of 4.

★42. One factor is 2. The product is 14. What is the other factor?

★43. 8 is a multiple of what numbers?

Logical Reasoning

1. This picture frame is 8 inches by 10 inches. How many snapshots that are 4 inches by 5 inches can you fit in it?

2. What size frame would you need to hold six pictures that are 3 inches by 4 inches?

Multiplication Properties: Mental Math

You can use a special property of multiplication and addition to help find products.

Order Property	$\begin{array}{r} 7 \\ \times 5 \\ \hline 35 \end{array}$	$\begin{array}{r} 5 \\ \times 7 \\ \hline 35 \end{array}$	You can multiply in either order. The product does not change.
Property of One	$\begin{array}{r} 8 \\ \times 1 \\ \hline 8 \end{array}$	$\begin{array}{r} 1 \\ \times 8 \\ \hline 8 \end{array}$	If one factor is 1, the product equals the other factor.
Property of Zero	$\begin{array}{r} 0 \\ \times 6 \\ \hline 0 \end{array}$	$\begin{array}{r} 6 \\ \times 0 \\ \hline 0 \end{array}$	If one factor is 0, the product equals 0.

Grouping Property

$3 \times 2 \times 4 = \blacksquare$
$6 \times 4 = 24$

You can group factors in different ways.
The product does not change.

$3 \times 2 \times 4 = \blacksquare$
$3 \times 8 = 24$

Distributive Property

$2 \times (3 + 5) = \blacksquare$
$2 \times 8 = 16$

When one factor is a sum, you can add and then multiply.

$(2 \times 3) + (2 \times 5) = \blacksquare$
$6 + 10 = 16$

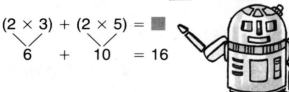

Or, you can multiply each addend and then add the products.

TRY THESE

Find the products.

1. $\begin{array}{r} 9 \\ \times 4 \\ \hline \end{array}$	**2.** $\begin{array}{r} 4 \\ \times 9 \\ \hline \end{array}$	**3.** $\begin{array}{r} 1 \\ \times 2 \\ \hline \end{array}$	**4.** $\begin{array}{r} 9 \\ \times 1 \\ \hline \end{array}$	**5.** $\begin{array}{r} 0 \\ \times 8 \\ \hline \end{array}$	**6.** $\begin{array}{r} 4 \\ \times 0 \\ \hline \end{array}$	**7.** $\begin{array}{r} 0 \\ \times 0 \\ \hline \end{array}$

Complete the number sentences.

8. $7 \times 6 = \blacksquare$

9. $9 \times 6 = \blacksquare$

10. $3 \times 2 \times 3 = \blacksquare$

11. $4 \times (3 + 1) = \blacksquare$

12. $3 \times (5 + 2) = \blacksquare$

13. $2 \times (4 + 3) = \blacksquare$

SKILLS PRACTICE _____

Multiply.

1. 1
   ×6

2. 8
   ×8

3. 0
   ×3

4. 5
   ×9

5. 7
   ×6

6. 4
   ×8

7. 0
   ×2

8. 6
   ×9

9. 5
   ×7

10. 4
    ×5

11. 9
    ×9

12. 0
    ×7

13. 5
    ×8

14. 1
    ×9

15. 8
    ×9

16. 9
    ×1

17. 8
    ×3

18. 5
    ×4

19. 7
    ×8

20. 0
    ×5

21. 9
    ×3

22. 3
    ×8

23. 9
    ×5

24. 7
    ×4

25. 6
    ×8

26. 6
    ×7

27. 8
    ×0

28. 3
    ×3

29. 7
    ×3

30. 5
    ×5

31. 2
    ×8

32. 7
    ×1

33. 5
    ×0

34. 9
    ×8

35. 6
    ×6

Complete the number sentences.

36. $6 \times 5 = \blacksquare$

37. $8 \times \blacksquare = 48$

38. $\blacksquare \times 7 = 56$

39. $3 \times 6 = \blacksquare$

40. $7 \times 1 \times 0 = \blacksquare$

41. $3 \times 2 \times 2 = \blacksquare$

42. $6 \times 1 \times 2 = \blacksquare$

43. $5 \times (1 + 1) = \blacksquare$

44. $2 \times (1 + 8) = \blacksquare$

45. $8 \times \blacksquare = 0$

46. $\blacksquare \times 3 = 3$

47. $7 \times 4 = 4 \times \blacksquare$

★48. $1 \times 389 = \blacksquare$

★49. $0 \times 462 = \blacksquare$

★50. $24 \times 77 = 77 \times \blacksquare$

★51. $6 \times (8 + 7) = \blacksquare$

★52. What number times 7 equals 63?

MIXED REVIEW

Add, subtract, or multiply.

1. 8
   +7

2. 5
   ×5

3. 16
   − 7

4. 9
   ×7

5. 7
   +8

6. 14
   − 8

7. 6
   ×6

8. $17 - 9 = \blacksquare$

9. $3 + 0 + 5 = \blacksquare$

10. $7 \times 0 \times 2 = \blacksquare$

Problem Solving Strategy

Choosing the Operation

When you plan how to solve a problem,
think carefully what operation to use.

A. The baseball manager spent $9 for
a bat and $8 for a glove. How
much money did she spend?

> **Add** to find
> the total amount.

$$\begin{array}{r} \$9 \\ +\ 8 \\ \hline \$17 \end{array}$$

The manager spent $17.

B. The store sells baseballs for $3
each. The coach wants to buy 6
baseballs. How much money does
he need?

> **Multiply** to find
> the total amount
> when each ball
> costs the same.

$$\begin{array}{r} \$3 \\ \times\ 6 \\ \hline \$18 \end{array}$$

The coach needs $18.

C. The coach gave the umpire all but
2 of the 6 baseballs he bought.
How many baseballs did he give to
the umpire?

> **Subtract** to find
> how many he gave.

$$\begin{array}{r} 6 \\ -2 \\ \hline 4 \end{array}$$

He gave 4 baseballs to the umpire.

TRY THESE

Choose the operation. Then solve.

1. An assembly line produces 8 pitching machines a day. How many pitching machines can 5 lines produce?

2. The school bought 8 baseball gloves last year and 9 gloves this year. How many gloves did the school buy in all?

3. Tracy had $9. She bought a baseball bat for $5. How much money did she have left?

4. Each team member received 4 free passes to each home game. There were 9 home games. How many passes did each member receive?

PROBLEM SOLVING PRACTICE

Choose the operation and solve.

1. A ticket to a soccer game costs $3. How much do 7 tickets cost?

2. A bike basket costs $5. How much do 3 baskets cost?

3. 5 tennis courts are being used. There are 4 players on each court. How many people are playing?

4. 2 wrestlers wrestle on each mat. 5 mats are being used. How many wrestlers are wrestling?

5. Each hockey team has 6 players. How many players do 7 teams have?

6. Each roller skate has 4 wheels. How many wheels are on 8 skates?

7. It costs $6 to rent skis, $3 to rent boots, and $1 for poles. How much does it cost in all to rent this equipment?

8. There were 8 baseball games on Tuesday and 7 baseball games on Wednesday. How many baseball games were there in all?

9. In 1891, the first basketball team had 9 players. Today, basketball teams have 5 players. How many more players were on the first basketball team?

★10. A ski lift ticket costs $9 for skiers over 12. It costs $7 for skiers under 12. How much do 3 "over 12" tickets cost? How much do 4 "under 12" tickets cost?

ON YOUR OWN

Make up a word problem for each number sentence.

1. $8 \times 5 = $ ▉

2. $8 + 5 = $ ▉

3. $8 - 5 = $ ▉

Division Facts

A. Paula has 12 balls of yarn. She needs 3 balls to make a sweater. How many sweaters can Paula make?

Divide to find *how many sets* when you know the number in all and the number in each set.

$$12 \div 3 = \blacksquare$$

in all   in each   sets
set

12 in all
3 in each set
$\blacksquare$ sets

Think multiplication.

$$\blacksquare \times 3 = 12$$

sets   in each   in all
set

Find the missing factor.

$$4 \times 3 = 12$$
$$\text{So,} \quad 12 \div 3 = 4.$$

Paula can make 4 sweaters.

B. You can write a division fact two ways.

$$18 \div 9 = 2 \qquad 9\overline{)18}^{\,2}$$

C. The numbers in a division fact have special names.

$$18 \div 9 = 2$$

Dividend Divisor Quotient

Divisor $9\overline{)18}$ Dividend   2 Quotient

TRY THESE

Divide. Find the missing factor.

1. 24 in all. 6 in each set.
   How many sets?

   $24 \div 6 = \blacksquare$ $\blacksquare \times 6 = 24$

2. 32 in all. 4 in each set.
   How many sets?

   $32 \div 4 = \blacksquare$ $\blacksquare \times 4 = 32$

Divide. Name the dividend, divisor, and quotient in each.

3. $3\overline{)9}$ 4. $8\overline{)40}$ 5. $7\overline{)14}$ 6. $9\overline{)36}$ 7. $4\overline{)28}$ 8. $6\overline{)36}$

SKILLS PRACTICE

Divide.

1. $2\overline{)14}$ 2. $4\overline{)16}$ 3. $3\overline{)15}$ 4. $5\overline{)30}$ 5. $6\overline{)18}$ 6. $7\overline{)42}$

7. $6\overline{)54}$ 8. $5\overline{)25}$ 9. $7\overline{)21}$ 10. $9\overline{)27}$ 11. $8\overline{)32}$ 12. $9\overline{)18}$

13. $4\overline{)8}$ 14. $3\overline{)24}$ 15. $5\overline{)45}$ 16. $8\overline{)48}$ 17. $4\overline{)36}$ 18. $7\overline{)28}$

19. $6\overline{)48}$ 20. $7\overline{)35}$ 21. $2\overline{)10}$ 22. $7\overline{)63}$ 23. $5\overline{)40}$ 24. $8\overline{)24}$

25. $4\overline{)12}$ 26. $8\overline{)16}$ 27. $9\overline{)81}$ 28. $5\overline{)10}$ 29. $2\overline{)12}$ 30. $8\overline{)64}$

31. $7\overline{)49}$ 32. $4\overline{)24}$ 33. $9\overline{)72}$ 34. $8\overline{)56}$ 35. $3\overline{)12}$ 36. $9\overline{)54}$

37. $6 \div 2 = \blacksquare$ 38. $28 \div 4 = \blacksquare$ 39. $45 \div 9 = \blacksquare$

40. $42 \div 6 = \blacksquare$ 41. $27 \div 3 = \blacksquare$ 42. $63 \div 9 = \blacksquare$

43. Find 30 divided by 6.

44. Find 56 divided by 7.

45. The divisor is 3. The dividend is 24. What is the quotient?

46. The divisor is 8. The dividend is 72. What is the quotient?

★47. The divisor is 9. The quotient is 4. What is the dividend?

★48. The dividend is 35. The quotient is 7. What is the divisor?

THINK!

Find the Rule

What does ∗ mean? Try to guess the rule. Then complete the number sentences.

$2 * 6 = 10$ $5 * 4 = 18$
$6 * 7 = 40$ $9 * 3 = 25$

1. $2 * 5 = \blacksquare$ 2. $6 * 1 = \blacksquare$

3. $7 * 8 = \blacksquare$ 4. $8 * 4 = \blacksquare$

Division Properties: Mental Math

You can use division properties to help find quotients.

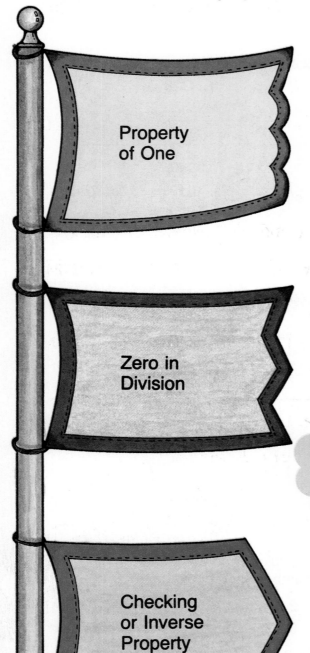

Property of One

Zero in Division

Checking or Inverse Property

When you divide by 1, the quotient is the same as the divisor.

$$9 \div 1 = 9 \qquad 1\overline{)4}\,^{4}$$

When you divide a number by itself, the quotient is 1.

$$8 \div 8 = 1 \qquad 2\overline{)2}\,^{1}$$

When you divide 0 by a number (not 0), the quotient is 0.

$$0 \div 7 = 0 \qquad 3\overline{)0}\,^{0}$$

WARNING Never divide a number by 0!

$$5 \div 0 = \blacksquare \qquad 0 \div 0 = \blacksquare$$

$\blacksquare \times 0 = 5$
No number works.

$\blacksquare \times 0 = 0$
Any number works, so there can't be one right answer.

Multiplication and division undo each other. You can use multiplication to check division.

$$9\overline{)72}\,^{8} \qquad \begin{array}{r} 9 \\ \times 8 \\ \hline 72 \end{array}\checkmark$$

TRY THESE

Can you do the division? If you can, give the quotient.

1. $1\overline{)8}$ **2.** $0\overline{)5}$ **3.** $5\overline{)0}$ **4.** $3\overline{)3}$ **5.** $0\overline{)9}$ **6.** $9\overline{)0}$

SKILLS PRACTICE

Divide.

1. $5\overline{)35}$ **2.** $1\overline{)9}$ **3.** $4\overline{)0}$ **4.** $6\overline{)12}$ **5.** $8\overline{)8}$ **6.** $3\overline{)21}$

7. $8\overline{)72}$ **8.** $7\overline{)56}$ **9.** $9\overline{)9}$ **10.** $1\overline{)7}$ **11.** $4\overline{)32}$ **12.** $7\overline{)0}$

13. $1\overline{)4}$ **14.** $9\overline{)54}$ **15.** $6\overline{)42}$ **16.** $2\overline{)8}$ **17.** $3\overline{)24}$ **18.** $8\overline{)48}$

19. $9\overline{)81}$ **20.** $4\overline{)24}$ **21.** $5\overline{)5}$ **22.** $6\overline{)0}$ **23.** $8\overline{)24}$ **24.** $2\overline{)4}$

25. $7\overline{)7}$ **26.** $5\overline{)45}$ **27.** $6\overline{)36}$ **28.** $2\overline{)18}$ **29.** $9\overline{)72}$ **30.** $6\overline{)24}$

31. $36 \div 4 =$    **32.** $1 \div 1 =$ ■   **33.** $35 \div 7 =$ ■

★**34.** $0 \div 93 =$ ■   ★**35.** $59 \div 59 =$ ■   ★**36.** $76 \div 1 =$ ■

PROBLEM SOLVING

37. Karl had 9 fish. He put 1 fish in each bowl. How many bowls did he use?

38. Loni had 6 snails. She put 6 snails in each fish tank. How many fish tanks did she use?

THINK!

Using a Calculator

Try this division problem on a calculator.

$$73 \div 0 = ■$$

What does the calculator show?

Problem Solving

Uses of Division

A. You can divide to find *how many sets* when you know how many in all and how many in each set.

The pet store has 14 rabbits. The storekeeper wants to put 2 rabbits in each hutch. How many hutches will she need?

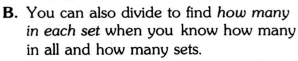

14 in all
2 in each set
■ sets

$$\begin{array}{r} 7 \leftarrow \text{sets} \\ \text{in each set} \rightarrow 2\overline{)14} \leftarrow \text{in all} \end{array}$$

Check. $\begin{array}{r} 2 \\ \times 7 \\ \hline 14 \end{array}$ ✓

She needs *7 hutches*.

B. You can also divide to find *how many in each set* when you know how many in all and how many sets.

The pet store has 18 tropical fish. The storekeeper has 3 fish tanks. She wants to put the same number of fish in each tank. How many fish should she put in each tank?

18 in all
3 sets
■ in each set

$$\begin{array}{r} 6 \leftarrow \text{in each set} \\ \text{sets} \rightarrow 3\overline{)18} \leftarrow \text{in all} \end{array}$$

Check. $\begin{array}{r} 3 \\ \times 6 \\ \hline 18 \end{array}$ ✓

She should put *6 fish in each tank*.

TRY THESE

Tell whether you must find *how many sets* or *how many in each set*. Then solve the problems.

1. A pet store received 20 canaries and put 4 canaries in each cage. How many cages were filled?

2. The pet store ordered 72 cat collars. There are 8 collars in each box. How many boxes are there?

3. There are 35 boxes of birdseed on 5 shelves. The same number of boxes are on each shelf. How many boxes are on each shelf?

4. The storekeeper puts 48 dog leashes on 6 hooks. She puts the same number of leashes on each hook. How many are on each hook?

PROBLEM SOLVING PRACTICE

Solve each problem.

1. The pet store has 27 mice. They are in 3 large cages with the same number of mice in each cage. How many mice are in each cage?

2. Yesterday the pet store sold 4 small dog bones, 3 medium bones, and 6 large bones. How many bones did the store sell in all?

3. On Saturday 4 dogs had the same number of puppies. There were 24 puppies in all. How many puppies did each dog have?

4. The pet store has 56 goldfish. The storekeeper can put 8 goldfish in a tank. How many tanks can the storekeeper fill?

5. The storekeeper ordered 30 kilograms of dog food. She stored the dog food in containers that hold 6 kilograms. How many containers did she fill?

★6. Carla started training her puppy when it was 8 weeks old. She gave a 5-minute lesson 4 times a day. How many minutes a day did she train her dog?

ON YOUR OWN

Make up two word problems for each division fact.

One problem should ask *how many sets.* The other one should ask *how many in each set.*

1. $8\overline{)16}$ 2. $3\overline{)15}$ 3. $6\overline{)42}$

Using a Calculator

You can illustrate properties on your calculator.

Order Property of Addition:

| 8 | + | 4 | = | **12.** |

| 4 | + | 8 | = | **12.** |

Zero Property of Subtraction:

| 5 | − | 5 | = | **0.** |

| 3 | − | 0 | = | **3.** |

Multiplication Property of One:

| 9 | × | 1 | = | **9.** |

Zero in Division:

| 0 | ÷ | 4 | = | **0.** |

Addition and Subtraction:

| 4 | + | 6 | = | − | 6 | = | **4.** |

> The display will show 10 .

Multiplication and Division:

| 2 | 8 | ÷ | 7 | = | × | 7 | = | **28.** |

> The display will show 4 .

The | M+ | key adds the displayed number to the calculator's memory.

The | MR | key displays the number that has been placed in memory.

Distributive Property:

4 × (6 + 1) = ■

| 6 | + | 1 | = | M+ |

> Add 6 + 1 = 7.
> Place 7 in memory.

| 4 | × | MR | = | **28.** |

(4 × 6) + (4 × 1) = ■

| 4 | × | 6 | = | M+ |

| 4 | × | 1 | = | M+ | MR | **28.** |

Tell which calculator keys you would press to find each answer.

1. 3 + 8 = ■   **2.** 8 + 3 = ■   **3.** 1 × 5 = ■   **4.** 0 ÷ 3 = ■

5. 2 × (3 + 4) = ■   **6.** (2 × 3) + (2 × 4) = ■

Add. (*pages 2–3, 6–7*)

1.	2.	3.	4.	5.	6.	7.
5 +7	8 +4	9 +0	5 +9	7 1 +5	5 3 +4	8 1 +7

8. 7 + 6 = ▓ **9.** 9 + 7 = ▓ **10.** ▓ + 8 = 12 **11.** 2 + 4 + 5 = ▓

Subtract. (*pages 4–7*)

12.	13.	14.	15.	16.	17.	18.
12 − 9	11 − 7	14 − 9	8 − 0	10 − 7	13 − 9	15 − 6

19. 12 − 5 = ▓ **20.** 13 − 6 = ▓ **21.** 13 − 4 = ▓ **22.** 7 − ▓ = 0

Multiply. (*pages 14–17*)

23.	24.	25.	26.	27.	28.	29.
7 ×5	1 ×4	5 ×9	1 ×3	4 ×7	3 ×6	2 ×3

30. 6 × 9 = ▓ **31.** 8 × 7 = ▓ **32.** 9 × 9 = ▓ **33.** 5 × 1 = ▓

Divide. (*pages 20–23*)

34. 4)‾12 **35.** 7)‾21 **36.** 3)‾12 **37.** 6)‾30 **38.** 9)‾45 **39.** 2)‾10

40. 18 ÷ 9 = ▓ **41.** 0 ÷ 7 = ▓ **42.** 32 ÷ 8 = ▓ **43.** 81 ÷ 9 = ▓

Complete the number sentences. (*pages 16–17*)

44. 2 × (3 + 5) = ▓ **45.** 5 × (1 + 5) = ▓ **46.** 4 × (3 + 2) = ▓

Solve the problems. (*pages 6–7, 12–13, 22–25*)

47. Danny bought 12 potatoes. He used 9 potatoes. How many did he have left?

48. Ed used 6 cans of orange juice and 8 cans of water. How many cans did he use?

49. Mrs. Fowler bought 8 cartons of milk. She used 2 cartons every day. How many days did the milk last?

50. Leni bought 7 chickens. Each chicken cost $3. How much did she spend in all?

Reinforcement

More Help with Addition

6 +8 14	8 +6 14
8 +0 8	0 +6 6

1. 4
+9

2. 8
+9

3. 9
+1

4. 7
+9

5. 8
+8

6. 9
+6

7. 6
+5

8. 3
+7

9. 7
+7

10. 0
+9

11. 6
+6

12. 1
+8

More Help with Subtraction

12 − 9 3	12 − 3 9
9 −0 9	7 −7 0

13. 13
− 5

14. 16
− 7

15. 18
− 9

16. 7
− 0

17. 16
− 8

18. 11
− 6

19. 16
− 9

20. 13
− 9

21. 14
− 7

22. 17
− 8

23. 10
− 4

24. 12
− 8

More Help with Multiplication

5 ×3 15	3 ×5 15
7 ×0 0	1 ×6 6

25. 7
×7

26. 6
×0

27. 8
×6

28. 9
×4

29. 9
×7

30. 8
×5

31. 7
×6

32. 9
×9

33. 9
×1

34. 4
×6

35. 7
×8

36. 9
×6

More Help with Division

$6\overline{)18}$ ³	$5\overline{)5}$ ¹
$3\overline{)0}$ ⁰	$1\overline{)4}$ ⁴

37. $6\overline{)54}$

38. $9\overline{)27}$

39. $3\overline{)9}$

40. $7\overline{)28}$

41. $5\overline{)20}$

42. $8\overline{)24}$

43. $5\overline{)45}$

44. $7\overline{)7}$

45. $2\overline{)8}$

46. $1\overline{)5}$

47. $6\overline{)24}$

48. $4\overline{)0}$

Grouping with Parentheses and Brackets

A. ( ) are *parentheses.* Parentheses are used to group numbers. They tell you what to do first.

$4 \times (2 + 3) = \blacksquare$

$4 \times \quad 5 \quad = 20$

$(4 \times 2) + 3 = \blacksquare$

$8 \quad + 3 = 11$

B. When two sets of parentheses are used, first work inside the set on the left. Then work inside the set on the right.

$(3 + 6) \times (14 - 6) = \blacksquare$

$9 \quad \times \quad 8 \quad = 72$

C. [ ] are *brackets.* When parentheses and brackets are used, work inside the parentheses first.

$6 + [(10 - 7) \times 3] = \blacksquare$

$6 + [\quad 3 \quad \times 3] = \blacksquare$

$6 + \quad 9 \quad = 15$

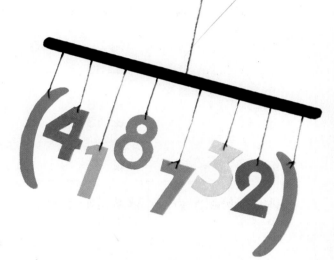

Complete.

1. $(18 - 9) \times 2 = \blacksquare$

2. $18 - (9 \times 2) = \blacksquare$

3. $6 + (11 - 8) + 4 = \blacksquare$

4. $(3 \times 5) - (4 \times 2) = \blacksquare$

5. $14 \div (8 - 1) = \blacksquare$

6. $(7 + 9) \div (3 + 1) = \blacksquare$

7. $(16 - 9) \times (3 + 6) = \blacksquare$

8. $(14 - 5) + (3 \times 3) = \blacksquare$

9. $5 \times [6 + (12 - 9)] = \blacksquare$

10. $[(6 + 7) - 4] \times 4 = \blacksquare$

Copy each exercise. Place parentheses, or parentheses and brackets, to make the answer correct.

11. $8 + 3 \times 2 = 14$

12. $9 - 2 + 1 \times 3 = 0$

13. $12 - 7 \times 16 - 8 = 40$

14. $5 \times 11 - 8 - 6 = 9$

15. $2 + 6 \times 7 = 56$

16. $12 \div 6 - 1 \times 3 = 4$

Cumulative Review

Choose the correct answer.

1.
$$9$$
$$+7$$
a. 63
b. 16
c. 15
d. 2

2.
$$9$$
$$\times 7$$
a. 63
b. 16
c. 72
d. 64

3.
$$8$$
$$-3$$
a. 24
b. 5
c. 11
d. 18

4. $4\overline{)32}$
a. 6
b. 7
c. 8
d. 9

5.
$$6$$
$$\times 7$$
a. 13
b. 28
c. 56
d. 42

6.
$$4$$
$$+9$$
a. 36
b. 14
c. 28
d. 13

7. $8\overline{)48}$
a. 6
b. 7
c. 8
d. 9

8.
$$14$$
$$-9$$
a. 6
b. 23
c. 5
d. 22

9. $7 + 6 =$ ▮
a. 42
b. 56
c. 13
d. 15

10. $6 \times 9 =$ ▮
a. 15
b. 69
c. 56
d. 54

11. $27 \div 9 =$ ▮
a. 18
b. 3
c. 4
d. 36

12. $12 - 7 =$ ▮
a. 19
b. 5
c. 4
d. 7

13. Amy bought 9 pens. She spent $3 for each pen. How much did she spend in all?

a. $12   b. $9
c. $6   d. $27

14. Phil has $7 in one pocket and $5 in another pocket. How much does he have in all?

a. $2   b. $12
c. $14   d. $35

15. Sam had 8 apples. After he gave some apples to Ken, he had 5 apples left. How many did he give to Ken?

a. 5 apples   b. 3 apples
c. 13 apples   d. 40 apples

16. Vera's garden has 6 rows, each with the same number of pumpkins. There are 42 pumpkins in all. How many are in each row?

a. 5 pumpkins   b. 36 pumpkins
c. 7 pumpkins   d. 8 pumpkins

2

Place Value

SOME AMERICAN SPACE TRAVEL FIRSTS

Year	Astronaut	Accomplishment
1961	Alan B. Shepard, Jr.	First American in space
1965	Edward H. White	First American to walk in space
1969	Neil A. Armstrong	First person to walk on the moon
1983	Sally Ride	First American woman in space

Hundreds, Tens, and Ones

Stamps are often sold in rolls or sheets of 100, strips of 10, or individually.

You can use the digits 0–9 to write *standard numerals* for all whole numbers.

3 hundreds   4 tens   6 ones

Hundreds	Tens	Ones
3	4	6

The *digit* 3 in the **hundreds place** means 3 hundreds.
The digit 4 in the **tens place** means 4 tens.
The digit 6 in the **ones place** means 6 ones.

You can write this number in different ways.

Standard numeral: 346   **Expanded form:** 300 + 40 + 6

Words: three hundred forty-six

TRY THESE

Write the standard numeral.

1.

2.

3. 600 + 90 + 7   4. 700 + 8

5. four hundred forty-six   6. five hundred sixty

Name the place of the digit 9. Then give the meaning of the digit 9.

7. 893   8. 904   9. 49   10. 295   11. 933   12. 349

Follow the directions.

13. Write 727 in words.   14. Write 409 in words.

15. Write 843 in expanded form.   16. Write 271 in expanded form.

SKILLS PRACTICE _____

Write the standard numeral.

1. ▦▦ |||| ▪ ▪

2. ▦ ||| ▫▫▫▫ / ▫▫▫▫

3. three hundred twenty-four

4. eight hundred eleven

5. 600 + 30

6. 400 + 4

Name the place of the digit 6.

7. 635   **8.** 365   **9.** 536   **10.** 165   **11.** 706   **12.** 647

Give the meaning of the digit 5.

13. 257   **14.** 805   **15.** 350   **16.** 56   **17.** 500   **18.** 516

Match.

19. 308

20. 38

21. 380

22. 383

a. 30 + 8

b. 300 + 80 + 3

c. 300 + 80

d. 300 + 8

Write in words.

23. 450   **24.** 900   **25.** 462   **26.** 707

Use the three digits to write all of the three-digit numerals you can.

27. 2, 4, 6   **28.** 4, 5, 7   ★**29.** 3, 0, 3

PROBLEM SOLVING _____

30. Carlos bought 2 rolls of 100 stamps, 4 strips of 10 stamps, and 3 extra stamps. How many stamps did he buy?

31. Martha bought 3 rolls of 100 stamps, 5 strips of 10 stamps, and 8 extra stamps. How many stamps did she buy?

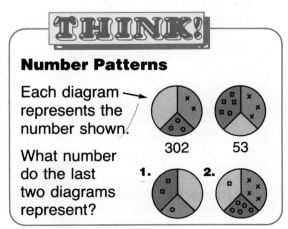

THINK!

Number Patterns

Each diagram represents the number shown.

302   53

What number do the last two diagrams represent?

1.   **2.**

Upside-down answers 7. hundreds place 13. 5 tens 1. 242

Homework   page 402

33

Thousands

The University of Michigan Stadium in Ann Arbor, Michigan, has a capacity of 101,701 people.

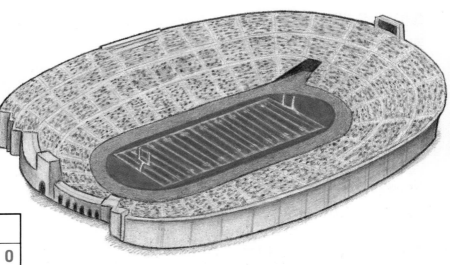

Thousands			Ones		
H	T	O	H	T	O
3	7	8	0	6	4

1 thousand = 10 hundreds

A comma separates the **ones period** from the **thousands period.**

3 in the **hundred-thousands place** means 3 hundred-thousands.
7 in the **ten-thousands place** means 7 ten-thousands.
8 in the **thousands place** means 8 thousands.

Standard numeral: 378,064
Expanded form: 300,000 + 70,000 + 8,000 + 60 + 4
Words: three hundred seventy-eight thousand, sixty-four

TRY THESE

Name the place of the digit 7. Then give the meaning of the digit 7.

1. 17,035
2. 48,079
3. 763,249
4. 81,725
5. 274,563

Write the standard numeral.

6. seven hundred forty-one thousand, eight hundred eleven

7. five hundred four thousand, three hundred seventy-nine

8. 200,000 + 70,000 + 1,000 + 500 + 60 + 2

9. 700,000 + 60,000 + 5,000 + 40 + 3

Write in words. Then write in expanded form.

10. 700,200
11. 83,095
12. 123,740
13. 750,000
14. 234,567

SKILLS PRACTICE

Name the place of the digit 8.

1. 82,165   **2.** 820,237   **3.** 1,682   **4.** 91,814

Give the meaning of the digit 4.

5. 4,876   **6.** 40,790   **7.** 300,400   **8.** 400,060

Write the standard numeral.

9. 600,000 + 90,000 + 2,000 + 500 + 80 + 7
10. 50,000 + 7,000 + 200 + 60
11. 70,000 + 10 + 6
12. three hundred seven thousand, three hundred seventy-six
13. eighty-six thousand, ten
14. nine hundred seventy-five thousand, one hundred forty-four

Write in expanded form.

15. 623,145   **16.** 92,801   **17.** 4,589   **18.** 702,006

Write in words.

19. 70,070   **20.** 150,650   **21.** 2,080   **22.** 100,001

Follow the directions.

23. Write the standard numeral with digits that mean 2 ten-thousands, 9 thousands, 4 hundreds, 4 tens, 2 ones.
24. Write the standard 6-digit numeral with 1 in the hundred-thousands place, 5 in the thousands place, 6 in the tens place, and nines in all other places.

Use the four digits to write the smallest and the largest four-digit standard numeral.

25. 6, 2, 7, 1   **26.** 9, 6, 3, 2   ★**27.** 4, 7, 4, 7   ★**28.** 5, 0, 8, 3

THINK!

Inputs and Outputs

Input	10	15	20	25	30	35	40	45
Output	3	4	5	6	?	?	?	?

Try to discover the rule that gives the output number for each input number. Then complete the table.

Comparing and Ordering Numbers

A. You can use a **number line** to **compare** whole numbers.

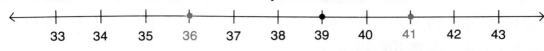

33 34 35 36 37 38 39 40 41 42 43

36 is to the left of 41.   41 is to the right of 36.
36 is *less than* 41.   41 is *greater than* 36.
    36 < 41   41 > 36

> The point is toward the smaller number.

39 is *equal to* 39.
    39 = 39

B. You can also compare whole numbers without using a number line.

> Compare 7,254 and 7,283.

Step 1 Write the whole numbers so their ones digits line up.

    7 , 2 5 4
    7 , 2 8 3

Step 2 Start at the left. Look at each pair of digits.

    7 , 2 5 4
    7 , 2 8 3   same

Step 3 Move to the right until you find different digits.

    7 , 2 5 4
    7 , 2 8 3   different

Step 4 Compare these digits.

    5 < 8 **so** 7,254 < 7,283
    8 > 5 **so** 7,283 > 7,254

C. List 14,753; 2,987; and 14,760 in order from least to greatest.
Start at the left.   Now compare 14,753 and 14,760.

            1 4,7 5 3   1 4,7 5 3
0 < 1   2,9 8 7   1 4,7 6 0   6 > 5
            1 4,7 6 0

2,987 is the least.   14,760 is the greatest.

Least to greatest: 2,987; 14,753; 14,760

TRY THESE

Write >, <, or = for ●.

1. 24 ● 36

2. 573 ● 53

3. 6,847 ● 6,837

4. 279,482 ● 275,309

5. 136,479 ● 13,582

6. 23,174 ● 23,735

Write the numbers in order from least to greatest.

7. 77; 67; 17

8. 123; 231; 132; 213

9. 2,618; 4,715; 4,714; 3,019

SKILLS PRACTICE

Write >, <, or = for ●.

1. 72 ● 79

2. 53 ● 61

3. 193 ● 174

4. 2,139 ● 2,139

5. 35,657 ● 35,429

6. 174,263 ● 175,249

7. 293 ● 2,935

8. 704,863 ● 705,863

9. 641,111 ● 64,111

Write the numbers in order from least to greatest.

10. 78; 58; 28

11. 243; 314; 212; 197

12. 4,379; 2,168; 4,286; 3,174

13. 24,275; 21,652; 24,197

Write the numbers in order from greatest to least.

14. 721; 714; 724

15. 18,259; 18,136; 18,263

16. 18,023; 6,247; 18,032

17. 41,276; 45,475; 45,489; 41,274

PROBLEM SOLVING

18. The mileage on a blue used car was 26,279. The mileage on a black used car was 62,279. Which car had the higher mileage?

19. Mr. D'Elia wants to buy a car that has been driven less than 35,000 miles. Which car should he buy?

Car A   34,989 miles
Car B   36,000 miles

THINK!

Number Clues
Find the number that fits all the clues.

1. It is less than 5 × 4.
It is greater than 8 × 2.
It is a multiple of 6.

2. It is less than 8 × 5.
7 is in the ones place.
It is greater than 4 × 9.

Rounding Numbers

A. A cup of corn soup has 153 calories.
A cup of tomato soup has 155 calories.
A cup of pea soup has 158 calories.

About how many calories does each have?
Round to the **nearest ten.**

153 is closer to 150 than 160.
Round 153 down to 150.

158 is nearer to 160 than 150.
Round 158 up to 160.

155 is as near 150 as 160.
Round 155 up to 160.

> **When a number is exactly in the middle, round up.**

A cup of corn soup has *about* 150 calories.
A cup of tomato soup has *about* 160 calories.
A cup of pea soup has *about* 160 calories.

B. Round 3,487 to the **nearest hundred.**

Find the hundreds place.
Look at the digit to its right.

$$3,4\overset{\uparrow}{8}7$$
$$8 > 5$$

Round 3,487 *up* to 3,500.

C. Round 3,487 to the **nearest thousand.**

Find the thousands place.
Look at the digit to its right.

$$3,\overset{\uparrow}{4}87$$
$$4 < 5$$

Round 3,487 *down* to 3,000.

D. Round 235,000 to the **nearest ten-thousand.**

Find the ten-thousands place.
Look at the digit to its right.

$$23\overset{\uparrow}{5},000$$
$$5 = 5$$

Round 235,000 *up* to 240,000.

E. Round 235,471 to the **nearest hundred-thousand.**

Find the hundred-thousands place.
Look at the digit to its right.

$$2\overset{\uparrow}{3}5,471$$
$$3 < 5$$

Round 235,471 *down* to 200,000.

F. Rounding to the **nearest dollar** is like rounding to the nearest hundred. Find the number of dollars. Look at the digit to its right.

Round $2.38 to $2.00.   Round $23.87 to $24.00.   Round $17.50 to $18.00.

$3 < 5$ $8 > 5$ $5 = 5$

TRY THESE

Round to the nearest ten; nearest hundred; nearest thousand.

1. 4,753   **2.** 6,739   **3.** 4,450   **4.** 9,872   **5.** 16,250   **6.** 283,527

Round to the nearest ten-thousand; nearest hundred-thousand.

7. 563,000   **8.** 394,251   **9.** 457,329   **10.** 714,500   **11.** 245,000

SKILLS PRACTICE

Round to the nearest ten.

1. 94   **2.** 173   **3.** 4,716   **4.** 12,182   **5.** 146,654

Round to the nearest hundred.

6. 238   **7.** 6,582   **8.** 7,853   **9.** 14,235   **10.** 417,018

Round to the nearest thousand.

11. 2,468   **12.** 7,500   **13.** 9,979   **14.** 18,364   **15.** 804,800

Round to the nearest ten-thousand.

16. 58,699   **17.** 139,400   **18.** 19,000   **19.** 624,378   **20.** 20,000

Round to the nearest hundred-thousand.

21. 243,625   **22.** 257,977   **23.** 150,000   **24.** 392,000   **25.** 898,000

Round to the nearest dollar. Think of rounding to hundreds.

26. $2.79   **27.** $5.06   **28.** $18.90   **29.** $3.54   **30.** $59.62

Round to the nearest thousand.

31. 975   **32.** 500   **33.** 499

Which digits could you use in place of the ■ to make each statement true?

★**34.** 1 ■ 5, 832 rounded to the nearest hundred-thousand is 100,000.

★**35.** 1 ■ 5, 832 rounded to the nearest hundred-thousand is 200,000.

Logical Reasoning

A teacher wrote a four-digit number on the chalkboard and asked Dan, Fran, and Stan to round the number.
Dan said, "I rounded it down to 7,000." Fran said, "I rounded it up to 7,400."
Stan said, "6 is in the ones place, so I rounded it to 7,390."
What number did the teacher write?

Problem Solving Strategy

Guess and Check

Sometimes, solving a problem requires more than deciding to add, subtract, multiply, or divide. It may make more sense to **guess** an answer and then **check** to see if your guess is correct.

Maria is two years older than Pablo. Bob is four years younger than Maria. The sum of Bob's age and Pablo's age is 14. How old are these students?

Guess Maria's age. Try 7.
Then Pablo's age would be 7 − 2 = 5 and Bob's age would be 7 − 4 = 3.

Check.
Is Bob's age + Pablo's age = 14?
5 + 3 = 8   Too small!

Guess a greater age for Maria. Try 10.
Then Pablo's age would be 8 and Bob's age would be 6.

Check.
Is 8 + 6 = 14?   Yes.

Maria's age is 10, Pablo's age is 8, and Bob's is 6.

Solve by guess and check.

1. Alice is 3 times as old as her brother. A year ago, she was 4 times as old. How old are Alice and her brother now?

2. Mel is 2 years older than Belle and 3 years younger than Nell. The sum of Belle's age and Mel's age is 16. How old is each?

3. There are two jugs of water. One jug holds 9 cups more than the other. Together they hold 17 cups of water. How much does each jug hold?

4. Carl has some quarters in his hand. In his pocket there are 2 times as many quarters. In all, Carl has 12 quarters. How many quarters are in his pocket?

Challenge Problems   page 457

Problem Solving Project

Data in Pictographs

A *pictograph* shows information in picture form. The pictograph below shows the number of pieces of mail handled at a post office in one month.

Mail Handled in September	
Each ▥ stands for 100,000 pieces of mail. Each ▯ stands for 50,000 pieces of mail.	
First Class Mail	▥ ▥ ▥ ▥ ▥ ▥ ▥ ▥ ▥ ▯
Second Class Mail	▥ ▥ ▥ ▥ ▥
Third Class Mail	▥ ▥ ▥ ▥ ▥
Special Delivery	▥
Express Mail	▥ ▥
Other	▥ ▥ ▥ ▥ ▥ ▯

The number of First Class pieces is 950,000.

1. How many pieces of Express Mail were handled?

2. How many pieces of Third Class Mail were handled?

3. Of which kind of mail did the post office handle the fewest pieces?

4. The post office handled about the same number of pieces for two kinds of mail. Which two kinds were they?

5. For which kind of mail were the most pieces handled?

6. Do you think these numbers are exact figures or estimates?

ON YOUR OWN

Make a pictograph from the data in this table. Let ▥ stand for 100,000 pieces of mail. Make up two problems that can be solved using your pictograph.

Mail Handled	
Type of Mail	Number of Pieces
Magazines	400,000
Books (hardcover)	100,000
Newspapers	500,000
Books (softcover)	200,000

Millions

A.

Millions			Thousands			Ones		
H	T	O	H	T	O	H	T	O
6	2	5	1	0	4	8	3	7

1 million = 10 hundred-thousands

Commas separate the periods to make it easy to read numerals.

6 in the **hundred-millions place** means 6 hundred-millions.
2 in the **ten-millions place** means 2 ten-millions.
5 in the **millions place** means 5 millions.

Standard numeral: 625,104,837

Expanded form: 600,000,000 + 20,000,000 + 5,000,000 + 100,000 + 4,000 + 800 + 30 + 7

Words: six hundred twenty-five million, one hundred four thousand, eight hundred thirty-seven

B. You can compare millions as you did thousands.

63,254,002   5 < 8   So   63,254,002 < 63,281,579
63,281,579   8 > 5   63,281,579 > 63,254,002

TRY THESE

Name the place of the digit 2 in each standard numeral.

1. 52,306,094   **2.** 724,361,100   **3.** 5,426,847   **4.** 200,000,000

Tell what 5 means in each numeral.

5. 352,231,417   **6.** 4,058,746   **7.** 520,924,000   **8.** 35,096,164

Write the standard numeral.

9. twelve million, two hundred forty

10. 200,000,000 + 9,000,000 + 40,000 + 5,000 + 800 + 20 + 7

Follow the directions.

11. Write 143,209,576 in words.   **12.** Write 654,007,405 in expanded form.

Compare. Use > and < to write two statements.

13. 7,060,054   **14.** 113,006,000   **15.** 18,889,460
    7,600,045   113,000,600   18,888,599

SKILLS PRACTICE _____

Name the place of the digit 3.

1. 301,266,881   2. 35,000,011   3. 9,304,866   4. 3,674,500

Give the meaning of the digit 4.

5. 24,009,808   6. 413,202,000   7. 40,500,000   8. 471,711

Write the standard numeral.

9. five hundred twenty-seven million, one hundred thousand, forty

10. eighty million, six hundred sixty thousand, eight hundred

11. 200,000,000 + 80,000,000 + 5,000,000 + 30,000 + 5,000 + 400 + 90 + 6

12. 100,000,000 + 100,000 + 100

Match.

13. three million, four hundred thousand, two hundred five   a. 3,040,205

14. thirty million, forty thousand, two hundred five   b. 3,400,205

15. three million, forty thousand, two hundred five   c. 3,004,205

16. three million, four thousand, two hundred five   d. 30,040,205

Write in words. Then write in expanded form.

17. 5,050,500   18. 173,000,000   19. 20,000,060   20. 12,012,000

Write >, <, or = for ⬤.

21. 36,284,311 ⬤ 38,284,311   22. 485,249,087 ⬤ 485,147,684

23. 84,000,000 ⬤ 59,000,000   24. 25,785,326 ⬤ 895,726

MIXED REVIEW

Add, subtract, multiply, or divide.

1. 7
   +9

2. 4
    5
   +3

3. 11
   − 2

4. 3
   ×7

5. 8)‾40‾

6. 14
   − 5

7. 0
   ×6

8. 35 ÷ 5 = ▪   9. 9 + 7 = ▪   10. 4 − 4 = ▪   11. 8 × 7 = ▪

43

Billions

Pluto is the planet farthest from the sun in our solar system. Its average distance from the sun is 5,913,000,000 kilometers. If you traveled at a speed of 500 kilometers per hour, it would take you about 1,350 years to cover that distance.

A.

Billions			Millions			Thousands			Ones		
H	T	O	H	T	O	H	T	O	H	T	O
3	4	7	8	1	6	0	0	2	0	1	0

1 billion = 10 hundred-millions

3 in the **hundred-billions place** means 3 hundred-billions.

4 in the **ten-billions place** means 4 ten-billions.

7 in the **billions place** means 7 billions.

Standard numeral: 347,816,002,010

Words: three hundred forty-seven billion, eight hundred sixteen million, two thousand, ten

B. You can compare billions as you did millions.

173,801,200,450	3 < 6	So	173,801,200,450 < 176,240,179,000
176,240,179,000	6 > 3		176,240,179,000 > 173,801,200,450

TRY THESE

Name the place of the digit 4 in each numeral.

1. 24,607,807,832

2. 645,109,620,000

3. 400,000,000,000

Tell what 7 means in each numeral.

4. 272,351,841,632

5. 964,173,119,386

6. 700,248,000,123

Follow the directions.

7. Write the standard numeral for eighteen billion, one hundred million, three thousand, seven hundred fifty-six.

8. Write 525,400,090,732 in words.

Compare. Use > and < to write two statements.

9. 13,403,547,090
   13,430,547,090

10. 7,000,000,000
   6,999,999,999

11. 15,570,613,300
   15,570,613,030

SKILLS PRACTICE

Name the place of the digit 9.

1. 295,286,432,007   2. 8,649,267,314   3. 49,681,043,275

Give the meaning of the digit 6.

4. 16,040,878,000   5. 621,872,000,111   6. 60,000,000,000

Write the standard numeral.

7. five billion, two hundred million, six thousand

8. thirty-seven billion, three hundred forty million, eight thousand, seventy

9. four hundred billion, four hundred million, four hundred thousand, four hundred

Write in words.

10. 17,050,000,051   11. 90,000,080,000   12. 8,002,400,000

Write >, <, or = for ●.

13. 8,725,000,123 ● 8,752,000,123

14. 308,000,000,000 ● 308,000,000,000

15. 975,000,001,000 ● 957,000,000,000

16. 121,314,222,123 ● 89,769,909,999

PROBLEM SOLVING

Use the table to solve these problems.

Planet	Distance from Sun in Kilometers
Mercury	58,000,000
Venus	107,000,000
Earth	149,000,000
Mars	227,000,000

17. Is Earth or Mars nearer to the sun?

18. Is Earth or Venus farther from the sun?

19. Which of these planets is farthest from the sun?

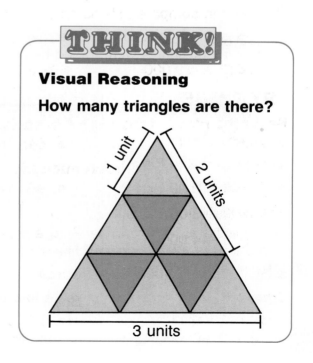

THINK!

Visual Reasoning

How many triangles are there?

1 unit

2 units

3 units

Problem Solving

Data from Tables and Graphs

Tables and *graphs* display data in different ways.

A. The numbers in this table tell how many *thousand* shares were traded. How many shares were traded between 12:00 and 1:00 P.M.?

Time	Shares Traded (in thousands)
10:00 –11:00 A.M.	934
11:00 –12:00	817
12:00 – 1:00 P.M.	610
1:00 – 2:00	907
2:00 – 3:00	682
3:00 – 4:00	751
Total	4,701

The final 3 zeros are missing.

610,000 shares were traded that hour.

B. In this graph the numbers are rounded to the nearest hundred-thousand. About how many shares were traded between 12:00 and 1:00 P.M.?

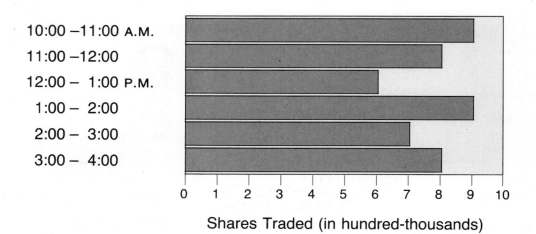

Shares Traded (in hundred-thousands)

About 600,000 shares were traded that hour.

TRY THESE

Answer the questions. First use the table in A. Then use the graph in B.

1. How many shares were traded between 2:00 and 3:00 P.M.?
2. Between which hours were the most shares traded?
3. Between which hours were the same number of shares traded?

Compare the sources.

4. Does the table or the graph give you more exact data?
5. Is it easier to compare data on the table or on the graph?
6. What accounts for the difference in your answers to questions 1–3 when you use the graph rather than the table?

PROBLEM SOLVING PRACTICE

Use the data in the table to answer the questions.

Computer Stock	
Day	Shares Traded (in thousands)
Monday	462
Tuesday	625
Wednesday	474
Thursday	623
Friday	459
Total	2,643

1. On which day were the most shares traded? How many?
2. On which day were the fewest shares traded? How many?
3. Were more shares traded on Tuesday or Thursday?
4. Were more shares traded on Wednesday or Friday?
5. Were more shares traded on Monday or Friday?
6. List the numbers of shares sold daily from least to greatest.
7. How many shares were traded that week?

ON YOUR OWN

Use the data in the table. Round each number to the nearest hundred-thousand. Make a graph that shows the shares traded each day. Show **Days** at the left and **Shares Traded (in hundred-thousands)** at the bottom.

Computers and How They Work

There are many computers around us. This chart shows several types:

Name	Number in Use	Approximate Cost	Uses
Supercomputers	about 100	$20,000,000	Government, business
Mainframe	thousands	$1,000,000	Government, business
Minicomputers	more than 100,000	$10,000–$100,000	Business
Microcomputers	millions	$100–$10,000	Home, school
Microprocessors	many millions	varies	Inside common machines

All of these computers work in similar ways. A computer system requires *input* information. An *input device* such as a keyboard accepts the input. The input is processed by the *Central Processing Unit* or CPU. The CPU has *two* parts, the *processor* and the *memory.* The processor calculates and retrieves information. The memory stores information. After the processing takes place the *output device,* such as a *screen* or a *printer,* displays the *output.*

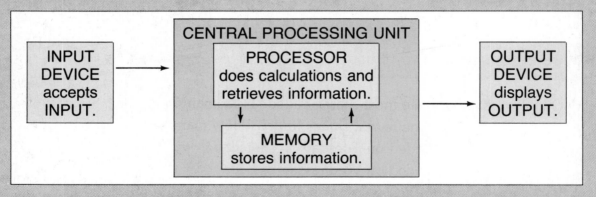

1. Are there more microcomputers or minicomputers in use today?

2. Which would cost more, a minicomputer or a microcomputer (also called a personal computer)?

3. Would mainframe computers and minicomputers be found more often in businesses or in homes?

4. What are the parts of a computer system?

5. Which part of the computer system accepts information?

Unit Review

Name the place of the digit 5. *(pages 32–35, 42–45)*

1. 75,631   **2.** 350,011,262,447   **3.** 51,600,724   **4.** 65,732,004,146

Give the meaning of the digit 7. *(pages 32–35, 42–45)*

5. 42,572   **6.** 17,003,429   **7.** 7,330,000,000   **8.** 8,071,342

Write in words. *(pages 32–35, 42–45)*

9. 4,329,680   **10.** 80,000,570,000

Write the standard numeral. *(pages 32–35, 42–45)*

11. eighteen billion, seven million, six thousand, four

12. one hundred thirty-seven million, five hundred fifty thousand

Write >, <, or = for ●. *(pages 36–37)*

13. 8,493 ● 8,943   **14.** 17,080 ● 17,800   **15.** 400,900 ● 490,000

16. 15,480,300 ● 14,580,300   **17.** 7,988,432,000 ● 7,432,988,000

Round to the nearest ten. Nearest hundred. Nearest thousand.
(pages 38–39)

18. 7,073   **19.** 1,566   **20.** 47,389   **21.** 43,712   **22.** 663,325

Round to the nearest ten-thousand. Nearest hundred-thousand.
(pages 38–39)

23. 381,227   **24.** 388,886   **25.** 701,159   **26.** 598,241   **27.** 605,773

Round to the nearest dollar. *(pages 38–39)*

28. $4.81   **29.** $11.50   **30.** $27.49   **31.** $3.29   **32.** $17.17

Use the data in the table to solve the problems. *(pages 46–47)*

33. Were there more visitors in April or in May?

34. Which month had the greatest number of visitors?

35. Which month had the smallest number of visitors?

Future World Park	
Month	**Number of Visitors (in thousands)**
April	311
May	641
June	288
Total	1,240

49

Reinforcement

More Help with Place Value

Millions			Thousands			Ones		
H	T	O	H	T	O	H	T	O
4	2	8	5	1	6	0	3	3

4 in the hundred-millions place means 4 hundred-millions.

Standard Numeral: 4,300,250,908

Words: four billion,
three hundred million,
two hundred fifty thousand,
nine hundred eight

Name the place of the digit 7.

1. 673,440,220
2. 400,357,298

What does the digit 7 mean?

3. 4,070,000
4. 9,702,000,000

Write the standard numeral.

5. seven billion, five hundred thousand
6. nineteen million, two hundred fifty-four thousand, eighty

Write in words.

7. 80,290,000,000
8. 4,039,400,000

More Help with Comparing and Rounding

4, 3 8 2, 5 6 0

4, 8 9 2, 6 5 0

3 < 8   so

4,382,560 < 4,892,650

257,814

To the nearest thousand:
258,000

To the nearest hundred:
257,800

Write >, <, or = for ●.

9. 45,698 ● 54,698
10. 3,498,000,000 ● 2,999,000,000
11. 17,468,400 ● 17,648,400

Round to the nearest hundred and to the nearest thousand.

12. 168,814   13. 246,195   14. 361,280

Round to the nearest dollar.

15. $7.98
16. $8.29
17. $7.39
18. $7.50

Roman Numerals

Many centuries ago, the Romans used letters to name numbers. This is how they wrote the numerals for 1 through 10 and for the multiples of 10.

Notice that the Romans never wrote any letter more than three times in a row.

VI means 1 more than 5, or 6.
IX means 1 less than 10, or 9.
XL means 10 less than 50, or 40.
XC means 10 less than 100, or 90.

They used C's to write multiples of 100 and M's to write multiples of 1,000.

| 100 C | 200 CC | 400 CD | 100 less than 500 | 500 D | 1,000 M | 3,000 MMM |

Study these Roman numerals.

20 + 6	90 + 8	300 + 50	400 + 50 + 9	3,000 + 900 + 40
XXVI	XCVIII	CCCL	CDLIX	MMMCMXL

What number does each Roman numeral name?

1. XII   **2.** XXXIV   **3.** XLVII   **4.** LXXV   **5.** XCIV   **6.** CX

7. CXC   **8.** CCXXII   **9.** CCCLXXI   **10.** CDXXXV   **11.** MML   **12.** MCMLXIII

Write the Roman numeral for each.

13. 11   **14.** 36   **15.** 63   **16.** 82   **17.** 99   **18.** 125

19. 192   **20.** 276   **21.** 348   **22.** 444   **23.** 984   **24.** 3,900

25. your age   **26.** your age in 20 years

Cumulative Review

Choose the correct answer.

1. Find the numeral for four million, two hundred.

  a. 4,020,000
  b. 4,200,000
  c. 4,000,200
  d. not given

2. Complete.
    59,297 ● 59,300

  a. >
  b. <
  c. =

3. Find six hundred nineteen million, eight hundred forty-three.

  a. 619,843
  b. 619,843,000
  c. 619,000,843
  d. 619,084,300

4.   7
   ×8

  a. 15
  b. 54
  c. 63
  d. not given

---

5. What does the digit 3 mean in 938,762?

  a. 3 thousands
  b. 3 hundred-thousands
  c. 3 ten-thousands
  d. not given

6. Complete.
    456,014 ● 98,751

  a. >
  b. <
  c. =

7. Round 135 to the nearest hundred.

  a. 100
  b. 130
  c. 140
  d. not given

8.   9
   −9

  a. 18
  b. 0
  c. 81
  d. not given

---

9. $3 + 2 + 7 =$ ▧

  a. 327
  b. 57
  c. 12
  d. not given

10. $17 − 9 =$ ▧

  a. 26
  b. 9
  c. 17
  d. not given

11. Round 687 to the nearest ten.

  a. 700
  b. 690
  c. 680
  d. not given

12.   8
   ×9

  a. 72
  b. 63
  c. 81
  d. not given

---

13. In which year did the factory have the greatest number of workers?

Year	Number of workers
1960	9,416
1965	11,009
1970	10,671
1975	11,006

  a. 1965
  b. 1970
  c. 1975
  d. not given

14. Kim bought 6 packages of note pads. Each package contained 8 pads. How many note pads did Kim buy?

  a. 14 pads
  b. 48 pads
  c. 54 pads
  d. not given

3 Addition and Subtraction

BUSES, PASSENGERS, AND MILEAGE

Type of Bus	Number in U.S.	Passengers	Total Mileage
Intercity	21,000	375 million *yearly*	1 billion miles
Local	60,000	$4\frac{1}{2}$ billion *yearly*	$1\frac{3}{4}$ billion miles
School buses	330,000	$22\frac{1}{2}$ million *daily*	Not Available

Addition

A. Steve has 35 fish in his aquarium.
Ginny has 27 fish.
How many fish do Steve and
Ginny have in all?

Add to find how many in all.

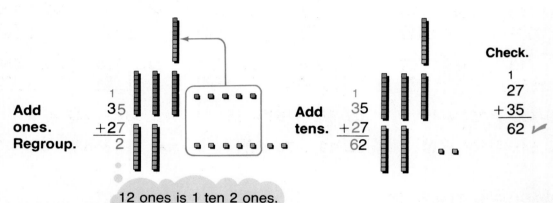

Add ones. Regroup.

$$
\begin{array}{r}
1 \\
35 \\
+27 \\
\hline
2
\end{array}
$$

Add tens.

$$
\begin{array}{r}
1 \\
35 \\
+27 \\
\hline
62
\end{array}
$$

Check.

$$
\begin{array}{r}
1 \\
27 \\
+35 \\
\hline
62 \checkmark
\end{array}
$$

12 ones is 1 ten 2 ones.

Steve and Ginny have 62 fish in all.

B. You may have to regroup more than once.

Add ones. Regroup.

$$
\begin{array}{r}
1 \\
768 \\
+896 \\
\hline
4
\end{array}
$$

Add tens. Regroup.

$$
\begin{array}{r}
1\,1 \\
768 \\
+896 \\
\hline
64
\end{array}
$$

Add hundreds.

$$
\begin{array}{r}
1\,1 \\
768 \\
+896 \\
\hline
1{,}664
\end{array}
$$

16 hundreds is 1 thousand, 6 hundreds.

TRY THESE

Add. Check your answers.

1.
$$
\begin{array}{r}
375 \\
+124 \\
\hline
\end{array}
$$

2.
$$
\begin{array}{r}
74 \\
+98 \\
\hline
\end{array}
$$

3.
$$
\begin{array}{r}
206 \\
+765 \\
\hline
\end{array}
$$

4.
$$
\begin{array}{r}
111 \\
+709 \\
\hline
\end{array}
$$

5.
$$
\begin{array}{r}
25 \\
+74 \\
\hline
\end{array}
$$

6.
$$
\begin{array}{r}
235 \\
+\ 56 \\
\hline
\end{array}
$$

7. 42 + 79 = ■

8. 157 + 286 = ■

9. 87 + 596 = ■

SKILLS PRACTICE

Find the sums.

1. 27 + 65	**2.** 433 + 758	**3.** 907 + 580	**4.** 686 + 100	**5.** 520 + 14	**6.** 436 + 74
7. 787 + 156	**8.** 35 + 6	**9.** 271 + 224	**10.** 63 + 65	**11.** 876 + 606	**12.** 943 + 280
13. 80 + 493	**14.** 625 + 15	**15.** 164 + 911	**16.** 7 + 153	**17.** 92 + 18	**18.** 68 + 225
19. 513 + 241	**20.** 570 + 655	**21.** 97 + 83	**22.** 563 + 905	**23.** 591 + 408	**24.** 392 + 728
25. 427 + 183	**26.** 82 + 78	**27.** 868 + 65	**28.** 111 + 222	**29.** 776 + 54	**30.** 556 + 479

31. 743 + 957 = ■   **32.** 937 + 85 = ■   **33.** 561 + 117 = ■

34. 345 + 506 = ■   **35.** 19 + 75 = ■   **36.** 144 + 82 = ■

PROBLEM SOLVING

37. 36 butterfly fish and 28 angelfish were in a pet shop fish tank. How many fish were in the tank all together?

★38. There were 2 large tanks with 313 snails in one and 398 in the other. How many snails were there in all?

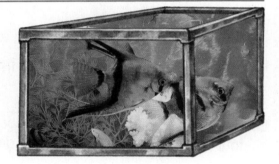

THINK!

Mental Math

Use addition facts to find the sums in your head.

6 + 9 = 15	3 + 7 = 10	8 + 5 = 13	4 + 8 = 12
16 + 9 = 25	13 + 7 = 20	18 + 5 = ■	24 + 8 = ■
26 + 9 = ■	23 + 7 = ■	28 + 5 = ■	34 + 8 = ■

Adding More Than Two Numbers

A. Mrs. Clark's class collected 216 aluminum cans. Mr. Wong's class collected 308 aluminum cans. Ms. Hudson's class collected 139 aluminum cans. How many cans did the classes collect in all?

Add ones.

$$
\begin{array}{r}
\overset{2}{2}16 \\
308 \\
+139 \\
\hline 3
\end{array}
\qquad
\begin{array}{r}
6 \\
+\ 8 \\
\hline 14 \\
+\ 9 \\
\hline 23
\end{array}
$$

Add tens.

$$
\begin{array}{r}
\overset{2}{2}16 \\
308 \\
+139 \\
\hline 63
\end{array}
\qquad
\begin{array}{r}
2 \\
+1 \\
\hline 3 \\
+0 \\
\hline 3 \\
+3 \\
\hline 6
\end{array}
$$

Add hundreds.

$$
\begin{array}{r}
\overset{2}{2}16 \\
308 \\
+139 \\
\hline 663
\end{array}
\qquad
\begin{array}{r}
2 \\
+3 \\
\hline 5 \\
+1 \\
\hline 6
\end{array}
$$

The classes collected 663 cans in all.

B. The table shows the number of bottles collected by students in four classes. How many bottles did the students collect?

Class	Bottles Collected
Grade 3	74
Grade 4	53
Grade 5	78
Grade 6	66

$$
\begin{array}{r}
\overset{2}{7}4 \\
53 \\
78 \\
+66 \\
\hline 1
\end{array}
\qquad
\begin{array}{r}
6 \\
+\ 4 \\
\hline 10 \\
+\ 8 \\
\hline 18 \\
+\ 3 \\
\hline 21
\end{array}
$$

$$
\begin{array}{r}
\overset{2}{7}4 \\
53 \\
78 \\
+66 \\
\hline 271
\end{array}
\qquad
\begin{array}{r}
7 \\
+7 \\
\hline 14 \\
+\ 6 \\
\hline 20 \\
+\ 5 \\
\hline 25 \\
+\ 2 \\
\hline 27
\end{array}
$$

> **Look for tens or other easy combinations.**

The students collected 271 bottles.

Add.

1.	2.	3.	4.	5.	6.
54 78 +69	48 26 +74	435 94 +126	380 50 +480	295 375 + 52	180 293 75 +355

SKILLS PRACTICE

Add.

1.	2.	3.	4.	5.	6.
73 82 +54	27 39 +64	342 67 + 39	58 97 +86	278 467 +426	189 52 + 41

7.	8.	9.	10.	11.	12.
700 800 +900	359 17 + 34	78 98 +34	640 890 +640	15 566 +804	107 304 +204

13.	14.	15.	16.	17.	18.
482 64 53 +136	50 80 70 +90	167 84 75 +298	370 439 564 +275	867 869 99 + 87	361 375 203 +559

19. $42 + 324 + 69 = $ ■

20. $248 + 326 + 47 + 142 = $ ■

21. $251 + 6 + 42 = $ ■

★22. $300 + 500 + 220 + 750 + 900 = $ ■

PROBLEM SOLVING

23. This table shows the number of newspapers collected by 3 classes. How many newspapers did they collect all together?

24. Whose class collected the most newspapers?

Teacher	Number of newspapers
Mrs. Silver	362
Mr. Bennett	280
Mrs. Springs	315

THINK!

Number Patterns

Try to find the pattern. Then write the next three numbers.

1. 9, 20, 31, 42, ■, ■, ■

2. 3, 5, 8, 12, 17, 23, ■, ■, ■

Adding Larger Numbers

A. The Book Nook sold 4,712 cookbooks in December and 2,564 cookbooks in January. How many cookbooks were sold in those two months?

Add to find how many in all.

Add ones.	Add tens.	Add hundreds.	Add thousands.
		1	1
4,712	4,712	4,712	4,712
+2,564	+2,564	+2,564	+2,564
6	76	276	7,276

The Book Nook sold 7,276 cookbooks in December and January.

B. When you add large numbers, you may have to regroup many times.

$$\begin{array}{r} 1\ \ 11 \\ 74,159 \\ +\ \ 6,387 \\ \hline 80,546 \end{array}$$

$$\begin{array}{r} 1111 \\ 374,832 \\ +695,487 \\ \hline 1,070,319 \end{array}$$

C. Add money the same way. Remember the $ and decimal point.

$$\begin{array}{r} 1 \\ \$10.95 \\ +\ \ 12.53 \\ \hline \$23.48 \end{array}$$

TRY THESE

Add.

1.
$$\begin{array}{r} 6,745 \\ +2,409 \end{array}$$

2.
$$\begin{array}{r} 47,826 \\ +34,915 \end{array}$$

3.
$$\begin{array}{r} 717,282 \\ +674,519 \end{array}$$

4.
$$\begin{array}{r} \$5.28 \\ +\ \ 6.95 \end{array}$$

5.
$$\begin{array}{r} \$27.63 \\ +\ \ 48.37 \end{array}$$

6. $3,491 + 8,567 = $ ■

7. $54,309 + 5,264 = $ ■

8. $\$467.58 + \$326.77 = $ ■

SKILLS PRACTICE

Add.

1. 3,759 +16,816	**2.** 7,834 +7,926	**3.** 16,375 +25,199	**4.** 346,951 + 52,356	**5.** $234.35 + 68.68
6. 457,302 +794,867	**7.** 67,200 +66,300	**8.** $380.00 + 51.00	**9.** 4,863 +68,232	**10.** $17.60 + 8.49
11. 78,546 +39,458	**12.** 653,207 +906,718	**13.** 31,859 + 637	**14.** 4,863 +75,892	**15.** $5,389.26 + 1,472.88
16. $27.13 + 38.96	**17.** 735,876 + 28,931	**18.** 67,510 +59,994	**19.** 35,000 +72,000	**20.** 49,673 + 6,796
21. 843,000 +236,800	**22.** 69,500 + 8,500	**23.** 48,657 253,909 + 72,096	**24.** 28,765 102,458 + 3,581	**25.** 16,808 432,000 + 5,594

26. $3,257 + 28,963 = \blacksquare$ **27.** $653,295 + 87,300 = \blacksquare$ **28.** $189.26 + $37.99 = \blacksquare$

PROBLEM SOLVING

29. The Open Door bookstore has 12,526 paperback and 7,840 hardcover books. How many books does it have in all?

30. Richard bought a book for $12.98 and a chess set for $14.49. How much did he spend in all?

31. The first printing of *The Life of the Whale* consisted of 153,600 copies and the second printing, 78,700 copies. How many copies were printed?

★**32.** The bookstore sold 7,651 books during June, 9,538 books during July, and 8,157 books during August. How many books did it sell during the three months?

THINK!

Logical Reasoning

Find the missing numbers.

1. 3 4 , ■ 8 1 + ■ 8 , 4 6 ■ 5 2 , 7 4 8	**2.** 6 3 ■ , 8 0 ■ + ■ 9 2 , ■ 2 7 1 , 2 2 8 , 3 3 6	**3.** $ 9 , ■ 8 ■ . 9 5 + 4 ■ 3 . ■ 8 $ 9 , 8 4 0 . 0 3

Estimating Sums: Mental Math

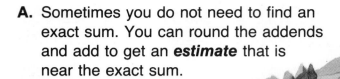

A. Sometimes you do not need to find an exact sum. You can round the addends and add to get an **estimate** that is near the exact sum.

Ann's family drove 372 miles on Saturday and 345 miles on Sunday. *About* how far did they drive in all?

Round to the leftmost place.

$$
\begin{array}{r}
3\,7\,2 \\
+\,3\,4\,5 \\
\end{array}
\qquad
\begin{array}{r}
4\,0\,0 \\
+\,3\,0\,0 \\
\hline
7\,0\,0 \\
\end{array}
$$

Ann's family drove *about* 700 miles. They drove exactly 717 miles.

B. This quick estimation method works with larger numbers, too.

$$
\begin{array}{r}
4\,,8\,5\,3 \\
+\,2\,,7\,6\,6 \\
\end{array}
\qquad
\begin{array}{r}
5\,,0\,0\,0 \\
+\,3\,,0\,0\,0 \\
\hline
8\,,0\,0\,0 \\
\end{array}
$$

The exact sum is 7,619.

$$
\begin{array}{r}
2\,1\,,0\,8\,7 \\
1\,,3\,5\,6 \\
+\,4\,7\,,8\,9\,1 \\
\end{array}
\qquad
\begin{array}{r}
2\,0\,,0\,0\,0 \\
0 \\
+\,5\,0\,,0\,0\,0 \\
\hline
7\,0\,,0\,0\,0 \\
\end{array}
$$

The exact sum is 70,334.

C. If you want a more precise estimate, round to a place farther to the right.

$$
\begin{array}{r}
4\,,8\,5\,3 \\
+\,2\,,7\,6\,6 \\
\end{array}
\qquad
\begin{array}{r}
4\,,9\,0\,0 \\
+\,2\,,8\,0\,0 \\
\hline
7\,,7\,0\,0 \\
\end{array}
$$

D. When you estimate money sums, you often round to the nearest dollar.

$$
\begin{array}{r}
\$\,4\,8\,.5\,3 \\
+\,\,2\,7\,.6\,6 \\
\end{array}
\qquad
\begin{array}{r}
\$\,4\,9\,.0\,0 \\
+\,\,2\,8\,.0\,0 \\
\hline
\$\,7\,7\,.0\,0 \\
\end{array}
$$

TRY THESE

A. Estimate by rounding to the leftmost place.
B. Estimate by rounding to the next place to the right.
C. Find the exact sum.
D. Compare the estimates with the exact sum.

1. 675 +106	**2.** 4,306 +2,497	**3.** 7,504 + 783	**4.** 256 +3,724	**5.** 24,331 +23,906

SKILLS PRACTICE

Estimate by rounding to the leftmost place.

1. 3,867 +5,020	**2.** 3,528 + 247	**3.** 21,572 +76,888	**4.** 69,478 +15,260	**5.** 175,000 + 9,876

Estimate by rounding to the second place from the left.

6. 3,867 +5,020	**7.** 3,528 + 247	**8.** 21,572 +76,888	**9.** 69,478 +15,260	**10.** 175,000 + 9,876

Estimate. Then find the exact sum.

11. 860 +570	**12.** $136.23 + 645.08	**13.** 75,923 683,876 + 28,644	**14.** $81.09 4.33 + 2.88	**15.** 182,679 24,832 +435,261

16. $46.39 + $21.89 = ■ **17.** 53 + 65 + 21 = ■ **18.** 84,956 + 7,380 = ■

PROBLEM SOLVING

Estimate to check your answer.

19. Mrs. Nishio drove 1,473 miles on a business trip. She came home by plane, a flight of 1,220 miles. How far did she travel in all?

★20. A plane flew 382 miles from Chattanooga to St. Louis. It then flew 477 miles from St. Louis to Minneapolis. Returning from Minneapolis to Chattanooga, it flew 826 miles. How far did it fly in all?

Reasoning with Money

Wayne buys towels on sale. The towels cost $8 each if you buy 5 or fewer, and $7 each if you buy more than 5. Wayne gives the clerk $50 and gets $1 in change. How many towels did he buy?

SPECIAL SALE

Problem Solving

Estimates and Answers

A. Some problems require only an estimate for an answer.

About how many people lived in New Hampshire in 1977?

$$
\begin{array}{r}
3\,0\,6{,}489 \\
+\ 5\,4\,2{,}511 \\
\end{array}
\qquad
\begin{array}{r}
300{,}000 \\
+\,500{,}000 \\
\hline
800{,}000 \\
\end{array}
$$

About 800,000 people in all.

POPULATIONS IN 1977		
State	In Cities	Outside Cities
New Hampshire	306,489	542,511
Maine	252,805	832,195
Rhode Island	867,680	67,320

B. Some problems require exact answers. Start with a quick estimate to get a good idea of how big your exact answer should be.

In 1790, how many people lived in the three states shown in the table?

POPULATIONS IN 1790	
State	Population
Massachusetts	378,787
New Hampshire	141,885
Vermont	85,425
TOTAL	?

	Estimate	Exact Sum
Massachusetts	400 thousand	378,787
New Hampshire	100 thousand	141,885
Vermont	+100 thousand	+ 85,425
TOTAL	600 thousand	606,097

Reasonable

A quick estimate can also help you decide if you pushed the right buttons on a calculator!

TRY THESE

Use data from the table in A.

1. About how many people lived outside cities in all three states in 1977? Exactly how many people lived there?

2. Estimate and then use your calculator to find how many people in all lived in New Hampshire and Rhode Island.

PROBLEM SOLVING PRACTICE _____

Use data from this table to solve each problem.

PEOPLE'S JOBS IN 1979					
	Vermont	**New Hampshire**	**Maine**	**Connecticut**	**Rhode Island**
Manufacturing	41,010	94,340	105,159	395,604	122,067
Community Service	38,324	58,623	56,333	229,110	68,845
Trade	34,370	67,785	75,460	255,925	74,589
Government	30,895	49,905	74,812	177,053	57,012

1. About how many people worked in government in Rhode Island and Connecticut?

2. How many people worked in community service in Maine and Rhode Island?

3. How many people worked in manufacturing in Vermont and Connecticut?

4. Did more people have manufacturing jobs in New Hampshire or in Maine?

5. About how many people worked in trade jobs in Vermont and New Hampshire?

6. In Maine, how many people worked in manufacturing or in trade?

7. About how many people worked in New Hampshire all together?

8. About how many people worked in government in all 5 states?

9. In Connecticut, how many people had jobs in fields other than government?

★10. Estimate and then use your calculator: How many people worked in Maine? in Vermont? In which state did more people work?

ON YOUR OWN

1. Choose a state. Use the data for manufacturing jobs and trade jobs. Make up a problem that asks for an exact answer.

2. Use the data for community service jobs in two states. Make up a problem that asks for an estimate.

Problem Solving Strategy

Solve a Simpler Problem

In a tree nursery there are straight one-meter paths between the young trees as shown in the picture. A chipmunk wants to go from the apple tree to the lilac tree. If it stays on the paths, the shortest way is 5 meters. How many different ways can the chipmunk go and travel just 5 meters?

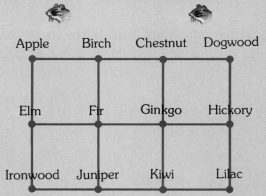

Start with a simpler problem. Look for patterns.

Apple to Birch
or
Apple to Elm

1 meter
1 way

Apple to Fir

2 meters
2 ways

Apple to Kiwi

4 meters
6 ways

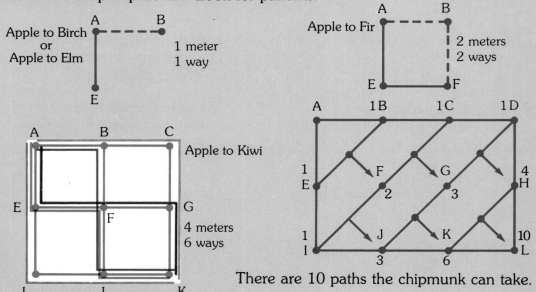

There are 10 paths the chipmunk can take.

1. If there were another row of trees as shown, how many different shortest paths would there be from the apple to the pear tree? How long would these paths be?

Apple B C D
E F G H
I J K L
M N O Pear

2. If the nursery size were increased as shown, how many shortest paths would there be from the apple to the yew tree? How long would they be?

Apple B C D E
F G H I J
K L M N O
P Q R S T
U V W X Yew

Problem Solving Project

Sales Tax

In many states, you have to pay *state sales tax* when you buy something. Stores often have a tax table to help salespeople find the amount of sales tax to charge. The rate of sales tax varies from state to state. This table is based on a rate of $.05 for every $1.00.

SALES TAX TABLE (5%)

Amount	Tax	Amount	Tax	Amount	Tax	Amount	Tax
$ .01 – .09	$.00	$2.50–2.69	$.13	$5.10–5.29	$.26	$7.70–7.89	$.39
.10 – .29	.01	2.70–2.89	.14	5.30–5.49	.27	7.90–8.09	.40
.30 – .49	.02	2.90–3.09	.15	5.50–5.69	.28	8.10–8.29	.41
.50 – .69	.03	3.10–3.29	.16	5.70–5.89	.29	8.30–8.49	.42
.70 – .89	.04	3.30–3.49	.17	5.90–6.09	.30	8.50–8.69	.43
.90–1.09	.05	3.50–3.69	.18	6.10–6.29	.31	8.70–8.89	.44
1.10–1.29	.06	3.70–3.89	.19	6.30–6.49	.32	8.90–9.09	.45
1.30–1.49	.07	3.90–4.09	.20	6.50–6.69	.33	9.10–9.29	.46
1.50–1.69	.08	4.10–4.29	.21	6.70–6.89	.34	9.30–9.49	.47
1.70–1.89	.09	4.30–4.49	.22	6.90–7.09	.35	9.50–9.69	.48
1.90–2.09	.10	4.50–4.69	.23	7.10–7.29	.36	9.70–9.89	.49
2.10–2.29	.11	4.70–4.89	.24	7.30–7.49	.37	9.90–10.00	.50
2.30–2.49	.12	4.90–5.09	.25	7.50–7.69	.38		

Cook's Nook

Quantity	Description	Price	Amount
1	Pan	$ 7.99	$ 7.99
1	Pot Holder	$ .59	$ .59
1	Mug	$ 1.25	$ 1.25
		Subtotal	$ 9.83
		Tax	.49
		Total	$ 10.32

The *subtotal* is $9.83.
  $9.83 is between $9.70 and $9.89. The tax is $.49.

Add the tax to the subtotal to find the *total cost.*
  $9.83 + $.49 = $10.32
  The total cost is $10.32.

Find the amount of the sales tax and the total cost.

1. $.75
2. $.15
3. $.90
4. $3.00
5. $4.89
6. $2.70
7. $8.19
8. $10.00
9. $9.79
10. $7.55

ON YOUR OWN

Data Search

Does your state have a sales tax? What things are taxable in your state? What things are not taxable?

If your state has a sales tax, get a tax table for your state. How much tax would you have to pay on the amounts in Exercises 1-10?

Subtraction

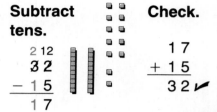

A. Jerry saw 32 sea gulls.
15 sea gulls flew away.
How many sea gulls were left?

Subtract to find how many were left.

Regroup.	Subtract ones.	Subtract tens.	Check.
2 12 3̶ 2 − 1 5	2 12 3̶ 2 − 1 5 7	2 12 3̶ 2 − 1 5 1 7	1 7 + 1 5 3 2 ✔

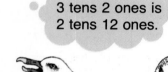

3 tens 2 ones is
2 tens 12 ones.

17 sea gulls were left.

B. You may have to regroup more than once.

Regroup. Subtract ones.	Regroup. Subtract tens.	Subtract hundreds.
4 16 3 5̶ 6̶ − 1 6 9 7	14 2 4 16 3̶ 5̶ 6̶ − 1 6 9 8 7	14 2 4 16 3̶ 5̶ 6̶ − 1 6 9 1 8 7

TRY THESE

1. 38 −16	2. 52 −29	3. 465 −262	4. 951 −489	5. 872 −365	6. 394 − 56

7. 58 − 23 = ■   **8.** 674 − 230 = ■   **9.** 858 − 75 = ■

SKILLS PRACTICE

1.   94
   − 61

2.   47
   − 43

3.   254
   − 144

4.   862
   − 490

5.   73
   − 8

6.   392
   − 64

7.   585
   − 493

8.   86
   − 9

9.   753
   − 695

10.   118
   − 18

11.   74
   − 63

12.   368
   − 80

13.   56
   − 29

14.   438
   − 143

15.   862
   − 75

16.   427
   − 114

17.   895
   − 197

18.   246
   − 141

19. 75 − 16 = ■

20. 297 − 163 = ■

21. 198 − 89 = ■

22. 35 − 7 = ■

23. 142 − 120 = ■

24. 634 − 27 = ■

PROBLEM SOLVING

25. A gray whale is 14 meters long. A blue whale is 44 meters long. How much longer is the blue whale than the gray whale?

26. There are 65 kinds of toothed whales. There are 10 kinds of toothless whales. How many kinds of whales are there?

27. A baby seal has a mass of 22 kilograms. An adult seal has a mass of 115 kilograms. How much less is the mass of the baby seal?

★28. A shark has 2 rows of teeth. Each row contains 56 teeth. How many teeth does the shark have in all? People have 32 teeth. How many more teeth do sharks have?

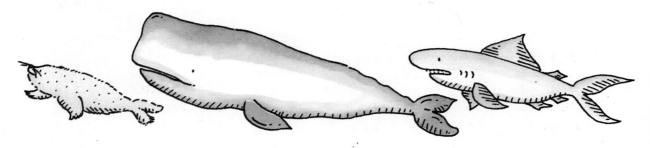

MIXED REVIEW

Add or subtract.

1.   37
   + 18

2.   74
   − 34

3.   857
   − 95

4.   119
   + 81

5.   113
   − 67

6.   338
   + 251

Subtracting Larger Numbers

A. Last month, the Great Falls Camping Company sold 7,217 canvas knapsacks and 3,583 nylon knapsacks. How many more canvas knapsacks than nylon ones did the company sell?

Subtract to find how many more.

Subtract ones.	**Regroup. Subtract tens.**	**Regroup. Subtract hundreds.**	**Subtract thousands.**
	1 11	11 6 ⅟ 11	11 6 ⅟ 11
7 , 2 1 7	7 , 2 ⅟ 7	7 , 2 ⅟ 7	7 , 2 ⅟ 7
− 3 , 5 8 3	− 3 , 5 8 3	− 3 , 5 8 3	− 3 , 5 8 3
4	3 4	6 3 4	3 , 6 3 4

The company sold 3,634 more canvas knapsacks.

B. When you subtract larger numbers, you may have to regroup many times.

```
        11
1 13 3  ⅟ 16
2 3 4 , 2 6 7
−   4 3 , 9 8 2
1 9 0 , 2 8 5
```

```
         15
   8 5  14 10
2 9 6 , 5 0 8
−     8 , 9 7 4
2 8 7 , 5 3 4
```

C. Subtract money the same way. Remember the $ and decimal point.

```
    8 12  6 15
$ 9 2 . 7 5
−  7 6 . 4 9
$ 1 6 . 2 6
```

TRY THESE

Subtract.

1. 1,847
    − 938

2. 15,639
    − 13,852

3. 736,599
    − 542,877

4. $98.66
    − 72.99

5. $352.74
    −   70.86

6. 7,453 − 6,481 = ■

7. 45,872 − 695 = ■

8. $579.62 − $42.85 = ■

SKILLS PRACTICE

Subtract.

1. 4,623
 −2,714

2. 865,474
 −478,366

3. $92.77
 − 65.23

4. $639.98
 − 440.49

5. 68,341
 −29,347

6. $632.84
 − 47.36

7. 666,672
 −648,745

8. 894,635
 −109,648

9. 323,561
 − 40,870

10. 9,324
 − 847

11. 87,991
 −68,096

12. $485.67
 − 94.04

13. 871,529
 − 4,066

14. 58,438
 −28,757

15. 48,865
 − 997

16. 38,167 − 788 = ▦

17. 931,475 − 642,088 = ▦

18. 453,841 − 149,720 = ▦

19. $854.83 − $407.04 = ▦

PROBLEM SOLVING

20. Dan is climbing Mount Mitchell. He has already climbed 5,250 feet. He must climb 6,684 feet in all. How much farther must he climb?

21. Mount Rainier is 14,410 feet above sea level. Mount Hood is 11,235 feet above sea level. How much higher is Mount Rainier?

22. A canvas knapsack costs $24.99. A nylon knapsack costs $18.75. How much cheaper is the nylon knapsack?

★23. Mrs. Garcia bought a sleeping bag for $52.76 and a camping stove for $37.24. How much did she spend? She gave the clerk $100.00. How much money should she get back?

THINK!

Recording Data

Copy and complete this record to show how many camp stoves Western Stove Company made, shipped, and had on hand each day.

Date	Made	Shipped	On Hand
June 5			3,926
June 6		753	3,173
June 7	298		▦
June 8		109	▦
June 9	451		▦
June 10		615	▦

Subtracting Across Zeros

A. Sometimes you may have to regroup several times before you can subtract the ones.

The Casitas Dam in California is 2,000 feet long. The Hoover Dam in Nevada is 1,242 feet long. How much longer is the Casitas Dam?

Regroup.	**Regroup again.**	**Regroup again.**	**Subtract.**
1 10 2,Ø0 0 −1,2 4 2	9 1 10 10 2,Ø Ø 0 −1,2 4 2	9 9 1 10 10 10 2,Ø Ø Ø −1,2 4 2	9 9 1 10 10 10 2,Ø Ø Ø −1,2 4 2 7 5 8

The Casitas Dam is 758 feet longer.

B. Sometimes when you regroup, the first digit becomes 0.

Regroup.	**Subtract.**
9 9 9 0 10 10 10 10 1 Ø,Ø Ø Ø − 8,6 2 3	9 9 9 0 10 10 10 10 1 Ø,Ø Ø Ø − 8,6 2 3 1,3 7 7

Here are some more examples of subtracting across zeros.

C.
9
4 10 10
5,Ø Ø 8
−2,3 7 4
2,6 3 4

D.
9 9 11
5 10 10 10 13
4 6 Ø,Ø 2 3
−1 4 5,7 2 8
3 1 4,2 9 5

Subtract.

1. 7,000 −3,263	**2.** 500 − 74	**3.** 15,008 − 9,382	**4.** 435,106 − 22,535	**5.** $600.00 − 47.99

SKILLS PRACTICE

Subtract.

1. 40,000 − 26,232	2. 900 − 894	3. 507 − 398	4. $60.00 − 48.75	5. 10,651 − 6,187
6. 7,000 − 3,243	7. 499,007 − 237,488	8. $80.00 − 47.36	9. 830,000 − 186,254	10. 700 − 328
11. 50,000 − 23,574	12. 196,002 − 8,374	13. 48,392 − 9,889	14. 17,546 − 8,291	15. $500.00 − 96.88
16. 10,054 − 1,457	17. 7,000 − 4,837	18. 558,921 − 482,030	19. 60,066 − 438	20. 900,000 − 4,854
21. $100.02 − 64.47	22. 92,604 − 66,235	23. 100,000 − 15,206	24. 619,457 − 239,817	25. 84,791 − 7,799

26. $63,940 - 961 = \blacksquare$

27. $\$846.02 - \$67.43 = \blacksquare$

28. $8,000 - 21 = \blacksquare$

29. $\$7,043.07 - \$6,823.89 = \blacksquare$

30. $923,475 - 27,596 = \blacksquare$

31. $109,001 - 9,999 = \blacksquare$

PROBLEM SOLVING

32. The San Luis Dam is 18,000 feet long. The Grand Coulee Dam is 4,173 feet long. How much longer is the San Luis Dam?

33. The Oroville Dam is 742 feet high. The Hoover Dam is 726 feet high. How much higher is the Oroville Dam?

34. The Arrowrock Dam was built in 1915. The Pyramid Dam was built in 1973. How many years later was the Pyramid Dam built?

★35. Alex built a model of a dam as a science project. He used 4 boards that were each 3 feet long, and 4 that were each 2 feet long. How many feet of boards did he use?

THINK!

Logical Reasoning

Find the missing digits in this subtraction.

$$\begin{array}{r} 1,0\;0\;0 \\ -\quad 4\;\blacklozenge\;\bullet \\ \hline \blacktriangle\;0\;\blacklozenge \end{array}$$

$\blacklozenge + \bullet = 10$

$\blacktriangle + \blacklozenge = 14$

Estimating Differences: Mental Math

A. Sometimes you need to find an *estimate* of a difference. You can round the numbers and subtract to get a number that is near the exact difference.

Hurricane Jason was 925 kilometers from Nassau and 472 kilometers from Savannah. *About* how much closer to Savannah was the hurricane?

Round to the leftmost place.

$$
\begin{array}{r}
9|25 \\
-4|72 \\
\hline
\end{array}
\qquad
\begin{array}{r}
900 \\
-500 \\
\hline
400
\end{array}
$$

The hurricane was *about* 400 kilometers closer to Savannah. It was exactly 453 kilometers closer.

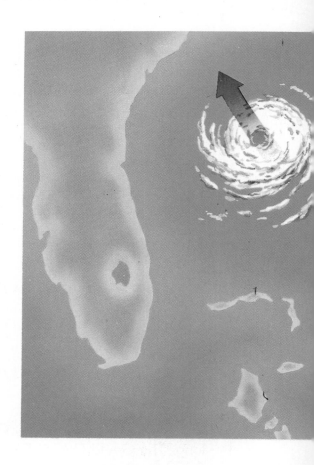

B. Estimate.

$$
\begin{array}{r}
3,|882 \\
-1,|316 \\
\hline
\end{array}
\qquad
\begin{array}{r}
4,000 \\
-1,000 \\
\hline
3,000
\end{array}
\qquad\qquad
\begin{array}{r}
6|19,342 \\
+|58,397 \\
\hline
\end{array}
\qquad
\begin{array}{r}
600,000 \\
-100,000 \\
\hline
500,000
\end{array}
$$

C. If you want a more precise estimate, round to a place farther to the right.

$$
\begin{array}{rcr}
3,|8|82 & \rightarrow & 3,900 \\
-1,|3|16 & \rightarrow & -1,300 \\
\hline
& & 2,600
\end{array}
$$

D. When you estimate money differences, you often round to the nearest dollar.

$$
\begin{array}{rcr}
\$64.21 & \rightarrow & \$64.00 \\
-\ 11.38 & \rightarrow & -11.00 \\
\hline
& & \$53.00
\end{array}
$$

TRY THESE

Estimate by rounding to the leftmost place. Next estimate by rounding to the next place to the right. Finally find the exact difference.

1.	2.	3.	4.	5.
374 − 211	4,603 − 3,274	34,537 − 9,305	51,629 − 18,421	143,800 − 76,214

SKILLS PRACTICE

Estimate by rounding to the leftmost place.

1.	2.	3.	4.	5.
5,743 − 878	9,954 − 2,642	873 − 82	43,007 − 21,368	573,694 − 517,580

Estimate by rounding to the second place from the left.

6.	7.	8.	9.	10.
5,743 − 878	9,954 − 2,642	873 − 82	43,007 − 21,368	573,694 − 517,580

Estimate. Then find the exact difference.

11.	12.	13.	14.	15.
8,267 − 3,775	$264.48 − 17.83	46,627 − 33,300	182,679 − 111,824	683,876 − 28,644

16. $81.35 − $66.86 = ■   **17.** 5,080 − 3,080 = ■   **18.** $80.00 − $.80 = ■

PROBLEM SOLVING

Estimate to check your answer.

19. A weather station reports a blizzard 423 kilometers from Winnipeg. The next day, the blizzard is only 87 kilometers from Winnipeg. How far has the blizzard traveled?

★20. Hurricane Rosa travels 642 kilometers over water and 93 kilometers over land. Hurricane Sam travels 438 kilometers over water and 130 kilometers over land. Which hurricane travels farther? How much farther?

MIXED REVIEW

Write >, <, or = for ●.

1. 10,486 ● 9,312   **2.** 53,679 ● 58,679   **3.** 742,831 ● 781,620

Add, subtract, multiply, or divide.

4.	5.	6.	7.	8.	9.	10.
8 ×7	11 − 3	4 +9	2 ×6	5)10	7 +6	6)24

Problem Solving

Working with Larger Numbers

When very large numbers are used, they are often rounded to the nearest million or billion. You often see numbers in this form in newspapers and magazines.

A. The new state budget was cut by $185 million. The city budget was cut by $23 million. How much was the total cut in the budgets?

Add to find the total of the budget cuts.

$$\begin{array}{r} \overset{1}{\$185,000,000} \\ +\ \ \ 23,000,000 \\ \hline \$208,000,000 \end{array} \quad \text{or} \quad \begin{array}{r} \overset{1}{\$185 \text{ million}} \\ +\ \ \ 23 \text{ million} \\ \hline \$208 \text{ million} \end{array}$$

The total cut in the budgets was $208,000,000 or $208 million.

B. Receipts of the U.S. Internal Revenue Service in 1945 were $43,902,001,929. Receipts in 1960 were $91,774,802,823. About how much higher were receipts in 1960?

$$\begin{array}{r} \$9\boxed{1},774,802,823 \quad \longrightarrow \quad \$92 \text{ billion} \\ -\ 4\boxed{3},902,001,929 \quad \longrightarrow \quad -\ 44 \text{ billion} \\ \hline \$48 \text{ billion} \end{array}$$

Receipts were about $48 billion higher in 1960.

TRY THESE

Add or subtract.

1.   432 million
   + 298 million

2.   895 million
   − 644 million

3.   611 billion
   + 92 billion

4.   617,000,000
   − 288,000,000

Estimate the sum or difference.

5.   11,205,773
   − 5,882,149

6.   76,551,603,411
   − 40,871,933,716

7.   8,226,113,502
   + 2,997,224,673

74   **Addition and Subtraction**

PROBLEM SOLVING PRACTICE

1. An aircraft manufacturer received a $3-billion order from the Air Force and a $2-billion order from the Army. How much larger was the first order?

2. A state government issued bonds worth $150 million in May and another $130 million in June to finance schools. How much were all the bonds issued worth?

3. A city's budget included $7,124,129 for police and $1,880,746 for sanitation. About how much more money was included for police than for sanitation?

4. A city's budget was increased by $37 million for education and by $84 million for construction. What was the total budget increase?

5. A city's budget must be cut by $311 million. The budget for transportation has been cut by $67 million. How much more must be cut from the city's budget?

6. In 1982, U.S. exports to Italy were worth $4,616,000,000. U.S. exports to Switzerland that year were worth $2,707,000,000. About how much more were exports to Italy worth?

7. A state expects to receive $200,000,000 in taxes this year. So far, $47,903,168 in taxes has been received. About how much more tax money does the state expect to receive?

★8. A state's budget is $9 billion. Of that amount, $370 million is for highways and $852 million is for housing. How much of the total budget is *not* for highways or housing?

ON YOUR OWN

Find out how much a city or town near you has budgeted for police, sanitation, and firefighting this year. Round the amounts if necessary. Make up two problems that can be solved by adding or subtracting the rounded numbers.

Problem Solving

Too Much Information

English is one of the world's most common languages. It is spoken by 409 million people. Mandarin, a language of China, is spoken by 755 million people. There are 275 million speakers of Spanish in Spain and in North and South America. Hindustani, widely spoken in India and Pakistan, is used by 352 million people. There are 121 million speakers of Japanese and 280 million speakers of Russian. In Africa, two widely used languages are Swahili, with 35 million speakers, and Hausa, with 27 million speakers.

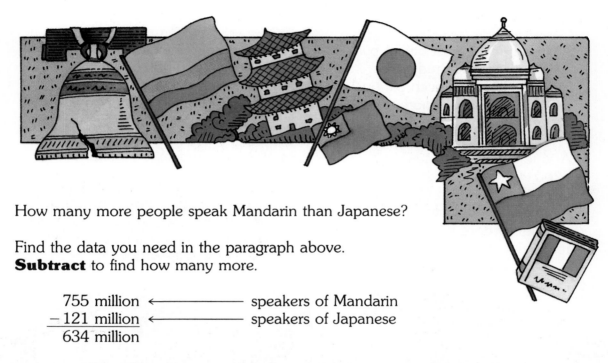

How many more people speak Mandarin than Japanese?

Find the data you need in the paragraph above.
Subtract to find how many more.

$$\begin{array}{r} 755 \text{ million} \longleftarrow \text{speakers of Mandarin} \\ -\ 121 \text{ million} \longleftarrow \text{speakers of Japanese} \\ \hline 634 \text{ million} \end{array}$$

There are 634 million more speakers of Mandarin than of Japanese.

TRY THESE

Use the data in the paragraph above. Solve.

1. Are there more speakers of Hindustani or of Spanish?

2. How many more people speak Swahili than Hausa?

3. Are there more speakers of Russian or of English?

4. How many people in all speak Japanese or Mandarin?

PROBLEM SOLVING PRACTICE

Some languages are spoken by fewer than 10 million people. Examples are Norwegian, which has 5 million speakers; Kongo, with 2 million speakers; Hebrew, with 3 million; and Swedish, with 9 million.

Use the data in the paragraph above and in the paragraph on page 76. Solve.

1. Name three languages that are spoken by more than 300 million people.

2. Name two languages that are spoken by fewer than 5 million people.

3. How many more people speak Swedish than Norwegian?

4. How many more people speak Hausa than Kongo?

5. How many people speak either English or Spanish?

6. How many people in all speak Norwegian or Swedish?

7. How many more speakers are there of Hindustani than of Hebrew?

8. Are there more speakers of Kongo or of Swahili?

★9. How many people in all speak either Russian, Japanese, English, or Swahili?

★10. How many people in all speak either Kongo, Hausa, or Swahili? Are there more people who speak any of those languages or more speakers of English?

ON YOUR OWN

Data Search

Find out how many people speak French and how many people speak Italian. Make up two problems that use the data you found.

Problem Solving with Calculators

Carrie wanted to buy 4 small cans of paint and 3 brushes at the paint store. Each can cost $2.95 and so did each brush. Carrie had $20. She used her calculator to see if she had enough money. She entered:

| 4 | + | 3 | × | 2 | . | 9 | 5 | = |. She got [12.85].

Her answer did not seem correct, so she estimated.

Estimate.

2.95 2.95 2.95 2.95   2.95 2.95 2.95

about $12   about $9

about $21

With her calculator, Carrie needs to enter information this way:

| 4 | + | 3 | = | × | 2 | . | 9 | 5 | = | [20.65].

Carrie needed $.65 more.

Solve the problem on your calculator to see how your calculator works. Read the instruction booklet that came with your calculator to learn the rules for solving problems.

Solve these problems. Be sure to enter information the correct way for your calculator. Estimate to check.

1. Later, Carrie bought 7 large cans of blue paint and 2 large cans of red paint. Each can cost $11.25. What was the total cost?

2. Carrie kept 5 of the 9 cans and returned the rest for a refund. At $11.25 a can, how much was her refund?

3. Carrie bought a roll of wallpaper for $10.89 and 3 tubes of paste at $3.79 each. How much did she spend?

Unit Review

Estimate. Then find the exact sum.   (*pages 54–58, 60–61*)

1. 54 +37	2. 666 +738	3. $9.83 + 3.37	4. 1,342 +2,447	5. 7,648 + 534

6. 12,379 +28,610	7. 83,248 + 3,436	8. $78.97 + 3.13	9. 604,315 +173,429	10. 12,763 89,247 + 3,822

Estimate. Then find the exact difference.   (*pages 66–73*)

11. 97 −39	12. 931 −740	13. $9.37 − 2.18	14. 5,300 −1,739	15. 6,149 − 362

16. 23,740 − 8,613	17. 92,103 −76,972	18. 19,004 − 9,005	19. $69.35 − 4.91	20. 643,201 −213,614

Solve.   (*pages 62–63, 74–75*)

21. Southern Union Railroad had 48,720 rail cars. The company bought an additional 12,475 rail cars. How many rail cars did the company then have in all?

22. In one year, 5 million passengers used LaGuardia Airport and 3 million passengers used Newark Airport. How many passengers in all used LaGuardia and Newark?

23. In one year, 648,007 planes landed at the Santa Ana Airport and 497,922 planes landed at the San Jose Municipal Airport. How many more planes landed at the Santa Ana Airport?

24. In one year, 351,642 planes landed at LaGuardia Airport and 335,473 planes landed at John F. Kennedy Airport. How many planes in all landed at these two airports?

25. In one year, 7 million passengers used O'Hare Airport in Chicago and 3 million passengers used Logan Airport in Boston. How many more passengers used O'Hare Airport?

26. In 1984, Southern Union Railroad carried 23 million passengers. In 1985, the railroad carried 37 million passengers. How many more passengers did the railroad carry in 1985?

More Help with Addition

```
 I I
286
+ 98
384
```

```
 I  I I
4,965
+2,635
7,600
```

```
   I  I  I  I
506,987
+835,625
1,342,612
```

```
   I  I  I2
26,295
1,839
+78,557
106,691
```

Add.

1.
```
    79
   +27
```
2.
```
    345
   + 86
```
3.
```
    342
   +931
```
4.
```
    672
   +429
```

5.
```
   4,639
  +3,209
```
6.
```
   9,807
  + 633
```
7.
```
   6,001
  +7,999
```
8.
```
   3,124
  + 975
```

9.
```
  29,377
 +62,434
```
10.
```
  12,988
 +97,622
```
11.
```
  343,129
 +277,483
```
12.
```
  842,010
 +937,614
```

13.
```
    23
    49
   + 7
```
14.
```
    124
    395
   + 16
```
15.
```
   1,932
    421
  +  25
```
16.
```
  734,094
   76,982
  +    26
```

More Help with Subtraction

```
  7 14
3 8 4
-  6 7
3 1 7
```

```
  4  11 15
5,2 5 8
-2,9 8 3
2,275
```

```
  12 10
1 2 0 15 26
2 3 1,5 3 6
- 1 6 2,9 2 8
68,608
```

```
  9 15 12
6 10 8 1 10
7 0 6,3 0 0
- 2 8 8,9 2 0
417,380
```

Subtract.

17.
```
    295
   - 69
```
18.
```
    784
   -639
```
19.
```
    93
   -74
```
20.
```
    972
   -683
```

21.
```
   8,632
  -7,248
```
22.
```
   3,410
  -3,369
```
23.
```
   9,103
  -2,744
```
24.
```
   7,123
  -6,924
```

25.
```
  28,293
 -21,407
```
26.
```
  95,324
 -61,743
```
27.
```
  103,053
 -102,040
```
28.
```
  703,429
 -612,143
```

29.
```
    700
   - 29
```
30.
```
   6,060
  - 123
```
31.
```
  80,000
 -62,419
```
32.
```
  830,000
 -429,136
```

Working with Sets

A. You can use circles to represent sets of objects.

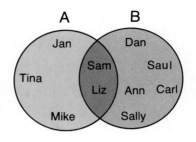

A is the set of students with red shirts.
B is the set of students with blue pants.

The circles show that:
A = {Tina, Jan, Sam, Liz, Mike}
B = {Dan, Saul, Carl, Ann, Sally, Liz, Sam}

B. The students who have *both* red shirts and blue pants form the *intersection* of the two sets.

Write: A ∩ B   Read: the intersection of A and B

A ∩ B = {Sam, Liz}

C. The students who have *either* red shirts *or* blue pants (including those in both sets) form the *union* of the two sets.

Write: A ∪ B   Read: the union of A and B

A ∪ B = {Tina, Jan, Sam, Liz, Mike, Dan, Saul, Carl, Ann, Sally}

List the numbers in each set. Use the symbol { }.

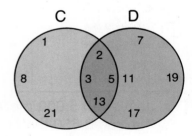

1. C

2. D

3. C ∩ D

4. C ∪ D

5. numbers in C, but not in D

Draw circles to show these two sets.

X = {0, 5, 10, 15, 20}
Y = {1, 3, 5, 7, 9, 11, 13, 15, 17, 19}

List the numbers in each set.

6. X ∩ Y

7. X ∪ Y

8. numbers in X, but not in Y

Cumulative Review

Choose the correct answer.

1. 4
     ×7

a. 11
b. 35
c. 28
d. not above

2. 962
    −559

a. 417
b. 403
c. 413
d. not above

3. Round 89,517 to the nearest thousand.

a. 80,000
b. 89,000
c. 90,000
d. not above

4. 86
    +35

a. 51
b. 111
c. 131
d. not above

5. Complete.
89,999 ⬤ 9,000

a. >
b. <
c. =

6. $8 \times 0 = $ ■

a. 8
b. 0
c. 80
d. not above

7. Write the standard numeral for eight million, nine hundred thousand.

a. 8,009,000
b. 8,000,900
c. 8,900
d. not above

8. $509 + 37 + 8 = $ ■

a. 554
b. 544
c. 546
d. not above

9. $512.98
    −   8.79

a. $516.21
b. $521.77
c. $504.19
d. not above

10. 152,726
     + 16,448

a. 168,164
b. 169,174
c. 179,274
d. not above

11. 243,006
     −104,129

a. 241,123
b. 138,987
c. 138,877
d. not above

12. $2,000 - 148 = $ ■

a. 1,852
b. 1,480
c. 2,148
d. not above

13. Jamie ran 5,000 meters. Tim ran 2,650 meters. How much farther than Tim did Jamie run?

a. 3,750 meters
b. 2,350 meters
c. 2,450 meters
d. not above

14. The balance in Ms. Gannon's bank account was $459.76. She made a deposit of $68.50. What is the balance in her account now?

a. $391.26
b. $411.26
c. $528.26
d. not above

4 Multiplication

FIFTY YEARS OF GROWTH OF U.S. AIRLINE CARRIERS

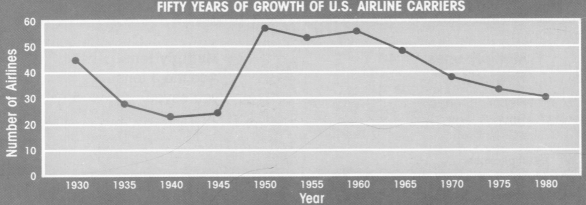

Multiplying 2-digit Numbers

A. A baker has 3 ovens. He is baking 32 loaves of bread in each oven. How many loaves of bread is he baking in all?

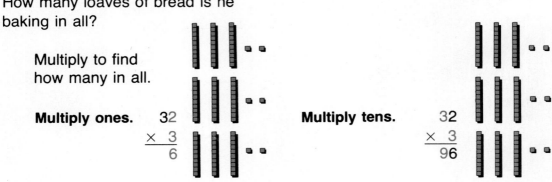

Multiply to find how many in all.

Multiply ones.
$$\begin{array}{r} 32 \\ \times\ 3 \\ \hline 6 \end{array}$$

Multiply tens.
$$\begin{array}{r} 32 \\ \times\ 3 \\ \hline 96 \end{array}$$

He is baking 96 loaves of bread in all.

B. Sometimes you must regroup ones and save.

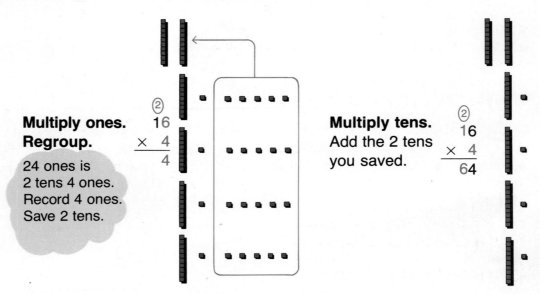

Multiply ones. Regroup.
$$\begin{array}{r} \overset{②}{16} \\ \times\ 4 \\ \hline 4 \end{array}$$

24 ones is 2 tens 4 ones. Record 4 ones. Save 2 tens.

Multiply tens. Add the 2 tens you saved.
$$\begin{array}{r} \overset{②}{16} \\ \times\ 4 \\ \hline 64 \end{array}$$

C. Sometimes you must regroup both ones and tens.

Multiply ones. Regroup.
$$\begin{array}{r} \overset{③}{47} \\ \times\ 5 \\ \hline 5 \end{array}$$

Record 5 ones. Save 3 tens.

Multiply tens. Add the 3 tens you saved.
$$\begin{array}{r} \overset{③}{47} \\ \times\ 5 \\ \hline 235 \end{array}$$

TRY THESE

Find the products.

1. $\begin{array}{r} 23 \\ \times\ 3 \\ \hline \end{array}$

2. $\begin{array}{r} 17 \\ \times\ 5 \\ \hline \end{array}$

3. $\begin{array}{r} 42 \\ \times\ 3 \\ \hline \end{array}$

4. $\begin{array}{r} 36 \\ \times\ 4 \\ \hline \end{array}$

5. $\begin{array}{r} 58 \\ \times\ 7 \\ \hline \end{array}$

6. $\begin{array}{r} 29 \\ \times\ 8 \\ \hline \end{array}$

7. $9 \times 61 = \blacksquare$

8. $2 \times 90 = \blacksquare$

9. $5 \times 89 = \blacksquare$

SKILLS PRACTICE

Multiply.

1. $\begin{array}{r} 34 \\ \times\ 2 \\ \hline \end{array}$

2. $\begin{array}{r} 62 \\ \times\ 3 \\ \hline \end{array}$

3. $\begin{array}{r} 71 \\ \times\ 4 \\ \hline \end{array}$

4. $\begin{array}{r} 54 \\ \times\ 2 \\ \hline \end{array}$

5. $\begin{array}{r} 11 \\ \times\ 9 \\ \hline \end{array}$

6. $\begin{array}{r} 80 \\ \times\ 6 \\ \hline \end{array}$

7. $\begin{array}{r} 28 \\ \times\ 3 \\ \hline \end{array}$

8. $\begin{array}{r} 19 \\ \times\ 4 \\ \hline \end{array}$

9. $\begin{array}{r} 35 \\ \times\ 5 \\ \hline \end{array}$

10. $\begin{array}{r} 59 \\ \times\ 4 \\ \hline \end{array}$

11. $\begin{array}{r} 63 \\ \times\ 7 \\ \hline \end{array}$

12. $\begin{array}{r} 74 \\ \times\ 8 \\ \hline \end{array}$

13. $\begin{array}{r} 83 \\ \times\ 7 \\ \hline \end{array}$

14. $\begin{array}{r} 62 \\ \times\ 4 \\ \hline \end{array}$

15. $\begin{array}{r} 94 \\ \times\ 3 \\ \hline \end{array}$

16. $\begin{array}{r} 27 \\ \times\ 9 \\ \hline \end{array}$

17. $\begin{array}{r} 42 \\ \times\ 4 \\ \hline \end{array}$

18. $\begin{array}{r} 98 \\ \times\ 8 \\ \hline \end{array}$

19. $3 \times 26 = \blacksquare$

20. $4 \times 25 = \blacksquare$

21. $8 \times 78 = \blacksquare$

PROBLEM SOLVING

22. The baker had 8 trays of rolls. There were 24 rolls on each tray. How many rolls were there in all?

★23. The bakery had 9 boxes of rolls with 48 rolls in each box. How many rolls in all? 415 rolls were sold. How many were left?

THINK!

Perimeter as a Product

The figure shown is a square.
Write a number sentence using multiplication
to find the perimeter of the figure.

47 m

Multiplying Larger Numbers

A. Mr. and Mrs. Anno use 4 subway tokens to go to their shop daily. They worked 328 days last year. How many tokens did they use?

Multiply ones.
```
    ③
  328
×   4
    2
```

Multiply tens. Add the 3 tens you saved.
```
  ①③
  328
×   4
   12
```

Multiply hundreds. Add the 1 hundred you saved.
```
  ①③
  328
×   4
1,312
```

Mr. and Mrs. Anno used 1,312 tokens.

B. 6 × 2,075 = ■
```
   ④③
  2,075
×     6
 12,450
```

C. 56,350 × 5 = 5 × 56,350 = ■
```
   ③①②
   56,350
×       5
  281,750
```

D. One monthly commutation pass costs $32.90. How much will 5 passes cost?
```
    ①④
  $32.90
×      5
 $164.50
```

Don't forget the $ and . in the answer.

5 passes will cost $164.50.

TRY THESE

Multiply.

1.
```
  352
×   4
```

2.
```
  705
×   6
```

3.
```
  8,257
×     4
```

4.
```
  $28.05
×      6
```

5.
```
         3
× 39,087
```

6. 8 × 634 = ■

7. 9,472 × 4 = ■

8. 8 × $148.69 = ■

SKILLS PRACTICE

Multiply.

1. 284 × 7
2. 152 × 6
3. 846 × 2
4. 375 × 4
5. 960 × 8

6. $136.60 × 6
7. 2,573 × 3
8. 8,974 × 4
9. $42.13 × 2
10. 8,062 × 5

11. 1,062 × 5
12. 25,143 × 9
13. 416 × 6
14. 8 × 246
15. $56.82 × 7

16. 51,023 × 8
17. 79,000 × 2
18. 348 × 8
19. 43,120 × 5
20. 5,903 × 4

21. 93,000 × 5
22. 63,895 × 9
23. 3 × 7,088
24. $4.59 × 6
25. 64,587 × 8

26. 6 × 7,071 = ■
27. 490 × 5 = ■
28. 8 × $281.09 = ■

PROBLEM SOLVING

Copy and complete this record of sales of skates by Mr. Anno's Company.

	Type	Pairs Sold	Cost per Pair	Total Cost
29.	Plain	9	$28.95	■
30.	Fancy	6	$35.50	■
31.	Extra Fancy	4	$41.98	■

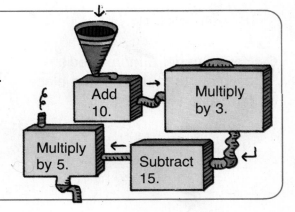

THINK!

Mental Math

Suppose you have a machine like this. When you put in 3, it gives you 120.

What number does the machine give you when you put in:

1. 2?   2. 7?   3. 12?   4. 20?

Add 10.

Multiply by 3.

Multiply by 5.

Subtract 15.

Estimating Products: Mental Math

A. Often you do not need to find an exact answer. You can *estimate* by rounding the factors to the leftmost place and multiplying.

A manufacturer shipped 5,175 boxes of paint brushes. There were 8 brushes in each box. *About* how many brushes were shipped?

Estimate.

$$\begin{array}{r} 5,175 \\ \times \quad 8 \\ \hline \end{array}$$

$$\begin{array}{r} 5,000 \\ \times \quad 8 \\ \hline 40,000 \end{array}$$

The manufacturer shipped *about* 40,000 brushes. Exactly 41,400 brushes were shipped.

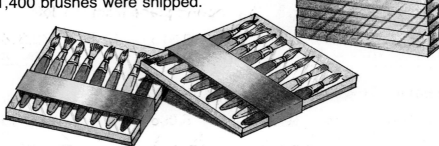

B. This quick estimation method works with larger numbers, too.

$$\begin{array}{r} 68,414 \\ \times \quad 5 \\ \hline \end{array}$$

$$\begin{array}{r} 70,000 \\ \times \quad 5 \\ \hline 350,000 \end{array}$$

$$\begin{array}{r} 227,793 \\ \times \quad 9 \\ \hline \end{array}$$

$$\begin{array}{r} 200,000 \\ \times \quad 9 \\ \hline 1,800,000 \end{array}$$

The exact product is 342,070.

The exact product is 2,050,137.

C. You may get a more precise estimate by rounding to a place farther to the right.

$$\begin{array}{r} 68,414 \\ \times \quad 5 \\ \hline \end{array}$$

$$\begin{array}{r} 68,000 \\ \times \quad 5 \\ \hline 340,000 \end{array}$$

D. When you estimate money products, you often round to the nearest dollar.

$$\begin{array}{r} \$817.69 \\ \times \quad 3 \\ \hline \end{array}$$

$$\begin{array}{r} \$818.00 \\ \times \quad 3 \\ \hline \$2,454.00 \end{array}$$

TRY THESE

A. Estimate by rounding to the leftmost place.
B. Estimate by rounding to the next place to the right.
C. Find the exact product.
D. Compare the estimates with the exact product.

1.	2.	3.	4.	5.
3,912	738	16,604	25,519	681,132
× 4	× 7	× 3	× 6	× 2

SKILLS PRACTICE

Estimate by rounding to the leftmost place.

1.	2.	3.	4.	5.
5,077	40,316	3,316	142,318	873,331
× 8	× 5	× 4	× 8	× 9

Estimate by rounding to the second place from the left.

6.	7.	8.	9.	10.
5,077	40,316	3,316	142,318	873,331
× 8	× 5	× 4	× 8	× 9

Estimate. Then find the exact product.

11.	12.	13.	14.	15.
3,440	$9.04	5,066	$411.83	1,207
× 6	× 7	× 9	× 2	× 3

16.	17.	18.	19.	20.
66,629	24,419	$1,211.63	200,113	624,409
× 3	× 5	× 7	× 8	× 4

PROBLEM SOLVING

Solve. Estimate to check your answer.

21. A manufacturer ships 28,350 erasers each month. How many erasers does the manufacturer ship in 9 months?

★22. An art club has 6 members. Each member buys an easel for $183.95 and a paint set for $76.59. How much does the whole club spend?

MIXED REVIEW

Add, subtract, multiply, or divide.

1.	2.	3.	4.	5.	6.
17	6	6)18	5	8	9)45
− 9	×6		+9	+0	

Problem Solving

Labeling Answers

A. A train has 7 boxcars. Each boxcar holds 1,540 kilograms (kg) of grain. How much grain is the train hauling?

③②
$$\begin{array}{r} 1,540 \\ \times \quad 7 \\ \hline 10,780 \end{array}$$

The train is hauling 10,780 kg of grain.

same label as one of the factors

1,540 kg

1,540 kg

1,540 kg

1,540 kg

1,540 kg

1,540 kg

1,540 kg

7 sets   1,540 in each set

B. A train traveled at a speed of 96 kilometers per hour (km/h). It ran for 5 hours. How far did it travel in all?

③
$$\begin{array}{r} 96 \\ \times \ 5 \\ \hline 480 \end{array}$$

The train traveled 480 km in all.

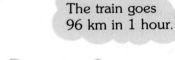

The train goes 96 km in 1 hour.

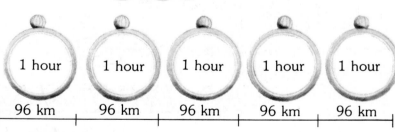

| 1 hour | 1 hour | 1 hour | 1 hour | 1 hour |

| 96 km | 96 km | 96 km | 96 km | 96 km |

TRY THESE

1. A plane travels at a speed of 935 km/h. How far does it travel in 6 hours?

2. A train has 19 boxcars. Each boxcar holds 3 metric tons of tomatoes. How many metric tons of tomatoes is the train hauling in all?

PROBLEM SOLVING PRACTICE

Use the five steps to solve each problem.

1. 3 planes take off. Each carries 3,580 kg of freight. How many kilograms of freight do they carry all together?

2. A train traveled 1,077 km from Atlanta to Baltimore. Then it traveled 301 km from Baltimore to New York City. How far did it travel in all?

3. A rocket travels 7,274 km/h. How far does the rocket travel in 9 hours?

4. A rocket travels 9 kilometers per second. How far does the rocket travel in 185 seconds?

5. It takes 6 hours to fly from New York to Los Angeles. It takes 14 hours to fly from New York to Hawaii. How much longer does it take to fly from New York to Hawaii?

6. A train traveled for 4 hours at 98 km/h to get from Cincinnati to Cleveland. How far did the train travel?

7. A plane flew for 7 hours at 913 km/h from Mexico City to Montreal. How far is Mexico City from Montreal?

8. The *Loco Express* has 16 cars. The *Cornhusker Local* has 8 cars. How many more cars does the *Loco Express* have?

★9. Mrs. Dempsey flew her plane for 3 hours at 392 km/h. How far did she fly? In 6 months, Mr. Shorter walked for 268 hours at 5 km/h. How far did he walk? Who traveled farther? How much farther?

★10. Mr. Allison flew for 6 hours at 825 km/h. How far did he fly? Then he drove for 5 hours at 80 km/h. How far did he drive? How far did he travel all together?

ON YOUR OWN

The Wheatland Whizz has 4 boxcars. The train travels at 87 km/h for 6 hours. It carries 2,100 kg of wheat in each boxcar.

Make up two problems using the data above.

For one problem, the answer should have the same label as one of the factors. For the second problem, the answer should have a different label from either factor.

Problem Solving Strategy

Find a Pattern

Sometimes a problem has numbers that form a pattern.
When you *find the pattern,* you can decide how to solve the problem.

Mr. Cabrini, the president of a large cabinet factory, wants to notify all his
employees that the company is closed because of a blizzard. He calls 5 employees.
Each of them agrees to call 3 more employees. Every person who is called is asked
to call 3 more employees. How many people are notified in the third round of calls?

Make a table to help in finding the pattern.

Round of calls	1	2	3	4	5
Employees	5	15	45	▪	▪

3 × 5   3 × 15

In the third round of calls, 45 people are notified of the closing.

Solve.

1. How many people are notified of
the closing on the fourth round of
calls?

2. On which round of calls are 405
people notified of the closing?

3. How many people are notified of
the closing on the seventh round of
calls?

4. When the fourth round of calls is
completed, how many people besides
Mr. Cabrini know of the closing?

Challenge Problems   page 458

Problem Solving Project

Keeping a Checkbook

A checkbook is a record of the amounts deposited in an account or withdrawn from it. When you write a **check,** you **subtract** the amount from the balance. When you make a **deposit,** you **add** the amount to the balance.

Mr. Burger kept this checkbook record.

Check No.	Date	Pay to	Amount of Check	Amount of Deposit	Balance $375.26
411	6/16	Edna's Food Store	$ 33.19		$342.07
	6/17	Deposit		$180.00	$522.07
412	6/19	Gracie's Dept. Store	$162.74		▩
413	6/28	Video World	$ 41.13		▩
	7/3	Deposit		$200.00	▩

To find his balance on June 16, Mr. Burger subtracted $33.19 from his previous balance.

$375.26 ···· • previous balance
− 33.19 ···· • amount of check 411
$342.07 ···· • balance on June 16

To find his balance on June 17, Mr. Burger added the amount of the deposit to his last balance.

$342.07 ···· • last balance
+ 180.00 ···· • amount of deposit
$522.07 ···· • balance on June 17

1. What was Mr. Burger's balance after he wrote the check to Gracie's Department Store?

2. What was his balance after he wrote the check to Video World?

3. What was his balance after the deposit he made on July 3?

ON YOUR OWN

Pretend you are Mr. Burger. Suppose you make a deposit on July 8 and write a check to Sturdy Shoe Company on July 10. Choose amounts for the deposit and the check. Write the next two lines in the check register. (Be sure *not* to write a check for more than the balance.)

Multiplying by Multiples of 10

A. Roger packed 10 jars of worms for a fishing trip. Each jar contained 6 worms. How many worms did Roger pack?

Find 10 × 6.

$$\begin{array}{r} 10 \\ \times\ 6 \\ \hline 60 \end{array} \quad \text{so} \quad \begin{array}{r} 6 \\ \times 10 \\ \hline 60 \end{array}$$

When you change the order of the factors, you do not change the product.

You can use a shortcut to multiply any number by 10.

$$\begin{array}{r} 42 \\ \times 10 \\ \hline 420 \end{array} \quad \begin{array}{r} 785 \\ \times\ 10 \\ \hline 7{,}850 \end{array} \quad \begin{array}{r} 6{,}359 \\ \times\ \ \ \ 10 \\ \hline 63{,}590 \end{array}$$

Shortcut

To multiply by 10, write a 0 in the ones place. Write the other digits to the left.

B. Claire works in the store at the boat dock. She has 30 boxes. There are 275 fishing flies in each box. How many flies does she have?

30 boxes are 3 sets of 10 boxes.

In **1 set of 10 boxes**

$$\begin{array}{r} 275 \\ \times\ 10 \\ \hline 2{,}750 \end{array}$$

In **3 sets of 10 boxes**

$$\begin{array}{r} 2{,}750 \\ \times\ \ \ \ 3 \\ \hline 8{,}250 \end{array}$$

Claire has 8,250 fishing flies.

You can use this shortcut to find 30 × 275.

Shortcut

To multiply by a multiple of 10, write 0 in the ones place. Then multiply by the tens.

Step 1

$$\begin{array}{r} 275 \\ \times\ \ 30 \\ \hline 0 \end{array}$$

Step 2

$$\begin{array}{r} \overset{2\,1}{275} \\ \times\ \ 30 \\ \hline 8{,}250 \end{array}$$

TRY THESE

Multiply.

1.
$$\begin{array}{r} 6 \\ \times 10 \end{array}$$

2.
$$\begin{array}{r} 43 \\ \times 10 \end{array}$$

3.
$$\begin{array}{r} 684 \\ \times\ 10 \end{array}$$

4.
$$\begin{array}{r} \$47.00 \\ \times\ \ \ \ \ 10 \end{array}$$

5.
$$\begin{array}{r} 2{,}603 \\ \times\ \ \ \ \ 10 \end{array}$$

Multiply.

1. 36
×10

2. 8
×10

3. 370
× 10

4. 5,275
× 10

5. 7,304
× 10

6. 15
×30

7. 123
× 40

8. $3.41
× 20

9. 46
×80

10. 6,382
× 50

11. 380
× 70

12. $13.24
× 50

13. 2,158
× 70

14. 8,000
× 20

15. 1,678
× 40

16. 586
× 30

17. 9,400
× 10

18. 357
× 90

19. 4,008
× 50

20. 6,355
× 40

21. 60 × 82 = ■

22. 70 × 1,250 = ■

23. 10 × 7,346 = ■

PROBLEM SOLVING _____

24. 38 ships are in the fleet. Each ship has 10 sails. How many sails does the fleet have all together?

25. A ship can carry 10 metric tons of fish in each of its 3 holds. How many metric tons of fish can it carry each trip?

THINK!

Making Logical Choices

All 3 of these boxes have wrong labels. Tell how to re-label them correctly by opening only 1 box and looking at only 1 item in that box.

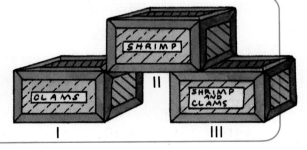

Multiplying by 2-digit Numbers

A. A store received 34 cartons of eggs. There were 12 eggs in each carton. How many eggs were there all together?

In 4 cartons:
4 × 12

```
  12
 ×34
  48 ← 4 × 12
```

In 30 cartons:
30 × 12

```
  12
 ×34
  48 ←  4 × 12
 360 ← 30 × 12
```

In 34 cartons:
48 + 360

```
  12
 ×34
  48 ←  4 × 12
 360 ← 30 × 12
 408 ← 34 × 12
```

There were 408 eggs in all.

B. 42 × 5,201 = ▧

Step 1
Multiply by 2.

```
  5,201
 ×   42
 10 402
```

Step 2
Multiply by 40.

```
  5,201
 ×   42
 10 402
208 040
```

Step 3
Add.

```
   5,201
 ×    42
  10 402
 208 040
 218,442
```

C. You can estimate before you multiply. Your estimate will help you decide whether your answer is reasonable.

	Estimate	Exact

```
  532        500        532
×  27       ×  30      ×  27
          15,000       3 724
                       10 64
                      14,364
```

The answer is reasonable.

Estimate. Then multiply.

1. 432
      × 32

2. 7,102
      ×   24

3. 4,340
      ×   12

4. $7.11
      ×   38

5. 3,042
      ×   21

6. 30 × 803 = ▪

7. 5,213 × 23 = ▪

8. 49 × 8,010 = ▪

SKILLS PRACTICE

Multiply.

1. 81
      ×58

2. 62
      ×24

3. 234
      × 12

4. 1,001
      ×   19

5. 83
      ×13

6. 6,212
      ×   42

7. 643
      ×   20

8. $7.40
      ×   22

9. 3,112
      ×   43

10. 2,493
       ×   11

11. 4,010
       ×   88

12. 7,212
       ×   14

13. 9,685
       ×   10

14. 6,103
       ×   20

★15.   14
        ×921

Estimate. Then multiply.

16. 42 × 92 = ▪

17. 34 × 802 = ▪

18. 67 × 4,100 = ▪

19. 31 × 8,203 = ▪

20. 10 × 39,467 = ▪

21. 601 × 91 = ▪

PROBLEM SOLVING

22. A store has 22 boxes of beans. Each box holds 144 packages of beans. How many packages of beans does the store have?

★23. A supermarket received 1,065 boxes of soap. In 1 week, all but 58 boxes were sold. How many boxes were sold?

THINK!

Logical Reasoning
How many 22¢ stamps are there in a dozen?

More Multiplication

A. An airline owns 28 airplanes.
Each airplane has 324 seats.
How many seats do these airplanes
have in all?

Estimate.
$30 \times 300 = 9,000$

Step 1
Multiply
by 8.

Cross out
your saves
before you
multiply again.

324
× 28
2 592

Step 2
Multiply
by 20.

324
× 28
2 592
6 480

Step 3
Add.

324
× 28
2 592
6 480
9,072

The airplanes have 9,072 seats in all.

Estimate.
$80 \times \$40 = \$3,200$

B. Multiply $39.52 by 78.

Step 1

$ 3 9.5 2
× 7 8
3 1 6 1 6

Step 2

$ 3 9.5 2
× 7 8
3 1 6 1 6
2 7 6 6 4 0

Step 3

$ 3 9.5 2
× 7 8
3 1 6 1 6
2 7 6 6 4 0
$ 3,0 8 2.5 6

TRY THESE

Multiply.

1. 52
×48

2. $3.82
× 43

3. 811
× 57

4. 3,180
× 89

5. 73
×9,023

6. $30 \times 189 =$ ■

7. $3,807 \times 35 =$ ■

8. $40 \times 900 =$ ■

SKILLS PRACTICE

Multiply.

1. 493
    × 71

2. 63
    × 53

3. 30
    × 285

4. 39
    × 2,820

5. 712
    × 63

6. 543
    × 13

7. $4.12
    × 48

8. 43
    × 263

9. 6,220
    × 32

10. 396
    × 71

11. $9.20
    × 38

12. 124
    × 76

13. 13
    × 5,070

14. $1.35
    × 64

15. 1,073
    × 48

16. 36 × 148 = ■

17. 65 × 5,380 = ■

18. 93 × 3,029 = ■

19. 52 × 97 = ■

20. 39 × 217 = ■

21. 88 × $32.68 = ■

PROBLEM SOLVING

22. A company bought 72 airline tickets. Each ticket cost $52.40. How much did the company spend all together for tickets?

23. 37 planes took off from the airport. Each had 13 flight attendants. How many flight attendants were there in all?

24. There were 147 passengers on a flight. During the flight, 81 passengers watched a movie. How many passengers did not watch the movie?

★25. One plane has 362 seats. Another has 267. How many more seats does the first have? How many more passengers can it carry in 13 trips?

MIXED REVIEW

Round to the nearest thousand.

1. 3,726
2. 1,493
3. 27,547
4. 56,493
5. 512,643

Round to the nearest hundred-thousand.

6. 279,513
7. 949,605
8. 842,519
9. 756,214
10. 427,912

Add or subtract.

11. 5,368 − 2,189 = ■
12. 84,712 + 3,684 = ■

Multiplying by Multiples of 100

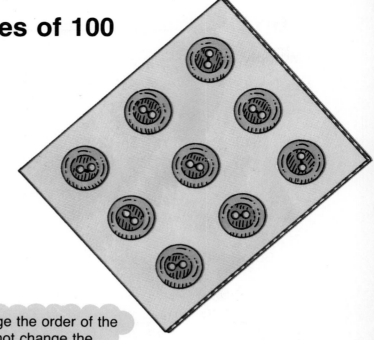

A. Mrs. Antico is responsible for shipping cards of buttons. If she ships 100 cards with 9 buttons on each, how many buttons does she ship?

$$100 \times 9 = \blacksquare$$

$$\begin{array}{r} 100 \\ \times \quad 9 \\ \hline 900 \end{array}$$ so $$\begin{array}{r} 9 \\ \times 100 \\ \hline 900 \end{array}$$

When you change the order of the factors, you do not change the product.

Shortcut

To multiply by 100, write 0's in the ones place *and* in the tens place. Write the other digits to the left.

$$\begin{array}{r} 15 \\ \times 100 \\ \hline 1,500 \end{array}$$ $$\begin{array}{r} 380 \\ \times 100 \\ \hline 38,000 \end{array}$$ $$\begin{array}{r} 7,256 \\ \times \quad 100 \\ \hline 725,600 \end{array}$$

B. You can work with multiples of 100 as you do with multiples of 10.

$$\begin{array}{r} \overset{⑤②}{283} \\ \times \quad 70 \\ \hline 19,810 \end{array}$$ Write a 0. Multiply 7 × 283.

$$\begin{array}{r} \overset{⑤②}{283} \\ \times 700 \\ \hline 198,100 \end{array}$$ Write two 0's. Multiply 7 × 283.

Shortcut

To multiply by a multiple of 100, write two 0's. Then multiply by the hundreds.

$$\begin{array}{r} 600 \\ \times 400 \\ \hline 240,000 \end{array}$$ $$\begin{array}{r} \overset{①\ ①}{4,635} \\ \times \quad 200 \\ \hline 927,000 \end{array}$$

TRY THESE

Multiply.

1. $\begin{array}{r} 386 \\ \times\,100 \end{array}$
2. $\begin{array}{r} 386 \\ \times\,400 \end{array}$
3. $\begin{array}{r} \$73.08 \\ \times\quad 200 \end{array}$
4. $\begin{array}{r} 6{,}280 \\ \times\quad 500 \end{array}$
5. $\begin{array}{r} 9{,}000 \\ \times\quad 800 \end{array}$

6. $400 \times 526 = $    7. $700 \times 2{,}300 = $ ■   8. $500 \times 4{,}800 = $ ■

SKILLS PRACTICE

Multiply.

1. $\begin{array}{r} 78 \\ \times\,100 \end{array}$
2. $\begin{array}{r} 340 \\ \times\,100 \end{array}$
3. $\begin{array}{r} \$47.65 \\ \times\quad 100 \end{array}$
4. $\begin{array}{r} 3{,}060 \\ \times\quad 100 \end{array}$
5. $\begin{array}{r} 2{,}000 \\ \times\quad 100 \end{array}$

6. $\begin{array}{r} 2{,}060 \\ \times\quad 700 \end{array}$
7. $\begin{array}{r} 4{,}510 \\ \times\quad 200 \end{array}$
8. $\begin{array}{r} 600 \\ \times\,7{,}420 \end{array}$
9. $\begin{array}{r} 5{,}000 \\ \times\quad 300 \end{array}$
10. $\begin{array}{r} 8{,}000 \\ \times\quad 900 \end{array}$

11. $800 \times 1{,}600 = $ ■   12. $400 \times 6{,}000 = $ ■   13. $700 \times 5{,}395 = $ ■

PROBLEM SOLVING

14. A store has 300 boxes of thread. Each contains 75 spools. How many spools are there in all?

★15. A store sold 200 cards of buttons in May and 400 cards of buttons in June. Each card had 12 buttons. How many buttons did the store sell in May and June?

THINK!

Exponents and Powers

| Exponent is 5. | There are 5 factors. |

$2^5 = 2 \times 2 \times 2 \times 2 \times 2 = 32$ 2^5 or 32 is the fifth power of 2.

| Each factor is 2. |

$10^3 = 10 \times 10 \times 10 = 1{,}000$ 10^3 or 1,000 is the third power of 10.

Complete.

1. $7 \times 7 = $ ■ or ■   2. $4 \times 4 \times 4 = $ ■ or ■

Multiplying by 3-digit Numbers

There are 612 spools of wire at a construction site. Each spool holds 1,125 meters of wire. How many meters of wire are at the construction site?

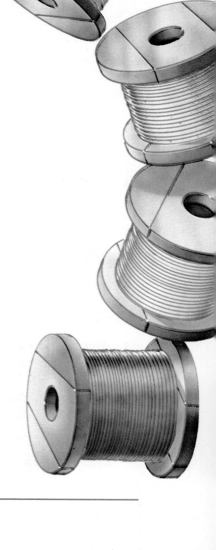

Use estimation first.

$$
\begin{array}{r}
\boxed{1},125 \\
\times \ \boxed{6}12 \\
\end{array}
\qquad
\begin{array}{r}
1,000 \\
\times \quad 600 \\
\hline
600,000
\end{array}
$$

Then find the exact answer.

Step 1	Step 2	Step 3	Step 4
Multiply by 2.	Multiply by 10.	Multiply by 600.	Add.

Step 1

$$
\begin{array}{r}
① \\
1,125 \\
\times 612 \\
\hline
2\ 250
\end{array}
$$

Step 2

$$
\begin{array}{r}
1,125 \\
\times \ 612 \\
\hline
2\ 250 \\
11\ 250
\end{array}
$$

Step 3

$$
\begin{array}{r}
①③ \\
1,125 \\
\times \quad 612 \\
\hline
2\ 250 \\
11\ 250 \\
675\ 000
\end{array}
$$

Step 4

$$
\begin{array}{r}
①③ \\
1,125 \\
\times \quad 612 \\
\hline
2\ 250 \\
11\ 250 \\
675\ 000 \\
\hline
688,500
\end{array}
$$

There are 688,500 meters of wire at the construction site. Since the estimate was 600,000, the answer is reasonable.

TRY THESE

Estimate. Then find the exact answer.

1. $\begin{array}{r} 632 \\ \times 548 \\ \hline \end{array}$

2. $\begin{array}{r} 509 \\ \times 731 \\ \hline \end{array}$

3. $\begin{array}{r} 2,088 \\ \times \quad 492 \\ \hline \end{array}$

4. $\begin{array}{r} 7,559 \\ \times \quad 663 \\ \hline \end{array}$

5. $\begin{array}{r} \$3.10 \\ \times 853 \\ \hline \end{array}$

6. $1,392 \times 781 = \blacksquare$

7. $632 \times 748 = \blacksquare$

8. $1,172 \times 935 = \blacksquare$

9. $247 \times \$5.16 = \blacksquare$

10. $319 \times 1,568 = \blacksquare$

11. $824 \times 4,990 = \blacksquare$

Estimate. Then find the exact answer.

1.	348	2.	753	3.	2,709	4.	$58.39	5.	736
	×256		×182		× 693		× 227		×400

6.	2,796	7.	3,704	8.	1,594	9.	930	10.	748
	× 358		× 636		× 252		×628		×593

11.	7,502	12.	482	13.	6,496	14.	$7.89	15.	2,500
	× 287		×366		× 532		× 596		× 763

16.	$60.02	17.	261	18.	3,886	19.	301	★20.	980
	× 133		×754		× 372		×1,605		×980

21. 643 × 2,008 = ■   **22.** 728 × 600 = ■   **23.** 496 × 8,941 = ■

PROBLEM SOLVING

24. A construction worker earned $10.85 for each hour he worked. One month, he worked 156 hours. How much did he earn that month?

★25. A wall will have 126 rows of bricks. Each row will contain 294 bricks. How many bricks will be used for the wall? There are 35,000 bricks already at the site. How many more are needed?

THINK!

Compute

There are 60 minutes in one hour. There are 24 hours in one day. There are 365 days in one year. How many minutes are there in one year? A leap year has one extra day. How many minutes are there in a leap year?

Multiplying with Zeros

A. The average reading speed for an adult is 255 words per minute. How many words can an adult read in 120 minutes?

255 × 120 = ■
About 300 × 100 = 30,000

```
    255
  × 120
      0
```

120 has 0 ones. No need to multiply by ones. Write the zero.

Multiply by 20.	**Multiply by 100.**	**Add.**
⓪①①	ⓧⓧⓧ	ⓧⓧⓧ
255	255	255
× 120	× 120	× 120
5 100	5 100	5 100
	25 500	25 500
		30,600

An adult can read 30,600 words in 120 minutes.

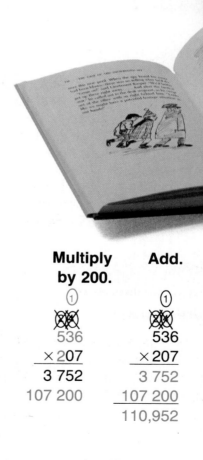

B. Find: 207 × 536

Multiply by 7.		**Multiply by 200.**	**Add.**
②④		①	①
536		ⓧⓧⓧ	ⓧⓧⓧ
×207		536	536
3 752		×207	×207
		3 752	3 752
		107 200	107 200
			110,952

207 has 0 tens. No need to multiply by tens. Write the zero.

Multiply. Estimate to check your answers.

1. 483
    ×370

2. 756
    ×508

3. $41.07
    ×   690

4. 5,432
    × 760

5. 680
    ×204

6. 810 × 532 = ■   7. 302 × 1,501 = ■   8. 450 × 986 = ■

SKILLS PRACTICE _____

Multiply.

1.   297
     × 301

2.   784
     × 670

3.   4,263
     × 215

4. $75.68
     ×   390

5.   4,033
     ×   637

6.   7,482
     ×   536

7. $9.51
     ×   808

8.   6,390
     ×   540

9.   5,817
     ×   613

10. 7,060
     ×   109

11. 580 × 946 = ■   12. 606 × 3,407 = ■   13. 208 × 3,694 = ■

PROBLEM SOLVING _____

14. Sally read at the rate of 225 words per minute for 75 minutes. How many words did she read?

15. Dan read a play of 279 pages. Then he read a book of 328 pages. How many pages did he read?

16. Mr. Alfonzo has read the newspaper for 45 minutes. He was reading 350 words per minute. How many words did he read?

★17. Donna read 217 pages of a book containing 320 pages. How many pages does she still have to read? There is an average of 305 words per page. How many words has she read?

THINK!

Vowel Patterns

Count how many times the vowel "a" occurs in problems 14–17 above. Then count how many times the vowels "e," "i," "o," and "u" occur in the problems. Make a tally table. Which vowel is used most often? Make a bar graph from your data.

Problem Solving

Order Forms

The Potter family ordered its supply of camping equipment from a catalog.

They filled out the **order form** shown below. They estimated about how much their order would cost.

Then they multiplied **Quantity × Price Each** to find the **Total Price** for each item.

After adding the total prices of all the items ordered, they looked up the 5% (5 *percent*) **sales tax** in the table below.

Tent 39S23 **$89.50**

Backpack 43F27 **$21.89**

Lantern 36R29 **$34.95**

Sleeping bag 39A73 **$42.35**

Cooking fuel 27X51 **$.89**

Camp stove 65Y39 **$39.50**

Canteen 36B19 **$8.50**

GIVE COMPLETE ORDERING INFORMATION

Name of Item	Catalog Number	Quantity	Price Each	Total Price	Estimat
Tent	39S23	1	$89.50	$89.50	$ 90
Sleeping bag	39A73	3	$42.35	$127.05	130
Camp stove	65Y39	1	$39.50	$39.50	40
Lantern	36R29	2	$34.95	$69.90	70
Canteen	36B19	4	$8.50	$34.00	+ 30
		Total For Merchandise		$359.95	$360
		5% Sales Tax		$18.00	
		Handling Charge		$2.00	
		Total Amount Enclosed		$379.95	

5% SALES TAX

Price	Tax
$359.70–359.89	$17.99
$359.90–360.09	$18.00
$360.10–360.29	$18.01

$359.95 is between $359.90 and $360.09.

TRY THESE

Copy and complete this order form. Use the sales tax table at the bottom of this page.

Name of Item	Catalog Number	Quantity	Price Each	Total Price	Estimate.
Lantern		3	$34.95		$105
Backpack		2	$21.89		44
	27X51	12			12
	36B19	5			45
		Total for Merchandise			$206
		5% Sales Tax			
		Handling Charge	$2.00		
		Total Amount Enclosed			

PROBLEM SOLVING PRACTICE

Copy and complete this order form.

Name of Item	Catalog Number	Quantity	Price Each	Total Price
Sleeping bag		2	$42.35	
Camp stove		1	$39.50	
	27X51	15		
	39S23	1		
	36R29	3		
Backpack		2		
		Total for Merchandise		
		5% Sales Tax		
		Handling Charge	$2.00	
		Total Amount Enclosed		

5% SALES TAX

Price	Tax
$201.70–201.89	$10.09
$201.90–202.09	$10.10
$202.10–202.29	$10.11
$375.10–375.29	$18.76
$375.30–375.49	$18.77
$375.50–375.69	$18.78

ON YOUR OWN

Your family wants to order ten items from the camping supply catalog. You have $190 to spend, and you can buy more than one of each item. First make a list. Then estimate to see if you can buy everything. If not, decide what you can buy. Make an order form. (Do not include sales tax.)

Algorithms and Flowcharts

Computers do only what they are told to do. They require step-by-step instructions. Two step-by-step methods of giving instructions are *algorithms* and *flowcharts*.

A payroll clerk keeps a record of workers' earnings. At the end of each week, the clerk must find each worker's *total pay*. Here is a *payroll record* for 4 part-time workers:

Worker's Name	Hours Worked						Pay Per Hour	Total Pay
	M	Tu	W	Th	F	Total		
A. Quigley	3	2	0	3	8		$4.15	
T. Jeffries	4	0	0	4	4		$3.80	
S. White	4	2	2	6	0		$2.95	
M. Garcia	0	6	7	0	7		$3.70	

To find how much a worker has earned in a week, the payroll clerk could use an algorithm or a flowchart.

Algorithm

Step 1 Find the sum of the numbers of hours worked during the week.

Step 2 Write the sum in the column marked Total.

Step 3 Find the product of the total hours and the pay per hour.

Step 4 Write the product in the column marked Total Pay.

1. How do the directions in the flowchart differ from those in the algorithm?

2. Does the algorithm or the flowchart appear to be more efficient to use?

3. Use the flowchart or the algorithm to find Total Pay for the workers above.

Flowchart

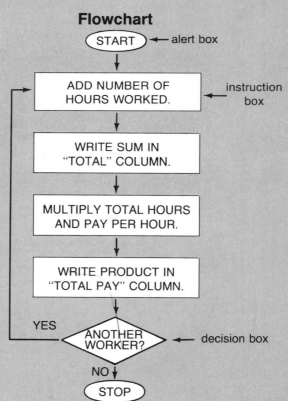

Unit Review

Multiply. *(pages 84–87)*

1. 32 × 4	**2.** 4,583 × 7	**3.** $3.49 × 8	**4.** 83,258 × 4	**5.** 9 ×1,105

6. 45 × 3 = ▨   **7.** 7 × $29.08 = ▨   **8.** 9 × 27,208 = ▨

Multiply. *(pages 94–95, 100–101)*

9. 315 × 10	**10.** $2.45 × 40	**11.** 3,876 × 20	**12.** 892 ×100	**13.** 2,812 × 600

14. $43.50 × 10 = ▨   **15.** 100 × 240 = ▨   **16.** 500 × 8,600 = ▨

Estimate. Then find the exact answer. *(pages 88–89, 96–97, 102–103)*

17. 82 ×23	**18.** 71 ×49	**19.** 386 × 44	**20.** 4,613 × 38	**21.** $2.42 × 16

Multiply. *(pages 102–105)*

22. 297 ×132	**23.** 758 ×286	**24.** 3,251 × 443	**25.** 6,419 × 528	**26.** 341 ×618

27. 314 × 747 = ▨   **28.** 283 × 5,993 = ▨   **29.** 940 × 1,200 = ▨

Solve the problems. *(pages 90–91)*

30. An airplane traveled for 3 hours at 817 km/h. How far did the plane travel?

31. A car has a mass of 1,400 kg. What is the total mass of a shipment of 350 cars?

32. How much would it cost to fill a 60-liter tank if gas costs $.35 per liter?

33. How far can a car travel in 9 hours if it is driven at an average speed of 88 km/h?

More Help with Multiplication

```
  ④
  38
× 6
 228
```

```
  ①②
  248
×  31
  248  ← 1 × 248
 7440  ← 30 × 248
 7,688 ← 31 × 248
```

Cross out the saves.

```
  ②③⑧
  486
× 395
  2 430  ← 5 × 486
 43 740  ← 90 × 486
145 800  ← 300 × 486
191,970 ← 395 × 486
```

304 has 0 tens. No need to multiply by tens.

```
  ②③
  ⑧⑥
  675
× 304
  2 700
202 500
205,200
```

Multiply.

1.	26 × 5	2.	43 × 7	3.	23 × 2	4.	341 × 6

5. 652 × 4
6. 2,683 × 8
7. 48 × 9
8. 6,809 × 7

9. 342 × 52
10. 58 × 21
11. 213 × 26
12. 703 × 93

13. 5,014 × 28
14. 2,321 × 35
15. 38 × 41
16. 683 × 14

17. 694 × 783
18. 495 × 526
19. 672 × 357
20. 794 × 152

21. 6,109 × 734
22. 7,986 × 454
23. 3,251 × 518
24. 972 × 635

25. 749 × 605
26. 532 × 540
27. 6,135 × 750
28. 163 × 207

29. 9,563 × 406
30. 7,582 × 360
31. 873 × 110
32. 4,459 × 908

Expanded Forms

A. You can write *expanded forms* for a *standard numeral.* Use the meaning of the digits to help you.

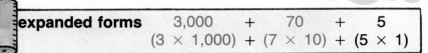

3 thousands   0 hundreds
7 tens   5 ones

standard numeral   3,075

expanded forms   3,000   +   70   +   5
(3 × 1,000) + (7 × 10) + (5 × 1)

You don't need
to show the
0 hundreds.

B. You can write a standard numeral for a number shown in expanded form. Use multiplication and addition.

(7 × 100,000) + (4 × 10,000) + (3 × 100) + (8 × 1) **expanded form**

Step 1
Multiply.   700,000   +   40,000   +   300   +   8

Step 2
Add.   700,000 + 40,000 + 300 + 8 = 740,308

standard numeral

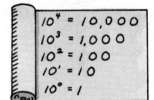

$10^4 = 10,000$
$10^3 = 1,000$
$10^2 = 100$
$10^1 = 10$
$10^0 = 1$

C. You can use exponential notation for expanded form. To write 34,672 with exponents, first write

(3 × 10,000) + (4 × 1,000) + (6 × 100) + (7 × 10) + (2 × 1)

Then use exponents.

$(3 \times 10^4) + (4 \times 10^3) + (6 \times 10^2) + (7 \times 10^1) + (2 \times 10^0)$

Write the expanded form in two ways. First use multiplication and addition. Then use exponents.

1. 43,718   **2.** 129,562   **3.** 6,700,208   **4.** 30,501,090

Write the standard numeral for each.

5. 4,000 + 800 + 90 + 5   **6.** $(3 \times 10^4) + (5 \times 10^3) + (6 \times 10^2)$

7. (2 × 10,000) + (6 × 1,000) + (4 × 100) + (3 × 10) + (5 × 1)

8. $(8 \times 10^5) + (4 \times 10^2) + (9 \times 10^0)$ **9.** 5,000,000 + 20,000 + 8,000 + 60

Cumulative Review

**Choose the correct answer. Use NG if the correct answer is *not given.*

1.   6,145
      − 233

a. 1,431,785
b. 6,112
c. 5,912
d. NG

2.   72
      ×18

a. 648
b. 1,296
c. 1,366
d. NG

3. Round $128.49
to the nearest
dollar.

a. $130
b. $129
c. $128
d. NG

4. 49,006 + 98 = ■

a. 49,104
b. 147,006
c. 49,986
d. NG

5.   3,906
      ×   7

a. 21,342
b. 27,342
c. 216,342
d. NG

6. Complete.
43,596 ● 43,596

a. >
b. <
c. =

7.   17
      − 9

a. 153
b. 8
c. 633
d. NG

8.   562
      × 60

a. 5,620
b. 3,372
c. 30,620
d. NG

9.   6,898
      + 316

a. 2,179,768
b. 317,308
c. 7,214
d. NG

10.   450
       ×206

a. 11,700
b. 92,700
c. 1,170
d. NG

11. 10 × 6,190 = ■

a. 61,900
b. 6,190
c. 6,200
d. NG

12. Name the place
of the digit 6
in 5,326,407.

a. millions
b. hundreds
c. thousands
d. NG

13. Eddy's boat cruises at the rate
of 20 knots per hour. How many
knots can it travel in 76 hours?

a. 1,520 knots
b. 96 knots
c. 152 knots
d. NG

14. Lupe sold 74 tickets. Charlene sold
69 tickets. Jackie sold 58 tickets. How
many tickets did they sell in all?

a. 141 tickets
b. 1,110 tickets
c. 201 tickets
d. NG

5

Dividing by Ones

NUMBER OF RECREATIONAL VEHICLES SOLD IN THE U.S.

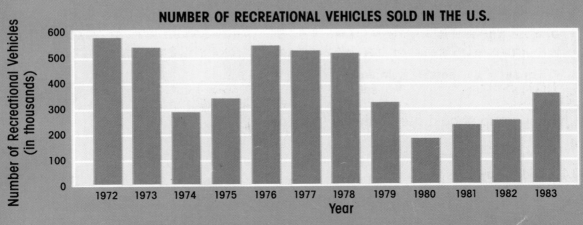

Reviewing Division Facts

A. There are 24 students in the science lab. Ms. Buono wants to make lab groups of 4. How many lab groups can she make?

Remember, you can divide to find how many sets when you know the number in all and the number in each set.

$$24 \div 4 = \blacksquare$$

in all   **in each set**   **sets**

Think multiplication.

$$\blacksquare \times 4 = 24$$

sets   **in each set**   **in all**

$$24 \div 4 = 6$$

Ms. Buono can make 6 lab groups.

B. You can also divide to find how many in each set when you know the number in all and the number of sets.

Ms. Buono has 48 leaves. She wants to give each of her 6 lab groups the same number of leaves. How many leaves should each group get?

$$48 \div 6 = 8 \quad \text{or} \quad 6\overline{)48} \;^{8}$$

in all   **sets**   **in each set**

Each group should get 8 leaves.

TRY THESE

Divide. What multiplication exercise will help you?

1. $40 \div 8 = \blacksquare$ **2.** $54 \div 9 = \blacksquare$ **3.** $24 \div 6 = \blacksquare$

4. $54 \div 6 = \blacksquare$ **5.** $18 \div 3 = \blacksquare$ **6.** $14 \div 2 = \blacksquare$

Divide.

7. $6\overline{)36}$ **8.** $4\overline{)28}$ **9.** $9\overline{)36}$ **10.** $7\overline{)14}$ **11.** $6\overline{)42}$ **12.** $3\overline{)9}$

SKILLS PRACTICE

Divide.

1. $7\overline{)42}$ **2.** $6\overline{)18}$ **3.** $5\overline{)30}$ **4.** $3\overline{)15}$ **5.** $4\overline{)16}$ **6.** $2\overline{)14}$

7. $9\overline{)18}$ **8.** $8\overline{)32}$ **9.** $9\overline{)27}$ **10.** $7\overline{)21}$ **11.** $5\overline{)25}$ **12.** $6\overline{)54}$

13. $7\overline{)28}$ **14.** $4\overline{)36}$ **15.** $8\overline{)48}$ **16.** $5\overline{)45}$ **17.** $3\overline{)24}$ **18.** $4\overline{)8}$

19. $8\overline{)24}$ **20.** $5\overline{)40}$ **21.** $7\overline{)63}$ **22.** $2\overline{)10}$ **23.** $7\overline{)35}$ **24.** $6\overline{)48}$

25. $8\overline{)64}$ **26.** $2\overline{)12}$ **27.** $5\overline{)10}$ **28.** $9\overline{)81}$ **29.** $8\overline{)16}$ **30.** $4\overline{)12}$

31. $9\overline{)54}$ **32.** $3\overline{)12}$ **33.** $8\overline{)56}$ **34.** $9\overline{)72}$ **35.** $4\overline{)24}$ **36.** $7\overline{)49}$

37. $10 \div 2 = \blacksquare$ **38.** $28 \div 7 = \blacksquare$ **39.** $45 \div 9 = \blacksquare$

40. $42 \div 7 = \blacksquare$ **41.** $24 \div 3 = \blacksquare$ **★42.** $63 \div 9 = \blacksquare$

PROBLEM SOLVING

Write the division fact. Solve the problem.

43. 24 lab workbooks in all
6 lab groups
How many books for each group?

44. 21 frogs
3 in each box
How many boxes?

45. 54 slides
6 boxes
How many in each box?

THINK!

Even and Odd

Ms. Buono bought some test tubes. The test tubes were sold in boxes of 6 each. She bought an even number of boxes. There were 8 tables in the lab and she put 8 test tubes on each of an odd number of tables. She used all the test tubes. How many test tubes did she buy?

Using Division Facts

A. Division facts can help you solve harder problems mentally.

A classroom set of 30 calculators costs $150. How much does each calculator cost?

$$150 \div 30 = \blacksquare$$ Use division facts.
$$150 \div 30 = 5$$ Think: $15 \div 3 = 5$

Check: $30 \times 5 = 150$

Each calculator costs $5.

B. Look at the number of zeros.

$$3,600 \div 90 = \blacksquare$$ Think:
$$3,600 \div 90 = 40$$ $36 \div 9 = 4$
$$2 - 1 = 1$$

$$63,000 \div 70 = \blacksquare$$ Think:
$$63,000 \div 70 = 900$$ $63 \div 7 = 9$
$$3 - 1 = 2$$

C. Division facts can help you estimate answers for harder problems. It is helpful to estimate your answers to see if the answer you get on a calculator is reasonable.

The River Street School ordered 32 computers for the computer room. The total bill was $21,440.96. How much did each computer cost?

Calculator

$$21,440.96 \div 32 = \blacksquare$$

670.03

Estimate

$$21,000 \div 30 = \blacksquare$$ $21 \div 3 = 7$
$$21,000 \div 30 = 700$$
$$3 - 1 = 2$$

The calculator answer of $670.03 is reasonable.

TRY THESE

Use mental math to find the answer.

1. 560 ÷ 7 = ■
2. 5,600 ÷ 7 = ■
3. 56,000 ÷ 70 = ■
4. 3,600 ÷ 900 = ■
5. 54,000 ÷ 600 = ■
6. 15,000 ÷ 3 = ■

Tell if each answer is reasonable.

7. 721 ÷ 87 = ■ | 80.1111 |
   720 ÷ 90

8. 3,854 ÷ 48 = ■ | 80.2916 |
   4,000 ÷ 50

SKILLS PRACTICE

Use mental math to find the answer.

1. 800 ÷ 4 = ■
2. 64,000 ÷ 8 = ■
3. 490 ÷ 7 = ■
4. 36,000 ÷ 6 = ■
5. 900 ÷ 30 = ■
6. 8,100 ÷ 9 = ■
7. 500,000 ÷ 5 = ■
8. 5,400 ÷ 90 = ■
9. 1,000 ÷ 20 = ■
10. 63,000 ÷ 700 = ■
★11. 440,000 ÷ 400 = ■
★12. 720,000 ÷ 600 = ■

Tell if each answer is reasonable.

13. 983 ÷ 52 = ■ | 18.9038 |
14. 6,312 ÷ 91 = ■ | 693.62641 |
15. 643 ÷ 79 = ■ | 0.81392 |
★16. 55,437,890 ÷ 553 = ■
    | 100249.34 |

PROBLEM SOLVING

Use mental math and division facts to find the answers.

17. Mrs. Cantrell ordered 56,000 disks for her company. They were to be shipped to 80 locations. If each location got the same number, how many disks did each get?

18. A computer was used for 15,000 hours with only 3 service calls. On average, how many hours did the computer operate before needing a service call?

THINK!

Mental Math

Compute mentally. Think about multiplication and division properties.

$$(8 - 8) ÷ 11 × (42 ÷ 1) = ■$$

Dividing 2-digit Numbers

A. Mr. Libresco has 89 nails. He needs 8 nails to make a model table. How many model tables can he make? Will he have any nails left over?

Divide: 8)89

Divide the 8 tens.	Multiply. Subtract and compare.	Divide the 9 ones.	Multiply. Subtract and compare.
$\begin{array}{r} 1 \\ 8\overline{)89} \end{array}$	$\begin{array}{r} 1 \\ 8\overline{)89} \\ \underline{8} \\ 0 \end{array}$ $1 \times 8 = 8$ $8 - 8 = 0$	$\begin{array}{r} 11 \\ 8\overline{)89} \\ \underline{8}\downarrow \\ 09 \end{array}$	$\begin{array}{r} 11 \text{ R1} \\ 8\overline{)89} \\ \underline{8} \\ 09 \\ \underline{8} \\ 1 \end{array}$ $1 \times 8 = 8$

$1 < 8$
The remainder is 1.

Mr. Libresco can make 11 model tables. He will have 1 nail left over.

B. You can check a division by multiplying and adding.

$$\begin{array}{r} 11 \leftarrow \textbf{quotient} \\ \underline{\times\ 8} \leftarrow \textbf{divisor} \\ 88 \\ \underline{+\ 1} \leftarrow \textbf{remainder} \\ 89\ \checkmark \end{array}$$

This number should equal the dividend.

C. When the remainder is 0, you do not need to record it.

$$\begin{array}{r} 16 \\ 6\overline{)96} \\ \underline{6} \\ 36 \\ \underline{36} \\ 0 \end{array}$$

no need to record the remainder

$96 \div 6 = 16$

TRY THESE

Divide. Check your answers.

1. 4)84   **2.** 7)79   **3.** 5)75   **4.** 3)53   **5.** 6)92   **6.** 2)58   **7.** 6)67

8. 3)64   **9.** 4)96   **10.** 6)71   **11.** 9)99   **12.** 3)88   **13.** 5)84   **14.** 7)84

15. $36 \div 3 = \blacksquare$ **16.** $76 \div 4 = \blacksquare$ **17.** $75 \div 5 = \blacksquare$

SKILLS PRACTICE

Divide. Check your answers.

1. $2\overline{)47}$
2. $7\overline{)83}$
3. $5\overline{)58}$
4. $6\overline{)75}$
5. $8\overline{)94}$
6. $3\overline{)80}$

7. $4\overline{)76}$
8. $6\overline{)66}$
9. $3\overline{)98}$
10. $5\overline{)88}$
11. $4\overline{)87}$
12. $2\overline{)97}$

13. $1\overline{)38}$
14. $3\overline{)40}$
15. $7\overline{)92}$
16. $8\overline{)92}$
17. $5\overline{)65}$
18. $6\overline{)99}$

19. $5\overline{)56}$
20. $4\overline{)68}$
21. $6\overline{)69}$
22. $7\overline{)84}$
23. $2\overline{)44}$
24. $3\overline{)77}$

25. $4\overline{)48}$
26. $7\overline{)99}$
27. $2\overline{)79}$
28. $6\overline{)73}$
29. $3\overline{)87}$
30. $5\overline{)95}$

31. $66 \div 3 = $ ■
32. $57 \div 3 = $ ■
33. $52 \div 4 = $ ■

34. $85 \div 5 = $ ■
35. $78 \div 6 = $ ■
36. $92 \div 2 = $ ■

37. $13 \div 1 = $ ■
38. $96 \div 8 = $ ■
★39. $0 \div 47 = $ ■

40. The dividend is 42. The divisor is 2. What is the quotient?

41. The dividend is 57. The divisor is 5. What is the quotient? What is the remainder?

★42. The dividend is 81. The quotient is 27. What is the divisor?

PROBLEM SOLVING

43. When he makes model chairs, Mr. Libresco uses 4 legs on each chair. If he has 63 legs, how many chairs can he make? How many legs will be left over?

★44. To make model houses, Nicole uses 4 strips of wood for the walls, 2 strips for the roof, and 1 strip for the floors. She has 88 strips of wood. How many houses can she make? How many strips will be left over?

THINK!

Visual Perception

These 12 coins are arranged in 4 rows with 4 coins in each row. How can you arrange the 12 coins in 4 rows with 5 coins in each row? (Think about stacking some of the coins.)

Placing Digits in the Quotient

Before you divide, decide whether you can divide tens. Decide by comparing the divisor with the tens digit of the dividend.

A. Maria has 62 slides. She wants to put them in boxes that hold 9 slides each. How many boxes can she fill? How many slides will be left over?

Compare.

$9\overline{)62}$ 6 < 9
not enough
tens

Regroup. Start with ones.

$9\overline{)62}$ 6 tens 2 ones is 62 ones.

Divide ones.

$$\begin{array}{r} 6\ \text{R8} \\ 9\overline{)62} \\ \underline{54} \\ 8 \end{array}$$

Maria can fill 6 boxes.
There will be 8 slides left over.

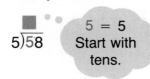

B. Jim is mounting snapshots in his album. He can put 5 snapshots on each page. If he has 58 snapshots, how many pages can he fill? How many snapshots will be left over?

Compare.

$5\overline{)58}$ 5 = 5
Start with tens.

Divide tens.

$$\begin{array}{r} 1 \\ 5\overline{)58} \\ \underline{5} \\ 0 \end{array}$$

1 × 5 = 5

5 − 5 = 0

Divide ones.

$$\begin{array}{r} 11\ \text{R3} \\ 5\overline{)58} \\ \underline{5}\downarrow \\ 08 \\ \underline{5} \\ 3 \end{array}$$

Jim can fill 11 pages in his album.
There will be 3 snapshots left over.

120   **Dividing by Ones**

TRY THESE

Tell whether the digit is placed correctly in the quotient.

1. $6\overline{)38}$ with 6
2. $4\overline{)75}$ with 1
3. $7\overline{)85}$ with 1
4. $2\overline{)91}$ with 4
5. $3\overline{)66}$ with 2
6. $8\overline{)53}$ with 6

Divide.

7. $24 \div 8 = \blacksquare$
8. $68 \div 4 = \blacksquare$
9. $63 \div 7 = \blacksquare$

SKILLS PRACTICE

Divide. Check your answers.

1. $5\overline{)48}$
2. $9\overline{)88}$
3. $3\overline{)47}$
4. $2\overline{)13}$
5. $6\overline{)51}$
6. $4\overline{)33}$

7. $7\overline{)55}$
8. $4\overline{)19}$
9. $7\overline{)65}$
10. $5\overline{)31}$
11. $3\overline{)51}$
12. $2\overline{)27}$

13. $8\overline{)41}$
14. $7\overline{)89}$
15. $4\overline{)32}$
16. $3\overline{)94}$
17. $9\overline{)75}$
18. $5\overline{)27}$

19. $2\overline{)19}$
20. $5\overline{)39}$
21. $3\overline{)16}$
22. $4\overline{)23}$
23. $5\overline{)77}$
24. $8\overline{)78}$

25. $3\overline{)29}$
26. $9\overline{)41}$
27. $8\overline{)89}$
28. $2\overline{)38}$
29. $9\overline{)38}$
30. $7\overline{)59}$

31. $40 \div 8 = \blacksquare$
32. $48 \div 4 = \blacksquare$
33. $35 \div 5 = \blacksquare$

Complete.

★34. $7\overline{)4\blacksquare}$ with 6 R3
★35. $9\overline{)6\blacksquare}$ with ■ R1
★36. $8\overline{)7\blacksquare}$ with ■ R4

PROBLEM SOLVING

37. Jim plans to take 50 snapshots on his vacation. If his vacation lasts 6 days, how many snapshots should he take each day? How many extra snapshots would he need to take on the last day?

★38. Rita wants to take 70 photographs. She can take 8 photographs with each roll of film. How many rolls of film does she need? How many pictures will be unused on the last roll?

THINK!

Addition Riddle

Here are six lines. How can you add five lines to make nine?

$$| \quad | \quad | \quad | \quad | \quad |$$

Zeros in Division

Sometimes you must write zero in the quotient.

A. An airline has 64 flight attendants. On each airplane 6 attendants are needed. How many airplanes can have a full crew? How many flight attendants will be left over?

Divide tens.

$$\begin{array}{r} 1 \\ 6\overline{)64} \\ \underline{6} \\ 0 \end{array}$$

$1 \times 6 = 6$

$6 - 6 = 0$

Bring down 4 ones.

$$\begin{array}{r} 1 \\ 6\overline{)64} \\ \underline{6}\downarrow \\ 04 \end{array}$$

Divide ones.

$$\begin{array}{r} 10 \text{ R4} \\ 6\overline{)64} \\ \underline{6} \\ 04 \\ \underline{0} \\ 4 \end{array}$$

$$\begin{array}{r} 0 \text{ R4} \\ 6\overline{)4} \end{array}$$

There are enough flight attendants for full crews for 10 planes. 4 flight attendants will be left over.

B. Checking your answer will remind you to record zeros in the quotient.

Check:
$$\begin{array}{r} 10 \text{ R4} \\ 6\overline{)64} \end{array}$$

$$\begin{array}{r} 10 \\ \times\ 6 \\ \hline 60 \\ +\ 4 \\ \hline 64 \end{array}$$

C. $30 \div 3 = \blacksquare$

Remember that when zero is divided by a non-zero number, the result is zero.

$$\begin{array}{r} 10 \\ 3\overline{)30} \\ \underline{3} \\ 00 \\ \underline{0} \\ 0 \end{array}$$

no need to record a remainder of 0

$30 \div 3 = 10$

TRY THESE

Divide. Watch out for zeros.

1. $5\overline{)80}$ **2.** $3\overline{)31}$ **3.** $4\overline{)83}$ **4.** $2\overline{)20}$ **5.** $7\overline{)75}$ **6.** $8\overline{)90}$

SKILLS PRACTICE

Divide. Check your answers.

1. $5\overline{)50}$
2. $3\overline{)60}$
3. $4\overline{)42}$
4. $1\overline{)20}$
5. $7\overline{)71}$
6. $9\overline{)90}$

7. $6\overline{)61}$
8. $4\overline{)80}$
9. $5\overline{)64}$
10. $9\overline{)95}$
11. $8\overline{)90}$
12. $2\overline{)81}$

13. $3\overline{)33}$
14. $7\overline{)50}$
15. $4\overline{)60}$
16. $9\overline{)60}$
17. $6\overline{)20}$
18. $5\overline{)79}$

19. $5\overline{)34}$
20. $5\overline{)68}$
21. $3\overline{)40}$
22. $2\overline{)51}$
23. $8\overline{)63}$
24. $1\overline{)40}$

25. $8\overline{)70}$
26. $3\overline{)90}$
27. $2\overline{)41}$
28. $7\overline{)40}$
29. $4\overline{)50}$
30. $5\overline{)62}$

31. $60 \div 2 = \blacksquare$
32. $52 \div 4 = \blacksquare$
33. $30 \div 6 = \blacksquare$

34. $72 \div 3 = \blacksquare$
35. $90 \div 9 = \blacksquare$
36. $55 \div 5 = \blacksquare$

★37. The dividend is 80. The quotient is 40. What is the divisor?

PROBLEM SOLVING

38. An airline has 8 flights per week between Dallas and Miami. This week, it has 82 cans of juice to serve on that route. How many cans of juice can be served on each flight? How many cans will be left over?

★39. The flight attendants on a jet plane served meals to all the passengers. The plane was full. There were 12 first-class seats in rows of 4. There were 126 coach seats in rows of 6. How many rows of seats did the attendants serve?

THINK!

Remainder Clues

What two-digit number satisfies all the clues?

- When it is divided by 9, the remainder is 4.
- When it is divided by 5, the remainder is 1.
- When it is divided by 7, the remainder is 6.

Problem Solving

Too Much Information

When problems occur in the real world, the information you need for solving them is often mixed in with extra information. You need to sort out the needed data before you can solve the problem.

Read each problem carefully. Decide which data you really need to solve the problem.

A. Rickey spent $120 for skin-diving equipment and $60 for skin-diving lessons. He was charged $5 per lesson. How many skin-diving lessons did Rickey take?

> per means for each

To find out how many lessons you do not need to know the cost of the skin-diving equipment.

$60 in all

$5 for each

■ lessons

$$\begin{array}{r} 12 \\ 5\overline{)60} \\ \underline{5} \\ 10 \\ \underline{10} \\ 0 \end{array}$$

Rickey took 12 lessons.

B. Rickey took 9 hours to paint each fishing boat. He charged $27 for each boat. Rickey painted 4 boats. How much did he charge per hour to paint the fishing boats?

To find the charge per hour, you do not need the number of boats.

$27 in all

9 hours

■ for each hour

$$9\overline{)27}^{3}$$

Rickey charged $3 per hour.

Tell which information you do not need. Then solve the problems.

1. Four members of a diving club rented a boat for 8 hours. They were charged $12 per hour for the boat. What was the total charge?

2. The diving club members have $74 to spend to fill their air tanks. Each air tank can be filled in 3 minutes. It costs $2 to fill each tank. How many tanks can they fill?

3. Sally stayed in a camp site that cost $4 per day. She paid $56. How many days did she stay?

4. Sally and her family rented 4 diving masks for $15. They also paid a deposit fee of $4. How much did they pay in all?

PROBLEM SOLVING PRACTICE

Tell which information you do not need. Then solve the problems.

1. The diving club members rented a car and drove 46 km to the ocean. They kept the car for 3 days and paid $66. What was the charge per day?

2. The diving club members bought jars of grease for $6 each. They spent $72 in all. How many jars of grease did they buy?

3. Barney had $100. He bought 3 air regulators for $85. How much money did he have left?

4. A net for collecting shells costs $7. A diving watch costs $85. Find the cost of 13 nets.

5. During one summer Barney spent $90 for diving lessons and $125 for diving equipment. A diving lesson costs $9 per hour. How many hours did he take lessons?

6. During one summer the diving store sold 52 diving tanks and 68 life preserver vests. Each tank cost $125. How much did the store receive for the diving tanks?

7. A snorkel is a short tube used for breathing under water. Marie had $32 to buy snorkels. Each snorkel cost $5. How many snorkels could she buy?

8. The diving club members rented an underwater movie camera for $53 and a still camera for $24. They bought film for $37. How much did they spend to rent the cameras?

ON YOUR OWN

Make up two problems that use different data from this situation:

Eight members of the diving club each bought goggles for $9.
Four members took diving lessons at $11 per lesson.
Three members rented a boat for 3 hours at $6 per hour.

Make an Organized List

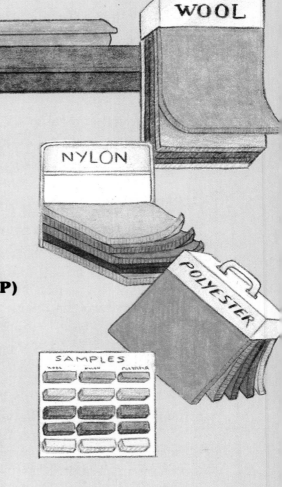

Everett is buying wall-to-wall carpet. He can buy carpet made from wool, nylon, or polyester fiber. He can buy it in gold, beige, rust, olive, or cream. In how many ways can he choose carpeting?

To be sure of counting all the possible choices, **make an organized list.** For each type of fiber, list the colors in which Everett could buy that fiber.

Fiber:	**wool (W)**	**nylon (N)**	**polyester (P)**
	W, G	N, G	P, G
	W, B	N, B	P, B
	W, R	N, R	P, R
	W, O	N, O	P, O
	W, C	N, C	P, C

There are 15 combinations of fiber and color. Everett can choose carpeting in 15 ways.

Solve.

1. If Everett decides not to buy cream-colored carpet because it will be too hard to keep it clean, how many choices will he have left?

2. Everett also plans to buy drapes. He can choose gray, beige, yellow, or blue drapes of acrylic or cotton. In how many ways can he choose drapes?

3. Enrique is choosing paint for his kitchen. He will paint the walls light green, tan, yellow, rose, off-white, or sky blue. He will paint the ceiling white or beige. In how many ways can he choose the paint?

4. Jeannette is buying wall tiles. She can buy ceramic or vinyl tiles in pink, black, yellow, or tan. Vinyl tiles also come in red. In how many ways can she choose the tiles?

Problem Solving **Project**

Data from Cash Register Tapes

When you buy something at a supermarket, you are given a *cash register tape*. This tape shows how much you have paid for your purchases. If you should decide to return something, you will usually need to have your cash register tape.

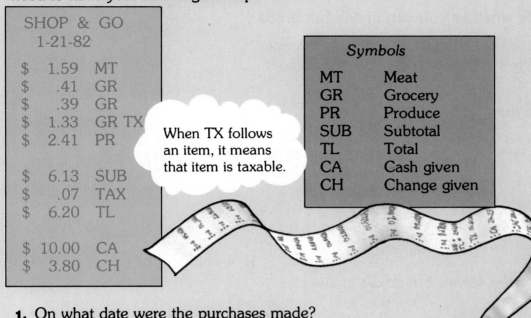

```
SHOP & GO
  1-21-82

$   1.59   MT
$    .41   GR
$    .39   GR
$   1.33   GR TX
$   2.41   PR

$   6.13   SUB
$    .07   TAX
$   6.20   TL

$  10.00   CA
$   3.80   CH
```

When TX follows an item, it means that item is taxable.

Symbols

MT	Meat
GR	Grocery
PR	Produce
SUB	Subtotal
TL	Total
CA	Cash given
CH	Change given

1. On what date were the purchases made?

2. How many grocery items were bought?

3. Sales tax was paid on one item. What was the cost of that item? How much tax was charged?

4. What was the total cost?

5. How much money did the customer give the sales clerk?

6. How much change did the customer receive?

ON YOUR OWN

Collect some cash register tapes from stores in your city or town. What information is included on these slips? How is this information shown?

The information which is printed on the cash register tape is also stored in the cash register. How do store managers use this information?

127

Dividing 3-digit Numbers

A. A store orders 872 turtleneck sweaters. The sweaters come in boxes of 4 each. How many boxes of sweaters does the store receive?

Decide whether you can divide hundreds.

■ · · · · ·
4)872

$4 < 8$
Start dividing with hundreds.

Divide hundreds.	**Divide tens.**	**Divide ones.**
2 4)872 8 0	21 4)872 8↓ 07 4 3	218 4)872 8 07 4↓ 32 32 0

The store receives 218 boxes of sweaters.

B. The store has 3 employees to put price tags on scarves. If there are 227 scarves and each employee tags the same number of scarves, how many must each employee tag? How many scarves would be left over?

Decide whether you can divide hundreds.	**Divide tens.**	**Divide ones.**
■ · · · 3)227	7 3)227 21 1	75 R2 3)227 21↓ 17 15 2

$2 < 3$
Not enough hundreds. Start with tens.

Each employee must tag 75 scarves. There would be 2 scarves left over.

TRY THESE

Divide. Check your answers.

1. 3)491   2. 4)537   3. 7)684   4. 6)79   5. 3)251   6. 2)178

7. $632 \div 4 =$ ■   8. $944 \div 8 =$ ■   9. $875 \div 7 =$ ■

SKILLS PRACTICE

Divide.

1. 4)943   2. 3)461   3. 5)362   4. 4)625   5. 7)920   6. 5)432

7. 3)279   8. 3)852   9. 4)79   10. 6)452   11. 6)800   12. 7)301

13. 4)507   14. 6)84   15. 3)403   16. 8)704   17. 3)794   18. 2)75

19. 6)474   20. 5)95   21. 8)210   22. 4)179   23. 6)522   24. 5)721

25. 9)475   26. 4)706   27. 2)759   28. 9)836   29. 5)713   30. 6)804

31. 8)53   32. 8)432   33. 5)675   34. 4)893   35. 7)801   36. 4)378

37. $771 \div 3 =$ ■   38. $632 \div 8 =$ ■   39. $78 \div 6 =$ ■

40. $399 \div 7 =$ ■   41. $975 \div 5 =$ ■   42. $668 \div 4 =$ ■

PROBLEM SOLVING

A clothing manufacturer packs T-shirts in boxes. A box holds 4 large T-shirts, 6 medium T-shirts, or 8 small T-shirts. Use a calculator to complete the record to show how many boxes are needed.

	Number of T-shirts	Number in each box	Number of boxes
	104 large	4	26
43.	222 medium	6	■
44.	328 small	8	■
45.	696 medium	6	■
46.	928 large	4	■
47.	744 small	8	■

THINK!

Visual Perception

How many triangles of any size are in this figure?

Zeros in the Quotient

It is important to record zeros in the quotient. If you don't, you may get 21 as an answer when the correct answer is 201 or 210.

A. The school auditorium has 805 folding chairs. For a concert, the chairs are to be grouped in 4 sections with the same number of chairs in each. How many chairs will be in each section? How many chairs will be left over?

Divide: 4)805

```
  201 R1
4)805
  8
  00    ← Don't stop yet!
   0       You haven't divided
  05       the tens or the ones.
   4
   1
```

There will be 201 chairs in each section and 1 chair left over.

B. $8.40 ÷ 4 =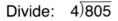

```
   $2.10
4)$8.40
  8
  0 4    ← Don't stop too soon!
    4       Be sure to divide the
   00       tens and the ones.
    0
    0
```

Remember to record the dollar sign and point in the quotient.

C. Find 800 ÷ 4.

```
  200
4)800
  8
  00   ← Both of these steps
   0      are important!
  00   ←
   0
   0
```

TRY THESE

Divide. Check your answers.

1. $3\overline{)207}$
2. $5\overline{)350}$
3. $2\overline{)801}$
4. $2\overline{)365}$
5. $6\overline{)80}$
6. $4\overline{)830}$

7. $540 \div 6 = \blacksquare$
8. $846 \div 2 = \blacksquare$
9. $\$4.50 \div 3 = \blacksquare$

SKILLS PRACTICE

Divide.

1. $3\overline{)927}$
2. $5\overline{)850}$
3. $2\overline{)380}$
4. $3\overline{)160}$
5. $3\overline{)96}$
6. $4\overline{)250}$

7. $5\overline{)349}$
8. $2\overline{)160}$
9. $9\overline{)410}$
10. $6\overline{)485}$
11. $5\overline{)600}$
12. $2\overline{)186}$

13. $7\overline{)68}$
14. $3\overline{)920}$
15. $3\overline{)651}$
16. $5\overline{)760}$
17. $2\overline{)57}$
18. $4\overline{)363}$

19. $2\overline{)101}$
20. $3\overline{)52}$
21. $4\overline{)340}$
22. $6\overline{)785}$
23. $4\overline{)484}$
24. $2\overline{)600}$

25. $3\overline{)429}$
26. $9\overline{)638}$
27. $7\overline{)900}$
28. $3\overline{)751}$
29. $2\overline{)561}$
30. $4\overline{)856}$

31. $8\overline{)300}$
32. $2\overline{)436}$
33. $2\overline{)143}$
34. $3\overline{)249}$
35. $7\overline{)719}$
36. $9\overline{)813}$

37. $500 \div 4 = \blacksquare$
38. $760 \div 4 = \blacksquare$
39. $63 \div 3 = \blacksquare$
40. $\$5.80 \div 5 = \blacksquare$
41. $\$1.80 \div 3 = \blacksquare$
42. $\$8.14 \div 2 = \blacksquare$

PROBLEM SOLVING

43. There are 150 sheets of music. Each member of the chorus gets 3 sheets. How many members of the chorus are there?

44. The school jazz band gave a concert. 385 people attended. 9 people were in the band. How many people were there in all?

45. Mr. Ramos paid a total of $9.00 for tickets to the concert. He bought 6 tickets. What was the price of each ticket?

★46. There were 300 people in the city chorus. There were the same number of men as women. How many men were in the chorus?

THINK!

A Measurement Riddle

What is bought by the yard but worn out by the foot?

Mental Math: Short Division and Estimation

A. When you divide by a 1-digit divisor, you can do much of the work in your head.

SHORT DIVISION

Divide hundreds. Regroup.

$$\begin{array}{r} 1 \\ 4\overline{)6^273} \end{array}$$

$1 \times 4 = 4$
$6 - 4 = 2$

Divide tens. Regroup.

$$\begin{array}{r} 1\ 6 \\ 4\overline{)6^27^33} \end{array}$$

$6 \times 4 = 24$
$27 - 24 = 3$

Divide ones. Write the remainder.

$$\begin{array}{r} 1\ 6\ 8\ R1 \\ 4\overline{)6^27^33} \end{array}$$

$8 \times 4 = 32$
$33 - 32 = 1$

B. There are many ways to estimate the answer to a division problem. The method you choose should depend on how close an estimate you need.

ESTIMATING QUOTIENTS

Mr. Wilson has $628 to spend on 3 beds for his family. *About* how much can he spend on each bed?

| Method 1 |

Sometimes you estimate by rounding the dividend.

$3\overline{)628}$ 628 rounds to 600.   About $200
        $600 \div 3 = 200$

| Method 2 |

Sometimes it is better to pick a number close to the dividend that is easy to divide mentally.

$3\overline{)628}$ 628 is close to 630.
        $630 \div 3 = 210$

About $210

| Method 3 |

It may be easier to break up the dividend and work with two or more numbers.

$3\overline{)628}$ $628 = 600 + 28$
        $600 \div 3 = 200$
        $28 \div 3$ is about 9.
        $200 + 9 = 209$

About $209

TRY THESE

Estimate the quotient. Then use short division to find the exact answer.

1. $5\overline{)550}$ 2. $3\overline{)97}$ 3. $3\overline{)911}$ 4. $8\overline{)99}$ 5. $2\overline{)137}$ 6. $4\overline{)608}$

7. $7\overline{)97}$ 8. $5\overline{)832}$ 9. $4\overline{)308}$ 10. $2\overline{)316}$ 11. $9\overline{)407}$ 12. $7\overline{)364}$

SKILLS PRACTICE

Estimate the quotient. Then use short division to find the exact answer.

1. $2\overline{)39}$ 2. $8\overline{)304}$ 3. $5\overline{)97}$ 4. $9\overline{)124}$ 5. $3\overline{)72}$ 6. $7\overline{)183}$

7. $6\overline{)80}$ 8. $3\overline{)48}$ 9. $3\overline{)148}$ 10. $4\overline{)920}$ 11. $9\overline{)996}$ 12. $5\overline{)261}$

13. $9\overline{)819}$ 14. $6\overline{)219}$ 15. $2\overline{)714}$ 16. $5\overline{)666}$ 17. $5\overline{)870}$ 18. $7\overline{)896}$

19. $3\overline{)495}$ 20. $8\overline{)408}$ 21. $4\overline{)381}$ 22. $6\overline{)407}$ 23. $6\overline{)663}$ 24. $2\overline{)740}$

25. $115 \div 5 = \blacksquare$ 26. $63 \div 3 = \blacksquare$ 27. $126 \div 9 = \blacksquare$

28. $777 \div 7 = \blacksquare$ ★29. $455 \div \blacksquare = 65$ ★30. $552 \div \blacksquare = 138$

31. The dividend is 864. The divisor is 8. What is the quotient?

★32. The divisor is 4. The quotient is 94. What is the dividend?

PROBLEM SOLVING

33. A truck carries 7 sofas, which have a total mass of 896 kilograms. About how much mass does each sofa have?

34. A store sold 4 chairs for a total of $372. About how much did it receive for each chair?

35. Three cushions fill the length of a 265-cm sofa. About how long is each cushion if all have the same length?

36. Mrs. Nash needs a set of 5 chairs. She can buy a set for $316 or a different set for $383. If she does not want to spend more than $70 per chair, can she buy one of the sets?

THINK!

Making a List

A book has 250 pages. If the pages are numbered consecutively from 1 to 250, how many digits are used in all?

Dividing Larger Numbers

You can divide larger numbers just as you divide
2- and 3-digit numbers.

A. Mrs. Lee went on a diet for 7 days. The food she ate
contained a total of 9,835 calories. The food she ate
contained the same number of calories each day.
How many calories did her food contain each day?

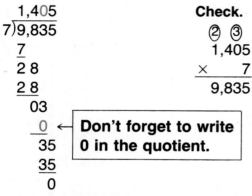

```
  1,405
7)9,835
  7
  2 8
  2 8
  03
   0  ← Don't forget to write
  35    0 in the quotient.
  35
   0
```

Check.
```
   ② ③
   1,405
 ×     7
   9,835 ✔
```

Her food contained 1,405 calories each day.

B. Divide 20,278 by 4.
Estimate to predict how big
your answer should be.

Round 20,278 to 20,000.
20 thousand ÷ 4 = 5 thousand
About 5,000

4 > 2

not enough ten-thousands
Start by dividing the
20 thousands.

```
     5,069 R2
4)20,278
  20
   0 2
     0
    27
    24
    38
    36
     2
```

Check.
```
    ②③
   5,069
 ×     4
  20,276
 +     2
  20,278 ✔
```

TRY THESE

Estimate. Then find the exact answer.

1. 3)8,245   **2.** 7)5,054   **3.** 5)90,000   **4.** 4)31,200   **5.** 2)16,851

6. 6,035 ÷ 5 = ■   **7.** $42.00 ÷ 6 = ■   **8.** $54.72 ÷ 6 = ■

SKILLS PRACTICE

Divide.

1. $2\overline{)7{,}328}$ 2. $3\overline{)4{,}680}$ 3. $5\overline{)730}$ 4. $6\overline{)9{,}552}$ 5. $8\overline{)4{,}300}$

6. $5\overline{)4{,}137}$ 7. $6\overline{)5{,}000}$ 8. $5\overline{)6{,}075}$ 9. $2\overline{)183}$ 10. $4\overline{)9{,}000}$

11. $6\overline{)6{,}390}$ 12. $2\overline{)73}$ 13. $3\overline{)2{,}410}$ 14. $9\overline{)909}$ 15. $2\overline{)10{,}120}$

16. $7\overline{)12{,}600}$ 17. $9\overline{)18{,}360}$ 18. $8\overline{)9{,}520}$ 19. $9\overline{)800}$ 20. $4\overline{)26{,}340}$

21. $7\overline{)9{,}500}$ 22. $3\overline{)62{,}400}$ 23. $6\overline{)3{,}163}$ 24. $8\overline{)46{,}392}$ 25. $2\overline{)80{,}000}$

26. $5{,}406 \div 6 = \blacksquare$ 27. $30{,}037 \div 7 = \blacksquare$ 28. $3{,}933 \div 9 = \blacksquare$

29. $\$63.40 \div 4 = \blacksquare$ 30. $\$85.28 \div 4 = \blacksquare$ 31. $\$80.00 \div 5 = \blacksquare$

PROBLEM SOLVING

32. Mr. Antonio went on a diet for 5 days. The food he ate contained a total of 10,625 Calories. He ate the same amount each day. How many Calories were in the food he ate each day?

★**33.** Randy ate a large sandwich for lunch. It had 3 slices of bread with 65 Calories in each slice. There were 165 Calories in the roast beef, 105 Calories in the cheese, and 15 Calories in the mustard. How many Calories were in the sandwich?

MIXED REVIEW

Add, subtract, or multiply.

1. $\begin{array}{r} 4{,}792 \\ \times\quad 84 \\ \hline \end{array}$ 2. $\begin{array}{r} 56{,}382 \\ +43{,}679 \\ \hline \end{array}$ 3. $\begin{array}{r} 3{,}186 \\ \times\quad 549 \\ \hline \end{array}$ 4. $\begin{array}{r} 86{,}004 \\ -37{,}219 \\ \hline \end{array}$ 5. $\begin{array}{r} 384{,}792 \\ +568{,}407 \\ \hline \end{array}$

Write >, <, or = for ⬤.

6. $2{,}857 \; \bullet \; 2{,}846$ 7. $23{,}486 \; \bullet \; 23{,}496$ 8. $2{,}354{,}717 \; \bullet \; 2{,}354{,}717$

Problem Solving

Answers in Division

All problems below use this division.
Each has a different answer.

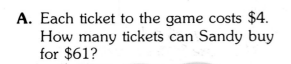

$$\begin{array}{r} 15 \\ 4\overline{)61} \\ \underline{4} \\ 21 \\ \underline{20} \\ 1 \end{array}$$

A. Each ticket to the game costs $4.
How many tickets can Sandy buy
for $61?

> You can only buy whole tickets.
> No need to give the remainder.

Sandy can buy 15 tickets.

B. 61 students are going to the game.
4 students can ride in each car.
How many cars are needed?

> 15 cars would leave 1 student
> behind! One more car is needed.

16 cars are needed.

C. The ticket office was open a total
of 61 hours for the 4 games this
year. It was open the same amount
of time for each game. How many
hours was the office open for each
game?

$$\begin{array}{r} 15\frac{1}{4} \leftarrow \\ 4\overline{)61} \\ \underline{4} \\ 21 \\ \underline{20} \\ 1 \end{array}$$

> All 61 hours were used.
> No hours were left over.

1 hour

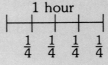

$$\frac{1}{4} \quad \frac{1}{4} \quad \frac{1}{4} \quad \frac{1}{4}$$

The office was open
$15\frac{1}{4}$ hours for each game.

$15\frac{1}{4}$ **is a
mixed numeral.**

1 hour for 4 games
is
$\frac{1}{4}$ hour for each game.

TRY THESE

1. Dan's family wants to buy tickets to this season's basketball games. Each ticket costs $5. How many tickets can they buy with $52?

2. Each basketball team has 5 players. How many teams can be formed with 52 players? How many players will be left over?

3. The team spent 52 hours in all practicing for 5 games. They practiced the same amount of time for each game. How long did they practice for each game?

4. The basketball coach wants to order 52 uniforms. There are 5 uniforms in each box. How many boxes must he order so that *every* player can have a uniform?

PROBLEM SOLVING PRACTICE

Solve. Make sure your answer is appropriate.

1. Each row of the stands can seat 9 people. How many rows must be used to seat 350 people?

2. Each bag will hold 4 basketballs. There are 27 basketballs in all. How many bags can be filled? How many basketballs will be left over?

3. 285 tickets to the game were sold. Each ticket cost $5. How much was collected for all the tickets?

4. The cheerleaders took 125 pennants to the game. They sold all but 9. How many did they sell?

5. David bought a pennant for $2.00 and a program for $1.75. How much money did he spend?

6. The coach has $150 to buy new basketballs. Each ball costs $7. How many basketballs can he buy?

7. The cheerleaders had 51 feet of streamer paper. They cut the streamer into 8 pieces. Each piece was the same length. How long was each piece?

8. The cheerleaders had to take 125 pennants to the game. 8 pennants filled each box. How many boxes did they need to pack all the pennants?

★9. Tom scored 2 more points than Jim. Jim scored 8 more points than Lorenzo. Lorenzo scored 16 points. How many points did Jim score? How many points did Tom score?

★10. Tom keeps in shape by riding a bike. He can ride a mile in 6 minutes. How far can he ride in 18 minutes? How far can he ride in 25 minutes?

ON YOUR OWN

Make up three problems that use this division: $59 \div 7 = $ ■

The problems should have different answers: 8, $8\frac{3}{7}$, and 9.

Problem Solving

Finding Averages

A. This bar graph shows the heights of some waterfalls in the United States and Canada.

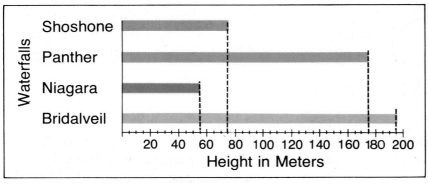

The **average** height of these waterfalls can be found in two steps.

Step 1
Add to find
the total.

$$\begin{array}{r} 3\,2 \\ 75 \\ 175 \\ 55 \\ +195 \\ \hline 500 \end{array}$$ Shoshone
Panther
Niagara
Bridalveil

Step 2
Divide the total
by the number
of waterfalls.

$$\begin{array}{r} 125 \\ 4\overline{)500} \end{array}$$

The average height of the waterfalls is 125 meters.

B. Pablo was saving money for a trip to Niagara Falls. He worked for 4 weeks and earned a total of $324. What were his **average** weekly earnings?

Divide the total earnings
by the number of weeks.

$$\begin{array}{r} 81 \\ 4\overline{)324} \end{array}$$

Pablo's average weekly earnings were $81.

C. Pablo flew from Los Angeles to New York in 5 hours. The distance is 4,625 kilometers (km). What was the **average** speed of the plane? Give your answer in kilometers per hour (km/h).

Divide the total
number of kilometers
by the number of hours.

$$\begin{array}{r} 925 \\ 5\overline{)4,625} \end{array}$$

The average speed of the plane was 925 km/h.

TRY THESE

1. Mr. Sanchez drove for 7 hours. He drove 553 km. What was his average speed?

2. Mr. Sanchez drove 2,312 km in 4 days. What was the average number of kilometers he drove each day?

3. A used-car dealer sold 4 cars at prices of $4,100; $6,300; $5,800; and $4,900. What was the average price of the cars?

4. Mr. Sanchez bought 7 glasses of juice in different places. He paid 30¢, 35¢, 45¢, 40¢, 55¢, 35¢, and 40¢. What was the average price?

PROBLEM SOLVING PRACTICE

Solve.

1. Mrs. Sloan spent $68.40 for 6 tanks of gas. What was the average cost of filling the tank?

2. Mrs. Sloan spent $63 for meals. She ate 9 meals. What was the average cost of these meals?

3. On Monday, the high temperature was 20°C. On Tuesday, it was 28°C. On Wednesday, it was 33°C. What was the average high temperature for these 3 days?

4. Mrs. Sloan drove 651 km on Monday, 582 km on Tuesday, and 624 km on Wednesday. What was the average number of kilometers she traveled each day?

5. Mr. Rizzo took his family to visit his mother. She lives 260 km away. Mr. Rizzo made the trip in 4 hours. What was his average speed?

6. Mr. Rizzo bought 5 presents to take to his mother. He spent $41.25. What was the average cost of these presents?

7. Mr. Rizzo watched his hometown team play 3 basketball games. He paid $1.50 for each ticket. How much did he spend in all?

8. In 3 games, the team scored 68 points, 62 points, and 74 points. What was the team's average score?

★9. The attendance for the 3 games was 475, 388, and 421. What was the average attendance for these games? What would have been the average attendance if Mr. Rizzo hadn't gone to these 3 games?

★10. Mr. Rizzo's hometown football team scored 14 points, 17 points, 24 points, and 13 points in preseason games. What was their average score during the preseason?

ON YOUR OWN

Make up a problem that uses the average of 92, 77, and 80.
Make up a second problem that uses the average of 92, 77, 80, and 83. Solve both.

Calculator Division with Remainders

The Old Mill Bakery puts 6 rolls in a package.
If they bake 9,657 rolls, how many packages can they fill?
How many rolls will be left over?

Find 9,657 ÷ 6 on your calculator.

| 9 | 6 | 5 | 7 | ÷ | 6 | = | 1609.5 |

The whole number part of the quotient is 1,609. To find the remainder, multiply 1,609 by the divisor: 1,609 × 6. Then subtract the product from the dividend, 9,657.

| 6 | × | 1 | 6 | 0 | 9 | M+ |
| 9 | 6 | 5 | 7 | − | MR | M 3. |

> Place the product, 9,654, in the calculator's memory.

They can fill 1,609 packages. There will be 3 rolls left over.

Warning: Before starting another problem in which you will want to use memory, clear what is already there.

Press: MR M−

Suppose 8 packages are shipped in a carton. How many cartons can be filled? How many packages will be left over?

| 1 | 6 | 0 | 9 | ÷ | 8 | = | 201.125 |

The whole number part of the quotient is 201. To find the remainder, multiply 8 × 201 and subtract the product from 1,609.

| 8 | × | 2 | 0 | 1 | M+ |
| 1 | 6 | 0 | 9 | − | MR | M 1. |

> Place the product, 1,608, in the calculator's memory.

They can fill 201 cartons. There will be 1 package left over.

Use your calculator to solve these problems.

1. The Sunny Bakery produced 7,250 loaves of bread one week. If 4 loaves are packed in a box, how many boxes were filled? How many loaves were left over? If 8 boxes fit in a carton, how many cartons were filled? How many boxes were left over?

2. The Flower Bakery packs loaves of French bread 5 in a bag. If there are 3,859 loaves, how many bags are needed to pack all the loaves? If 9 bags fit in a carton, how many cartons will be completely filled? How many bags will be left over?

Unit Review

Divide. *(pages 114–123)*

1. $5\overline{)35}$ 2. $9\overline{)63}$ 3. $4\overline{)36}$ 4. $6\overline{)24}$ 5. $8\overline{)8}$ 6. $7\overline{)0}$

7. $3\overline{)37}$ 8. $4\overline{)59}$ 9. $6\overline{)68}$ 10. $3\overline{)35}$ 11. $4\overline{)72}$ 12. $5\overline{)63}$

13. $8\overline{)87}$ 14. $5\overline{)92}$ 15. $7\overline{)77}$ 16. $3\overline{)74}$ 17. $4\overline{)84}$ 18. $6\overline{)80}$

19. $64 \div 8 = $ ■   20. $0 \div 4 = $ ■   21. $72 \div 3 = $ ■

Divide. *(pages 128–133)*

22. $6\overline{)215}$ 23. $2\overline{)672}$ 24. $8\overline{)885}$ 25. $4\overline{)191}$ 26. $3\overline{)676}$ 27. $2\overline{)489}$

28. $3\overline{)900}$ 29. $6\overline{)517}$ 30. $4\overline{)829}$ 31. $4\overline{)210}$ 32. $7\overline{)847}$ 33. $3\overline{)908}$

34. $505 \div 5 = $ ■   35. $272 \div 4 = $ ■   36. $\$10.00 \div 4 = $ ■

Divide. *(pages 134–135)*

37. $3\overline{)4,587}$ 38. $6\overline{)6,734}$ 39. $4\overline{)2,863}$ 40. $5\overline{)7,154}$

41. $4\overline{)37,262}$ 42. $7\overline{)16,100}$ 43. $6\overline{)3,694}$ 44. $5\overline{)12,527}$

45. $7,749 \div 7 = $ ■   46. $52,200 \div 8 = $ ■   47. $4,404 \div 6 = $ ■

Solve the problems. *(pages 124–125, 136–139)*

48. There are 122 steers in the rodeo. Joe can put 8 steers in each corral. How many corrals does he need to hold all the steers?

49. Each adult ticket to the rodeo costs $4. Each child's ticket costs $2. How many adult tickets can John buy with $58?

50. The attendance for the 5 days of the rodeo was 1,020; 990; 1,100; 1,050; and 1,035. What was the average attendance at the rodeo for these 5 days?

51. The stablehand used 21 pounds of corn. She put the same amount of corn in 8 horses' feeders. How many pounds of corn did she put in each feeder?

141

More Help with Division

Divide.

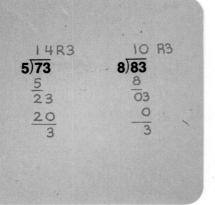

$$5\overline{)73} \quad 14R3$$
$$\underline{5}$$
$$23$$
$$\underline{20}$$
$$3$$

$$8\overline{)83} \quad 10\ R3$$
$$\underline{8}$$
$$03$$
$$\underline{0}$$
$$3$$

1. $5\overline{)75}$
2. $5\overline{)56}$
3. $6\overline{)68}$
4. $4\overline{)74}$

5. $3\overline{)38}$
6. $3\overline{)93}$
7. $2\overline{)26}$
8. $7\overline{)88}$

9. $4\overline{)36}$
10. $9\overline{)74}$
11. $6\overline{)52}$
12. $8\overline{)56}$

13. $6\overline{)74}$
14. $3\overline{)33}$
15. $8\overline{)58}$
16. $5\overline{)47}$

17. $2\overline{)65}$
18. $8\overline{)64}$
19. $7\overline{)66}$
20. $7\overline{)42}$

$$4\overline{)2,896} \quad 724$$
$$\underline{2\ 8} \quad \leftarrow \boxed{7 \times 4 = 28}$$
$$09$$
$$\underline{8} \quad \leftarrow \boxed{2 \times 4 = 8}$$
$$16$$
$$\underline{16} \quad \leftarrow \boxed{4 \times 4 = 16}$$
$$0$$

21. $5\overline{)115}$
22. $6\overline{)676}$
23. $7\overline{)225}$
24. $3\overline{)376}$

25. $8\overline{)899}$
26. $3\overline{)339}$
27. $4\overline{)189}$
28. $5\overline{)666}$

29. $7\overline{)782}$
30. $9\overline{)326}$
31. $3\overline{)372}$
32. $5\overline{)712}$

33. $4\overline{)8,457}$
34. $6\overline{)1,476}$
35. $5\overline{)7,362}$
36. $9\overline{)6,399}$

37. $7\overline{)8,949}$
38. $3\overline{)2,194}$
39. $2\overline{)8,694}$
40. $8\overline{)9,857}$

$$2\overline{)6,180} \quad 3,090$$
$$\underline{6} \quad \leftarrow \boxed{3 \times 2 = 6}$$
$$01$$
$$\underline{0} \quad \leftarrow \boxed{0 \times 2 = 0}$$
$$18$$
$$\underline{18} \quad \leftarrow \boxed{9 \times 2 = 18}$$
$$00$$
$$\underline{0} \quad \leftarrow \boxed{0 \times 2 = 0}$$
$$0$$

41. $6\overline{)240}$
42. $9\overline{)98}$
43. $7\overline{)749}$
44. $8\overline{)883}$

45. $5\overline{)544}$
46. $3\overline{)62}$
47. $6\overline{)725}$
48. $2\overline{)602}$

49. $7\overline{)8,614}$
50. $4\overline{)4,400}$
51. $4\overline{)83}$
52. $5\overline{)400}$

53. $9\overline{)8,109}$
54. $2\overline{)6,201}$
55. $8\overline{)4,818}$
56. $7\overline{)7,843}$

57. $6\overline{)3,600}$
58. $4\overline{)8,405}$
59. $5\overline{)6,200}$
60. $8\overline{)6,409}$

Divisibility

When division gives a 0 remainder, the dividend is *divisible by* the divisor.

$$\begin{array}{r} 36 \text{ R}0 \\ 2\overline{)72} \end{array}$$

divisible by 2

$$\begin{array}{r} 36 \text{ R}1 \\ 2\overline{)73} \end{array}$$

not divisible by 2

Even numbers are divisible by 2.

Odd numbers are not divisible by 2.

It is easy to find whether a number is divisible by 2, 5, 10, or 3 without having to divide.

A. divisible by 2 — 0, 2, 4, 6, 8, 10, 12, 14, 16, 18, 20, 22, 24, 26, 28, 30,

A number is divisible by 2 if its last digit is 0, 2, 4, 6, or 8.

B. divisible by 5 — 0, 5, 10, 15, 20, 25, 30, 35, 40,

A number is divisible by 5 if its last digit is 0 or 5.

C. divisible by 10 — 10, 20, 30, 40, 50, 60, 70, 80, 90,

A number is divisible by 10 if its last digit is 0.

$$1 + 2 = 3 \qquad 2 + 4 = 6 \qquad 3 + 6 = 9$$

D. divisible by 3 — 3, 6, 9, 12, 15, 18, 21, 24, 27, 30, 33, 36,

A number is divisible by 3 if the sum of its digits is divisible by 3.

Which of these numbers are divisible by 2? by 5? by 10? by 3?

1. 72   **2.** 93   **3.** 105   **4.** 483   **5.** 1,000   **6.** 2,304

7. 234   **8.** 465   **9.** 612   **10.** 3,420   **11.** 6,280   **12.** 8,115

Cumulative Review

Choose the correct answer.

1. 39 + 973 = ▨

a. 1,363
b. 39,973
c. 37,947
d. 1,012

2. 47 × 83 = ▨

a. 130
b. 3,901
c. 913
d. 3,781

3. $30.00 − $2.98 = ▨

a. $28.12
b. $.20
c. $27.02
d. $32.98

4. 306 ÷ 9 = ▨

a. 297
b. 315
c. 2,754
d. 34

5. 426
    ×180

a. 76,680
b. 38,340
c. 7,668
d. 3,834

6. 7)‾54‾

a. 8
b. 7
c. 7 R5
d. 8 R2

7. Round 99,493 to the nearest thousand.

a. 99,500
b. 99,490
c. 100,000
d. 99,000

8. 6)‾2,440‾

a. 46 R4
b. 406 R4
c. 4 R4
d. 4 R40

9.   97
       249
    +8,586

a. 8,822
b. 8,932
c. 9,932
d. 8,712

10. 8 × $19.72 = ▨

a. $157.76
b. $15,776
c. $1,577.6
d. $15.776

11. Complete.
    9,999 ⬤ 10,000

a. =
b. >
c. <

12. 8)‾79‾

a. 9
b. 1 R1
c. 10 R2
d. 9 R7

13. 8 airplanes will fit into each hangar. There are 195 airplanes. How many hangars must be built to house all of the airplanes?

a. 24 hangars
b. 24 hangars, 3 airplanes left over
c. 24 $\frac{3}{8}$ hangars
d. 25 hangars

14. Each bus can carry 56 people. The city has 492 buses. How many people could ride these buses at the same time?

a. 548 people
b. 5,412 people
c. 27,552 people
d. 436 people

144   **Dividing by Ones**

6 Time, Money, Measurement

RAILROAD TRACK LENGTH IN LEADING RAILROAD COUNTRIES

Country	Track Length $\oplus$ = 10,000 miles of track
Australia	⊕ ⊕ ⊕
Canada	⊕ ⊕ ⊕ ⊕
China	⊕ ⊕ ⊕
India	⊕ ⊕ ⊕ ⊕
Russia	⊕ ⊕ ⊕ ⊕ ⊕ ⊕ ⊕ ⊕ ⊕
United States	⊕ ⊕

Telling Time

A. You can read this time as minutes *past* the hour or minutes *to* the next hour.

50 minutes *past* 2   two-fifty   10 minutes *to* 3

Write this time as 2:50.

B. There are 60 minutes in one hour.   There are 24 hours in a day.

The minute hand goes around the clock once in an hour.

The hour hand goes around the clock twice in one day.

Use **A.M.** to write times between 12:00 midnight and 12:00 noon.

Use **P.M.** to write times between 12:00 noon and 12:00 midnight.

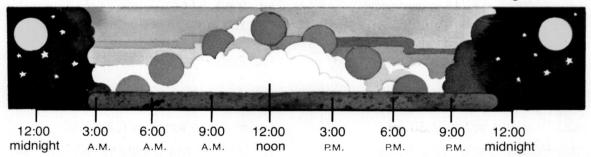

| 12:00 midnight | 3:00 A.M. | 6:00 A.M. | 9:00 A.M. | 12:00 noon | 3:00 P.M. | 6:00 P.M. | 9:00 P.M. | 12:00 midnight |

TRY THESE

Read each clock.

1.

■ : ■

■ minutes to ■

2.

■ : ■

■ minutes to ■

3.

■ : ■

■ minutes past ■

SKILLS PRACTICE

Read each clock.

1.

■ : ■

■ minutes past ■

2.

■ : ■

■ minutes past ■

3.

■ : ■

■ minutes to ■

4.

■ : ■

■ minutes past ■

5.

■ : ■

■ minutes to ■

6.

■ : ■

■ minutes to ■

Match the times.

7. 2:45   a. 17 minutes to 5
8. 8:25   b. 25 minutes to 2
9. 4:43   c. 15 minutes to 3
10. 1:35   d. 14 minutes past 12
11. 12:14   e. 20 minutes to 8
12. 7:40   f. 25 minutes past 8

Is it light or dark outside at:

13. 9:05 A.M.
14. 3:35 P.M.
15. 2:40 A.M.
16. 12:00 noon
17. 11:20 P.M.
18. 2:30 P.M.

Use A.M. or P.M. to complete each sentence.

19. The sun set at 7:30 ■.

20. Sue ate lunch at 12:30 ■.

21. Ed ate dinner at 5:30 ■.

22. George ate breakfast at 8:00 ■.

THINK!

Visual Reasoning

The minute hand of this clock has two dots on it, A and B. While the minute hand goes around the clock once, what shape is traced by dot A? By dot B? Which point moves faster, A or B?

Homework   page 421

Elapsed Time: Hours or Minutes

A. Find the time:

5 hours *after* 10:40 A.M.

2 hours
to
12:40 P.M.

3 hours
after
12:40 P.M.

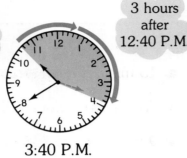

3:40 P.M.

8 hours *before* 5:20 P.M.

3 hours
before
12:20 P.M.

5 hours
back to
12:20 P.M.

9:20 A.M.

B. Find the time:

35 minutes *after* 3:40 P.M.

20 minutes
to
4:00 P.M.

15 minutes
after
4:00 P.M.

4:15 P.M.

50 minutes *before* 9:20 A.M.

30 minutes
before
9:00 A.M.

20 minutes
back to
9:00 A.M.

8:30 A.M.

C. Find the time:

between 7:25 A.M. and 2:25 P.M.

5 hours
to
12:25 P.M.

2 hours
after
12:25 P.M.

5 + 2 = 7
7 hours between

between 2:25 P.M. and 3:10 P.M.

35 minutes
to
3:00 P.M.

10 minutes
after
3:00 P.M.

35 + 10 = 45
45 minutes between

TRY THESE

Find the time.

1. 2 hours after 8:15 A.M.

2. 40 minutes before 5:35 P.M.

3. between 1:20 A.M. and 8:20 A.M.

4. between 4:40 P.M. and 5:20 P.M.

SKILLS PRACTICE

Find the time.

1. 7 hours after 6:30 P.M.

2. 15 minutes after 11:25 A.M.

3. 3 hours before 2:05 A.M.

4. 55 minutes before 4:20 P.M.

5. 35 minutes after 6:50 A.M.

6. 9 hours before 7:25 A.M.

7. between 6:10 A.M. and 2:10 P.M.

8. between 9:20 A.M. and 10:00 A.M.

9. between 5:30 P.M. and 6:05 P.M.

10. between 11:55 P.M. and 3:55 A.M.

★11. 15 hours after 1:30 A.M.

★12. between 7:20 A.M. and 9:20 P.M.

PROBLEM SOLVING

13. Mr. Chen's train leaves at 8:15 A.M. It takes him 25 minutes to go from his home to the station. At what time must he leave home?

★14. Both Bob and Carlos left the airport at 5:15 P.M. It took Bob 45 minutes to get home. It took Carlos 5 minutes longer. When did Bob get home? When did Carlos get home?

THINK!

Arithmetic on a Clock

If you add on the clock face, 7 + 8 = 3. Do each addition on the clock face.

1. 7 + 9 = ▪   **2.** 5 + 10 = ▪   **3.** 5 + 8 = ▪

There is no 0 when you add on a clock. But there is a number that has a property like the zero property.

4. 8 + ___?___ = 8   **5.** ___?___ + 5 = 5

What clock number has this property?

Elapsed Time: Hours and Minutes

Find the time:

A. 5 hours 35 minutes *after* 10:40 A.M.

Step 1 Work with hours.

5 hours after 10:40 A.M. is 3:40 P.M.

Step 2 Work with minutes.

35 minutes after 3:40 P.M. is 4:15 P.M.

10:40 A.M.

4:15 P.M.

B. 8 hours 50 minutes *before* 5:20 P.M.

Step 1 Work with hours.

8 hours before 5:20 P.M. is 9:20 A.M.

Step 2 Work with minutes.

50 minutes before 9:20 A.M. is 8:30 A.M.

5:20 P.M.

8:30 A.M.

C. *Between* 7:25 A.M. and 3:10 P.M.

3:25 is after 3:10. Use 2:25.

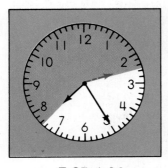

7:25 A.M.

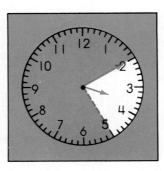

3:10 P.M.

Step 1 Work with hours.

Between 7:25 A.M. and 2:25 P.M. there are 7 hours.

Step 2 Work with minutes.

Between 2:25 P.M. and 3:10 P.M. there are 45 minutes.

Between 7:25 A.M. and 3:10 P.M. there are 7 hours 45 minutes.

TRY THESE

Find the time.

1. 1 hour 30 minutes after 10:20 A.M.   **2.** 2 hours 5 minutes before 4:15 P.M.

3. between 1:30 A.M. and 6:35 A.M.   **4.** between 8:15 P.M. and 12:45 A.M.

SKILLS PRACTICE

Find the time.

1. 4 hours 20 minutes before 8:10 P.M.   **2.** 7 hours 35 minutes after 8:15 A.M.

3. between 10:25 A.M. and 12:10 P.M.   **4.** between 6:50 P.M. and 3:15 A.M.

5. 5 hours 50 minutes after 9:20 A.M.   **6.** 10 hours 5 minutes after 3:55 A.M.

7. 9 hours 30 minutes before 5:20 P.M.   **8.** 1 hour 45 minutes before 1:10 A.M.

9. between 7:30 A.M. and 2:15 P.M.   **10.** between 3:40 P.M. and 5:20 A.M.

PROBLEM SOLVING

Use this schedule to solve the problems.

11. How long does it take to go from Boston to New York?

12. How long does the flight stay in New York?

13. How long does it take to go from New York to Atlanta?

FLIGHT 208 BOSTON TO ATLANTA WITH STOPS IN NEW YORK AND WASHINGTON		
City	**Arrive**	**Depart**
Boston	——	8:40 A.M.
New York	9:25 A.M.	10:15 A.M.
Washington	11:05 A.M.	12:10 P.M.
Atlanta	2:35 P.M.	——

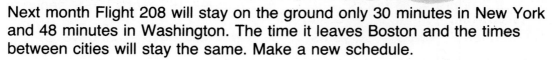

Making a Table

Next month Flight 208 will stay on the ground only 30 minutes in New York and 48 minutes in Washington. The time it leaves Boston and the times between cities will stay the same. Make a new schedule.

Units of Time

A. Use the table and multiply to change larger units of time to smaller units.

> 1 minute = 60 seconds
> 1 hour = 60 minutes
> 1 day = 24 hours
> 1 week = 7 days
> 1 year = 12 months
> 1 century = 100 years

B. 7 hours = ■ minutes

7 hours = 7 × 1 hour
= 7 × 60 minutes
= 420 minutes

C. 9 days = ■ hours

9 days = 9 × 1 day
= 9 × 24 hours
= 216 hours

D. 3 years 8 months = ■ months

Step 1 Change 3 years to months.

3 years = 3 × 1 year
= 3 × 12 months
= 36 months

Step 2 Add the months.

3 years 8 months = 36 months + 8 months
= 44 months

E. Not all months have the same number of days.

31 days	January, March, May, July, August, October, December
30 days	April, June, September, November
28 days	February (29 days in leap years—every four years)

TRY THESE

Complete.

1. 5 weeks = ■ days

2. 8 centuries = ■ years

3. 4 days 3 hours = ■ hours

4. 2 minutes 14 seconds = ■ seconds

5. 3 centuries 27 years = ■ years

6. 6 weeks 5 days = ■ days

7. January and July each have ■ days.

8. Except for leap year, February has ■ days.

SKILLS PRACTICE _____

Complete.

1. 9 minutes = ■ seconds
2. 7 days = ■ hours
3. 5 years = ■ months
4. 20 centuries = ■ years
5. 12 weeks = ■ days
6. 24 hours = ■ minutes
7. 4 hours 20 minutes = ■ minutes
8. 4 weeks 3 days = ■ days
9. 4 minutes 12 seconds = ■ seconds
10. 19 centuries 85 years = ■ years
11. 5 days 12 hours = ■ hours
12. 3 years 6 months = ■ months
13. 10 minutes 10 seconds = ■ seconds
14. 2 centuries 96 years = ■ years
15. 5 hours 6 minutes = ■ minutes
16. 1 day 18 hours = ■ hours
★17. 1 day = ■ minutes
★18. 1 week = ■ hours
19. In leap year, February has ■ days.
20. April and March have ■ days in all.
21. There are ■ months that have 30 days.
22. December and January each have ■ days.

PROBLEM SOLVING _____

23. How many days are in the first 4 months of a year? a leap year?

24. How many days are in the last 4 months of a year? a leap year?

★25. 1 regular year = 365 days
1 leap year = 366 days

How many days are there in 3 years that include 1 leap year?

★26. How many days are in 52 weeks? Is the relation between weeks and years, 1 year = 52 weeks, exact or a "good estimate"?

$$\boxed{\text{MIXED REVIEW}}$$

Write the standard numerals.

1. sixty thousand, three
2. four million, twenty thousand

Add, subtract, or multiply.

3.	4.	5.	6.	7.
3,411	$146.82	775	$16.42	4,003
× 18	− 97.03	+11,430	× 50	−1,009

Money

A. You can name or show the value of amounts of money by using a *cents sign* (¢) or a *dollar sign* ($) and *decimal point* (.).

| 1¢ | $.01 | | 5¢ | $.05 | | 10¢ | $.10 | | 25¢ | $.25 | | 50¢ | $.50 |
| penny | | | nickel | | | dime | | | quarter | | | half-dollar | |

| 100¢ | $1.00 | 500¢ | $5.00 | 1,000¢ | $10.00 | 2,000¢ | $20.00 |
| 1-dollar bill | | 5-dollar bill | | 10-dollar bill | | 20-dollar bill | |

B. To count money, start by counting the bills or coins that are worth the most.

| | $20.00 | +$5.00 | +$1.00 | +50¢ | +25¢ | +5¢ |
| Count | $20.00 | $25.00 | $26.00 | $26.50 | $26.75 | $26.80 |

TRY THESE

How much money?

1.

2.

3. 6 dollars, 1 quarter, 2 dimes, 6 pennies

4. 4 dollars, 3 quarters, 1 nickel, 7 pennies

5. 2 dollars, 2 quarters, 2 dimes, 2 nickels

SKILLS PRACTICE _____

Use a dollar sign and decimal point to show the amount.

1.

2.

3.

4.

5. 2 dollars, 3 quarters,
   1 dime, 3 nickels

6. 1 half-dollar, 1 quarter,
   3 dimes, 6 pennies

7. 3 dollars, 3 quarters,
   3 dimes, 3 pennies

8. 17 dollars, 1 half-dollar,
   3 quarters, 4 dimes

Find the total value.

	$20	$10	$5	$1	HD	Q	D	N	P	Total Value
9.		3	2				5	1		■
10.		1		2				3	2	■
11.			4	4			4		4	■
12.	1	2			1	1			1	■
13.	1	2	3	4				3		■

Which is worth more?

14. 5 quarters or 15 nickels

15. 3 dimes and 2 nickels or 2 quarters

★16. 1 dollar, 3 dimes, 4 nickels
   or 1 dollar, 2 quarters

★17. 2 dollars, 4 quarters, 15 dimes,
   10 nickels or 1 five-dollar bill

THINK!

Research Project

Find the name of the person pictured and value of each of the coins or bills shown above. What is the total value of the coins and bills shown?

Problem Solving

Making Change

A. Some cash registers show only the total amount you spent.

Georgia bought a game that cost $6.20.
She gave the clerk $20.00.
How much should she get back?

The clerk started with the cost and continued counting:

smallest first		+5¢	+25¢	+50¢	+$1.00	+$1.00	+$1.00	+$10.00
Count:	**$6.20**	**$6.25**	**$6.50**	**$7.00**	**$8.00**	**$9.00**	**$10.00**	**$20.00**
	Cost							

Georgia received 1 nickel, 1 quarter, 1 half-dollar, 3 dollar bills, and 1 ten-dollar bill, or $13.80 in change.

B. Some registers show how much money you get back.

Georgia bought another game that cost $6.20.
She gave the clerk $20.00.
How should the clerk count out what she gets back?

The cash register showed the price, how much Georgia gave, and the change she should get back.
This time the clerk counted in this way:

largest first	$10.00	+ $1.00	+ $1.00	+ $1.00	+ 50¢	+ 25¢	+ 5¢
Count:	**$10.00**	**$11.00**	**$12.00**	**$13.00**	**$13.50**	**$13.75**	**$13.80**

Georgia received 1 ten-dollar bill, 3 dollar bills, 1 half-dollar, 1 quarter, and 1 nickel, or $13.80 in change.

TRY THESE

Count out the change.

1. $11.15

Given:

+10¢ +25¢ +50¢ +$1.00 +$1.00 +$1.00 +$5.00

Count: $11.15   What change should you get?

2. After a purchase, the register showed that you should get $12.45 back.
What change should you get? Use the largest possible bills and coins.

Count: $10.00

PROBLEM SOLVING PRACTICE

1. Marie bought an iron that cost
$17.50 and gave the clerk $20.
How should the clerk count out
the change?

★2. Mrs. Mandel bought a lamp for $5.65.
She gave the clerk a ten-dollar bill.
The cash register had no quarters.
What change did she get?

**Copy and complete the table. Use the least number
of coins and bills to make change.**

	Cost	Given								
3.	$3.42	$5.00								
4.	$14.20	$20.00								
5.	$.83	$5.00								
6.	$9.72	$10.00								

ON YOUR OWN

Find the price of something you would like to buy. Decide
what money you might use to pay for it. Make up a problem
about the change you would get.

Problem Solving Strategy

Working Backwards

Sometimes a problem tells you the total amount a person can spend. **Working backwards** may help you find which things the person can buy.

Sandy wants to buy 2 pairs of socks at $3 each and a pair of jeans at $16. She has $20. Can she buy the socks and jeans?

Work backwards.

$20	amount Sandy has
− 16	cost of jeans
$ 4	amount left after she buys the jeans

Sale! Sale! Sale!

socks	$3.00
jeans	$16.00
handkerchiefs	$3.50
scarves	$9.00
hats	$8.00
ties	$3.50

Two pairs of socks at $3 each cost $6, which is more than $4. Sandy cannot buy the socks and jeans.

1. Can Sandy buy 1 pair of socks and the jeans with her $20?

2. Suppose Sandy had $25. Could she buy 2 pairs of socks and a pair of jeans?

3. Chet wants 4 handkerchiefs and 2 scarves. Can he buy them with $30?

4. If Chet buys only 3 handkerchiefs, can he still buy 2 scarves?

5. Dino must buy a hat. What is the greatest number of ties he can also buy if he has $25?

6. Joan wants to buy a tie and a scarf for each of her 3 brothers. She has $35. Can she afford all of these?

Problem Solving Project

Time Zones

This map shows the **time zones** of the United States. The clocks show you what time it will be in each zone when it is noon, Mountain Time.

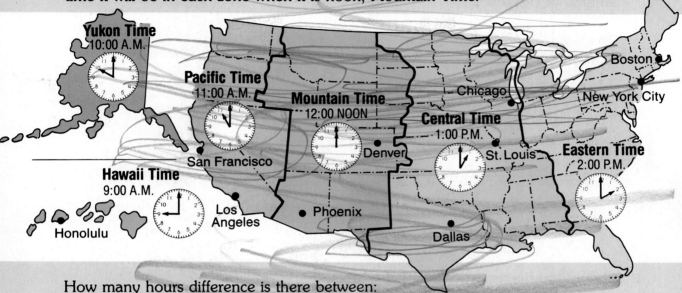

How many hours difference is there between:

1. Central Time and Pacific Time?

2. Hawaii Time and Eastern Time?

When it is 4:00 P.M. in Denver, what time is it in:

3. Boston?

4. Los Angeles?

5. Honolulu?

Complete this airplane schedule.

	Leaves		Flight Time	Arrives	
6.	New York City	9:00 A.M.	6 hours	Los Angeles	▮
7.	Chicago	11:30 A.M.	3 hours	Phoenix	▮
8.	San Francisco	12:00 noon	3 hours 30 minutes	St. Louis	▮
9.	Dallas	5:30 P.M.	3 hours 30 minutes	Boston	▮

ON YOUR OWN

Data Search

Find out why the earth is divided into time zones. Find a map that shows the time zones for the entire world. How many time zones are there in all? Where does the time change from one day to the next?

Centimeter and Millimeter

A. The *centimeter* (cm) is a metric unit used to measure small lengths or distances.

The width of a postage stamp is about 2 centimeters.

This ruler is marked in centimeters. The length of this nail *to the nearest centimeter* is 8 cm.

between 7 and 8 cm
nearer 8

B. The *millimeter* (mm) is a metric unit used to measure smaller lengths or distances.

The width of this letter is about 1 millimeter.

i
1 mm

10 millimeters = 1 centimeter

C. The length of this paper clip may be measured in millimeters or centimeters.

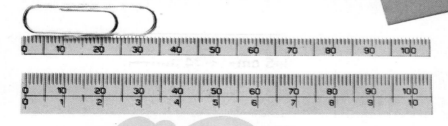

about
34 mm
or
3 cm 4 mm

3 cm = 30 mm
3 cm 4 mm = 30 mm + 4 mm = 34 mm

TRY THESE

1. Name some lengths or distances you would measure using centimeters or millimeters.

Measure the length and width of each. Measure to the nearest centimeter. Then measure to the nearest millimeter.

2.

3.

4.

SKILLS PRACTICE

Measure the length and width of each. Measure to the nearest centimeter. Then measure to the nearest millimeter.

1.

2.

3.

Measure to the nearest centimeter. Then measure to the nearest millimeter.

4. the width of a ribbon

5. the height of a paint jar

6. the length of a crayon

7. the distance across a nickel

Select the answer that seems reasonable.

8. The thickness of a lamp cord is about ____.
   a. 30 cm   **b.** 30 mm   **c.** 3 mm

9. The length of a new pencil is about ____.
   a. 16 mm   **b.** 16 cm   **c.** 160 cm

10. The width of this book is about ____.
   a. 30 mm   **b.** 300 mm   **c.** 300 cm

★11. The distance a snail crawls is about ____ in 1 minute.
   a. 80 cm   **b.** 8 cm   **c.** 8 mm

THINK!

Visual Perception

Danny had a 20-cm strip of paper. He cut off a piece 5 cm long and a piece 74 mm long. How much was left?

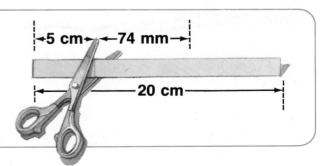

Meter and Kilometer

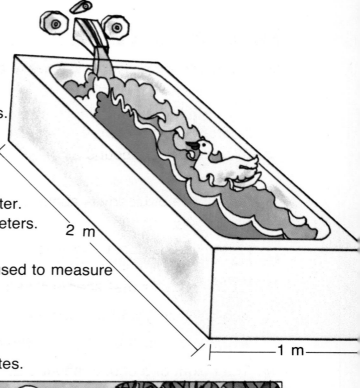

A. The *meter* (m) is another metric unit used to measure lengths or distances.

> **100 centimeters = 1 meter**
> **1,000 millimeters = 1 meter**

The width of a bathtub is about 1 meter.
The length of a bathtub is about 2 meters.

2 m

1 m

B. The *kilometer* (km) is a metric unit used to measure longer lengths or distances.

> **1,000 meters = 1 kilometer**

You can walk 1 km in about 10 minutes.

The distance from San Francisco to Washington, D.C., is about 3,900 km.

TRY THESE

1. Name some lengths or distances you would measure using meters.

2. Name some lengths or distances you would measure using kilometers.

Use m or km to complete each sentence.

3. The Columbia River is about 2,000 _____ long.

4. The height of a classroom is about 3 _____.

5. The length of a car is about 5 _____ long.

6. The runners who completed the race ran about 15 _____.

7. If Sue walked to school, it would be about 2 _____.

8. A work table is about 1 _____ wide and 2 _____ long.

SKILLS PRACTICE

Use mm, cm, m, or km to complete each sentence.

1. The Red River is about 2,000 ▧ long.

2. The width of a classroom is about 7 ▧.

3. A thumbtack is about 8 ▧ across.

4. A butterfly's body is about 2 ▧ long.

5. The Statue of Liberty is about 46 ▧ high.

6. The English Channel is about 560 ▧ long.

7. A doorknob is about 5 ▧ across.

8. A staple is about 12 ▧ long.

Select the answer that seems reasonable.

9. The distance from San Francisco to Honolulu is about _____.

   a. 3,800 m   **b.** 3,800 km   **c.** 380 cm

10. The height of a door is about _____.
    a. 2 m   **b.** 2 mm   **c.** 20 cm

11. The distance across a half-dollar is about _____.
    a. 30 cm   **b.** 3 mm   **c.** 3 cm

12. A baseball bat is about _____ long.
    a. 1 m   **b.** 10 mm   **c.** 10 cm

13. From New York City to Los Angeles is about _____.
    a. 3,900 m   **b.** 3,900 km   **c.** 39,000 cm

THINK!

Estimating Time

If you can walk about 1 kilometer in 10 minutes, about how long would it take you to walk from San Francisco to Washington, D.C.? (Find the distance on page 162.)

Other Metric Units

A. The *liter* (L) and *milliliter* (mL) are metric units used to measure liquid volume and to tell how much a container will hold.

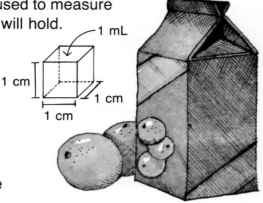

One milliliter (1 mL) of water will fill a cube that is 1 cm long, 1 cm high, and 1 cm wide.

A liter is used to measure larger amounts.

> **1,000 milliliters = 1 liter**

A carton of juice holds about 1 liter.

B. The *gram* (g), *kilogram* (kg), and *metric ton* are metric units used to measure mass.

paper clip
mass about 1 g

1 mL of water
mass 1 g

> **1,000 grams = 1 kilogram**

The mass of this book is about 1 kg.
One liter of water also has a mass of 1 kg.

> **1,000 kilograms = 1 metric ton**

A compact car has a mass of about 1 metric ton.

C. The *degree Celsius* (°C) is a metric unit used to measure temperature.

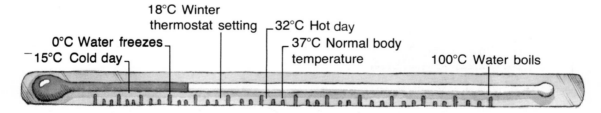

18°C Winter thermostat setting   ⌐32°C Hot day
0°C Water freezes⌐   ⌐37°C Normal body temperature
⁻15°C Cold day⌐   100°C Water boils

TRY THESE

1. Name some things whose volumes you could measure in liters.

2. Name some things whose masses you could measure in metric tons.

3. Name some things you could do if the outside temperature were ⁻5°C; 28°C.

Match to show which unit you would use to measure:

1. mass of a bottle cap
2. temperature at the beach
3. volume of liquid in a bottle of shampoo
4. mass of a dog
5. mass of an airplane

a. metric ton
b. degrees Celsius
c. kilogram
d. gram
e. milliliter

Use mL, L, g, or kg to complete each sentence.

6. The volume of water in a fish tank is about 37 _____ of water.
7. A frog has a mass about 140 _____.
8. A toaster has a mass of about 2 _____.
9. There are about 150 _____ of orange juice in a small glass.

Select the answer that seems reasonable.

10. A hamster has a mass of about _____.
    a. 14 g   b. 140 g   c. 1,400 g

11. A hippopotamus has a mass of about _____.
    a. 1 metric ton   b. 10 metric tons   c. 100 metric tons

12. The temperature inside a refrigerator is about _____.
    a. 50°C   b. 15°C   c. 5°C

THINK!

Measuring Out Amounts

Suppose you have these two pails.

1. How can you use the pails to measure out 4 L of water?

2. How can you use the pails to measure out 5 L of water?

Changing Metric Units Mentally

You can use the relations between metric units to change from
one unit to another mentally.

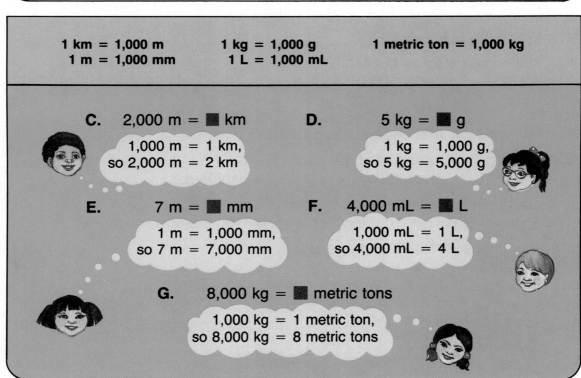

1 m = 100 cm   **1 cm = 10 mm**

A.   3 m = ■ cm   **B.**   60 mm = ■ cm

Think.   1 m = 100 cm,   10 mm = 1 cm,
so 3 m = 3 × 100 = 300 cm   so 60 mm = 6 × 1 cm = 6 cm

1 km = 1,000 m   **1 kg = 1,000 g**   **1 metric ton = 1,000 kg**
1 m = 1,000 mm   **1 L = 1,000 mL**

C.   2,000 m = ■ km   **D.**   5 kg = ■ g

1,000 m = 1 km,   1 kg = 1,000 g,
so 2,000 m = 2 km   so 5 kg = 5,000 g

E.   7 m = ■ mm   **F.**   4,000 mL = ■ L

1 m = 1,000 mm,   1,000 mL = 1 L,
so 7 m = 7,000 mm   so 4,000 mL = 4 L

G.   8,000 kg = ■ metric tons

1,000 kg = 1 metric ton,
so 8,000 kg = 8 metric tons

TRY THESE

Complete these exercises mentally.

1. 9 m = ■ cm   **2.** 7 m = ■ mm   **3.** 8 cm = ■ mm

4. 8 kg = ■ g   **5.** 3,000 g = ■ kg   **6.** 4,000 kg = ■ metric tons

7. 5,000 mL = ■ L   **8.** 9 L = ■ mL   **9.** 3 metric tons = ■ kg

SKILLS PRACTICE _____

Complete these exercises mentally.

1. 3 kg = ▓ g   2. 8,000 mL = ▓ L   3. 5 metric tons = ▓ kg

4. 4 m = ▓ cm   5. 6 m = ▓ mm   6. 7,000 m = ▓ km

7. 90 mm = ▓ cm   8. 3 L = ▓ mL   9. 2,000 kg = ▓ metric tons

10. 4,000 g = ▓ kg   11. 200 cm = ▓ m   12. 9,000 mm = ▓ m

13. 8 km = ▓ m   14. 4 cm = ▓ mm   15. 7 L = ▓ mL

16. 500 cm = ▓ m   17. 5 m = ▓ mm   18. 7 metric tons = ▓ kg

19. 6 m = ▓ cm   20. 30 mm = ▓ cm   21. 2,000 mL = ▓ L

22. 7 kg = ▓ g   23. 15,000 m = ▓ km   ★24. 8 cm 6 mm = ▓ mm

PROBLEM SOLVING _____

25. Ken ran a 5,000-m race on the weekend. How many kilometers did he run?

26. The finish line was 3 m long. How many centimeters long was the finish line?

27. The runners drank 9 L of juice after the race. How many milliliters did they drink?

28. Lynn filmed the race. Her camera's mass was 3,000 g. What was its mass in kilograms?

★29. The tallest runner is 1 m 86 cm tall. How many centimeters tall is he?

★30. To practice for the race, Ken ran 8 km 675 m each day. How many meters did he run each day?

MIXED REVIEW

Round each amount to the nearest dollar.

1. $11.92   2. $36.49   3. $.51   4. $39.75   5. $.49

Divide.

6. 2)19   7. 6)54   8. 3)472   9. 6)5,278   10. 9)6,327

11. 978 ÷ 6 = ▓   12. $86.20 ÷ 5 = ▓   13. 14,932 ÷ 4 = ▓

Problem Solving

Finding Needed Facts

Sometimes you need to find some facts to solve a problem.

A. The problem below does not contain all the facts you need. You may remember the fact you need. For this problem, you can use the table on page 166.

Laura had 5 meters of string. She used 200 centimeters to tie packages. How many centimeters did she have left?

To find how many cm in 5 m, you need to know how many cm in 1 m.

1 m = 100 cm,
so 5 m = 500 cm

Subtract.

$$\begin{array}{r} 500 \text{ cm} \\ - 200 \text{ cm} \\ \hline 300 \text{ cm} \end{array}$$

Laura had 300 centimeters of string left.

B. Sometimes you can't find a fact you need to solve a problem.

The postage for the packages was $15.14.
Laura also bought some stamps. How much did she spend?

To solve this problem you must find the cost of the stamps.

TRY THESE

**Write the fact you need to find.
Solve the problem if you can.**

1. Walt's boat was 13 m long. Jean's boat was 60 cm shorter. How long was Jean's boat?

2. Joan needed some line for her rowboat. It cost $3.15 for 1 meter. How much did she spend?

3. The mass of a sailboat was 400 kg. The mass of a motorboat was 1 metric ton. What was the difference in mass?

4. Tyrone sailed for 3 hours on Saturday and for most of the afternoon on Sunday. How long did he sail in all?

PROBLEM SOLVING PRACTICE

What fact do you need to know to solve each problem? Solve the problem if you can.

1. Betty and Arnie were pitching horseshoes. Betty pitched a shoe 156 cm. Arnie pitched a shoe 2 m. How many centimeters farther did Arnie pitch the shoe?

2. Sara went bowling. She put a bowling ball with a mass of 2 kg and bowling shoes into a bag. What was the total mass in grams of the objects in the bag?

3. Ray went hiking. He hiked 2 km in the morning and 1,658 m in the afternoon. How many meters farther did he hike in the morning?

4. The campers used 2 L of water for drinking, 638 mL for cooking, and 250 mL for washing. How many milliliters of water were used in all?

5. A marina received a delivery of three boats. One boat had a mass of 785 kg, another had a mass of 352 kg, and the third had a mass of 1 metric ton. What was the total mass of the boats in kilograms?

★6. There were three sailboats at the marina. One had a yellow sail that was 6 m long; another had a white sail that was 3 m 30 cm long; the third had a blue sail. Which had the longest sail?

★7. Anna has skis that are 1 m 85 cm long. Her ski poles are 120 cm long. How much longer are her skis?

★8. Ed practiced horseback riding on a trail that was 1 km 500 m long. He rode the trail 4 times. How many meters did he ride in all?

ON YOUR OWN

Make up one problem about the pitcher and the glass. Make up another problem about the pitcher and the jug. Ask a classmate to solve your problems.

Inch, Half-Inch, Quarter-Inch, Eighth-Inch

A. The *inch* (in.) is a customary unit used to measure small lengths or distances.

A postage stamp is about 1 inch long.

B. Inch rulers can be used to measure to the nearest *inch, half-inch, quarter-inch,* or *eighth-inch.*

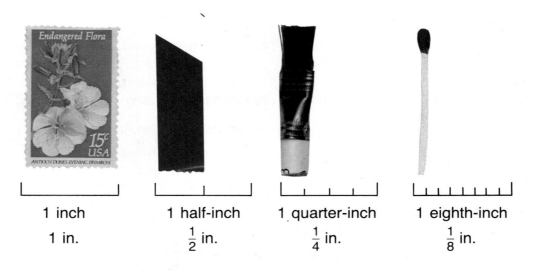

1 inch	1 half-inch	1 quarter-inch	1 eighth-inch
1 in.	$\frac{1}{2}$ in.	$\frac{1}{4}$ in.	$\frac{1}{8}$ in.

3 in. to the nearest inch

$2\frac{1}{2}$ in. to the nearest half-inch

$2\frac{3}{4}$ in. to the nearest quarter-inch

$2\frac{5}{8}$ in. to the nearest eighth-inch

TRY THESE

1. Name some things you could measure using inches, half-inches, quarter-inches, and eighth-inches.

2. Measure the length of a notebook page to the nearest inch, half-inch, quarter-inch, and eighth-inch.

SKILLS PRACTICE

Measure to the nearest quarter-inch.

1.

2.

3.

4.

Draw each.

5. a tack $\frac{3}{4}$ in. long

6. a key $3\frac{5}{8}$ in. long

7. a pencil $7\frac{1}{4}$ in. long

8. an eraser $2\frac{1}{8}$ in. long

Measure to the nearest quarter-inch.

9. the width of your hand

10. the length of your pen

Complete. Use the ruler below.

★11. The ruler is marked to show ▭-inches.

★12. Using the ruler, lengths can be given to the nearest ▭ .

★13. The length of the paper clip is ▭ to the nearest ▭ .

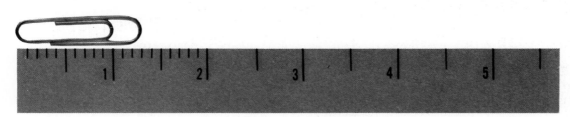

THINK!

Perimeter and Inches

Each stamp is about 1 inch on each side. What is the distance around each stamp or group of stamps?

1.
2.
3.
4.

Foot, Yard, and Mile

A. The *foot* (ft), *yard* (yd), and *mile* (mi) are other customary units used to measure lengths or distances.

> 1 foot = 12 inches
> 1 yard = 3 feet
> 1 mile = 1,760 yards

Here are some estimates of common lengths and distances.

The width of a door is about 3 ft.
The height of a door is about 7 ft.
The length of a "giant step" is about 1 yd.

The distance from San Francisco to Washington, D.C., is about 2,440 mi.

B. You can change the units used to report a length or distance.

9 ft = ▓ in.
9 ft = 9 × 1 ft ••• 1 ft = 12 in.
$\quad$ = 9 × 12 in.
$\quad$ = 108 in.

C. 4 mi 60 yd = ▓ yd

Step 1
Change 4 miles to yards.
4 mi = 4 × 1 mi
$\quad$ = 4 × 1,760 yd ••• 1 mi = 1,760 yd
$\quad$ = 7,040 yd

Step 2
Add the yards.
4 mi 60 yd
$\quad$ = 7,040 yd + 60 yd
$\quad$ = 7,100 yd

TRY THESE

1. Name some things you could measure in feet; yards; miles.

Estimate and measure to the nearest ft and to the nearest yd.

2. the total length of 9 of your normal steps

3. the total length of 9 of your "giant" steps

4. the length of your classroom

5. the width of your classroom

SKILLS PRACTICE

Use in., ft, yd, or mi to complete each estimate.

1. A long-jumper can jump about 5 ▓ .

2. An airplane can fly about 530 ▓ in one hour.

3. A large car is about 16 ▓ long.

4. The screen of a television is about 18 ▓ wide.

Copy and complete.

5. 8 yd = ▓ ft

6. 10 ft = ▓ in.

7. 3 mi = ▓ yd

8. 5 mi 500 yd = ▓ yd

9. 4 ft 9 in. = ▓ in.

★10. 8 yd 2 ft = ▓ in.

PROBLEM SOLVING

11. José jogged 2 mi. Then he ran 440 yd as fast as he could. How many yards did he go in all?

12. Karl high-jumped 5 ft 4 in. Mark high-jumped 61 in. Who jumped higher? How many inches higher?

13. In a relay race, Jan ran 1 mi, June ran 1 mi 220 yd, Mark ran 880 yd, and Teri ran 330 yd. How many yards in all was the race?

★14. Karl long-jumped 5 yd 2 ft. Mark's long jump was 14 ft 6 in. long. Who jumped farther? How many inches farther?

THINK!

Logical Reasoning

There is a saying:

Give someone an inch and he or she will take a mile.

How many more inches does the person take?

Units of Liquid Volume

A. The *fluid ounce* (fl oz), *cup, pint* (pt), *quart* (qt), and *gallon* (gal) are customary units used to measure liquid volume.

| 1 cup = 8 fl oz | 1 pt = 2 cups | 1 qt = 2 pt | 1 gal = 4 qt |

A small glass holds about 4 fl oz of orange juice.

A drinking glass holds about 1 cup of water.

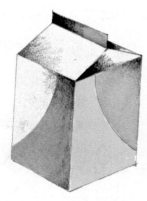

Milk is often sold in 1-qt containers.

A large bucket holds about 5 gal of water.

You can change the units used to report liquid volume.

B. 5 gal = ■ qt

Think.
1 gal = 4 qt

5 gal = 5 × 1 gal
= 5 × 4 qt
= 20 qt

C. 3 cups = ■ fl oz

1 cup = 8 fl oz

3 cups = 3 × 1 cup
= 3 × 8 fl oz
= 24 fl oz

D. 6 qt 3 pt = ■ pt

Step 1
Change 6 quarts to pints.

1 qt = 2 pt

6 qt = 6 × 1 qt
= 6 × 2 pt
= 12 pt

Step 2
Add the pints.
6 qt 3 pt = 12 pt + 3 pt
= 15 pt

TRY THESE

1. Name some things whose volume you would measure in fluid ounces; cups; pints; quarts; gallons.

2. 2 cups = ■   3. 2 qt = ■   4. 3 qt = ■

SKILLS PRACTICE

Use fl oz, cup, pt, qt, and gal to complete each estimate.

1. A bottle of hand lotion holds about 6 ■.

2. A kitchen sink holds about 5 ■ of water.

3. A jar of paste contains about 1 ■ of paste.

4. A saucepan will hold about 2 ■ of liquid.

Copy and complete.

5. 8 gal = ■ qt

6. 3 gal 2 qt = ■ qt

7. 2 cups 3 fl oz = ■ fl oz

8. 3 gal 1 qt = ■ qt

9. 5 gal 3 qt = ■ qt

10. 8 pt 1 cup = ■ cups

11. 8 cups = ■ fl oz

★12. 1 gal 1 pt = ■ pt

★13. 2 pt = ■ fl oz

PROBLEM SOLVING

14. The refreshment counter sold 16 pt of cider, 8 pt of juice, and 8 pt of milk. How many quarts of drinks did they sell?

★15. A pot contained 7 qt 1 pt of water. 4 qt of water were added. Then 3 qt 1 pt were added. How many pints of water were in the pot then?

THINK!

Comparing Liquid Volumes

Which holds the greatest amount of water?
Which holds the least amount?

A.
B.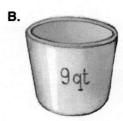
C.
D.

Other Customary Units

A. The *ounce* (oz), *pound* (lb), and *ton* are customary units of weight.

> **1 lb = 16 oz   1 ton = 2,000 lb**

An orange weighs about 5 oz.

A loaf of bread weighs about 1 lb.

A small car weighs about 1 ton.

You can change from one unit of weight to another.

B. 12 tons = ▨ lb

12 tons = 12 × 1 ton
= 12 × 2,000 lb
= 24,000 lb

> 1 ton = 2,000 lb

C. 9 lb 6 oz = ▨ oz

Step 1
Change 9 pounds to ounces.
9 lb = 9 × 1 lb
= 9 × 16 oz
= 144 oz

> 1 lb = 16 oz

Step 2
Add the ounces.
9 lb 6 oz = 144 oz + 6 oz
= 150 oz

D. The degree Fahrenheit (°F) is the customary unit of temperature.

90° hot day ——   — 98.6° normal body temperature   — 212° water boils

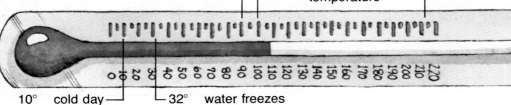

10° cold day ——   — 32° water freezes

TRY THESE

1. Name some things whose weights you could measure in ounces; pounds; tons.

2. Name some things you could do if the temperature outside were 25°F; 89°F.

SKILLS PRACTICE

Match to show what you could do outside at each temperature.

1. 97°F   **a.** go ice skating

2. 32°F   **b.** wear a light coat

3. 55°F   **c.** go swimming

4. ⁻5°F   **d.** wear a heavy coat or stay inside

Use oz, lb, or tons to complete each estimate.

5. A man weighs about 175 ▓.

6. A watermelon weighs about 15 ▓.

7. A slice of cheese weighs about 1 ▓.

8. A tractor weighs about 4 ▓.

Copy and complete.

9. 2 tons = ▓ lb

10. 3 lb 4 oz = ▓ oz

11. 5 tons 1,000 lb = ▓ lb

12. 8 lb 8 oz = ▓ oz

13. 2 tons 300 lb = ▓ lb

14. 7 tons = ▓ lb

PROBLEM SOLVING

15. Frank made granola. He used 1 lb of oatmeal, 13 oz of sunflower seeds, and 5 oz of raisins. How many ounces did the granola weigh?

★16. A bakery uses 1 ton of whole wheat flour and 550 lb of bran each week. How many more pounds of wheat than bran do they use in 1 week? in 4 weeks?

THINK!

Comparing Temperature Units

Water freezes at 0°C and boils at 100°C.
Water freezes at 32°F and boils at 212°F.
In which system is one degree a larger measure? Why?

Computers as Tools

Computers can make many business and daily life activities more efficient. Several programs have been developed for common uses.

A *word processing program* allows a person to use the computer keyboard as a typewriter to input the text or manuscript which then appears on the screen. With this program, changes or corrections can be made easily and then printed out.

With a *data base program,* a person can use the computer to store, reorganize, and retrieve vast amounts of information.

A *spreadsheet program* provides a table with columns and rows of numbers. A person can change information, and the program directs the computer to change affected information in the rows and columns of the spreadsheet. This small spreadsheet shows the sales, expenses, and profits of a store for two months:

2	A	B	C	D
3		Sales	Expenses	Profits
4	January	56,000	51,000	5,000
5	February	52,000	50,500	1,500
6	Total	$108,000	$101,500	$6,500

If the operator changes the February sales figures to $55,000, the spreadsheet program will automatically change all the affected totals and differences:

2	A	B	C	D
3		Sales	Expenses	Profits
4	January	56,000	51,000	5,000
5	February	55,000	50,500	4,500
6	Total	$111,000	$101,500	$9,500

1. Name one way that a data base program would be useful in a clothing store.

2. If the expenses for February were changed to $48,000, how would the spreadsheet above look?

3. Find out about other useful software programs for home or business use. Prepare a short report of one or two paragraphs that tells how the software is useful.

Unit Review

Find the time. (*pages 148–151*)

1. 7 hours after 5:40 A.M.

2. 55 minutes before 2:15 P.M.

3. between 8:45 A.M. and 3:05 P.M.

4. between 1:40 P.M. and 10:25 P.M.

Complete. (*pages 152–153*)

5. 5 hours 15 minutes = ▓ minutes

6. 4 years 8 months = ▓ months

7. 3 weeks 2 days = ▓ days

8. 1 day 9 hours = ▓ hours

Use a dollar sign to show the amount. (*pages 154–155*)

9. 3 dollars, 2 quarters, 1 dime

10. 8 dollars, 3 quarters, 5 nickels

Use mm, cm, m, or km to complete each sentence. (*pages 160–163*)

11. The letter m is about 3 ▓ wide.

12. A pen is about 16 ▓ long.

13. The distance between Chicago and St. Louis is about 470 ▓.

14. The length of a broom handle is about 1 ▓.

Use mL, L, g, or kg to complete each sentence. (*pages 164–165*)

15. A small bottle contains about 20 ▓ of perfume.

16. The mass of a roast chicken is about 3 ▓.

Complete. (*pages 166–167, 172–177*)

17. 9 L = ▓ mL

18. 7 kg = ▓ g

19. 400 cm = ▓ m

20. 5 cups = ▓ fl oz

21. 3 ft 4 in. = ▓ in.

22. 5 lb 3 oz = ▓ oz

Measure to the nearest quarter-inch. (*pages 170–171*)

23.

24.

Solve the problems if you can. (*pages 156–157, 168–169*)

25. If you buy a book for $1.75, what coins and bills should you receive from a $5 bill?

26. One freight train is 1 km long. Another train is 870 m long. How much longer is the first train?

179

Reinforcement

More Help with Time

3 hours 10 minutes = ☐ minutes

3 hours = 3×1 hour
= 3×60 minutes
= 180 minutes

3 hours 10 minutes
= 180 minutes +
10 minutes
= 190 minutes

Complete.

1. 9 hours = ☐ minutes

2. 5 days = ☐ hours

3. 8 years = ☐ months

4. 6 weeks = ☐ days

5. 4 minutes 8 seconds = ☐ seconds

6. 3 weeks 5 days = ☐ days

7. 2 years 4 months = ☐ months

8. 3 hours 14 minutes = ☐ minutes

More Help with Metric Measurement

9 m = ☐ cm

1 m = 100 cm

so 9 m = 900 cm

Complete.

9. 5 L = ☐ mL   10. 2,000 kg = ☐ metric tons

11. 7 m = ☐ cm   12. 80 mm = ☐ cm

13. 4,000 mL = ☐ L   14. 5 kg = ☐ g

More Help with Customary Measurement

4 ft 2 in. = ☐ in.
4 ft = 4×1 ft
4 ft = 4×12 in.
= 48 in.
4 ft 2 in. = 48 in. + 2 in.
= 50 in.

Complete.

15. 2 yd = ☐ ft   16. 5 ft = ☐ in.

17. 2 mi = ☐ yd   18. 9 ft = ☐ in.

19. 3 ft 5 in. = ☐ in.   20. 2 yd 2 ft = ☐ ft

Enrichment

Computing with Units of Time

You can add, subtract, or multiply with time measures.

A. Find (4 days 12 hours) + (6 days 7 hours).

Add hours.	4 days 12 hours	**Add days.**	4 days 12 hours
	+6 days 7 hours		+ 6 days 7 hours
	19 hours		10 days 19 hours

B. Some answers can be written in a simpler form.

Multiply seconds.

5 minutes 11 seconds
×7
77 seconds

Multiply minutes.

5 minutes 11 seconds
×7
35 minutes 77 seconds
or 36 minutes 17 seconds

77 seconds =
1 minute
17 seconds

C. When subtracting, you sometimes need to regroup first.

5 years 6 months
−2 years 3 months
3 years 3 months

6 > 3
No need to regroup

4 weeks 8 days
5 weeks 1 day
−3 weeks 4 days
1 week 4 days

Regroup 5 weeks 1 day as 4 weeks 8 days.

Add, subtract, or multiply.

1. 3 hours 15 minutes
×2

2. 7 years 8 months
+1 year 9 months

3. 5 years 40 weeks
−4 years 13 weeks

4. 12 minutes 50 seconds
+ 9 minutes 35 seconds

5. 4 days 10 hours
×3

6. 10 weeks 4 days
− 3 weeks 5 days

7. 4 days 12 hours 35 minutes
+   13 hours 40 minutes

8. 9 hours 11 minutes 40 seconds
−2 hours 30 minutes 20 seconds

9. (2 years 5 months) + (2 years 3 months) = ▇
10. (8 days 14 hours) − (7 days 3 hours) = ▇
11. (20 minutes) − (14 minutes 30 seconds) = ▇
12. (5 weeks 1 day) + (4 weeks 6 days) = ▇

Cumulative Review

Choose the correct answer.

1. $4\overline{)8{,}036}$

a. 29
b. 209
c. 2,009
d. not given

2.
$$\begin{array}{r} 216 \\ \times 148 \\ \hline \end{array}$$

a. 12,528
b. 31,968
c. 2,808
d. not given

3. $865 + 4{,}519 = \blacksquare$

a. 13,169
b. 8,654,519
c. 5,484
d. not given

4. Round 39,686 to the nearest ten.

a. 39,690
b. 39,700
c. 40,000
d. not given

5. Find the total value.

a. $15.35
b. $32.13
c. $40.55
d. not given

6. $5\overline{)1{,}276}$

a. 211 R1
b. 115 R6
c. 255
d. not given

7.
$$\begin{array}{r} 43{,}592 \\ -16{,}284 \\ \hline \end{array}$$

a. 27,308
b. 33,312
c. 37,318
d. not given

8. Find the time when you can see the sun.

a. 2:00 A.M.
b. 12:15 P.M.
c. 12:15 A.M.
d. not given

9. Complete.
46,019 ● 46,091

a. =
b. <
c. >

10. 1 week = 7 days
4 weeks 3 days = ■ days

a. 31 days
b. 43 days
c. 25 days
d. not given

11. $54 \times 6 = \blacksquare$

a. 9
b. 48
c. 324
d. not given

12. Find the numeral for six million, ninety.

a. 600,090
b. 6,000,090
c. 6,090
d. not given

13. Phyllis started to work at 10:40 A.M. She stopped working at 1:30 P.M. How much time did she work?

a. 9 hours 10 minutes
b. 3 hours 10 minutes
c. 2 hours 50 minutes
d. not given

14. Find the average of these scores: 53 points, 66 points, 45 points, 60 points.

a. 56 points
b. 70 points
c. 63 points
d. not given

182   Time, Money, Measurement

Problem Solving Situations

Selling Plants

You are going to sell plants in flowerpots at a flea market, but first you must buy the items at the plant nursery.

You must buy the same number of plants and flowerpots.

You have 3 sizes of each to choose from. What will you buy to make the most money?

Your Notes

Costs		
	Plants	**Flowerpots**
Small	$ 3	$ 5
Medium	$ 7	$11
Large	$13	$15

Selling Prices (plant *and* pot)

Small. $17
Medium $25
Large $41

Other Conditions

- You can spend up to $500.
- From past experience you know about how many you can sell of each:

  Small. 8–12
  Medium 10–15
  Large 5–9

Work in small groups to find answers and make decisions.

1. Suppose you buy 12 small plants and flowerpots, 15 medium plants and flowerpots, and 9 large plants and flowerpots. What is your total cost?

2. You bought some plants and flowerpots of the small size. The total cost was $88. How many plants did you buy?

3. Suppose you sell 9 small potted plants, 12 medium potted plants, and 7 large potted plants. How much profit did you make? (Think: Profit = Cost − Selling Price.)

4. Suppose you sold the same number of small potted plants as medium ones. In all, you received $336. How many medium potted plants did you sell?

5. What other things should you think about?

6. What size will you choose to make the most money?

Problem Solving Situations

Renting a Canoe

You and your older cousin want to rent a canoe.
Two rental plans are available. Which rental
plan will you choose?

Your Notes

Rental Plans

Plan A

$17 . . . for the first 2 hours
$ 6 . . . each additional hour
or part of an hour

Plan B

$ 9 . . . each hour for the first
3 hours
$ 4 . . . each additional hour or part
of an hour

Other Conditions

- You like to canoe between 3 and 6 hours.
- You can spend between $25 and $40.
- Both rental plans offer excellent canoes.

Work in small groups to find answers and make decisions.

1. Suppose you rent a canoe using plan A. You pick up the canoe at 9 A.M. and return it at 2:50 P.M. How much would you pay for renting the canoe?

2. Suppose you rent a canoe at 10 A.M. using plan B. You pay $31. What is the latest time that you could return the canoe?

3. Suppose you rent a canoe, using plan A, for 3 hours. The next day you use plan B for twice as much time. How much money would you pay for the 2 days?

4. Suppose you and a friend rent 2 canoes. You use plan A and your friend uses plan B. The rental charges for you and your friend are the same. How many hours did you rent the canoes?

5. What other things should you think about?

6. What rental plan will you choose?

Problem Solving Situations

Choosing a Delivery Route

You want to deliver newspapers and magazines after school. Each delivery route has the same number of customers. Which route will you choose?

Your Notes

Costs

Each newspaper costs 14¢.
Each magazine costs 39¢.
You sell a newspaper for 20¢.
You sell a magazine for 50¢.

Routes		
	Route #1	Route #2
Newspapers	34	25
Magazines	18	27

Other Conditions

- It takes 3 minutes to deliver a newspaper.
- It takes 7 minutes to deliver a magazine because you must put it in a wrapper.
- You do not deliver on weekends.
- You make the same tips on both routes.

Work in small groups to find answers and make decisions.

1. How much money can you make per day on Route #1?

2. How much money can you make per day on Route #2?

3. How much more money can you make on Route #2 for a 5-day week?

4. How many minutes will it take you to deliver newspapers and magazines each day on Route #1? on Route #2?

5. How much longer will it take you on Route #2 for a 5-day week?

6. What other things should you think about?

7. Which route will you choose?

Problem Solving Situations

Choosing Coins

The juice machine in school takes only quarters, dimes, and nickels. You must use exact change only. The cost of one container of juice is 45¢. What coins will you choose to use?

Your Notes

You can use 8 different combinations of coins. The smallest number of coins you can use is 3. The greatest number of coins you can use is 9.	**Other Conditions** • The machine does not give change. • The machine holds 200 juice containers when filled. • The machine works best when you use 5, 6, or 7 coins. • You rarely have nickels.

Work in small groups to find answers and make decisions.

1. What are the 8 different coin combinations you can use? (Hint: Make a list.)

Combination	Q	D	N	Number of coins
1	1	2	0	3
2				
3				
4				
5				
6				
7				
8				

2. Suppose the machine has sold 190 juice containers. How much more money will be put into the juice machine before it is empty?

3. What coins will you use if the number of dimes must be 2?

4. Which coin combinations work the best?

5. What other things should you think about?

6. What coins will you choose to use?

Planning a Bike-athon

You are planning to ride in a Bike-athon. Everyone must start from Rye and finish in Lee. You will raise 10¢ for each kilometer (km) you ride. Which route will you choose?

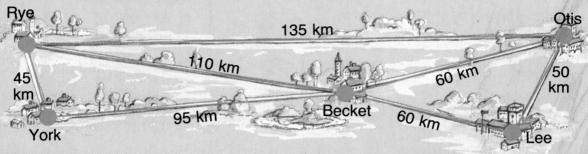

Your Notes

Rules for Bike-athon	Other Conditions
• You can only pass through a town once. • You can take any route from Rye to Lee. • You must wear a helmet. • No "drafting."	• You can ride at a rate of 25 km per hour. • The bike-athon starts at 8 A.M. • You get tired after 8 hours of riding.

Work in small groups to find answers and make decision.

1. How many different routes are there from Rye to Lee? Name them.

2. Suppose you biked from Rye to Lee via Becket. How much money did you raise?

3. If you biked 185 km, what route did you take and how much money did you raise?

4. What route would you take if you want to finish the bike-athon at 4 P.M.?

5. What is the difference in kilometers between the shortest and longest routes?

6. What other things should you think about?

7. What route will you take?

Problem Solving Situations

Do It Yourself?

You and your mother want to build a bookcase, but you do not have all the tools. You can hire a professional carpenter who will do the job for $27.50 per hour, or part of an hour, or you can buy the tools and do the job yourselves. What choice will you make?

Your Notes

Tool Prices	
Saw	$ 8.95
Hammer	$ 7.50
Screwdriver	$ 3.75
Stepladder	$29.90

Other Conditions

• The carpenter has all the tools.
• It will take you about 6 hours to do the job.
• It takes the carpenter between 2 and 3 hours to do the job.
• The carpenter guarantees the work for one year.

Work in small groups to find answers and make decisions.

1. You buy all the tools and give the clerk 3 twenty-dollar bills. How much change do you receive?

2. You buy only 3 of the tools you need. You give the clerk a fifty-dollar bill and get back $7.40 in change. Which tools did you buy?

3. If the carpenter begins the job at 8:15 A.M. and finishes at 10:30 A.M., how much money does the carpenter earn?

4. You and your mother's labor is worth $2.50 an hour. How much will the job cost if you do it yourself? (Hint: Remember the cost of all the tools you need.)

5. What other things should you think about?

6. Will you do the job yourself? Explain.

7 Dividing by Tens and Ones

HIGHLIGHTS IN THE HISTORY OF SHIPS

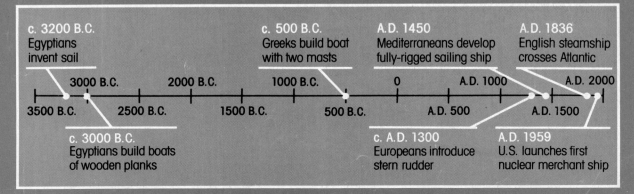

c. 3200 B.C.
Egyptians invent sail

c. 500 B.C.
Greeks build boat with two masts

A.D. 1450
Mediterraneans develop fully-rigged sailing ship

A.D. 1836
English steamship crosses Atlantic

3500 B.C. — 3000 B.C. — 2500 B.C. — 2000 B.C. — 1500 B.C. — 1000 B.C. — 500 B.C. — 0 — A.D. 500 — A.D. 1000 — A.D. 1500 — A.D. 2000

c. 3000 B.C.
Egyptians build boats of wooden planks

c. A.D. 1300
Europeans introduce stern rudder

A.D. 1959
U.S. launches first nuclear merchant ship

Divisors Less Than 10

A. A packaging machine puts 4 batteries in each package. If 250 batteries are put into the machine, how many packages will the machine make? How many batteries will be left over?

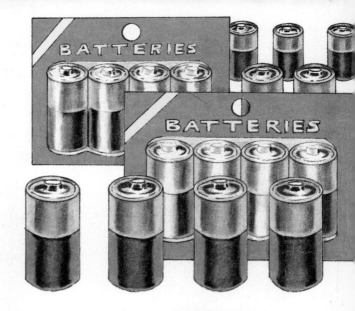

Divide: 4)250

Estimate.
250 is close to 240.
240 ÷ 4 = 60

Decide where to start.
Compare.

4)250   4 > 2
          Regroup.

■
4)**250**   4 < 25
          Start with
          tens.

Divide tens.

```
   6
4)250      6 × 4 = 24
  24
   1  ...  25 − 24 = 1
```

Regroup. Divide ones.

```
   62 R2
4)250
  24↓
   10    2 × 4 = 8
    8
    2    10 − 8 = 2
```

The machine will make 62 packages. There will be 2 batteries left over.

B. Find 3)72,019

Estimate.
72,000 ÷ 3 = 24,000

3 < 7
Start with
ten-thousands.

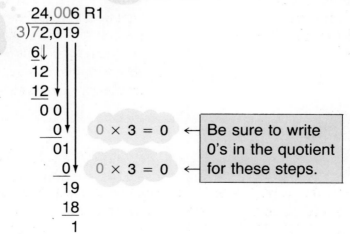

```
    24,006 R1
3)72,019
  6↓
  12
  12
   0 0
     0      0 × 3 = 0  ← Be sure to write
     01                   0's in the quotient
      0     0 × 3 = 0  ← for these steps.
     19
     18
      1
```

Check.

```
  1   1
  24,006
×      3
  72,018
+      1
  72,019 ✓
```

190   **Dividing by Tens and Ones**

TRY THESE

Estimate. Then divide. Check your answers.

1. $6\overline{)94}$ 2. $8\overline{)426}$ 3. $5\overline{)4,500}$ 4. $3\overline{)7,906}$ 5. $7\overline{)45,302}$

6. $288 \div 8 = \blacksquare$ 7. $7,896 \div 3 = \blacksquare$ 8. $\$486.12 \div 6 = \blacksquare$

SKILLS PRACTICE

Estimate. Then divide.

1. $8\overline{)178}$ 2. $5\overline{)4,540}$ 3. $6\overline{)82}$ 4. $4\overline{)\$53.60}$ 5. $8\overline{)897}$

6. $5\overline{)3,138}$ 7. $9\overline{)333}$ 8. $3\overline{)6,647}$ 9. $8\overline{)89}$ 10. $6\overline{)6,300}$

11. $7\overline{)72}$ 12. $3\overline{)19,570}$ 13. $3\overline{)322}$ 14. $4\overline{)2,346}$ 15. $5\overline{)75}$

16. $8\overline{)8,978}$ 17. $6\overline{)\$6.72}$ 18. $5\overline{)45,624}$ 19. $4\overline{)9,956}$ 20. $7\overline{)47,050}$

21. $6\overline{)420}$ 22. $7\overline{)7,900}$ 23. $8\overline{)64,974}$ 24. $9\overline{)2,700}$ 25. $4\overline{)14,505}$

26. $960 \div 3 = \blacksquare$ 27. $7,404 \div 6 = \blacksquare$ 28. $52,256 \div 8 = \blacksquare$

29. $\$30.52 \div 4 = \blacksquare$ 30. $\$64.64 \div 8 = \blacksquare$ 31. $\$456.20 \div 5 = \blacksquare$

PROBLEM SOLVING

32. Joan spent $15.50 for camera batteries. She bought 5 batteries. Each battery cost the same amount. How much did each battery cost?

33. Mr. Smith has 2,340 packages of batteries in his store. There are 4 batteries in each package. How many batteries does he have?

34. 8,266 batteries were made at the factory. 4 batteries were put in each package. How many packages were there? How many batteries were left over?

★35. Mr. Brown had 6,024 flashlight batteries in his store. Then he received a shipment of 8,238 batteries. How many batteries did he have in all? The batteries were in packages of 6 each. How many packages of batteries did he have?

THINK!

```
   4       6       8       4       ■
 3<>8    4<>9    4<>■    2<>6    6<>12
   6       6       2       ■       9
```

Finding Patterns

Find the pattern of the numbers at the corners of the first two diamonds. Then find the missing numbers for the other diamonds.

Dividing by Multiples of 10

A. An office building has 60 floors. Each floor has the same number of offices. There are 780 offices in the building. How many offices are on each floor?

Decide where to start.

$60\overline{)780}$ 60 > 7 Not enough hundreds. Regroup.

$60\overline{)780}$ 60 < 78 Start with tens.

Divide the tens.

$$\begin{array}{r} 1 \\ 60\overline{)780} \\ \underline{60} \\ 18 \end{array}$$

■ × 60 = 78 Use 1.

Divide the ones.

$$\begin{array}{r} 13 \\ 60\overline{)780} \\ \underline{60}\downarrow \\ 180 \\ \underline{180} \\ 0 \end{array}$$

■ × 60 = 180 Use 3.

There are 13 offices on each floor.

B. Find: $40\overline{)32,168}$

$40\overline{)32,168}$ 40 > 3 Regroup.

$40\overline{)32,168}$ 40 > 32 Regroup.

$40\overline{)32,168}$ 40 < 321 Start with hundreds.

$$\begin{array}{r} 804 \text{ R}8 \\ 40\overline{)32,168} \\ \underline{32\ 0}\downarrow \\ 16 \\ \underline{0}\downarrow \\ 168 \\ \underline{160} \\ 8 \end{array}$$

TRY THESE

Divide. Check your answers.

1. $20\overline{)840}$ **2.** $50\overline{)465}$ **3.** $70\overline{)9,360}$ **4.** $80\overline{)14,632}$

5. 630 ÷ 30 = ■   **6.** 5,400 ÷ 60 = ■   **7.** $84.20 ÷ 20 = ■

SKILLS PRACTICE

Divide.

1. $40\overline{)6,400}$ 2. $30\overline{)870}$ 3. $60\overline{)\$7.20}$ 4. $80\overline{)47,320}$

5. $50\overline{)2,806}$ 6. $60\overline{)960}$ 7. $10\overline{)80,600}$ 8. $20\overline{)\$68.00}$

9. $70\overline{)300}$ 10. $90\overline{)890}$ 11. $30\overline{)95,000}$ 12. $40\overline{)920}$

13. $30\overline{)1,940}$ 14. $20\overline{)9,000}$ 15. $80\overline{)14,900}$ 16. $50\overline{)9,325}$

17. $60\overline{)6,500}$ 18. $10\overline{)\$90.80}$ 19. $40\overline{)74,504}$ 20. $90\overline{)4,410}$

21. $40\overline{)86,975}$ 22. $50\overline{)93,000}$ 23. $30\overline{)9,600}$ 24. $70\overline{)40,000}$

25. $800 \div 20 = \blacksquare$ 26. $560 \div 80 = \blacksquare$ 27. $1,680 \div 60 = \blacksquare$

28. $\$95.00 \div 50 = \blacksquare$ 29. $\$780.00 \div 40 = \blacksquare$ 30. $\$548.10 \div 90 = \blacksquare$

PROBLEM SOLVING

31. A building has 30 floors. There are 6,420 windows in the building. Each floor has the same number of windows. How many windows are on each floor?

32. There are 62,400 light bulbs in use in a building. The building has 30 floors. Each floor has the same number of light bulbs. How many lights bulbs does each floor have?

33. There are 17,080 desks in an office building. There are 40 floors in the building. The same number of desks are on each floor. How many desks are on each floor?

★34. There are 20 offices on each floor of a building. There are 1,480 offices in all. How many floors are there? Each floor has 6 closets. How many closets are there?

THINK!

Division Patterns and Mental Math

Look for a pattern.

$\dfrac{24}{2\overline{)48}}$ $\dfrac{24}{20\overline{)480}}$	$\dfrac{29}{3\overline{)87}}$ $\dfrac{29}{30\overline{)870}}$	$\dfrac{9\ R3}{5\overline{)48}}$ $\dfrac{9\ R30}{50\overline{)480}}$

Explain how you can use the easier exercise to find the answer to the harder exercise.

Look at **TRY THESE** again. Do as many of the exercises as you can in your head.

Upside-down answers   1. 160   25. 40

Homework   page 428

153

2-digit Divisors

Rounding 2-digit divisors to the nearest
ten can help you find quotients.

A. The 38 students in class 5M plan to trim the
bushes in a local park. If there are 82 bushes
and each student trims the same number,
how many bushes must each student trim?
How many bushes will be left over?

Divide: $38\overline{)82}$

Round up to find a trial divisor.	**Use the trial divisor to estimate the quotient.**	**Multiply the real divisor by the estimate.**
40 $38\overline{)82}$	■ × 40 = 82 2 × 40 = 80 Use 2.	$\begin{array}{r} 2\ \text{R6} \\ 38\overline{)82} \\ \underline{76} \\ 6 \end{array}$ 6 < 38

Each student must trim 2 bushes. There will be 6 bushes left over.

B. The park has 53 flowerbeds, each with the
same number of flowers. If there are 2,756
flowers in all, how many flowers are in each bed?

Divide: $53\overline{)2,756}$

**Round down to find
a trial divisor.**

50 $53\overline{)2,756}$

Use the trial divisor to estimate the quotient.

■ × 50 = 270
5 × 50 = 250
Try 5.

**Divide tens. Multiply the
real divisor by the estimate.**

$\begin{array}{r} 5 \\ 53\overline{)2,756} \\ \underline{2\ 65} \\ 10 \end{array}$

**Regroup. Estimate again.
Divide ones.**

$\begin{array}{r} 52 \\ 50\quad 53\overline{)2,756} \\ \underline{2\ 65}\downarrow \\ 106 \\ \underline{106} \\ 0 \end{array}$

■ × 50 = 106
2 × 50 = 100
Try 2.

There are 52 flowers in each bed.

TRY THESE

Divide. Check your answers.

1. $23\overline{)78}$ **2.** $67\overline{)356}$ **3.** $43\overline{)995}$ **4.** $54\overline{)1{,}836}$ **5.** $32\overline{)9{,}920}$

6. $736 \div 32 = \blacksquare$ **7.** $3{,}328 \div 64 = \blacksquare$ **8.** $1{,}050 \div 42 = \blacksquare$

SKILLS PRACTICE

Divide.

1. $47\overline{)98}$ **2.** $72\overline{)794}$ **3.** $26\overline{)79}$ **4.** $57\overline{)7{,}020}$ **5.** $12\overline{)48}$

6. $23\overline{)512}$ **7.** $36\overline{)800}$ **8.** $74\overline{)9{,}847}$ **9.** $42\overline{)7{,}994}$ **10.** $23\overline{)98}$

11. $47\overline{)157}$ **12.** $46\overline{)1{,}078}$ **13.** $65\overline{)285}$ **14.** $92\overline{)\$8.28}$ **15.** $23\overline{)9{,}478}$

16. $75\overline{)995}$ **17.** $76\overline{)4{,}822}$ **18.** $57\overline{)2{,}469}$ **19.** $55\overline{)790}$ **20.** $34\overline{)886}$

21. $24\overline{)9{,}912}$ **22.** $22\overline{)770}$ **23.** $56\overline{)1{,}360}$ **24.** $31\overline{)\$89.90}$ **25.** $49\overline{)1{,}057}$

26. $33\overline{)528}$ **27.** $24\overline{)7{,}944}$ **28.** $54\overline{)394}$ **29.** $68\overline{)3{,}566}$ **30.** $53\overline{)7{,}000}$

31. $336 \div 21 = \blacksquare$ **32.** $714 \div 21 = \blacksquare$ **33.** $7{,}500 \div 60 = \blacksquare$

34. $4{,}752 \div 33 = \blacksquare$ **35.** $7{,}998 \div 93 = \blacksquare$ **36.** $9{,}632 \div 43 = \blacksquare$

PROBLEM SOLVING

37. The park received 270 wood slats to make benches. If each bench uses 12 slats, how many benches can be made? How many slats will be left over?

★38. The safari train at the park can carry 6 people in each of its 8 cars. What is the least number of times the train must run to carry 740 people?

THINK!

Visual Perception

Which figure satisfies both clues?
- It has an even number of sides.
- It has 5 lines of symmetry.

a.   **b.**   **c.**   **d.**

Revising Overestimates

When you round down, the first number you try
in the quotient may be too big.

A. The Lee family has 255 apples to put in sacks.
If 34 apples are put in each sack, how many
bags will be filled? How many apples will
be left over?

Divide: $34\overline{)255}$

**Round down to
estimate the quotient.**

$$\overset{30}{}\quad \overset{\blacksquare}{34\overline{)255}}$$

$\blacksquare \times 30 = 255$
$8 \times 30 = 240$
Try 8.

**Multiply the
real divisor.**

$$\overset{8}{34\overline{)255}}$$
272 too big

**Revise. Try a
smaller estimate.**

$$\overset{7\ R17}{34\overline{)255}}$$
$\underline{238}$
17 $17 < 34$

The family will fill 7 sacks. There will be 17 apples left over.

B. Workers on the Hanson farm picked 8,162 ears of corn in 14 days. What was
the average number of ears picked each day?

Divide to find the average: $14\overline{)8,162}$

**Round down.
Estimate.**

$$\overset{10}{}\quad \overset{\blacksquare}{14\overline{)8,162}}$$

$\blacksquare \times 10 = 81$
$8 \times 10 = 80$
Try 8.

**Multiply the
real divisor.**

$$\overset{8}{14\overline{)8,162}}$$
$11\ 2$ too big

**Revise your estimate as
many times as necessary.**

$7 \times 14 = 98$ too big
$6 \times 14 = 84$ too big
$5 \times 14 = 70$ $70 < 81$

Divide hundreds.

$$\overset{5}{14\overline{)8,162}}$$
$\underline{7\ 0}$
$1\ 1$

**Divide tens. Estimate.
Revise if necessary.**

$$\overset{58}{14\overline{)8,162}}$$
$\underline{7\ 0}\downarrow$
$1\ 16$
$\underline{1\ 12}$
4

$9 \times 14 = 126$ too big
$8 \times 14 = 112$ $112 < 116$

Divide ones.

$$\overset{583}{14\overline{)8,162}}$$
$\underline{7\ 0}\downarrow$
$1\ 16$
$\underline{1\ 12}\downarrow$
42
$\underline{42}$
0

The farm workers picked an average of 583 ears of corn each day.

TRY THESE

Divide. Check your answers.

1. $34\overline{)900}$ 2. $63\overline{)480}$ 3. $41\overline{)2,936}$ 4. $33\overline{)927}$ 5. $73\overline{)7,000}$

6. $1,804 \div 22 = $ ■   7. $600 \div 12 = $ ■   8. $3,100 \div 62 = $ ■

SKILLS PRACTICE

Divide.

1. $22\overline{)894}$ 2. $32\overline{)610}$ 3. $23\overline{)1,179}$ 4. $86\overline{)549}$ 5. $84\overline{)4,000}$

6. $79\overline{)4,700}$ 7. $62\overline{)8,000}$ 8. $51\overline{)768}$ 9. $33\overline{)9,000}$ 10. $11\overline{)759}$

11. $44\overline{)963}$ 12. $93\overline{)5,970}$ 13. $31\overline{)\$7.13}$ 14. $12\overline{)5,500}$ 15. $14\overline{)120}$

16. $43\overline{)7,000}$ 17. $64\overline{)520}$ 18. $52\overline{)2,500}$ 19. $22\overline{)837}$ 20. $54\overline{)8,300}$

21. $82\overline{)9,760}$ 22. $24\overline{)\$50.40}$ 23. $43\overline{)345}$ 24. $61\overline{)2,745}$ 25. $33\overline{)769}$

26. $32\overline{)8,700}$ 27. $13\overline{)5,300}$ 28. $24\overline{)6,530}$ 29. $44\overline{)9,999}$ 30. $42\overline{)875}$

31. $2,583 \div 41 = $ ■   32. $2,117 \div 73 = $ ■   33. $539 \div 11 = $ ■

34. $936 \div 52 = $ ■   35. $1,700 \div 34 = $ ■   36. $416 \div 13 = $ ■

PROBLEM SOLVING

37. Mr. Hanson shipped the same number of cartons of pears to each of 72 stores in a chain. He shipped 1,800 cartons in all. How many cartons did each store receive?

★38. A firm received 8,576 orders for oranges and grapefruit. There were 6,336 orders for oranges. How many orders were for grapefruit? The grapefruit orders were packed by 32 people. If each person packed the same number of orders, how many grapefruit did each person pack?

THINK!

A Coin Problem

Vin has an equal number of pennies, nickels, and dimes. Their total value is $1.60. How many of each coin does Vin have?

Revising Underestimates

When you round up, the first number you try in the quotient may be too small.

A. A shipping company must carry 1,432 cartons of candles in 15 vans. If each van carries the same number of cartons, how many will each carry? How many cartons will be left over?

Divide: $15\overline{)1{,}432}$

Round up. Estimate the quotient.

20

$15\overline{)1{,}432}$ ■

■ × 20 = 143
7 × 20 = 140
Try 7.

Multiply the real divisor.

$$
\begin{array}{r}
7 \\
15\overline{)1{,}432} \\
1\,05 \\
\hline
38
\end{array}
$$
too big

Revise. Try a larger estimate.

$$
\begin{array}{r}
8 \\
15\overline{)1{,}432} \\
1\,20 \\
\hline
23
\end{array}
$$
too big

Revise your estimate again.

$$
\begin{array}{r}
9 \\
15\overline{)1{,}432} \\
1\,35 \\
\hline
8
\end{array}
$$
8 < 15

Divide ones. Estimate. Revise if necessary.

$$
\begin{array}{r}
95\ \text{R7} \\
15\overline{)1{,}432} \\
1\,35\downarrow \\
\hline
82 \\
75 \\
\hline
7
\end{array}
$$

4 × 15 = 60   too small
5 × 15 = 75
6 × 15 = 90   too big

The remainder must be less than the divisor, 15.

Each van will carry 95 cartons. There will be 7 cartons left over.

B. Checking your answer will help you be sure you have revised your quotient estimates correctly.

$$
\begin{array}{r}
95 \\
\times\ 15 \\
\hline
475 \\
950 \\
\hline
1{,}425 \\
+\ \ \ 7 \\
\hline
1{,}432\ \checkmark
\end{array}
$$

TRY THESE

Divide. Check your answers.

1. 26)835 **2.** 67)545 **3.** 45)585 **4.** 77)1,853 **5.** 39)1,645

6. 204 ÷ 17 = ■ **7.** 468 ÷ 78 = ■ **8.** 5,100 ÷ 25 = ■

SKILLS PRACTICE

Divide.

1. 88)279 **2.** 26)470 **3.** 49)1,078 **4.** 16)266 **5.** 37)455

6. 53)6,473 **7.** 48)3,092 **8.** 28)3,397 **9.** 36)300 **10.** 59)418

11. 66)399 **12.** 83)435 **13.** 12)85 **14.** 89)277 **15.** 17)7,027

16. 55)391 **17.** 69)365 **18.** 35)318 **19.** 18)2,366 **20.** 27)2,242

21. 57)179 **22.** 48)1,504 **23.** 99)609 **24.** 76)7,608 **25.** 39)601

26. 25)1,405 **27.** 63)1,707 **28.** 47)449 **29.** 91)4,823 **30.** 58)2,746

31. 532 ÷ 28 = ■ **32.** 2,142 ÷ 34 = ■ **33.** 3,600 ÷ 45 = ■

34. 408 ÷ 17 = ■ **35.** 1,995 ÷ 57 = ■ **36.** 2,196 ÷ 36 = ■

PROBLEM SOLVING

37. A company has 927 candles to box. Each box holds 28 candles. How many boxes will be filled? How many candles will be left over?

★38. A gift store sold 9 scented candles and 8 unscented candles, each at the same price. $78.03 was received for all of them. What was the price per candle?

Reasoning about Sums

Find three consecutive numbers such that one half of their sum is 18.

Problem Solving **Strategy**

Make a Table

In a laboratory experiment, two seedlings are planted on the same day. Seedling A is 18 centimeters tall when planted, and seedling B is 9 centimeters tall. Seedling A grows 1 centimeter per week. Seedling B is given special fertilizer and grows 2 centimeters per week. After how many weeks will the seedlings be the same height? How tall will they be then?

To solve problems such as this one, it helps to **make a table.** List the heights of the two seedlings after each week.

End of Week	1	2	3	4	5	6	7	8	9	10	
Height of Seedling A	19	20	21	22	23	24	25	26	27	28	same heights
Height of Seedling B	11	13	15	17	19	21	23	25	27	29	

The two seedlings will have the same height after 9 weeks.
They will each be 27 centimeters tall at that time.

Solve. Extend the table above or make your own table.

1. After how many weeks will seedling B be 5 centimeters taller than seedling A?

2. How tall will seedling B be when seedling A is 37 centimeters tall?

3. Seedling C, 12 centimeters tall, was planted at the same time as A and B. It grew 3 centimeters per week. After how many weeks was seedling C the same height as seedling A?

4. How tall will seedling C be when seedling A and B are the same height?

200   **Dividing by Tens and Ones**

Data on Line Graphs

A line graph can be used to show information. This line graph shows
the number of gold and silver medals won by the United States
Team at the Summer Olympic Games from 1960 to 1976.

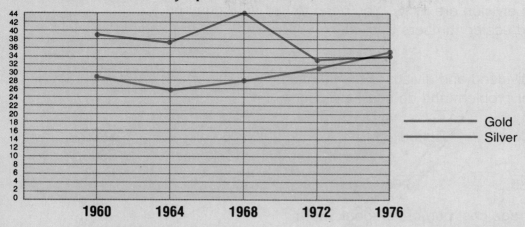

The *median* of a set of numbers is the middle number. To find the
median number of gold medals, arrange the numbers of gold medals
in order from smallest to largest and find the middle number.

33   34   ⟨37⟩   39   44

The median number of gold medals was 37.

The *range* of a set of numbers is the difference between the largest
number and the smallest number. To find the range of the numbers
of gold medals subtract the smallest number from the largest number.

$$44 - 33 = 11$$

The range of the number of gold medals was 11.

1. What was the greatest number of silver medals won?

2. What was the least number of silver medals won?

3. Find the median number of silver medals won.

4. Find the range of the numbers of silver medals won.

ON YOUR OWN

Data Search

Find the number of bronze medals won by the U.S. at the Summer Olympic Games
from 1960 to 1976. Draw a line graph to show this information. Find the median number
of bronze medals won. Find the range of the number of bronze medals won.

Estimating Quotients

A repair shop received $5,635 for 23 repair jobs. Estimate the average charge per job.

Estimates in division are tricky. You need to use your number sense to find easier numbers to divide.

A. Round dividend and divisor to the leftmost digit. Then think of an easier problem and do short division.

Round down.   Round up.

$$23\overline{)\$5,635} \longrightarrow 20\overline{)\$6,000}$$

$20\overline{)\$6,000}$ is the same as $2\overline{)\$600}$.

$$\frac{\$300}{2\overline{)\$600}}$$

The average cost per job is about $300.

B. You can often get a better estimate by rounding both numbers in the same direction.

Round both down.

$$23\overline{)\$5,635} \longrightarrow 20\overline{)\$5,000}$$

$20\overline{)\$5,000}$ is the same as $2\overline{)\$500}$.

$$\frac{\$250}{2\overline{)\$500}}$$

The average cost per job is about $250.

C. Another way to estimate is to find the first digit of the real quotient and then write zeros for the other digits.

$$\frac{2}{23\overline{)\$5,635}}$$
$$\underline{4\ 6}$$

■ × 23 = 56
Try 2.

$$\frac{\$\ 200}{23\overline{)\$5,635}}$$
$$\underline{4\ 6}$$

← Write zeros.

The average cost per job is about $200.

D. The *real* average cost per job is $245.
For this problem, method **B** gives the best estimate.

Estimate each quotient in three different ways. Then find the real quotient. Decide which estimate is the best.

1. $36\overline{)1,476}$ **2.** $52\overline{)8,424}$ **3.** $79\overline{)2,528}$ **4.** $47\overline{)8,272}$

SKILLS PRACTICE

Estimate each quotient. Then use your estimate to choose the correct answer.

1. $17\overline{)8,857}$ **2.** $64\overline{)1,472}$ **3.** $88\overline{)6,248}$ **4.** $53\overline{)6,466}$

a. 251	**a.** 23	**a.** 7	**a.** 122
b. 521	**b.** 235	**b.** 17	**b.** 222
c. 5,210	**c.** 253	**c.** 71	**c.** 1,220

Estimate each quotient. Then use your calculator to find the correct answer.

5. $13\overline{)2,886}$ **6.** $45\overline{)2,880}$ **7.** $65\overline{)7,995}$ **8.** $15\overline{)6,345}$ **9.** $12\overline{)4,284}$

10. $32\overline{)1,664}$ **11.** $14\overline{)6,328}$ **12.** $23\overline{)8,211}$ **13.** $85\overline{)2,040}$ **14.** $27\overline{)8,667}$

15. $23\overline{)3,013}$ **16.** $35\overline{)2,975}$ **17.** $39\overline{)1,287}$ ★**18.** $77\overline{)8,705}$ ★**19.** $15\overline{)4,790}$

20. $2,280 \div 95 = \blacksquare$ **21.** $1,444 \div 38 = \blacksquare$ ★**22.** $5,484 \div \blacksquare = 457$

PROBLEM SOLVING

23. Last week the repair shop paid wages of $6,696 to its 18 employees. Estimate the average weekly wage of an employee.

24. In 1985, the shop sold 3,588 stereo cables. Estimate the average number of cables sold per week. (1 year = 52 weeks)

MIXED REVIEW

What coins and bills should you get as change?

1. Cost: $3.98; Gave clerk: $5.00   **2.** Cost: $12.53; Gave clerk: $20.00

What time is it?

3. 2 hours after 9:45 A.M.   **4.** 15 minutes before 3:10 P.M.

5. 30 minutes after 11:55 P.M.   **6.** 4 hours 25 minutes before 2:15 A.M.

Dividing Larger Numbers

A factory printed 81,375 greeting cards. 75 cards were packed in each box. How many boxes were filled? How many cards were left over?

Divide: 81,375 ÷ 75 = ■

Estimate. About 80,000 ÷ 80 = 1,000.

Decide where to start.

$$75\overline{)81,375}$$ •••   75 > 8   Not enough ten-thousands. Regroup.

$$75\overline{)81,375}$$ •••   75 < 81 Start with thousands.

Divide the thousands.

```
      1
75)81,375
   75
    6
```

Divide the hundreds.

```
     1,0
75)81,375
   75 ↓
    6 3
      0
    6 3
```

Divide the tens.

```
    1,08
75)81,375
   75
    6 3
      0
    6 37
    6 00
      37
```

Divide the ones.

```
    1,085
75)81,375
   75
    6 3
      0
    6 37
    6 00
      375
      375
        0
```

Check.

```
    1,085
  ×    75
   5 425
   75 95
  81,375 ✔
```

1,085 boxes were filled. 0 cards were left over.

TRY THESE

Divide. Check your answers.

1. $23\overline{)94,765}$ 2. $37\overline{)2,788}$ 3. $54\overline{)20,750}$ 4. $47\overline{)97,000}$

5. $2,050 \div 82 =$ ■   6. $28,854 \div 63 =$ ■   7. $13,920 \div 96 =$ ■

SKILLS PRACTICE

Divide.

1. $13\overline{)64,856}$ 2. $36\overline{)2,384}$ 3. $24\overline{)848}$ 4. $16\overline{)39,503}$

5. $76\overline{)389}$ 6. $32\overline{)54,650}$ 7. $55\overline{)1,980}$ 8. $77\overline{)\$53.13}$

9. $61\overline{)42,259}$ 10. $27\overline{)5,951}$ 11. $92\overline{)12,100}$ 12. $33\overline{)296}$

13. $15\overline{)12,000}$ 14. $63\overline{)92,076}$ 15. $57\overline{)915}$ 16. $46\overline{)\$64.86}$

17. $34\overline{)81,650}$ 18. $42\overline{)760}$ 19. $56\overline{)83,700}$ 20. $85\overline{)87,125}$

21. $12\overline{)75,000}$ 22. $93\overline{)3,945}$ 23. $64\overline{)475}$ 24. $25\overline{)38,600}$

25. $98,986 \div 43 =$ ■   26. $70,080 \div 73 =$ ■   27. $10,164 \div 66 =$ ■

28. $5,488 \div 98 =$ ■   29. $602 \div 86 =$ ■   30. $49,938 \div 82 =$ ■

PROBLEM SOLVING

31. A factory produced 87,000 baseballs. They put 84 baseballs in each box. How many boxes did they fill? How many baseballs were left over?

★32. A bottling factory put 28,248 ounces of ketchup into 11-ounce bottles. How many bottles did they use? How many ounces of ketchup will fill 950 bottles?

THINK!

Methods of Payment
Suppose you want to buy a $220 bicycle. You can:
A. pay the full $220 now.
B. pay $70 now and make 16 additional monthly payments of $12 each.
C. pay $100 now and make 10 additional monthly payments of $15 each.
With which method would you pay the greatest total amount? Why might you use that method?

Changing Units

Sometimes you may need to change the units used to report a measure.
These tables of time units and customary units will help you.

Time Units	
1 minute	= 60 seconds
1 hour	= 60 minutes
1 day	= 24 hours
1 week	= 7 days
1 year	= 12 months

Customary Units		
1 foot (ft)	=	12 inches (in.)
1 yard (yd)	=	3 feet (ft)
1 pound (lb)	=	16 ounces (oz)
1 pint (pt)	=	2 cups
1 quart (qt)	=	2 pints (pt)
1 gallon (gal)	=	4 quarts (qt)

A. Multiply to change larger units to smaller units.

8 weeks = ■ days

> 1 week = 7 days
> 8 weeks = 8 × 7 days
> = 56 days

8 weeks = 56 days

C. Divide to change smaller units to larger units.

16 quarts = ■ gallons

> 4 qt = 1 gal
> 16 ÷ 4 qt = 4 gal

16 quarts = 4 gallons

B. Multiply and **add** to change mixed units to smaller units.

7 lb 3 oz = ■ oz

> 1 lb = 16 oz
> 7 lb = 7 × 16 oz
> = 112 oz

$$\begin{array}{r} 112 \text{ oz} \\ +3 \text{ oz} \\ \hline 115 \text{ oz} \end{array}$$

7 lb 3 oz = 115 oz

D. If there is a remainder, write it using the smaller unit.

400 min = ■ h ■ min

> 60 min = 1 h

$$\begin{array}{r} 6 \leftarrow \text{hours} \\ 60\overline{)400} \\ \underline{360} \\ 40 \leftarrow \text{minutes} \end{array}$$

400 minutes = 6 hours 40 minutes

TRY THESE

Use the tables to find the missing numbers.

1. 21 days = ◾ weeks
2. 13 gal = ◾ qt
3. 17 cups = ◾ pt ◾ cup
4. 3 days 17 hours = ◾ hours

SKILLS PRACTICE

Use the tables to find the missing numbers.

1. 6 weeks = ◾ days
2. 9 pt = ◾ qt ◾ pt
3. 5 lb = ◾ oz
4. 23 in. = ◾ ft ◾ in.
5. 15 minutes = ◾ seconds
6. 149 ft = ◾ yd ◾ ft
7. 523 oz = ◾ lb ◾ oz
8. 168 months = ◾ years
9. 7 yd 1 ft = ◾ ft
10. 4 gal 3 qt = ◾ qt
★11. 2 qt 1 pt = ◾ cups
★12. 1 week 5 days = ◾ hours

PROBLEM SOLVING

13. The camp dining hall is 96 ft long. How many yards long is it?

14. The volleyball net is 72 in. high. How many feet high is it?

15. Lucy was at summer camp for 7 weeks 2 days. For how many days was she at camp?

16. The campers drank 6 pt 1 cup of fruit juice. How many cups of juice did they drink?

★17. Eric put up his tent in 3 minutes. It took Dennis 205 seconds to put up his tent. Who took more time? How much more time?

★18. The cook put 4 oz of meat on each of 55 sandwiches. How many ounces did he use? How many 1-pound packages of meat did he have to open?

THINK!

Visual Perception

How can you divide the figure into 2 equal parts? 3 equal parts? 4 equal parts?

Problem Solving

Two-Step Problems

When you shop you often solve problems that require two steps.

A. If these cans of fruit are the same
size and quality, which store
gives the better buy?

Step 1 Find the cost per can at
Meyer's store.

$$\begin{array}{r} \$\ .51 \\ 4)\overline{\$2.05} \\ \underline{2\ 0} \\ 05 \\ \underline{4} \\ 1 \end{array}$$ ←**Stores always round up if
the remainder is not 0.**

The price at Meyer's is 52¢ per can.

Step 2 Compare: Milton's ⟶ 53¢ per can
Meyer's ⟶ 52¢ per can

52¢ < 53¢   Meyer's gives the better buy.
An estimate is not helpful for problems like this.

B. Jamie bought a roast for $7.50 and 8 melons for $1.26 each.
What was the total cost of what Jamie bought?

Think: Total cost is the cost of the roast + the cost of the melons.

$7.50 . . . 8 × $1.26 . . .

Estimate. 8 × ($1 + $.25) = ■
$8 + $2 = $10
$10 + $7.50 = $17.50

Step 1 Find the amount
for melons.

$$\begin{array}{r} ②④ \\ \$1.26 \\ \times\quad 8 \\ \hline \$10.08 \end{array}$$

Step 2 Find what was spent
in all.

$$\begin{array}{r} \$\ 7.50 \\ +\ 10.08 \\ \hline \$17.58 \end{array}$$

Jamie spent $17.58 in all.

208 **Dividing by Tens and Ones**

TRY THESE

Which is the better buy?

1. Apples: 12 for $1.49 or 1 for 14¢

2. Pickles: 1 for 35¢ or 4 for $1.45

Solve the problems.

3. Marty bought a pineapple for $2.75 and apple juice for $1.19. How much change did he receive from $10.00?

4. Cindy bought a tub of butter for $1.19, sunflower seeds for $1.69, and cheese for $2.13. How much did she spend?

5. Miguel had $8.75. He bought four avocados. Each avocado cost $.89. How much money did Miguel have left?

6. Glenia bought 6 oranges and a carton of sour cream. Each orange cost 19¢. The sour cream cost 73¢. How much did she spend?

PROBLEM SOLVING PRACTICE

Which is the better buy?

1. Peppers: 1 for 72¢ or 4 for $2.77

2. Oranges: 9 for $1.00 or 1 for 13¢

3. Rolls: 6 for 89¢ or 18¢ each

4. Muffins: 20¢ each or 12 for $2.60

Solve the problems.

5. Mr. Jacobs bought 2 lemons for 49¢ each and a grapefruit for 34¢. How much did he spend in all?

6. Ms. Lorenzo bought 4 jars of peach jelly. Each jar cost 53¢. How much did she spend in all?

7. Charles had $12.50. He bought a carton of milk for $1.09 and a turkey for $7.65. How much money did he have left?

8. Maria bought 6 nectarines. Each nectarine cost 13¢. She also bought a squash for $1.19. How much did she spend?

9. Ms. Owens bought jam for 49¢, popcorn for $1.29, and corn oil for $1.79. How much did she spend in all?

10. Mr. Brown bought 2 bunches of bananas. Each bunch cost $1.39. He gave the clerk $5.00. How much change should he receive?

★11. 3 pears cost 79¢. 4 peaches cost 89¢. Eddie bought 1 peach and 3 pears. How much did he spend?

★12. 3 rolls cost $1.15. Lucy bought 1 roll, a quart of juice for $.79, and a dozen eggs for $1.20. How much did she spend?

ON YOUR OWN

Data Search

Visit two neighborhood stores that sell the same item at different prices. Make a note of the prices. Calculate which store has the better buy. Do you think that store has the better buy on all items it sells?

Repeated Operations on a Calculator

Jan and Jon take the bus to school. They get special bus tokens that cost 79¢ each. Each has a $5 bill. How many tokens can each buy?

Jan and Jon use their calculators to find out. On some calculators if you press the ☐ button more than once after a calculation, the calculation you did is repeated.

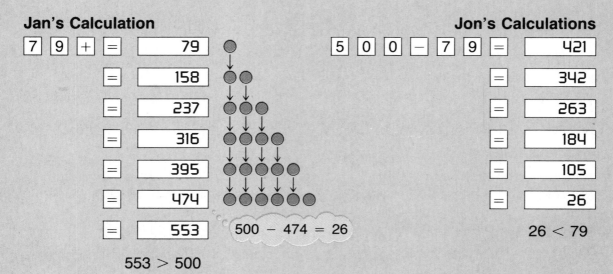

Jan's Calculation

7 9 + =	79
=	158
=	237
=	316
=	395
=	474
=	553

553 > 500

Jon's Calculations

5 0 0 − 7 9 =	421
=	342
=	263
=	184
=	105
=	26

26 < 79

500 − 474 = 26

Jan can buy 6 tokens and has 26¢ left over.

Jon can buy 6 tokens and has 26¢ left over.

If your calculator does not work this way, you will have to enter repeated operations.

Find each quotient and remainder by using repeated addition or subtraction.

1. 527 ÷ 66 = ■
2. 235 ÷ 27 = ■
3. 473 ÷ 68 = ■
4. 484 ÷ 75 = ■
5. 623 ÷ 83 = ■
6. 684 ÷ 81 = ■
7. 847 ÷ 95 = ■
8. 1,187 ÷ 54 = ■
9. 5,106 ÷ 43 = ■
10. 599 ÷ 81 = ■
11. 987 ÷ 72 = ■
12. 2,453 ÷ 37 = ■

Divide. *(pages 192–199, 204–205)*

1. $60\overline{)358}$ 2. $80\overline{)92,500}$ 3. $30\overline{)7,218}$ 4. $90\overline{)10,000}$ 5. $20\overline{)4,320}$

6. $25\overline{)598}$ 7. $42\overline{)9,682}$ 8. $12\overline{)39}$ 9. $53\overline{)7,765}$ 10. $15\overline{)167}$

11. $69\overline{)757}$ 12. $38\overline{)1,194}$ 13. $22\overline{)5,966}$ 14. $75\overline{)4,595}$ 15. $73\overline{)368}$

16. $38\overline{)109}$ 17. $46\overline{)362}$ 18. $24\overline{)97}$ 19. $69\overline{)7,273}$ 20. $35\overline{)3,392}$

21. $28\overline{)5,824}$ 22. $12\overline{)84}$ 23. $49\overline{)580}$ 24. $82\overline{)3,731}$ 25. $73\overline{)872}$

26. $17\overline{)4,600}$ 27. $34\overline{)3,704}$ 28. $19\overline{)53}$ 29. $23\overline{)492}$ 30. $64\overline{)1,991}$

31. $65\overline{)44,592}$ 32. $65\overline{)2,492}$ 33. $88\overline{)7,649}$ 34. $48\overline{)91,766}$

35. $50\overline{)32,717}$ 36. $26\overline{)26,000}$ 37. $83\overline{)74,504}$ 38. $48\overline{)5,380}$

39. $14\overline{)9,275}$ 40. $56\overline{)9,850}$ 41. $85\overline{)59,467}$ 42. $24\overline{)86,000}$

43. $3,952 \div 26 = $ ■   44. $\$33.15 \div 39 = $ ■   45. $792 \div 44 = $ ■

46. $24,576 \div 96 = $ ■   47. $22,940 \div 37 = $ ■   48. $1,410 \div 15 = $ ■

Estimate each quotient. Then use your estimate to choose the correct answer. *(pages 202–203)*

49. $66\overline{)6,204}$
   a. 9
   b. 40
   c. 94

50. $12\overline{)2,592}$
   a. 216
   b. 2,160
   c. 2,600

51. $35\overline{)20,300}$
   a. 580
   b. 853
   c. 8,500

52. $54\overline{)15,606}$
   a. 29
   b. 289
   c. 2,890

Solve the problems. *(pages 206–209)*

53. An apple tree is 6 yd 2 ft tall. How many feet tall is it?

54. Alice worked 480 minutes. How many hours did she work?

55. Marian bought 5 oranges and 1 nectarine. Each orange cost $.19, and each nectarine cost $.23. How much did she spend in all?

56. Rafael had $6.30. He bought some milk for $2.19 and a cucumber for 39¢. How much money did he have left?

Reinforcement

More Help with Division

Round 72 down to 70.

$$\begin{array}{r} 56\ R36 \\ 72\overline{)4,068} \\ 360 \\ \hline 468 \\ 432 \\ \hline 36 \end{array}$$

When you round down, your first estimate may be too large.

40

$$\begin{array}{r} 1,919\ R17 \\ 43\overline{)82,534} \\ 43 \\ \hline 395 \\ 387 \\ \hline 83 \\ 43 \\ \hline 404 \\ 387 \\ \hline 17 \end{array}$$

Round 28 up to 30.

$$\begin{array}{r} 126\ R22 \\ 28\overline{)3,550} \\ 28 \\ \hline 75 \\ 56 \\ \hline 190 \\ 168 \\ \hline 22 \end{array}$$

When you round up, your first estimate may be too small.

20

$$\begin{array}{r} 523\ R4 \\ 15\overline{)7,849} \\ 25 \\ \hline 34 \\ 30 \\ \hline 49 \\ 45 \\ \hline 4 \end{array}$$

Divide.

1. $43\overline{)6,889}$ **2.** $31\overline{)104}$ **3.** $14\overline{)169}$

4. $21\overline{)85}$ **5.** $52\overline{)6,399}$ **6.** $74\overline{)6,039}$

7. $11,160 \div 93 = \blacksquare$ **8.** $4,433 \div 11 = \blacksquare$

9. $34\overline{)9,320}$ **10.** $33\overline{)2,882}$ **11.** $44\overline{)1,726}$

12. $53\overline{)72,395}$ **13.** $63\overline{)12,900}$ **14.** $22\overline{)1,716}$

15. $2,914 \div 94 = \blacksquare$ **16.** $19,142 \div 34 = \blacksquare$

17. $46\overline{)8,350}$ **18.** $25\overline{)68}$ **19.** $56\overline{)894}$

20. $26\overline{)992}$ **21.** $87\overline{)3,995}$ **22.** $29\overline{)3,516}$

23. $89,870 \div 55 = \blacksquare$ **24.** $3,915 \div 87 = \blacksquare$

25. $68\overline{)549}$ **26.** $36\overline{)116}$ **27.** $77\overline{)5,400}$

28. $45\overline{)970}$ **29.** $36\overline{)8,680}$ **30.** $68\overline{)7,278}$

31. $1,672 \div 76 = \blacksquare$ **32.** $9,414 \div 18 = \blacksquare$

Enrichment

Base 5 Numerals

You can write a numeral in which the place values depend on powers of 5. This is a **base 5 numeral.**

Write 4,509 using powers of 5.

$$5^0 = 1$$
$$5^1 = 5$$
$$5^2 = 25$$
$$5^3 = 125$$
$$5^4 = 625$$
$$5^5 = 3,125$$
$$5^6 = 15,625$$
$$5^7 = 78,125$$

Step 1 Find the largest power of 5 less than or equal to 4,509.

$$5^5 < 4,509$$
$$5^6 > 4,509$$

Step 2 Divide 4,509 by that power of 5. Write a number sentence for 4,509 using the quotient and remainder.

$$
\begin{array}{r}
1 \text{ R}1,384 \\
5^5 \quad 3,125\overline{)4,509} \\
3,125 \\
\hline
1,384
\end{array}
$$

$$4,509 = 1 \times 5^5 + 1,384$$

Step 3 Divide the remainder by the next smallest power 5. Write another number sentence for 4,509 using the new quotient and remainder.

$$
\begin{array}{r}
2 \text{ R}134 \\
5^4 \quad 625\overline{)1,384} \\
1,250 \\
\hline
134
\end{array}
$$

$$4,509 = 1 \times 5^5 + 2 \times 5^4 + 134$$

Step 4 Continue in the same way until you divide by $5^0 = 1$. Be sure to record any quotient that is 0.

$$
\begin{array}{r}
1 \text{ R}9 \\
5^3 \quad 125\overline{)134} \\
125 \\
\hline
9
\end{array}
\qquad
\begin{array}{r}
0 \text{ R}9 \\
5^2 \quad 25\overline{)9} \\
0 \\
\hline
9
\end{array}
\quad \text{0 quotient}
$$

$$4,509 = 1 \times 5^5 + 2 \times 5^4 + 1 \times 5^3 + 9 \qquad 4,509 = 1 \times 5^5 + 2 \times 5^4 + 1 \times 5^3 + 0 \times 5^2 + 9$$

$$
\begin{array}{r}
1 \text{ R}4 \\
5^1 \quad 5\overline{)9} \\
5 \\
\hline
4
\end{array}
\qquad
\begin{aligned}
4 &= 4 \times 1 \\
&= 4 \times 5^0
\end{aligned}
$$

$$4,509 = 1 \times 5^5 + 2 \times 5^4 + 1 \times 5^3 + 0 \times 5^2 + 1 \times 5^1 + 4 \times 5^0$$

standard numeral ⟶ $4,509 = 121014$ ⟵ base 5 numeral
FIVE

Write a base 5 numeral for each standard numeral.

1. 3   **2.** 10   **3.** 11   **4.** 85   **5.** 634   **6.** 42,000

Write as a standard numeral.

7. 11_{FIVE}   **8.** 42_{FIVE}   **9.** 333_{FIVE}   **10.** 1000_{FIVE}   **11.** 42000_{FIVE}

Cumulative Review

Choose the correct answer.

1. 38,792
$-29,486$

a. 68,272
b. 11,278
c. 9,306
d. not above

2. 658
$\times 300$

a. 18,540
b. 19,740
c. 197,400
d. not above

3. $23\overline{)920}$

a. 40
b. 46
c. 44 R18
d. not above

4. $8 \times 7 = \blacksquare$

a. 54
b. 56
c. 87
d. not above

5. $5\overline{)70,416}$

a. 1,483 R1
b. 14,083 R1
c. 1,408 R1
d. not above

6. 846,518
$+192,634$

a. 1,049,252
b. 1,039,152
c. 938,142
d. not above

7. $9.00
$-\quad .79$

a. $1.10
b. $8.31
c. $8.21
d. not above

8. $60\overline{)65,415}$

a. 109 R15
b. 19 R15
c. 192 R3
d. not above

9. 86
$\times 62$

a. 5,332
b. 688
c. 6,844
d. not above

10. $86\overline{)7,139}$

a. 71 R25
b. 83 R1
c. 89 R19
d. not above

11. | 1 day |
| = **24 hours** |

3 days
4 hours
$= \blacksquare$ hours

a. 76 hours
b. 72 hours
c. 34 hours
d. not above

12. What does the digit 4 mean in 592,461?

a. 4 tens
b. 4 thousands
c. 4 hundreds
d. not above

13. 56 people can ride on each bus. How many buses must be used to carry 325 people?

a. 5 buses
b. 6 buses
c. 5 R45 buses
d. not above

14. Each ticket costs $8. Mr. Gerry has $75. How many tickets can he buy?

a. 9 R3 tickets
b. $9
c. 9 tickets
d. not above

8 Fractions

Transportation in San Francisco

The cable car is almost synonymous with San Francisco. The cars run on rails and are pulled by an endless moving cable under the street. The system has three lines and covers 10 miles. Recently the system was completely overhauled and has been declared a national historic landmark. Although a trip to San Francisco would be incomplete without a ride on these famous cars, the city can also be proud of the extensive 71-mile Bay Area Rapid Transit (BART) electric rail system. One branch of this system runs through the 5-mile Trans-Bay Tube under the San Francisco Bay between San Francisco and Oakland.

Fractions

A. You can write *fractions* for parts of sets or objects.

 1 of 3 ties is red.

$\frac{1}{3}$ of the set is red.

 $\frac{3}{5}$ of the scarf is red.

$\frac{1}{3}$ ← **numerator**
$\quad$ ← **denominator**

one-third

$\frac{3}{5}$ ← **numerator**
$\quad$ ← **denominator**

three-fifths

B. *Equivalent fractions* name the same part.

 $\frac{2}{3}$ of the packs or $\frac{6}{9}$

of the socks are red.

 $\frac{3}{4}$ or $\frac{6}{8}$ of the

bandanna is red.

To show that fractions are equivalent write:

$$\frac{2}{3} = \frac{6}{9}$$

$$\frac{3}{4} = \frac{6}{8}$$

C. *Number lines* or *fraction bars* can be used to show equivalent fractions.

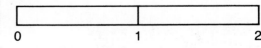

Ones

0 $\qquad$ 1 $\qquad$ 2

0 $\qquad$ 1 $\qquad$ 2

Halves

$\frac{0}{2}$ $\quad$ $\frac{1}{2}$ $\quad$ $\frac{2}{2}$ $\quad$ $\frac{3}{2}$ $\quad$ $\frac{4}{2}$

$\frac{0}{2}$ $\quad$ $\frac{1}{2}$ $\quad$ $\frac{2}{2}$ $\quad$ $\frac{3}{2}$ $\quad$ $\frac{4}{2}$

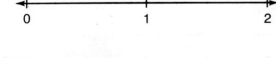

Fourths

$\frac{0}{4}$ $\frac{1}{4}$ $\frac{2}{4}$ $\frac{3}{4}$ $\frac{4}{4}$ $\frac{5}{4}$ $\frac{6}{4}$ $\frac{7}{4}$ $\frac{8}{4}$

$\frac{0}{4}$ $\frac{1}{4}$ $\frac{2}{4}$ $\frac{3}{4}$ $\frac{4}{4}$ $\frac{5}{4}$ $\frac{6}{4}$ $\frac{7}{4}$ $\frac{8}{4}$

TRY THESE

Give two equivalent fractions for the blue part.

1.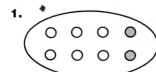

2.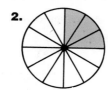

3.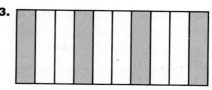

Use the fraction bars. Write a fraction equivalent to:

4. $\dfrac{2}{3}$ **5.** $\dfrac{0}{6}$ **6.** $\dfrac{3}{3}$

7. $\dfrac{1}{3}$ **8.** 1 **9.** $\dfrac{2}{6}$

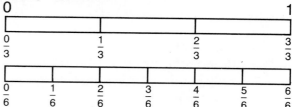

SKILLS PRACTICE

Give two equivalent fractions for the green part.

1.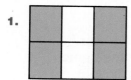

2.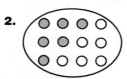

3.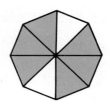

Use the number lines. Write a fraction equivalent to:

4. $\dfrac{6}{10}$ **5.** $\dfrac{7}{5}$ **6.** 1

7. $\dfrac{10}{5}$ **8.** $\dfrac{16}{10}$ **9.** $\dfrac{2}{5}$

Each set of fractions is equivalent. Draw pictures to find the missing number.

★10. $\dfrac{3}{4} = \dfrac{\blacksquare}{8}$

★11. $\dfrac{2}{5} = \dfrac{\blacksquare}{15}$

★12. $\dfrac{2}{3} = \dfrac{\blacksquare}{6} = \dfrac{6}{\blacksquare}$

THINK!

Equivalent Probabilities

Beth and Seth were playing a penny-toss game. Beth tossed 14 heads and 16 tails. Seth tossed 7 heads and 8 tails. Write a fraction for the number of heads in each set of tosses. What can you say about the fractions?

Multiplying to Find Equivalent Fractions

A. In art class, 5 students decided to paint a paper banner with the school colors. The banner was folded into 5 equal parts and the students planned to paint it like this:

$\dfrac{2}{5}$ = blue

Another group of 5 students offered to help. So the banner was folded to make 2 smaller pieces from each large piece.

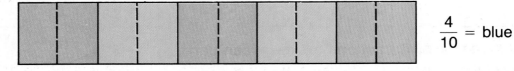

$\dfrac{4}{10}$ = blue

$$\frac{2}{5} = \frac{4}{10} \qquad \begin{array}{c} 2 \times 2 \\ \overline{5 \times 2} \end{array}$$

> **Multiplying both numerator and denominator by the same number gives an equivalent fraction.**

B. The students also put together sets of balloons. Each set contained 1 orange and 3 blue balloons. You can make lists of equivalent fractions to show the part of each set that is blue.

1 set	$\dfrac{3}{4}$	The numerator shows the number of blue balloons.
2 sets	$\dfrac{3 \times 2}{4 \times 2} = \dfrac{6}{8}$	
3 sets	$\dfrac{3 \times 3}{4 \times 3} = \dfrac{9}{12}$	
4 sets	$\dfrac{3 \times 4}{4 \times 4} = \dfrac{12}{16}$	

$$\frac{3}{4} = \frac{6}{8} = \frac{9}{12} = \frac{12}{16}$$

Copy and complete.

1. $\dfrac{3}{4} = \dfrac{3 \times 3}{4 \times 3} = \dfrac{\blacksquare}{\blacksquare}$

2. $\dfrac{1}{2} = \dfrac{\blacksquare}{6}$

3. $\dfrac{1}{3} = \dfrac{\blacksquare}{15}$

4. $\dfrac{2}{5} = \dfrac{\blacksquare}{15}$

Multiply the numerator and denominator by 2, 3, 4, and 5 to find lists of equivalent fractions.

5. $\dfrac{2}{3}$

6. $\dfrac{1}{5}$

7. $\dfrac{3}{4}$

8. $\dfrac{1}{6}$

9. $\dfrac{5}{8}$

SKILLS PRACTICE

Copy and complete.

1. $\dfrac{5}{6} = \dfrac{5 \times 3}{6 \times 3} = \dfrac{\blacksquare}{\blacksquare}$

2. $\dfrac{2}{5} = \dfrac{2 \times \blacksquare}{5 \times 4} = \dfrac{\blacksquare}{20}$

3. $\dfrac{1}{4} = \dfrac{1 \times \blacksquare}{4 \times 2} = \dfrac{\blacksquare}{8}$

4. $\dfrac{5}{8} = \dfrac{\blacksquare}{24}$

5. $\dfrac{9}{10} = \dfrac{\blacksquare}{20}$

6. $\dfrac{5}{5} = \dfrac{\blacksquare}{25}$

7. $\dfrac{0}{2} = \dfrac{\blacksquare}{8}$

★8. $\dfrac{4}{1} = \dfrac{\blacksquare}{3}$

Multiply the numerator and denominator by 4, 5, 6, 8, and 10 to find lists of equivalent fractions.

9. $\dfrac{1}{4}$

10. $\dfrac{3}{8}$

11. $\dfrac{2}{5}$

12. $\dfrac{5}{6}$

13. $\dfrac{3}{7}$

PROBLEM SOLVING

★14. In each row of 8 seats, 3 are reserved for teachers. Use equivalent fractions to find how many seats are reserved for teachers in 5 rows; in 10 rows.

★15. Each school softball team had 4 boys and 5 girls on it. Write equivalent fractions to show first the number of girls and then the number of boys on 2 teams; 3 teams; 4 teams.

THINK!

Cross Products

Here is an easy way to find out if two fractions are equivalent. Use the *cross product*.

> **Two fractions are equivalent if their cross products are equal.**

$5 \times 8 = 40$
$4 \times 10 = 40$

$\dfrac{4}{5}$ and $\dfrac{8}{10}$ are equivalent.

Write equal ($=$) or not equal ($\neq$). Use cross products.

1. $\dfrac{2}{3} \; \bullet \; \dfrac{6}{9}$

2. $\dfrac{4}{5} \; \bullet \; \dfrac{5}{6}$

3. $\dfrac{9}{15} \; \bullet \; \dfrac{15}{25}$

4. $\dfrac{14}{20} \; \bullet \; \dfrac{6}{7}$

Comparing and Ordering Fractions

A. To compare fractions with common denominators, compare the numerators.

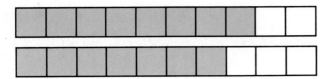

$\dfrac{8}{10}$ of the strip is red.

$\dfrac{7}{10}$ of the strip is blue.

$8 > 7$

$\dfrac{8}{10}$ is greater than $\dfrac{7}{10}$.

$\dfrac{8}{10} > \dfrac{7}{10}$

$7 < 8$

$\dfrac{7}{10}$ is less than $\dfrac{8}{10}$.

$\dfrac{7}{10} < \dfrac{8}{10}$

B. When fractions have unlike denominators, find equivalent fractions with a common denominator. Then compare.

Compare $\dfrac{5}{6}$ and $\dfrac{7}{8}$.

$\times 2$ $\times 3$ $\times 4$

$\dfrac{5}{6} = \dfrac{10}{12} = \dfrac{15}{18} = \dfrac{20}{24}$

$\times 2$ $\times 3$ $\times 4$

$\dfrac{7}{8} = \dfrac{14}{16} = \dfrac{21}{24} = \dfrac{28}{32}$

$\dfrac{20}{24} < \dfrac{21}{24}$ so $\dfrac{5}{6} < \dfrac{7}{8}$ and $\dfrac{21}{24} > \dfrac{20}{24}$ so $\dfrac{7}{8} > \dfrac{5}{6}$

C. Put $\dfrac{3}{4}, \dfrac{5}{6}$, and $\dfrac{2}{3}$ in order from least to greatest.

Use the lists.

$\dfrac{3}{4} = \dfrac{9}{12}$ $\dfrac{5}{6} = \dfrac{10}{12}$ $\dfrac{2}{3} = \dfrac{8}{12}$

$\dfrac{8}{12} < \dfrac{9}{12} < \dfrac{10}{12}$

$\dfrac{2}{3} < \dfrac{3}{4} < \dfrac{5}{6}$

$\dfrac{2}{3}, \dfrac{3}{4}, \dfrac{5}{6}$

Lists of Equivalent Fractions

$\times 2$ $\times 3$ $\times 4$ $\times 5$ $\times 6$

$\dfrac{1}{2} = \dfrac{2}{4} = \dfrac{3}{6} = \dfrac{4}{8} = \dfrac{5}{10} = \dfrac{6}{12}$

$\dfrac{2}{3} = \dfrac{4}{6} = \dfrac{6}{9} = \dfrac{8}{12} = \dfrac{10}{15} = \dfrac{12}{18}$

$\dfrac{3}{4} = \dfrac{6}{8} = \dfrac{9}{12} = \dfrac{12}{16} = \dfrac{15}{20} = \dfrac{18}{24}$

$\dfrac{4}{5} = \dfrac{8}{10} = \dfrac{12}{15} = \dfrac{16}{20} = \dfrac{20}{25} = \dfrac{24}{30}$

$\dfrac{5}{6} = \dfrac{10}{12} = \dfrac{15}{18} = \dfrac{20}{24} = \dfrac{25}{30} = \dfrac{30}{36}$

$\dfrac{5}{8} = \dfrac{10}{16} = \dfrac{15}{24} = \dfrac{20}{32} = \dfrac{25}{40} = \dfrac{30}{48}$

Write >, <, or = for ●. Use the lists of equivalent fractions on page 220.

1. $\frac{3}{4}$ ● $\frac{2}{3}$ 2. $\frac{1}{2}$ ● $\frac{5}{6}$ 3. $\frac{5}{8}$ ● $\frac{5}{6}$ 4. $\frac{7}{8}$ ● $\frac{3}{8}$

Use your own lists of equivalent fractions. Order from least to greatest.

5. $\frac{7}{10}, \frac{9}{10}$ 6. $\frac{3}{5}, \frac{8}{15}$ 7. $\frac{1}{6}, \frac{2}{9}, \frac{1}{3}$ 8. $\frac{3}{10}, \frac{2}{5}, \frac{4}{15}$

SKILLS PRACTICE

Write >, <, or = for ●. Use the lists of equivalent fractions on page 220.

1. $\frac{7}{12}$ ● $\frac{5}{12}$ 2. $\frac{5}{8}$ ● $\frac{3}{4}$ 3. $\frac{4}{6}$ ● $\frac{1}{2}$ 4. $\frac{9}{16}$ ● $\frac{6}{16}$

Use your own lists of equivalent fractions.

5. $\frac{2}{3}$ ● $\frac{9}{15}$ 6. $\frac{3}{8}$ ● $\frac{7}{8}$ 7. $\frac{5}{9}$ ● $\frac{2}{3}$ 8. $\frac{3}{4}$ ● $\frac{9}{10}$

Put in order from least to greatest.

9. $\frac{3}{5}, \frac{7}{8}, \frac{3}{4}$ 10. $\frac{5}{6}, \frac{3}{4}, \frac{7}{8}$ 11. $\frac{8}{9}, \frac{5}{6}, \frac{2}{3}$ ★12. $\frac{4}{7}, \frac{2}{5}, \frac{3}{4}, \frac{7}{8}$

PROBLEM SOLVING

13. Tom worked $\frac{1}{6}$ of a day. Barry worked $\frac{3}{8}$ of a day. Who worked longer?

14. Jan ran $\frac{3}{4}$ of a kilometer. Jean ran $\frac{4}{5}$ of a kilometer. Who ran the shorter distance?

THINK!

Comparing with Cross Products

Cross products can be used to compare fractions.

$\frac{3}{7} \times \frac{5}{9}$ The first cross product is $3 \times 9 = 27$. $27 < 35$
        The second cross product is $7 \times 5 = 35$.

First cross product $27 < 35$ Second cross product

First fraction $\rightarrow \frac{3}{7} < \frac{5}{9} \leftarrow$ Second fraction

Write >, <, or = for ●. Use cross products.

1. $\frac{4}{9}$ ● $\frac{4}{5}$ 2. $\frac{5}{6}$ ● $\frac{7}{8}$ 3. $\frac{3}{5}$ ● $\frac{6}{11}$ 4. $\frac{2}{3}$ ● $\frac{9}{14}$

Lowest Terms Fractions

A. What part of this set of stamps is bird stamps?

6 of the 8 stamps

$\frac{6}{8}$ of the set is bird stamps.

3 of the 4 sets of 2

$\frac{3}{4}$ of the set is bird stamps.

$\frac{6}{8} = \frac{3}{4}$ $6 = 3 \times 2$
$8 = 4 \times 2$

Since 2 is a factor of 6, and is also a factor of 8, 2 is called a **common factor** of 6 and 8.

> **To get an equivalent fraction, divide both numerator and denominator by a common factor.**

B. Divide to find a fraction equivalent to $\frac{12}{18}$.

2 is a common factor of 12 and 18.

$$\frac{12}{18} = \frac{12 \div 2}{18 \div 2} = \frac{6}{9}$$

But 6 and 9 have a common factor.

3 is a common factor of 6 and 9.

$$\frac{6}{9} = \frac{6 \div 3}{9 \div 3} = \frac{2}{3}$$

Both $\frac{2}{3}$ and $\frac{6}{9}$ are equivalent to $\frac{12}{18}$.

C. To find an equivalent fraction in *lowest terms* divide the numerator and denominator by their *greatest common factor.*

Find the lowest terms fraction for $\frac{16}{24}$.

Factors of 16: 1, 2, 4, 8, 16   Factors of 24: 1, 2, 3, 4, 6, 8, 12, 24

Greatest common factor of 16 and 24: 8

$$\frac{16}{24} = \frac{16 \div 8}{24 \div 8} = \frac{2}{3} \longleftarrow \text{lowest terms fraction}$$

TRY THESE

Divide to find an equivalent fraction.

1. $\dfrac{5}{15}$ 2. $\dfrac{6}{10}$ 3. $\dfrac{8}{16}$ 4. $\dfrac{9}{27}$ 5. $\dfrac{12}{14}$ 6. $\dfrac{8}{36}$

Find the greatest common factor of each pair of numbers.

7. 16 and 20   8. 6 and 15   9. 10 and 15   10. 14 and 21

Give the lowest terms fraction for each.

11. $\dfrac{16}{20}$ 12. $\dfrac{6}{15}$ 13. $\dfrac{10}{15}$ 14. $\dfrac{14}{21}$ 15. $\dfrac{4}{10}$ 16. $\dfrac{21}{14}$

SKILLS PRACTICE

Divide to find an equivalent fraction.

1. $\dfrac{9}{18}$ 2. $\dfrac{14}{21}$ 3. $\dfrac{4}{28}$ 4. $\dfrac{15}{25}$ 5. $\dfrac{15}{30}$ 6. $\dfrac{18}{27}$

Find the greatest common factor of each pair of numbers.

7. 15 and 24   8. 12 and 16   9. 9 and 12   10. 20 and 18

Give the lowest terms fraction for each.

11. $\dfrac{15}{24}$ 12. $\dfrac{12}{16}$ 13. $\dfrac{9}{12}$ 14. $\dfrac{16}{18}$ 15. $\dfrac{9}{15}$ 16. $\dfrac{12}{30}$

17. $\dfrac{15}{20}$ 18. $\dfrac{20}{24}$ 19. $\dfrac{4}{8}$ 20. $\dfrac{9}{13}$ 21. $\dfrac{5}{25}$ 22. $\dfrac{6}{18}$

23. $\dfrac{6}{9}$ 24. $\dfrac{14}{8}$ 25. $\dfrac{18}{24}$ 26. $\dfrac{24}{32}$ 27. $\dfrac{12}{20}$ ★28. $\dfrac{5}{7}$

PROBLEM SOLVING

Give the lowest terms fractions for answers.   **1 dozen = 12**

★29. Mr. Buono bought 1 dozen eggs. Of the dozen, 6 eggs were brown. What part of the eggs were brown?

★30. Mr. Buono used 4 of the eggs in an omelet. What part of the dozen eggs did he use?

MIXED REVIEW

Complete.

1. 9 kg = ■ g   2. 700 cm = ■ m   3. 5,000 mL = ■ L   4. 83 km = ■ m

Divide.

5. $9\overline{)495}$ 6. $18\overline{)7,436}$ 7. $95\overline{)3,565}$ 8. $5\overline{)1,785}$ 9. $80\overline{)16,080}$

Upside-down answers   11. $\dfrac{5}{8}$ 7. 3   1. $\dfrac{1}{2}$

223

Homework   page 433

Mixed and Standard Numerals

A. Individual boxes of cereal come in packs of 6. During one month, Dana used 17 boxes. How many packs did she use?

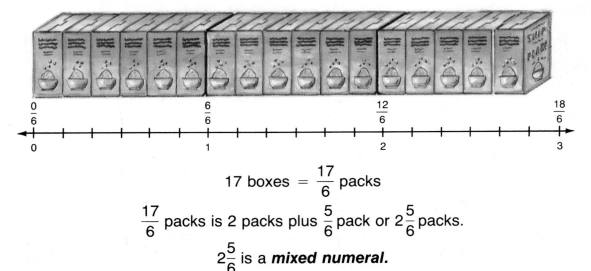

$$17 \text{ boxes} = \frac{17}{6} \text{ packs}$$

$\frac{17}{6}$ packs is 2 packs plus $\frac{5}{6}$ pack or $2\frac{5}{6}$ packs.

$2\frac{5}{6}$ is a ***mixed numeral.***

B. You can divide to find mixed or standard numerals.

$\frac{10}{3} = \blacksquare$

$$\begin{array}{r} 3\frac{1}{3} \\ 3\overline{)10} \\ \underline{9} \\ 1 \end{array}$$

Show the remainder as a fraction. The remainder is the numerator. The divisor is the denominator.

$$\frac{10}{3} = 3\frac{1}{3}$$

$\frac{12}{8} = \blacksquare$

$$\begin{array}{r} 1\frac{4}{8} \\ 8\overline{)12} \\ \underline{8} \\ 4 \end{array}$$

$\frac{4}{8}$ is not a lowest terms fraction.

$$\frac{12}{8} = 1\frac{4}{8} = 1\frac{1}{2}$$

$\frac{15}{5} = \blacksquare$

$$\begin{array}{r} 3 \\ 5\overline{)15} \\ \underline{15} \\ 0 \end{array}$$

$$\frac{15}{5} = 3$$

standard numeral

TRY THESE

Give a lowest terms mixed numeral or a standard numeral.

1. $\dfrac{7}{2}$ **2.** $\dfrac{6}{3}$ **3.** $\dfrac{15}{9}$ **4.** $\dfrac{0}{7}$ **5.** $\dfrac{5}{1}$ **6.** $\dfrac{14}{6}$

SKILLS PRACTICE

Give a lowest terms mixed numeral or a standard numeral.

1. $\dfrac{15}{6}$ **2.** $\dfrac{9}{2}$ **3.** $\dfrac{5}{3}$ **4.** $\dfrac{17}{5}$ **5.** $\dfrac{14}{4}$ **6.** $\dfrac{22}{8}$

7. $\dfrac{8}{2}$ **8.** $\dfrac{20}{3}$ **9.** $\dfrac{10}{1}$ **10.** $\dfrac{28}{7}$ **11.** $\dfrac{25}{10}$ **12.** $\dfrac{0}{9}$

13. $\dfrac{9}{4}$ **14.** $\dfrac{8}{5}$ **15.** $\dfrac{28}{16}$ **16.** $\dfrac{15}{8}$ **17.** $\dfrac{61}{9}$ **18.** $\dfrac{22}{4}$

19. $\dfrac{21}{9}$ **20.** $\dfrac{45}{5}$ **21.** $\dfrac{21}{16}$ **22.** $\dfrac{30}{10}$ **23.** $\dfrac{17}{10}$ **24.** $\dfrac{45}{6}$

25. $\dfrac{49}{8}$ **26.** $\dfrac{11}{6}$ **27.** $\dfrac{28}{10}$ **28.** $\dfrac{10}{7}$ **29.** $\dfrac{29}{12}$ **30.** $\dfrac{18}{6}$

31. $\dfrac{22}{12}$ **32.** $\dfrac{0}{11}$ **33.** $\dfrac{48}{15}$ **34.** $\dfrac{40}{8}$ ★**35.** $\dfrac{45}{45}$ ★**36.** $\dfrac{38}{1}$

PROBLEM SOLVING

37. Alicia collected 28 eggs. Each box holds 12 eggs. How many boxes of eggs did Alicia collect?

38. Alfred has 43 muffins. Each pack holds 8 muffins. How many packs does Alfred have?

THINK!

Logical Reasoning

$\dfrac{3}{4}$ hour is 45 minutes. How many minutes is:

1. $3\dfrac{3}{4}$ hours?   **2.** $4\dfrac{1}{4}$ hours?   **3.** $5\dfrac{1}{2}$ hours?

Addition: Common Denominators

A. Sarah filled $\frac{1}{5}$ of a pitcher with frozen orange juice and $\frac{3}{5}$ of the pitcher with water. What part of the pitcher did she fill in all?

$$\frac{1}{5} + \frac{3}{5} = \blacksquare$$

common denominator

$\frac{1}{5}$

$+\frac{3}{5}$

The picture shows that Sarah filled $\frac{4}{5}$ of the pitcher.

$$\frac{1}{5} + \frac{3}{5} = \frac{4}{5}$$

1 + 3

same denominator

> To add with fractions that have a common denominator:
> Add the numerators.
> Use the same denominator.

B. When you add, your sum may be a fraction, a mixed numeral, or a standard numeral.

$$\begin{array}{r} \frac{5}{8} \\ +\frac{1}{8} \\ \hline \frac{6}{8} = \frac{3}{4} \end{array}$$

$$\begin{array}{r} \frac{7}{9} \\ +\frac{5}{9} \\ \hline \frac{12}{9} = 1\frac{3}{9} = 1\frac{1}{3} \end{array}$$

$$\begin{array}{r} \frac{3}{4} \\ +\frac{5}{4} \\ \hline \frac{8}{4} = 2 \end{array}$$

Find the lowest terms fraction.

TRY THESE

Add. Give your answer in lowest terms.

1. $\frac{3}{7} + \frac{2}{7} = \blacksquare$

2. $\frac{4}{5} + \frac{3}{5} = \blacksquare$

3. $\frac{1}{2} + \frac{3}{2} = \blacksquare$

4. $\frac{3}{6} + \frac{1}{6} = \blacksquare$

5. $\frac{3}{4} + \frac{1}{4} = \blacksquare$

6. $\frac{7}{8} + \frac{6}{8} = \blacksquare$

7. $\frac{9}{10} + \frac{7}{10} = \blacksquare$

8. $\frac{5}{6} + \frac{7}{6} = \blacksquare$

9. $\frac{8}{9} + \frac{4}{9} = \blacksquare$

SKILLS PRACTICE

Add. Give your answer in lowest terms.

1. $\dfrac{5}{16} + \dfrac{9}{16} = $ ■

2. $\dfrac{3}{7} + \dfrac{4}{7} = $ ■

3. $\dfrac{6}{10} + \dfrac{7}{10} = $ ■

4. $\dfrac{3}{12} + \dfrac{8}{12} = $ ■

5. $\dfrac{4}{9} + \dfrac{2}{9} = $ ■

6. $\dfrac{8}{16} + \dfrac{7}{16} = $ ■

7. $\dfrac{2}{6} + \dfrac{3}{6} = $ ■

8. $\dfrac{7}{11} + \dfrac{3}{11} = $ ■

9. $\dfrac{5}{12} + \dfrac{1}{12} = $ ■

10. $\dfrac{7}{8} + \dfrac{7}{8} = $ ■

11. $\dfrac{9}{14} + \dfrac{12}{14} = $ ■

12. $\dfrac{9}{5} + \dfrac{11}{5} = $ ■

13. $\begin{array}{r} \frac{2}{9} \\ +\frac{5}{9} \\ \hline \end{array}$

14. $\begin{array}{r} \frac{5}{10} \\ +\frac{3}{10} \\ \hline \end{array}$

15. $\begin{array}{r} \frac{7}{4} \\ +\frac{5}{4} \\ \hline \end{array}$

16. $\begin{array}{r} \frac{5}{8} \\ +\frac{2}{8} \\ \hline \end{array}$

17. $\begin{array}{r} \frac{4}{5} \\ +\frac{7}{5} \\ \hline \end{array}$

18. $\begin{array}{r} \frac{9}{16} \\ +\frac{3}{16} \\ \hline \end{array}$

PROBLEM SOLVING

19. Inez mowed $\dfrac{3}{12}$ of the lawn before it started to rain. Later, she mowed $\dfrac{7}{12}$ of the lawn. What part of the lawn did she mow in all?

20. Matt raked $\dfrac{3}{7}$ of the lawn before lunch and an additional $\dfrac{3}{7}$ of the lawn after lunch. What part of the lawn did he rake in all?

★21. Donna used $\dfrac{1}{6}$ of a can of yellow paint, $\dfrac{5}{6}$ of a can of blue paint, and $\dfrac{3}{6}$ of a can of green paint. How many cans of paint did she use in all?

Mental Math

John had $24. He gave $\dfrac{1}{3}$ of his money to Jane and $\dfrac{1}{2}$ of what was left to Jan. How much money did each person have then?

Subtraction: Common Denominators

A. Before Mr. Sarti drove to work, the gas tank in his car was $\frac{5}{8}$ full. When he returned home, the tank was $\frac{2}{8}$ full. What part of a tank of gas did Mr. Sarti use?

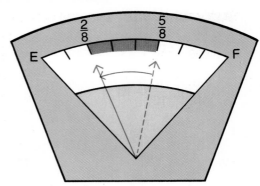

$$\frac{5}{8} - \frac{2}{8} = \blacksquare$$

common denominator

The picture shows that Mr. Sarti used $\frac{3}{8}$ of a tank of gas.

$$\frac{5}{8} - \frac{2}{8} = \frac{3}{8} \quad \cdots \quad 5 - 2$$

same denominator

> To subtract with fractions that have a common denominator:
> Subtract the numerators.
> Use the same denominator.

B. When you subtract, your difference may be a fraction, a mixed numeral, or a standard numeral.

$$\begin{array}{r} \frac{8}{9} \\ -\frac{2}{9} \\ \hline \frac{6}{9} = \frac{2}{3} \end{array} \qquad \begin{array}{r} \frac{11}{6} \\ -\frac{3}{6} \\ \hline \frac{8}{6} = 1\frac{2}{6} = 1\frac{1}{3} \end{array} \qquad \begin{array}{r} \frac{9}{2} \\ -\frac{3}{2} \\ \hline \frac{6}{2} = 3 \end{array}$$

Use a lowest terms fraction.

TRY THESE

Subtract. Give your answer in lowest terms.

1. $\frac{4}{5} - \frac{1}{5} = \blacksquare$

2. $\frac{7}{8} - \frac{5}{8} = \blacksquare$

3. $\frac{9}{4} - \frac{5}{4} = \blacksquare$

4. $\frac{11}{6} - \frac{4}{6} = \blacksquare$

5. $\frac{9}{7} - \frac{6}{7} = \blacksquare$

6. $\frac{19}{10} - \frac{7}{10} = \blacksquare$

7. $\frac{10}{9} - \frac{4}{9} = \blacksquare$

8. $\frac{14}{3} - \frac{5}{3} = \blacksquare$

9. $\frac{17}{12} - \frac{2}{12} = \blacksquare$

SKILLS PRACTICE

Subtract. Give your answer in lowest terms.

1. $\dfrac{13}{12} - \dfrac{5}{12} = $ ■

2. $\dfrac{9}{6} - \dfrac{4}{6} = $ ■

3. $\dfrac{15}{7} - \dfrac{5}{7} = $ ■

4. $\dfrac{8}{6} - \dfrac{5}{6} = $ ■

5. $\dfrac{3}{4} - \dfrac{2}{4} = $ ■

6. $\dfrac{23}{12} - \dfrac{5}{12} = $ ■

7. $\dfrac{7}{9} - \dfrac{7}{9} = $ ■

8. $\dfrac{15}{11} - \dfrac{2}{11} = $ ■

9. $\dfrac{13}{8} - \dfrac{3}{8} = $ ■

10. $\dfrac{10}{3}$
$-\dfrac{5}{3}$

11. $\dfrac{17}{15}$
$-\dfrac{4}{15}$

12. $\dfrac{11}{8}$
$-\dfrac{7}{8}$

13. $\dfrac{9}{4}$
$-\dfrac{1}{4}$

14. $\dfrac{9}{10}$
$-\dfrac{8}{10}$

15. $\dfrac{19}{9}$
$-\dfrac{4}{9}$

16. $\dfrac{15}{16}$
$-\dfrac{3}{16}$

17. $\dfrac{11}{8}$
$-\dfrac{6}{8}$

18. $\dfrac{23}{9}$
$-\dfrac{4}{9}$

19. $\dfrac{19}{15}$
$-\dfrac{7}{15}$

20. $\dfrac{12}{12}$
$-\dfrac{5}{12}$

21. $\dfrac{27}{10}$
$-\dfrac{3}{10}$

PROBLEM SOLVING

22. Joel jogged $\dfrac{5}{4}$ miles. Then he walked $\dfrac{1}{4}$ mile. How much farther did Joel jog than he walked?

23. David jogged $\dfrac{6}{11}$ mile. Richard jogged $\dfrac{19}{11}$ miles. How much farther did Richard jog than David?

24. Justine jogged $\dfrac{3}{8}$ mile in the morning and $\dfrac{4}{8}$ mile that evening. How far did she jog in all?

★25. Lois wants to jog 1 mile. She has already jogged $\dfrac{3}{5}$ mile. How much farther must she jog?

THINK!

Patterns

Pretend you have a whole loaf of bread and you give $\dfrac{1}{2}$ of it to a friend. You then give $\dfrac{1}{2}$ of what you have left to another friend. You continue to give away $\dfrac{1}{2}$ of what you have left each time. How many friends would you need to give away the whole loaf? (Draw pictures to help.)

Problem Solving

Using Fractions

A. Judy Sullivan is wiring two lamps for her den. She needs $\frac{5}{12}$ yard of wire for one and $\frac{11}{12}$ yard of wire for the other. How much wire does she need in all? Use a lowest terms fraction.

Add.

$$\frac{5}{12} + \frac{11}{12} = \frac{16}{12} = 1\frac{4}{12} = 1\frac{1}{3}$$

Judy needs $1\frac{1}{3}$ yards of wire.

B. Frank Sullivan had $\frac{3}{4}$ can of paint. He used $\frac{1}{4}$ can to paint a chair. How much paint did he have left?

Subtract.

$$\frac{3}{4} - \frac{1}{4} = \frac{2}{4} = \frac{1}{2}$$

Frank had $\frac{1}{2}$ can of paint left.

C. Mr. Sullivan used $\frac{4}{5}$ of a jar of wood stain on a cabinet. He used $\frac{2}{3}$ of a jar of the wood stain on a table. On which piece of furniture did he use more of the wood stain?

Compare.

cabinet: $\frac{4}{5} = \frac{12}{15}$

table: $\frac{2}{3} = \frac{10}{15}$ $\qquad \frac{12}{15} > \frac{10}{15}$ so $\frac{4}{5} > \frac{2}{3}$

He used more wood stain on the cabinet.

TRY THESE

1. Ms. Becker is rewiring a lamp. She works on the lamp for $\frac{1}{4}$ hour in the morning and $\frac{3}{4}$ hour in the afternoon. How long does she work in all?

2. Ms. Becker used $\frac{7}{8}$ yard of wire in the lamp base. She used $\frac{2}{3}$ yard of wire in the neck of the lamp. In which part did she use more wire?

PROBLEM SOLVING PRACTICE

1. Ron used two pieces of pipe in the kitchen. One piece was $\frac{7}{12}$ foot and the other was $\frac{11}{12}$ foot. How much pipe did he use in all?

2. Fran spent $\frac{5}{6}$ hour painting a desk in the morning. She spent $\frac{4}{6}$ hour painting in the afternoon. How much time did she spend in all?

3. It is $\frac{7}{10}$ mile from Larry's house to Hank's Hardware Haven. It is $\frac{2}{3}$ mile from Larry's house to Phil's Paint Place. Which store is closer to Larry's house?

4. Beth had a piece of wood that was $\frac{7}{8}$ inch thick. She had a nail that was $\frac{3}{8}$ inch long. How much thicker is the wood than the length of the nail?

5. Mr. Ryan bought $\frac{3}{4}$ foot of copper tubing and $\frac{5}{4}$ foot of aluminum tubing. How much longer is the aluminum tubing than the copper?

6. Vida and her brother James each wallpapered $\frac{3}{8}$ of a room. How much of the room did they wallpaper in all?

★7. The shelf over the sink is $\frac{5}{9}$ yard long. The shelf over the refrigerator is $\frac{2}{3}$ yard long. The shelf over the oven is $\frac{9}{12}$ yard long. Which shelf is the longest?

★8. Susan put tiles on $\frac{1}{5}$ of the floor. Jason put tiles on $\frac{2}{5}$ of the floor. How much more of the floor needs to be tiled?

ON YOUR OWN

Use the information about the three pieces of pipe in the drawing at the right. Make up two problems of your own.

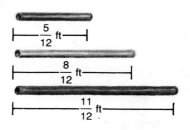

$\frac{5}{12}$ ft

$\frac{8}{12}$ ft

$\frac{11}{12}$ ft

Least Common Denominator

Sherlock said that $\frac{3}{4}$ of all mysteries are solved.

Watson said that $\frac{5}{6}$ of all mysteries are solved.

Who thinks more mysteries are solved?

A. Find fractions equivalent to $\frac{3}{4}$ and $\frac{5}{6}$ that have a common denominator. List multiples of 4 and 6.

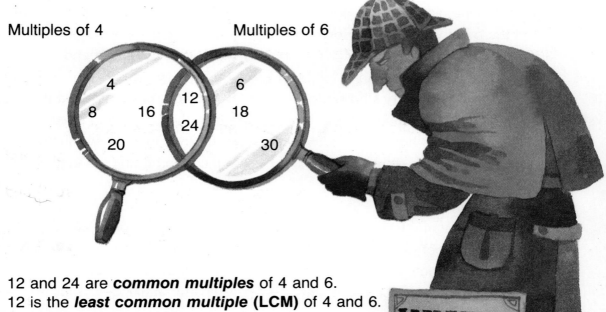

Multiples of 4   Multiples of 6

4   8   16   12   24   6   18   20   30

12 and 24 are **common multiples** of 4 and 6.
12 is the **least common multiple (LCM)** of 4 and 6.
Use the least common multiple for the
least common denominator (LCD).

$\frac{3}{4} = \frac{\blacksquare}{12}$ 4 × 3 $\frac{5}{6} = \frac{\blacksquare}{12}$ 6 × 2

$\frac{3}{4} = \frac{3 \times 3}{4 \times 3} = \frac{9}{12}$ $\frac{5}{6} = \frac{5 \times 2}{6 \times 2} = \frac{10}{12}$

WANTED
LCM
Known as
LCD

B. Compare $\frac{3}{4}$ and $\frac{5}{6}$.

$\frac{3}{4} = \frac{9}{12}$ $\frac{5}{6} = \frac{10}{12}$ $\frac{10}{12} > \frac{9}{12}$ so $\frac{5}{6} > \frac{3}{4}$

It's elementary. Watson thinks more mysteries are solved.

Find the least common multiple of each pair of numbers.

1. 6 and 9   **2.** 6 and 10   **3.** 4 and 5   **4.** 3 and 12   **5.** 3 and 8

Find equivalent fractions with the least common denominator for:

6. $\frac{5}{6}$ and $\frac{7}{9}$ **7.** $\frac{1}{6}$ and $\frac{3}{10}$ **8.** $\frac{3}{4}$ and $\frac{3}{5}$ **9.** $\frac{2}{3}$ and $\frac{3}{7}$ **10.** $\frac{1}{3}$ and $\frac{5}{8}$

Write $<$, $>$, or $=$ for ●.

11. $\frac{5}{6}$ ● $\frac{7}{9}$ **12.** $\frac{1}{6}$ ● $\frac{3}{10}$ **13.** $\frac{3}{4}$ ● $\frac{3}{5}$ **14.** $\frac{2}{3}$ ● $\frac{7}{12}$ **15.** $\frac{1}{3}$ ● $\frac{5}{8}$

SKILLS PRACTICE

Find the least common multiple of each pair of numbers.

1. 6 and 8   **2.** 3 and 4   **3.** 2 and 10   **4.** 5 and 6   **5.** 8 and 12

Find equivalent fractions with the least common denominator for:

6. $\frac{5}{6}$ and $\frac{5}{8}$ **7.** $\frac{2}{3}$ and $\frac{3}{4}$ **8.** $\frac{1}{2}$ and $\frac{3}{7}$ **9.** $\frac{3}{5}$ and $\frac{5}{6}$ **10.** $\frac{5}{8}$ and $\frac{7}{12}$

11. $\frac{1}{2}$ and $\frac{2}{3}$ **12.** $\frac{5}{6}$ and $\frac{7}{10}$ **13.** $\frac{1}{3}$ and $\frac{4}{5}$ **14.** $\frac{1}{10}$ and $\frac{2}{3}$ **15.** $\frac{1}{4}$ and $\frac{2}{5}$

Write $>$, $<$, or $=$ for ●.

16. $\frac{5}{6}$ ● $\frac{5}{8}$ **17.** $\frac{2}{3}$ ● $\frac{3}{4}$ **18.** $\frac{1}{2}$ ● $\frac{3}{10}$ **19.** $\frac{3}{5}$ ● $\frac{5}{6}$ **20.** $\frac{5}{8}$ ● $\frac{7}{12}$

21. $\frac{5}{11}$ ● $\frac{8}{11}$ **22.** $\frac{2}{9}$ ● $\frac{1}{6}$ **23.** $\frac{8}{10}$ ● $\frac{4}{5}$ ★**24.** $2\frac{1}{6}$ ● $3\frac{1}{9}$ ★**25.** $4\frac{1}{2}$ ● $4\frac{1}{5}$

THINK!

Mental Math

Here is a shortcut method for finding least common denominators.
- Look at the denominators.
- Find the multiples of the larger *in order*.
- Test each to see if it is a multiple of the smaller also. If it is, you have the least common denominator.

$\frac{3}{8}$ and $\frac{5}{6}$

Test: Multiple of 6?

$8 \times 1 = 8$ No
$8 \times 2 = 16$ No
$8 \times 3 = 24$ Yes

6×4

LCD = 24

Addition: Different Denominators

A. On Friday Jon papered $\frac{1}{6}$ of his room. On Saturday he papered $\frac{3}{5}$ of it. What part of his room did Jon paper?

The denominators are different.

Find the least common denominator.

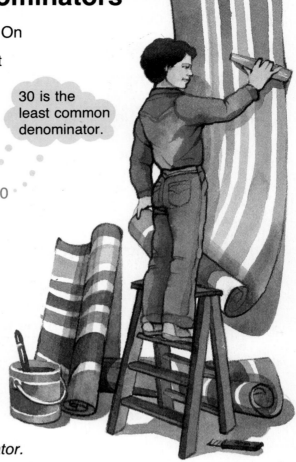

30 is the least common denominator.

   Multiples of 6: 6, 12, 18, 24, 30
   Multiples of 5: 5, 10, 15, 20, 25, 30

Write equivalent fractions using the least common denominator, 30.

Add.
$$\frac{1}{6} + \frac{3}{5} = \blacksquare$$
$$\downarrow \qquad \downarrow$$
$$\frac{5}{30} + \frac{18}{30} = \frac{23}{30}$$

Jon papered $\frac{23}{30}$ of his room.

B. Add. Use the *least common denominator.*
Write the answer in lowest terms.

$$\frac{1}{2} \rightarrow \frac{3}{6}$$
$$+\frac{1}{6} \rightarrow +\frac{1}{6}$$
$$\frac{4}{6} = \frac{2}{3}$$

The LCD is one of the given denominators.

$$\frac{7}{8} \rightarrow \frac{7}{8}$$
$$+\frac{3}{4} \rightarrow +\frac{6}{8}$$
$$\frac{13}{8} = 1\frac{5}{8}$$

The LCD is one of the given denominators.

$$\frac{3}{4} \rightarrow \frac{9}{12}$$
$$+\frac{7}{3} \rightarrow +\frac{28}{12}$$
$$\frac{37}{12} = 3\frac{1}{12}$$

TRY THESE

Add.

1. $\frac{1}{5} + \frac{3}{10} = \blacksquare$

2. $\frac{3}{4} + \frac{1}{6} = \blacksquare$

3. $\frac{7}{12} + \frac{2}{3} = \blacksquare$

4. $\frac{3}{4} + \frac{5}{8} = \blacksquare$

5. $\frac{8}{9} + \frac{4}{9} = \blacksquare$

6. $\frac{2}{9} + \frac{1}{6} = \blacksquare$

7. $\frac{2}{3} + \frac{3}{4} = \blacksquare$

8. $\frac{1}{2} + \frac{9}{10} = \blacksquare$

SKILLS PRACTICE

Add.

1. $\dfrac{3}{8} + \dfrac{1}{6} = \blacksquare$ 2. $\dfrac{2}{3} + \dfrac{1}{5} = \blacksquare$ 3. $\dfrac{1}{6} + \dfrac{7}{15} = \blacksquare$ 4. $\dfrac{3}{4} + \dfrac{4}{5} = \blacksquare$

5. $\dfrac{5}{12} + \dfrac{3}{8} = \blacksquare$ 6. $\dfrac{5}{6} + \dfrac{7}{12} = \blacksquare$ 7. $\dfrac{4}{9} + \dfrac{10}{18} = \blacksquare$ 8. $\dfrac{3}{4} + \dfrac{5}{6} = \blacksquare$

9. $\dfrac{3}{7} + \dfrac{1}{2} = \blacksquare$ 10. $\dfrac{4}{5} + \dfrac{4}{15} = \blacksquare$ 11. $\dfrac{5}{12} + \dfrac{7}{12} = \blacksquare$ 12. $\dfrac{7}{10} + \dfrac{3}{8} = \blacksquare$

13. $\dfrac{3}{4}$ 14. $\dfrac{1}{6}$ 15. $\dfrac{1}{9}$ 16. $\dfrac{3}{4}$ 17. $\dfrac{1}{6}$ 18. $\dfrac{5}{8}$
    $+\dfrac{5}{7}$ $+\dfrac{3}{10}$ $+\dfrac{5}{6}$ $+\dfrac{3}{20}$ $+\dfrac{3}{5}$ $+\dfrac{5}{6}$

19. $\dfrac{5}{8}$ 20. $\dfrac{9}{10}$ 21. $\dfrac{7}{8}$ 22. $\dfrac{1}{4}$ 23. $\dfrac{3}{10}$ 24. $\dfrac{5}{12}$
    $+\dfrac{1}{3}$ $+\dfrac{1}{4}$ $+\dfrac{9}{8}$ $+\dfrac{2}{3}$ $+\dfrac{4}{15}$ $+\dfrac{4}{9}$

PROBLEM SOLVING

25. Kate typed $\dfrac{3}{4}$ of her report before dinner and $\dfrac{1}{6}$ of her report after dinner. What part of her report had she typed?

26. Josh completed $\dfrac{1}{4}$ of his science project at home and $\dfrac{3}{10}$ of it at school. What part of his project had he completed?

27. Mel had to do $\dfrac{3}{5}$ page of math in class and $\dfrac{13}{15}$ page of math for homework. How many pages of math did he do?

★28. Joan read $\dfrac{1}{2}$ of a history book last week. She read another history book this week. How many history books did she read in all?

THINK!

Logical Reasoning

Marge had math homework on $\dfrac{2}{3}$ of the nights in September. She had English homework on $\dfrac{3}{5}$ of the nights in September. Can you tell how many nights she had math homework? English homework? Can you tell how many nights she had both?

SEPTEMBER

S	M	T	W	T	F	S
	1	2	3	4	5	6
7	8	9	10	11	12	13
14	15	16	17	18	19	20
21	22	23	24	25	26	27
28	29	30				

Subtraction: Different Denominators

A. Aretha bought $\frac{4}{5}$ yard of fabric.

She used $\frac{2}{3}$ yard to make a scarf.

How much fabric did Aretha have left?

The denominators are different.
Find the least common denominator.

15 is the least common denominator.

Multiples of 5: 5, 10, 15
Multiples of 3: 3, 6, 9, 12, 15

Write equivalent fractions using the
least common denominator, 15.

Subtract.

$$\frac{4}{5} - \frac{2}{3} = \blacksquare$$

$$\frac{12}{15} - \frac{10}{15} = \frac{2}{15}$$

Aretha had $\frac{2}{15}$ yard of fabric left.

B. Subtract. Use the least common denominator.
Write the answer as a lowest terms fraction.

$$\frac{5}{6} \rightarrow \frac{5}{6}$$
$$-\frac{1}{3} \rightarrow -\frac{2}{6}$$
$$\frac{3}{6} = \frac{1}{2}$$

The LCD is one of the given denominators.

$$\frac{11}{4} \rightarrow \frac{22}{8}$$
$$-\frac{7}{8} \rightarrow -\frac{7}{8}$$
$$\frac{15}{8} = 1\frac{7}{8}$$

The LCD is one of the given denominators.

$$\frac{9}{5} \rightarrow \frac{36}{20}$$
$$-\frac{3}{4} \rightarrow -\frac{15}{20}$$
$$\frac{21}{20} = 1\frac{1}{20}$$

TRY THESE

Subtract.

1. $\frac{11}{12} - \frac{1}{2} = \blacksquare$

2. $\frac{5}{6} - \frac{1}{4} = \blacksquare$

3. $\frac{11}{12} - \frac{5}{8} = \blacksquare$

4. $\frac{8}{5} - \frac{2}{10} = \blacksquare$

5. $\frac{3}{2} - \frac{2}{5} = \blacksquare$

6. $\frac{7}{6} - \frac{3}{10} = \blacksquare$

7. $\frac{13}{10} - \frac{7}{10} = \blacksquare$

8. $\frac{17}{12} - \frac{5}{8} = \blacksquare$

SKILLS PRACTICE

Subtract.

1. $\dfrac{5}{6} - \dfrac{4}{6} = $ █

2. $\dfrac{7}{8} - \dfrac{5}{6} = $ █

3. $\dfrac{3}{5} - \dfrac{1}{2} = $ █

4. $\dfrac{3}{10} - \dfrac{1}{4} = $ █

5. $\dfrac{8}{3} - \dfrac{7}{5} = $ █

6. $\dfrac{5}{12} - \dfrac{1}{4} = $ █

7. $\dfrac{7}{4} - \dfrac{1}{6} = $ █

8. $\dfrac{11}{12} - \dfrac{7}{12} = $ █

9. $\begin{array}{r} \dfrac{7}{6} \\ -\dfrac{2}{15} \\ \hline \end{array}$

10. $\begin{array}{r} \dfrac{2}{3} \\ -\dfrac{1}{2} \\ \hline \end{array}$

11. $\begin{array}{r} \dfrac{7}{8} \\ -\dfrac{5}{12} \\ \hline \end{array}$

12. $\begin{array}{r} \dfrac{7}{10} \\ -\dfrac{7}{10} \\ \hline \end{array}$

13. $\begin{array}{r} \dfrac{9}{10} \\ -\dfrac{2}{3} \\ \hline \end{array}$

14. $\begin{array}{r} \dfrac{11}{9} \\ -\dfrac{1}{12} \\ \hline \end{array}$

Add or subtract.

15. $\begin{array}{r} \dfrac{5}{6} \\ +\dfrac{7}{8} \\ \hline \end{array}$

16. $\begin{array}{r} \dfrac{7}{15} \\ +\dfrac{1}{3} \\ \hline \end{array}$

17. $\begin{array}{r} \dfrac{3}{4} \\ -\dfrac{2}{3} \\ \hline \end{array}$

18. $\begin{array}{r} \dfrac{9}{10} \\ -\dfrac{3}{4} \\ \hline \end{array}$

19. $\begin{array}{r} \dfrac{1}{2} \\ +\dfrac{5}{7} \\ \hline \end{array}$

20. $\begin{array}{r} \dfrac{11}{6} \\ -\dfrac{3}{10} \\ \hline \end{array}$

PROBLEM SOLVING

21. Denis bought $\dfrac{2}{5}$ yard of red ribbon and $\dfrac{3}{4}$ yard of blue ribbon. How much less red ribbon than blue ribbon did he buy?

22. Katrinka bought $\dfrac{9}{10}$ yard of material. She used $\dfrac{4}{5}$ yard to make a vest. How much material did she have left?

23. Maria used $\dfrac{7}{9}$ yard of green ribbon and $\dfrac{5}{12}$ yard of yellow ribbon. How much more green ribbon than yellow ribbon did she use?

★24. Barbara needed $\dfrac{1}{6}$ yard of lace to trim a collar. She needed $\dfrac{8}{9}$ yard to trim cuffs. How much lace did she need? Should she buy more or less than 1 yard?

THINK!

Patterns

Richard cut a piece of cloth in half. Then he cut one of the halves in half again. If he continues doing this, how many cuts will he make before getting a piece of cloth that is $\dfrac{1}{64}$ the size of the original?

Problem Solving Strategy

Find a Pattern

In Tech Town, each computer has one connecting line to each of the other computers. If there are 5 computers, how many connecting lines are there?

Start with easier numbers. Put the results in a table and try to find a pattern.

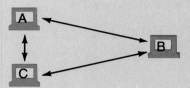

If there were only 1 computer, A, there would be 0 lines.

If there were 2 computers, A and B, there would be just 1 line.

If there were 3 computers, A, B, and C, there would be 3 lines.

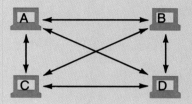

If there were 4 computers, A, B, C, and D, there would be 6 lines.

Make a table of the results.

First 1 line was added, then 2, then 3. Continue the pattern. For 5 computers, add 4 to the last answer.

$$6 + 4 = 10$$

If there are 5 computers, there are 10 connecting lines.

Number of Computers	Number of Lines
1	0 } Add 1
2	1 } Add 2
3	3 } Add 3
4	6
5	?

Solve.

1. How many connecting lines would there be for 7 computers?

2. How many connecting lines would there be for 11 computers?

3. How many computers would there be if there were 36 connecting lines?

4. An electrician counted 93 connections for 14 computers. Was the count correct? If not, what should it be?

Problem Solving Project

Fraction Nomographs

You can use a *nomograph* to add fractions.

Find $\frac{1}{2} + \frac{3}{8}$ using the nomograph shown at the right.

Place a ruler or sheet of paper so that the edge crosses $\frac{1}{2}$ on line A and $\frac{3}{8}$ on line B. Notice that the ruler crosses line C at the sum.

$$\frac{1}{2} + \frac{3}{8} = \frac{7}{8}$$

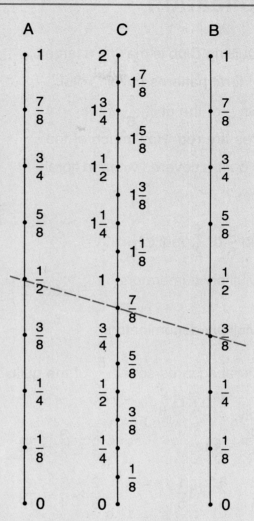

Use the nomograph to find each sum.

1. $\frac{1}{4} + \frac{1}{8}$

2. $\frac{3}{8} + \frac{5}{8}$

3. $\frac{3}{4} + \frac{1}{2}$

4. $\frac{7}{8} + \frac{3}{4}$

5. $\frac{1}{8} + \frac{3}{4}$

6. $\frac{5}{8} + \frac{7}{8}$

7. $\frac{1}{2} + \frac{5}{8}$

8. $\frac{3}{4} + \frac{3}{4}$

ON YOUR OWN

Construct your own nomograph. Draw three lines, each 6 inches long and 1 inch apart. Label them A, C, and B as above. Divide A and B into 6 equal parts and mark off 0, $\frac{1}{6}$, $\frac{1}{3}$, $\frac{1}{2}$, $\frac{2}{3}$, 1 on each. Divide line C into twelve equal parts and mark off 0, $\frac{1}{6}$, $\frac{1}{3}$, $\frac{1}{2}$, $\frac{2}{3}$, $\frac{5}{6}$, 1, $1\frac{1}{6}$, $1\frac{1}{3}$, $1\frac{1}{2}$, $1\frac{2}{3}$, $1\frac{5}{6}$, 2. Try some addition problems on your nomograph.

Use this idea to construct other nomographs.

239

Multiplication

A. The Quilting Club is making a large quilt. Floral patterns cover $\frac{1}{2}$ of it. On this $\frac{1}{2}$ of the quilt, $\frac{5}{6}$ of the squares are red. How much of the entire quilt is covered with red floral squares?

To find $\frac{5}{6}$ of $\frac{1}{2}$, multiply.

Multiply numerators. $\qquad \frac{5}{6} \times \frac{1}{2} = \frac{5}{}$

Multiply denominators. $\qquad \frac{5}{6} \times \frac{1}{2} = \frac{5}{12}$

Red floral squares cover $\frac{5}{12}$ of the quilt.

B. Multiply.

$3 \times \dfrac{2}{5} = \blacksquare$
$\downarrow$
$\dfrac{3}{1} \times \dfrac{2}{5} = \dfrac{6}{5} = 1\dfrac{1}{5}$

$\dfrac{2}{3} \times \dfrac{3}{4} = \blacksquare$

$\dfrac{2}{3} \times \dfrac{3}{4} = \dfrac{6}{12} = \dfrac{1}{2}$

$\dfrac{7}{8} \times \dfrac{5}{2} = \blacksquare$

$\dfrac{7}{8} \times \dfrac{5}{2} = \dfrac{35}{16} = 2\dfrac{3}{16}$

TRY THESE

Copy and complete.

1. $\dfrac{1}{2} \times \dfrac{3}{5} = \dfrac{\blacksquare \times \blacksquare}{2 \times 5} = \dfrac{\blacksquare}{10}$

2. $\dfrac{3}{4} \times \dfrac{5}{8} = \dfrac{3 \times 5}{\blacksquare \times \blacksquare} = \dfrac{15}{\blacksquare}$

3. $\dfrac{2}{3} \times \dfrac{5}{6} = \dfrac{\blacksquare \times \blacksquare}{3 \times 6} = \dfrac{\blacksquare}{18} = \dfrac{\blacksquare}{9}$

4. $\dfrac{3}{4} \times \dfrac{4}{5} = \dfrac{3 \times 4}{\blacksquare \times \blacksquare} = \dfrac{12}{\blacksquare} = \dfrac{3}{\blacksquare}$

5. $6 \times \dfrac{3}{5} = \dfrac{\blacksquare \times \blacksquare}{1 \times 5} = \dfrac{\blacksquare}{5} = 3\dfrac{\blacksquare}{5}$

6. $\dfrac{5}{2} \times 4 = \dfrac{5 \times 4}{\blacksquare \times \blacksquare} = \dfrac{20}{\blacksquare} = \blacksquare$

SKILLS PRACTICE

Multiply.

1. $\dfrac{2}{5} \times \dfrac{2}{3} = $ ■

2. $\dfrac{1}{2} \times \dfrac{3}{4} = $ ■

3. $\dfrac{5}{6} \times \dfrac{1}{3} = $ ■

4. $4 \times \dfrac{2}{5} = $ ■

5. $\dfrac{2}{3} \times 3 = $ ■

6. $\dfrac{3}{4} \times \dfrac{3}{4} = $ ■

7. $\dfrac{3}{4} \times \dfrac{1}{6} = $ ■

8. $\dfrac{5}{8} \times \dfrac{3}{2} = $ ■

9. $\dfrac{7}{10} \times \dfrac{2}{3} = $ ■

10. $5 \times \dfrac{2}{5} = $ ■

11. $\dfrac{3}{4} \times \dfrac{3}{10} = $ ■

12. $\dfrac{1}{8} \times \dfrac{4}{5} = $ ■

13. $\dfrac{5}{6} \times \dfrac{4}{5} = $ ■

14. $\dfrac{1}{2} \times \dfrac{7}{9} = $ ■

15. $\dfrac{1}{6} \times 7 = $ ■

16. $\dfrac{2}{3} \times \dfrac{7}{8} = $ ■

17. $\dfrac{5}{7} \times \dfrac{2}{3} = $ ■

18. $\dfrac{3}{8} \times \dfrac{5}{8} = $ ■

19. $\dfrac{7}{6} \times \dfrac{3}{2} = $ ■

20. $\dfrac{7}{8} \times \dfrac{8}{7} = $ ■

21. $2 \times \dfrac{5}{6} = $ ■

22. $\dfrac{9}{5} \times \dfrac{5}{4} = $ ■

23. $\dfrac{8}{9} \times 4 = $ ■

24. $\dfrac{8}{15} \times \dfrac{3}{4} = $ ■

PROBLEM SOLVING

25. David spends $\dfrac{2}{3}$ hour at lunch each day. How many hours does he spend at lunch in 5 days? How many hours does he spend at lunch in 10 days?

26. Brown tiles and white tiles cover $\dfrac{4}{5}$ of the cafeteria floor. Of these, $\dfrac{3}{4}$ are brown. What part of the cafeteria floor is covered with brown tiles?

★27. Each day, Luke eats $\dfrac{1}{2}$ cup of cottage cheese for breakfast and $\dfrac{3}{4}$ cup for lunch. How much cottage cheese does he eat in a week?

★28. Mai had $\dfrac{3}{4}$ quart of milk. She used $\dfrac{2}{3}$ of the milk. How much milk did she use? How much milk did she have left?

THINK!

A Multiplication Pattern

Multiply.

1. $\dfrac{3}{7} \times \dfrac{7}{3} = $ ■

2. $\dfrac{5}{8} \times \dfrac{8}{5} = $ ■

3. $\dfrac{17}{9} \times \dfrac{9}{17} = $ ■

4. $\dfrac{1}{6} \times \dfrac{6}{1} = $ ■

What do you notice?

Finding Parts of Numbers

A. There are 15 ivy plants in the greenhouse. $\frac{1}{3}$ belong to Mr. O'Brien. How many plants belong to Mr. O'Brien?

To find $\frac{1}{3}$ of a number you can divide the number by 3.

$$15 \div 3 = 5$$

To find $\frac{1}{3}$ of a number you can multiply the number by $\frac{1}{3}$.

$$\frac{15}{1} \times \frac{1}{3} = \frac{15}{3} = 5$$

Mr. O'Brien has 5 ivy plants.

B. There are 20 tulip plants in the greenhouse. $\frac{3}{4}$ of them belong to Mrs. Stein. How many belong to Mrs. Stein?

To find $\frac{3}{4}$ of a number you can divide the number by 4 and then multiply by 3.

$$20 \div 4 = 5$$
$$5 \times 3 = 15$$

To find $\frac{3}{4}$ of a number you can multiply the number by $\frac{3}{4}$.

$$\frac{20}{1} \times \frac{3}{4} = \frac{60}{4} = 15$$

Mrs. Stein has 15 tulip plants.

TRY THESE

Complete.

1. $\frac{1}{8}$ of $16 =$ ▓ **2.** $\frac{1}{5}$ of $20 =$ ▓ **3.** $\frac{1}{6}$ of $24 =$ ▓ **4.** $\frac{1}{3}$ of $21 =$ ▓

5. $\frac{2}{3}$ of $18 =$ ▓ **6.** $\frac{3}{4}$ of $24 =$ ▓ **7.** $\frac{2}{5}$ of $25 =$ ▓ **8.** $\frac{5}{6}$ of $30 =$ ▓

SKILLS PRACTICE

Complete.

1. $\frac{1}{2}$ of $14 =$ ▓ **2.** $\frac{3}{4}$ of $20 =$ ▓ **3.** $\frac{2}{5}$ of $15 =$ ▓ **4.** $\frac{1}{6}$ of $12 =$ ▓

5. $\frac{2}{3}$ of $27 =$ ▓ **6.** $\frac{3}{10}$ of $20 =$ ▓ **7.** $\frac{1}{4}$ of $36 =$ ▓ **8.** $\frac{4}{5}$ of $25 =$ ▓

9. $\frac{1}{10}$ of $30 =$ ▓ **10.** $\frac{5}{6}$ of $36 =$ ▓ **11.** $\frac{3}{8}$ of $24 =$ ▓ **12.** $\frac{2}{7}$ of $21 =$ ▓

13. $\frac{7}{8}$ of $40 =$ ▓ **14.** $\frac{9}{10}$ of $50 =$ ▓ **15.** $\frac{5}{9}$ of $99 =$ ▓ **16.** $\frac{6}{7}$ of $63 =$ ▓

PROBLEM SOLVING

17. There were 32 flowerpots in a shipment. Meg found that $\frac{3}{8}$ of them were broken. How many flowerpots were broken?

18. The plant store has 45 geranium plants. Of these, $\frac{3}{5}$ are flowering. How many geranium plants are flowering?

★19. On Saturday, the plant store had sales of $402. Hanging plants made up $\frac{1}{6}$ of the sales. How much money was not from hanging plants?

★20. The regular price of a hedge trimmer is $72. The store is having a $\frac{1}{4}$-off sale. What is the sale price of a hedge trimmer?

MIXED REVIEW

Add, subtract, multiply, or divide.

1. $7,463.18 \\ + 3,551.69$

2. $3,809 \\ \times \;\; 205$

3. $1,428 \\ - \;\; 819$

4. $3,257 \\ \times \;\; 362$

5. $563,715 \\ - \;\;\; 6,084$

6. $36 \div 6 =$ ▓   **7.** $543 \div 5 =$ ▓   **8.** $632 \div 4 =$ ▓

Division

A. Two numbers are *reciprocals* when their product is 1.

$$\frac{4}{5} \times \frac{5}{4} = \frac{20}{20} = 1 \qquad\qquad \frac{7}{1} \times \frac{1}{7} = \frac{7}{7} = 1$$

reciprocals   reciprocals

B. A pan of bread is $\frac{2}{3}$ full.

Each piece of bread is $\frac{1}{6}$ of the pan.

How many pieces of bread are there?

From the picture:

$$\frac{2}{3} \div \frac{1}{6} = 4$$

There are 4 pieces of bread.

To divide fractions, multiply by the reciprocal of the divisor.

To find $\frac{2}{3} \div \frac{1}{6}$ do $\frac{2}{3} \times \frac{6}{1} = \frac{12}{3} = 4$.

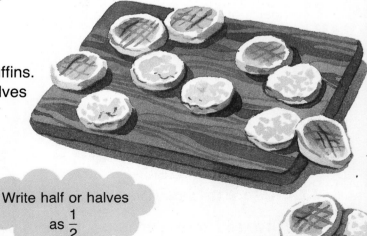

C. A package contains 6 English muffins. Each is cut in half. How many halves are there?

$$6 \div \frac{1}{2} = \frac{6}{1} \times \frac{2}{1} = \frac{12}{1} = 12$$

reciprocals

> Write half or halves as $\frac{1}{2}$

There are 12 muffin halves.

TRY THESE

Complete.

1. $\dfrac{3}{4} \div \dfrac{2}{3} = \dfrac{3}{4} \times \dfrac{3}{2} = $ ■

2. $3 \div \dfrac{3}{10} = \dfrac{3}{1} \times \dfrac{10}{3} = $ ■

Divide. Write the answer in lowest terms.

3. $\dfrac{2}{3} \div \dfrac{1}{2} = $ ■

4. $\dfrac{3}{4} \div \dfrac{5}{6} = $ ■

5. $\dfrac{7}{8} \div \dfrac{3}{4} = $ ■

6. $4 \div \dfrac{5}{6} = $ ■

SKILLS PRACTICE

Divide. Write the answer in lowest terms.

1. $\dfrac{2}{3} \div \dfrac{1}{8} = $ ■

2. $\dfrac{3}{4} \div \dfrac{1}{3} = $ ■

3. $\dfrac{5}{8} \div \dfrac{1}{4} = $ ■

4. $2 \div \dfrac{3}{4} = $ ■

5. $\dfrac{7}{9} \div \dfrac{9}{7} = $ ■

6. $\dfrac{7}{2} \div \dfrac{1}{2} = $ ■

7. $\dfrac{8}{5} \div \dfrac{2}{3} = $ ■

8. $\dfrac{3}{4} \div \dfrac{1}{16} = $ ■

9. $\dfrac{7}{6} \div \dfrac{2}{9} = $ ■

10. $\dfrac{8}{3} \div \dfrac{7}{6} = $ ■

11. $\dfrac{7}{8} \div \dfrac{1}{4} = $ ■

12. $8 \div \dfrac{3}{5} = $ ■

PROBLEM SOLVING

13. Terry has $\dfrac{3}{4}$ of a container of juice. Each serving is $\dfrac{1}{8}$ of the container. How many servings of juice can Terry make?

14. Jack uses $\dfrac{1}{5}$ of a package of cheese for each sandwich. How many sandwiches can Jack make from 4 packages?

★15. About $\dfrac{2}{3}$ of a store's customers use credit cards. About $\dfrac{1}{4}$ of these customers use the Quik Pay Card. What part of the store's customers use the Quik Pay Card? What part uses other cards?

★16. Lucy has $2\dfrac{1}{2}$ cups of raisins. She uses $\dfrac{1}{4}$ cup of raisins for each serving of cereal. How many servings can she make?

THINK!

Logical Reasoning

A.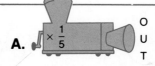

B.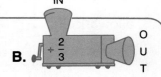

Put three fractions into each machine. Which machine produces smaller fractions? Which machine produces larger fractions?

Problem Solving Strategy

Choosing the Operation

A. Tim completed $\frac{2}{3}$ of a puzzle.

Then Jan completed $\frac{1}{4}$ of the puzzle.

What part of the puzzle did they complete in all?

Add.

$$\frac{2}{3} + \frac{1}{4} = \frac{8}{12} + \frac{3}{12} = \frac{11}{12}$$

They completed $\frac{11}{12}$ of the puzzle.

B. The puzzle has 240 pieces. Tim and Jan still had $\frac{1}{12}$ of the puzzle to complete.

How many pieces did they still have to put in?

Multiply.

$$\frac{1}{12} \times 240 = \blacksquare$$

$$\frac{1}{12} \times \frac{240}{1} = \frac{240}{12} = 20.$$

They still had to put in 20 pieces.

C. Tim spent $4 or $\frac{2}{3}$ of his allowance for a new puzzle. How much was his allowance?

Divide.

$$4 \div \frac{2}{3} = \frac{4}{1} \times \frac{3}{2} = \frac{12}{2} = 6$$

Tim's allowance was $6.

1. Jane completed $\frac{1}{3}$ of a puzzle. Fred completed $\frac{2}{5}$ of it. How much more of the puzzle did Fred complete?

2. A puzzle has 80 pieces. Larry put together $\frac{3}{4}$ of the puzzle. How many pieces did Larry put together?

3. There are 3 storage boxes. Each puzzle takes up $\frac{1}{4}$ box. How many puzzles can be stored?

4. Paul spent $\frac{1}{5}$ hour on the puzzle. Lynn spent $\frac{1}{3}$ hour. How much time did they spend in all?

PROBLEM SOLVING PRACTICE

Solve.

1. Anne had $\frac{1}{2}$ of a bag of marbles. A friend gave her $\frac{5}{8}$ of a bag of marbles. How many bags of marbles did Anne have then?

2. Carl had $\frac{3}{4}$ of a bag of marbles. Dan had $\frac{5}{6}$ of a bag of marbles. How much less of a bag did Carl have than Dan?

3. Danny is going to paint $\frac{3}{5}$ of a model car blue. He put on $\frac{2}{3}$ of the blue paint. What part of the car did he paint?

4. Ed completed $\frac{2}{5}$ of the puzzle and Nancy completed $\frac{1}{6}$ of the puzzle. What part of the puzzle did they complete in all?

5. Wanda uses $\frac{2}{3}$ of a tube of glue for each model airplane. How many airplanes can she make with 6 tubes of glue?

6. Bob had $\frac{3}{4}$ of a book to read. After he read for an hour, he had only $\frac{1}{6}$ of the book to read. What part of the book did he read?

7. When the game was over, $\frac{4}{5}$ of all the letters had been used. Maria used $\frac{1}{2}$ of these letters. What part of all the letters had Maria used?

★8. Pat jogged $\frac{7}{8}$ mile and Sally jogged $\frac{5}{6}$ mile. Who jogged the shorter distance? How much shorter?

ON YOUR OWN

Make up an addition and subtraction problem using the fractions $\frac{1}{3}$ and $\frac{7}{8}$.

Make up a multiplication and division problem using the fractions $\frac{3}{4}$ and $\frac{1}{2}$.

Problem Solving

Data from Circle Graphs

Ms. Mallory made a **circle graph** to show what part of her income she plans to spend for five different things.

Ms. Mallory's Budget

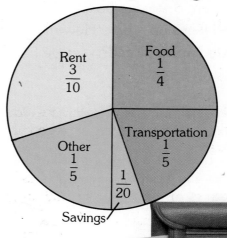

A. What part of her income does Ms. Mallory plan to spend for food and transportation?

Food: $\frac{1}{4}$ of her income

Transportation: $\frac{1}{5}$ of her income

Add to find what part in all.

$$\frac{1}{4} + \frac{1}{5} = \frac{5}{20} + \frac{4}{20} = \frac{9}{20}$$

Ms. Mallory plans to spend $\frac{9}{20}$ of her income for food and transportation.

B. Ms. Mallory's income each month is $1,500. How much does she pay for rent each month?

Rent: $\frac{3}{10}$ of her income

Income: $1,500

Multiply to find how much.

$$\frac{3}{10} \times 1,500 = \frac{3}{10} \times \frac{1,500}{1} = \frac{4,500}{10} = 450$$

Ms. Mallory pays $450 for rent each month.

248   **Fractions**

Use the circle graph on page 248 to solve the problems.

1. What part more of her income does Ms. Mallory plan to spend for rent than for savings?

2. Ms. Mallory's monthly income is $1,500. How much will be spent for "other" expenses each month?

PROBLEM SOLVING PRACTICE

Use this circle graph to solve these problems.

Mr. Cooper's Budget

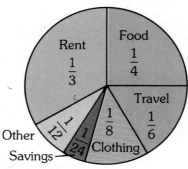

1. What part of his income does Mr. Cooper plan to spend for food or travel?

2. Does Mr. Cooper plan to spend more of his income for clothing or for rent? What part more?

3. What part less of his income does Mr. Cooper plan to spend for savings than for travel?

4. What part of his income does Mr. Cooper plan to spend in all for rent, food, and travel?

5. Mr. Cooper earns $1,440 each month. How much does he expect to spend for "other" expenses?

6. How much of his $1,440 monthly income should Mr. Cooper set aside for savings?

7. How much of his $1,440 monthly income does Mr. Cooper plan to spend for food?

★8. What is the sum of the fractions on Mr. Cooper's graph?

★9. How much of his $1,440 monthly income does Mr. Cooper expect to spend for rent? How much will he spend for rent in a year?

★10. Mr. Cooper got a pay raise to $1,464 each month. How much should he set aside for savings each month? each year?

ON YOUR OWN

Look in newspapers and magazines. Find examples of circle graphs that use fractions. Bring the graphs to class. Use the graphs and make up some questions for your classmates to answer.

An Algorithm for Finding the LCD

Computers can follow very complex algorithms. You may be surprised at how many steps there are to find a least common denominator. To find the LCD for two fractions with different denominators, a computer might be given instructions like these:

Step 1. Find the denominator of each fraction.

Step 2. Find multiples of each denominator that are less than 100.

Step 3. Find the common multiples of both.

Step 4. Find the least common multiple.

Step 5. If no common multiples, find multiples of each denominator less than 1,000.

Step 6. Go to Step 3.

Sometimes you do not use every step of an algorithm. To find the LCD of $\frac{3}{5}$ and $\frac{1}{6}$, you would use Steps 1, 2, 3, and 4. The output would be:

Step 1. 5 6

Step 2. 5 10 15 20 25 30 35 40 45 50 55 60 65 70 75 80 85 90 95
6 12 18 24 30 36 42 48 54 60 66 72 78 84 90 96

Step 3. 30 60 90

Step 4. 30

Use the algorithm to find the LCD of each pair of fractions. Show the output for each step.

1. $\frac{5}{9}$ and $\frac{2}{7}$

2. $\frac{2}{3}$ and $\frac{3}{11}$

3. $\frac{3}{4}$ and $\frac{1}{8}$

What steps in the algorithm would you use for each pair of the following fractions? What is the LCD?

4. $\frac{7}{10}$ and $\frac{2}{15}$

5. $\frac{4}{15}$ and $\frac{1}{32}$

6. $\frac{2}{9}$ and $\frac{3}{22}$

Unit Review

Copy and complete. (*pages 218–219, 222–223*)

1. $\dfrac{9}{12} = \dfrac{\blacksquare}{4}$
2. $\dfrac{5}{6} = \dfrac{\blacksquare}{18}$
3. $\dfrac{8}{20} = \dfrac{2}{\blacksquare}$
4. $\dfrac{2}{3} = \dfrac{8}{\blacksquare}$
5. $\dfrac{1}{2} = \dfrac{\blacksquare}{10}$

Write >, <, or = for ●. (*pages 220–221*)

6. $\dfrac{7}{10} \bullet \dfrac{3}{10}$
7. $\dfrac{1}{2} \bullet \dfrac{3}{8}$
8. $\dfrac{4}{5} \bullet \dfrac{5}{6}$
9. $\dfrac{1}{4} \bullet \dfrac{1}{6}$
10. $\dfrac{5}{9} \bullet \dfrac{2}{3}$

Give a lowest terms mixed numeral or a standard numeral. (*pages 224–225*)

11. $\dfrac{16}{3}$
12. $\dfrac{15}{5}$
13. $\dfrac{7}{2}$
14. $\dfrac{10}{6}$
15. $\dfrac{14}{7}$
16. $\dfrac{26}{8}$

Find equivalent fractions with the least common denominator. (*pages 232–233*)

17. $\dfrac{3}{4}$ and $\dfrac{2}{3}$
18. $\dfrac{1}{6}$ and $\dfrac{4}{9}$
19. $\dfrac{2}{5}$ and $\dfrac{1}{2}$
20. $\dfrac{1}{4}$ and $\dfrac{7}{10}$

Add or subtract. (*pages 226–229, 234–237*)

21. $\dfrac{1}{6} + \dfrac{3}{4} = \blacksquare$
22. $\dfrac{7}{8} - \dfrac{5}{6} = \blacksquare$
23. $\dfrac{3}{10} - \dfrac{1}{6} = \blacksquare$
24. $\dfrac{4}{5} + \dfrac{2}{3} = \blacksquare$

Multiply or divide. (*pages 240–245*)

25. $\dfrac{1}{2} \times \dfrac{3}{8} = \blacksquare$
26. $6 \div \dfrac{2}{3} = \blacksquare$
27. $\dfrac{3}{4} \div \dfrac{1}{8} = \blacksquare$
28. $\dfrac{9}{10} \times \dfrac{3}{4} = \blacksquare$

Solve the problems. (*pages 230–231, 246–249*)

29. Lisa drank $\dfrac{3}{4}$ glass of milk in the morning and afternoon. How much milk did she drink in all?

30. What part of her allowance in all does June plan to spend for clothing and entertainment?

31. June's allowance is $4 a week. How much does she plan to save each week?

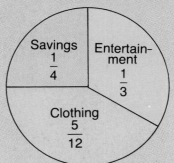

June's Allowance Budget

Savings $\dfrac{1}{4}$

Entertainment $\dfrac{1}{3}$

Clothing $\dfrac{5}{12}$

Reinforcement

More Help with Fractions

$$\frac{3}{4} + \frac{5}{6} = \blacksquare$$

Multiples of 6: 6, (12), 18
Multiples of 4: 4, 8, (12)

$$\frac{3}{4} + \frac{5}{6} = \frac{9}{12} + \frac{10}{12}$$

$$= \frac{19}{12}$$

$$1\frac{7}{12}$$
$$12\overline{)19}$$

$$= 1\frac{7}{12}$$

$$\frac{7}{10} \rightarrow \frac{7}{10}$$
$$-\frac{1}{2} \rightarrow -\frac{5}{10}$$
$$\frac{2}{10}$$

$$\frac{2 \div 2}{10 \div 2} = \frac{1}{5}$$

$$\frac{2}{10} = \frac{1}{5}$$

$$\frac{2}{3} \times \frac{4}{5} = \frac{2 \times 4}{3 \times 5} = \frac{8}{15}$$

$$\frac{2}{3} \div \frac{3}{4} = \frac{2}{3} \times \frac{4}{3}$$

$$= \frac{2 \times 4}{3 \times 3}$$

$$= \frac{8}{9}$$

Add or subtract.

1. $\frac{2}{9} + \frac{5}{9} = \blacksquare$

2. $\frac{7}{5} - \frac{3}{5} = \blacksquare$

3. $\frac{1}{3} + \frac{7}{12} = \blacksquare$

4. $\frac{4}{9} - \frac{1}{6} = \blacksquare$

5. $\frac{3}{4} + \frac{2}{3} = \blacksquare$

6. $\frac{7}{8} - \frac{3}{8} = \blacksquare$

7. $\begin{array}{r} \frac{7}{10} \\ + \frac{3}{10} \\ \hline \end{array}$

8. $\begin{array}{r} \frac{2}{3} \\ - \frac{3}{5} \\ \hline \end{array}$

9. $\begin{array}{r} \frac{3}{10} \\ + \frac{3}{4} \\ \hline \end{array}$

10. $\begin{array}{r} \frac{11}{12} \\ - \frac{1}{6} \\ \hline \end{array}$

11. $\begin{array}{r} \frac{1}{2} \\ + \frac{1}{6} \\ \hline \end{array}$

12. $\begin{array}{r} \frac{10}{11} \\ - \frac{4}{11} \\ \hline \end{array}$

13. $\begin{array}{r} \frac{1}{6} \\ + \frac{5}{8} \\ \hline \end{array}$

14. $\begin{array}{r} \frac{11}{10} \\ - \frac{3}{5} \\ \hline \end{array}$

Multiply.

15. $\frac{1}{2} \times \frac{1}{4} = \blacksquare$

16. $\frac{1}{4} \times \frac{7}{10} = \blacksquare$

17. $\frac{1}{10} \times \frac{2}{3} = \blacksquare$

18. $\frac{2}{5} \times \frac{3}{8} = \blacksquare$

19. $24 \times \frac{1}{5} = \blacksquare$

20. $18 \times \frac{2}{3} = \blacksquare$

Divide.

21. $4 \div \frac{3}{5} = \blacksquare$

22. $\frac{7}{8} \div \frac{1}{2} = \blacksquare$

23. $\frac{5}{6} \div \frac{5}{6} = \blacksquare$

24. $\frac{9}{10} \div \frac{1}{3} = \blacksquare$

Enrichment

Prime and Composite Numbers

A. A *prime number* has exactly two factors, 1 and the number itself.

> **Prime Numbers less than 10**

$$2 = 1 \times 2 \quad 3 = 1 \times 3 \quad 5 = 1 \times 5 \quad 7 = 1 \times 7$$

A *composite number* has more than two factors.

> **Composite Numbers less than 10**

$$4 = 1 \times 4 = 2 \times 2 \qquad 8 = 1 \times 8 = 2 \times 4$$
$$6 = 1 \times 6 = 2 \times 3 \qquad 9 = 1 \times 9 = 3 \times 3$$

1 is neither prime nor composite.

B. Here is an easy way to find all the prime numbers less than 50.

Step 1 Cross out 1, since it has only 1 factor.

Step 2 Cross out all multiples of 2 except 2.

Step 3 Cross out all multiples of 3 except 3.

Step 4 Cross out all multiples of 5 except 5.

~~1~~ 2 3 ~~4~~ 5 ~~6~~ 7 ~~8~~ ~~9~~ ~~10~~

11 ~~12~~ 13 ~~14~~ ~~15~~ ~~16~~ 17 ~~18~~ 19 ~~20~~

~~21~~ ~~22~~ 23 ~~24~~ ~~25~~ ~~26~~ ~~27~~ ~~28~~ 29 ~~30~~

31 ~~32~~ ~~33~~ ~~34~~ ~~35~~ ~~36~~ 37 ~~38~~ ~~39~~ ~~40~~

41 ~~42~~ 43 ~~44~~ ~~45~~ ~~46~~ 47 ~~48~~ ~~49~~ ~~50~~

Step 5 Cross out all multiples of 7 except 7.

All the numbers not crossed off are prime numbers.

1. List all the prime numbers less than 50.

2. Extend the chart to 100. Repeat steps 1–5 to find the rest of the prime numbers less than 100.

Cumulative Review

Choose the correct answer. Use NG if the correct answer is *not given*.

1. Round $4.52 to the nearest dollar.

a. $4.00
b. $5.00
c. $4.50
d. NG

2. 673
   $\times 409$

a. 32,977
b. 275,257
c. 8,749
d. NG

3. Which fraction is equivalent to $\frac{2}{3}$?

a. $\frac{2}{6}$ b. $\frac{4}{3}$
c. $\frac{6}{9}$ d. NG

4. $58\overline{)8,174}$

a. 140 R54
b. 163 R24
c. 141 R4
d. NG

5. $\frac{5}{9} + \frac{2}{9} = \blacksquare$

a. $\frac{7}{18}$ b. $\frac{52}{99}$
c. $\frac{7}{9}$ d. NG

6. 32,006
   $- 21,604$

a. 11,602
b. 10,402
c. 10,392
d. NG

7. $9 + 37 + 594 = \blacksquare$

a. 721
b. 1,864
c. 630
d. NG

8. $\frac{7}{8} - \frac{5}{6} = \blacksquare$

a. 1 b. $\frac{1}{24}$
c. $\frac{6}{7}$ d. NG

9. Find the total value.

a. $15.30
b. $25.90
c. $21.33
d. NG

10. $\frac{2}{5} \times \frac{1}{3} = \blacksquare$

a. $\frac{2}{15}$ b. $\frac{3}{8}$
c. $\frac{1}{2}$ d. NG

11. $16 - 8 = \blacksquare$

a. 2
b. 9
c. 8
d. NG

12. Find the time when it is dark.

a. 12:45 P.M.
b. 12:45 A.M.
c. 11:45 A.M.
d. NG

13. Mrs. Foster spends $\frac{2}{7}$ of her income for rent. How much does she spend for rent each month if her monthly income is $1,400?

a. $200   b. $280
c. $400   d. NG

14. Clare spent $32.40 in all. When she paid, she got $7.60 back as change. How much had she given the salesperson?

a. $40.00   b. $24.80
c. $10.84   d. NG

9 Adding and Subtracting with Decimals

TRUCKS (OTHER THAN PICKUPS) IN USE IN THE U.S.

Type	Number (in thousands)
Dump Trucks	452
Panel Trucks	4,519
Platform Trucks	1,779
Tank Trucks	272
Utility Trucks	201
Vans	887
All Others	471
Total	8,581

Table

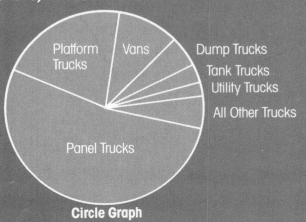

Circle Graph

Tenths

A. Hassan put wood panels on the wall. In one hour he put up $\frac{6}{10}$ of the panels. You can write a fraction or a decimal to show how much was completed.

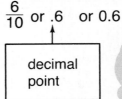

$\frac{6}{10}$ or .6   or 0.6

decimal point

You can write a zero before the decimal point for numbers less than one.

Standard decimal: .6 or 0.6

Words: six tenths *or* point six *or* zero point six

B. You can also use decimals to name whole numbers and other numbers greater than one.

Ones	Tenths
8	0

└decimal point

Tens	Ones	Tenths
2	3	5

└decimal point

Standard decimal: 8.0

Words: eight and zero tenths

23.5

twenty-three and five tenths

C. You can use a number line to show decimals as you do whole numbers and fractions.

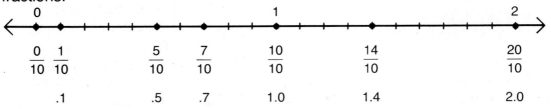

TRY THESE

Write a decimal to tell how much is shaded. Name the place of each digit. Then show each decimal on a number line.

1.   **2.**   **3.**

Write in words.

4. 4.6   **5.** 0.7   **6.** 23.2   **7.** 587.6   **8.** 32.0

Write the standard decimal.

9. 2 ones 6 tenths   **10.** 7 ones 5 tenths   **11.** $\frac{5}{10}$ **12.** $\frac{17}{10}$

SKILLS PRACTICE

Write a decimal to tell how much is shaded. Then name the place of each digit.

1.   **2.**   **3.**

Write in words.

4. 6.3   **5.** .2   **6.** 14.0   **7.** 9.1   **8.** 20.3

Write the standard decimal.

9. 3 tens 7 ones 3 tenths   **10.** 5 tens 7 tenths   **11.** 8 tens 6 ones

Write a decimal for each.

12. 5 in the ones place, 2 in the tenths place

13. 0 in the ones place, 7 in the tenths place

14. $65\frac{4}{10}$

15. ninety point seven

★16. nine thousand and nine tenths

Decimals in Your Life

Name at least three places you see decimals frequently. Think about clocks, cars, cash registers, newspapers. Compare your list with your classmates' lists.

Hundredths

A. Write a decimal to tell how much is shaded.

1

1

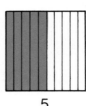
$\frac{5}{10}$

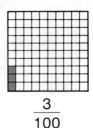
$\frac{3}{100}$

Ones	Tenths	Hundredths
2.	5	3

10 hundredths = 1 tenth

3 in the **hundredths place** means 3 hundredths.

2.53 squares are shaded.

$$\frac{5}{10} + \frac{3}{100} = \frac{50}{100} + \frac{3}{100} = \frac{53}{100}$$

Standard decimal: 2.53 ←

5 tenths 3 hundredths is 53 hundredths.

Words: two and fifty-three hundredths *or* two point five three

B. You can use decimals to name whole numbers and tenths or hundredths.

5 ones

5 ones 0 tenths
0 hundredths

8 ones
3 tenths

8 ones 3 tenths
0 hundredths

5 = 5.00

8.3 = 8.30

You must **be careful** when you write 0's in decimals.

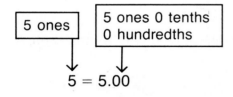

1.8 or 1.80

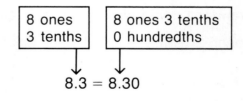

1.08

1.8 = 1.80

1.**0**8 names a smaller number than 1.80.

TRY THESE

**Write a decimal to tell how much is shaded.
Then name the place of each digit.**

1.   **2.**   **3.**

Write in words.

4. 3.75   **5.** 15.03   **6.** 15.30   **7.** 300.07   **8.** 57.83

Which name the same number?

9. 7.02, 7.20, 7.2   **10.** .5, .05, .50   **11.** 3.90, $3\frac{90}{100}$, 3.09

SKILLS PRACTICE

**Write a decimal to tell how much is shaded.
Then name the place of each digit.**

1.   **2.** 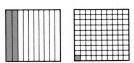   **3.**

Write in words.

4. 6.24   **5.** 7.07   **6.** 30.2   **7.** 2.02   **8.** 37.37

Write the standard decimal.

9. 2 ones 4 tenths 6 hundredths

10. 3 tens 5 ones 7 tenths hundredths

11. 4 hundredths

12. $6\frac{20}{100}$

13. eight tenths two hundredths

14. two tenths one hundredth

Which name the same number?

15. 17.00, 17, 17.0   **16.** 3.05, 3.50, 3.5

Write the standard decimal.

17. three and forty-eight hundredths

★**18.** fifty and five hundredths

THINK!

Check It Out

You usually use both fractions and decimals to write a check. Why do you think you use both? Which does the bank use?

Thousandths

A. In the picture, 1 hundredth is blue.

Divide 1 hundredth into 10 equal pieces.

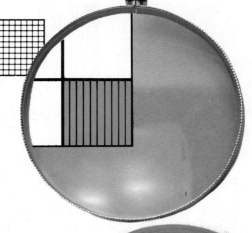

1 hundredth = 10 thousandths

B. Write a decimal to tell how much is shaded.

   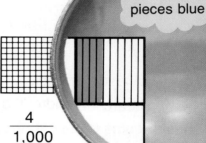

4 of 1,000 pieces blue

1 $\dfrac{5}{10}$ $\dfrac{7}{100}$ $\dfrac{4}{1,000}$

or $1\dfrac{574}{1,000}$

Ones	Tenths	Hundredths	Thousandths
1 .	5	7	4

↑
decimal point

Standard decimal: 1.574

Words: one and five hundred seventy-four thousandths *or* one point five seven four

TRY THESE

**Write a decimal to tell how much is shaded.
Then name the place of each digit.**

1.

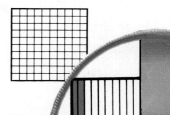

Write in words.

2. 6.41 **3.** 21.200 **4.** 17.070 **5.** 300.7 **6.** $39\frac{29}{100}$

Write the standard decimal.

7. 5 ones 2 tenths 1 hundredth 8 thousandths
8. 8 tens 4 ones 0 tenths 4 hundredths
9. 6 tenths 6 hundredths 6 thousandths

SKILLS PRACTICE

Write in words.

1. 0.147 **2.** 2.003 **3.** 11.100 **4.** 18.037 **5.** 30.1

6. 9.25 **7.** 63.4 **8.** 82.005 **9.** 1.010 **10.** 60.060

Write the standard decimal.

11. 7 ones 4 tenths 7 hundredths 4 thousandths

12. 1 tenth 5 hundredths 5 thousandths

13. 0 tenths 4 hundredths 6 thousandths

14. $24\frac{75}{1,000}$

Write the standard decimal.

15. three and two hundred forty-seven thousandths
16. twenty-three and seven hundred fourteen thousandths
17. one and sixty-four thousandths
18. four and six hundred thousandths
19. five and zero thousandths
20. five and fifty thousandths
★21. ten and ten thousandths
★22. ten and one hundred thousandths

Decimals and Measurement

A decimeter is 0.1 of a meter.
A centimeter is 0.01 of a meter.
A millimeter is 0.001 of a meter.

1. How many decimeters in a meter?
2. How many centimeters in a meter?
3. How many millimeters in a meter?
4. How many millimeters in a centimeter?

Comparing and Ordering with Decimals

A. Paula rode her bike 30.8 kilometers.
Peter rode his bike 30.54 kilometers.
Who rode farther?

Compare 30.8 and 30.54.

Use two steps.

Step 1   Write the decimal **with the decimals points lined up.**

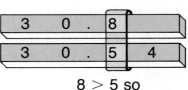

Step 2   Read from left to right until you find **different digits** in the **same place.** The decimal with the **greater digit** is **greater.**

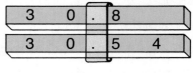

8 > 5 so
30.8 > 30.54 and 30.54 < 30.8

Paula rode farther.

B. Write >, <, or = for ⬤.

21 ⬤ 3.96

Write 21.0 for 21.   21.0
                            3.96

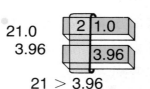

21 > 3.96

1.235 ⬤ 1.253

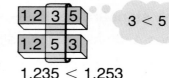

3 < 5

1.235 < 1.253

C. Write in order from greatest to least: 2.65; 2.8; 3.

Find the greatest.

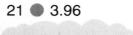

3 is the greatest.

Find the next greatest.

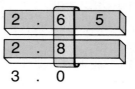

2.8 is the next greatest.

Greatest to least: 3; 2.8; 2.65

2.5   2.6   2.65   2.7   2.8   2.9   3

TRY THESE

Write >, <, or = for ⬤.

1. 2.7 ⬤ .27   **2.** 98 ⬤ 103.7   **3.** .006 ⬤ .016   **4.** 5.1 ⬤ 5.10

5. 1.0 ⬤ .80   **6.** 31 ⬤ 31.00   **7.** 11.8 ⬤ 9.68   **8.** 7.007 ⬤ 70.07

SKILLS PRACTICE

Write >, <, or = for ⬤.

1. .72 ⬤ .47   **2.** 2.136 ⬤ 2.316   **3.** 27 ⬤ 3.2   **4.** 1.00 ⬤ .99

5. .9 ⬤ .59   **6.** 45.36 ⬤ 43.56   **7.** 10.0 ⬤ 10   **8.** 250.0 ⬤ 25.00

9. 12.415 ⬤ 4.813   **10.** .445 ⬤ .45   **11.** 19.0 ⬤ 19.00   **12.** .03 ⬤ .03

13. 218 ⬤ 21.8   **14.** 14 ⬤ .41   **15.** .308 ⬤ .318   **16.** .41 ⬤ .39

17. 2.00 ⬤ 2.02   **18.** 12.003 ⬤ 12   **19.** 5.41 ⬤ 51.4   **20.** .7 ⬤ .700

21. .09 ⬤ 90   **22.** 7.20 ⬤ 7.02   **23.** 9.90 ⬤ 10   **24.** 3.926 ⬤ 3.41

25. 20.06 ⬤ 20   **26.** 9.2 ⬤ 87   **27.** 3.16 ⬤ 316   **28.** 6 ⬤ 7.0

Write in order from greatest to least.

29. .08; 2; 1.7   **30.** 3.08; 5; 4.633   ★**31.** .60; .06; 6.006; .606

MIXED REVIEW

Add or subtract.

1. $\dfrac{7}{12}$ **2.** $\dfrac{5}{12}$ **3.** $\dfrac{7}{9}$ **4.** $\dfrac{1}{3}$ **5.** $\dfrac{5}{6}$ **6.** $\dfrac{7}{8}$

$+\dfrac{1}{4}$ $-\dfrac{3}{12}$ $-\dfrac{1}{2}$ $+\dfrac{2}{7}$ $+\dfrac{7}{8}$ $-\dfrac{1}{12}$

Multiply.

7. $\dfrac{1}{2} \times \dfrac{4}{11} =$ ◼   **8.** $\dfrac{3}{8} \times \dfrac{4}{9} =$ ◼   **9.** $\dfrac{7}{3} \times \dfrac{9}{14} =$ ◼

Complete.

10. 9 lb = ◼ oz   **11.** 4 ft 10 in. = ◼ in.   **12.** 6 pt = ◼ cups

Rounding Decimals

A. Roy measured a carpet. It was 3.8 meters long. To the nearest meter, how long was the carpet?

Round 3.8 to the nearest one.

Circle the rounding place.

③ . 8

Look at the digit to the right.

③ . 8

8 > 5

5 or greater, round up.

Round 3.8 up to 4.

To the nearest meter, the carpet was 4 meters long.

B. You can use the same method to round to any place. Round 6.41 to the nearest tenth.

Circle the rounding place.

6 . ④ 1

Look at the digit to the right.

6 . ④ 1

1 < 5

Less than 5, round down.

Round 6.41 down to 6.4.

To the nearest tenth, 6.41 is 6.4.

C. Round 17.273 to the nearest hundredth.

1 7 . 2 ⑦ 3

3 < 5
Round down.

1 7 . 2 7

nearest hundredth

To the nearest tenth.

1 7 . ② 7 3

7 > 5
Round up.

1 7 . 3

nearest tenth

TRY THESE

Round to the nearest tenth; to the nearest one.

1. 7.52
2. 3.35
3. 7.04
4. 2.87
5. 5.05

Round to the nearest hundredth.

6. 17.277
7. 1.864
8. 6.423
9. 19.889
10. 21.053

Round to the nearest tenth; to the nearest one.

1. 9.46   2. .57   3. 13.12   4. 4.48   5. 7.16

6. 9.72   7. 17.42   8. 7.07   9. 8.631   10. 8.889

Round to the nearest hundredth; to the nearest tenth.

11. 1.592   12. 6.166   13. .662   14. 2.079   15. 2.821

16. 5.144   17. 1.679   18. 16.067   19. 5.318   20. .624

21. .069   22. 8.071   ★23. 9.031   ★24. 5.009   ★25. 3.499

PROBLEM SOLVING _____

26. A door is 2.76 meters high. Find the height of the door to the nearest tenth of a meter.

27. Paula has a green curtain 3.15 meters long and a gold curtain 3.8 meters long. Which curtain is shorter? Give the length of the shorter curtain to the nearest meter.

Working a Simpler Problem

There are 1,000 students and 1,000 lockers in the school.

The 1st student opens all lockers.
The 2nd student closes every 2nd one.
The 3rd student changes every 3rd one
   (opens if closed, closes if open).
The 4th student changes every 4th one.
The 5th student changes every 5th one.

....

The 1,000th student changes every 1,000th one.

Which lockers are open?

Hint: Solve the simpler problem with 16 lockers.
       Draw a picture.

Problem Solving Strategy

Mixed Strategies

Solve.

Use one of the strategies listed in the box, or use your own strategy.

> Draw a Picture
>
> Guess and Check
>
> Solve a Simpler Problem
>
> Work Backwards

1. Ginny's age is $\frac{3}{4}$ of Harry's. The sum of their ages is 21. How old are Ginny and Harry?

2. Ned has $120. He buys a $70 jacket. Can he also buy 3 shirts at $15 each? Could he buy 4 shirts?

3. Lisa rode her bike 11 kilometers east to the market. Then she rode 3 kilometers west to the bank. How far was she then from her starting place?

4. Mrs. Flynn earned $2,316 in March and $2,195 in April. She paid $525 rent each month. How much was left from her earnings for March and April after she paid her rent?

5. A decimal has 1 in the hundredths place. The number in the ones place is 4 more than the number in the hundredths place. There are no tenths. What is the number?

6. There were 726 adults and 365 children at the baseball game. There were 411 adults and 689 children at the basketball game. Which game had the greater attendance?

7. Mike's time in the 100-meter dash was 12.36 seconds. Theo's time was 11.87 seconds. Who ran the 100-meter dash faster?

8. Jim drove 7 blocks north, then 12 blocks west, then 7 blocks south. How far was he then from his starting place?

Problem Solving Project

Adjusting a Recipe

This recipe makes enough for 4 people.

Jan and Mark wanted to make enough salad for 6 people.

Step 1 They divided the amounts by 4, to find how much would be needed for 1 person.

Potato slices: 800 mL ÷ 4 = 200 mL

CHEESY POTATO SALAD
Serves 4

800 mL cooked potato slices
120 mL sliced celery
100 mL chopped onion
  8 bacon slices, cooked crisp
200 mL grated cheese
 80 mL mayonnaise

Step 2 They multiplied the amounts needed for 1 person by 6, to find how much would be needed for 6 people.

Potato slices: 6 × 200 mL = 1,200 mL

Copy and complete the table below. Show the amount of each ingredient Jan and Mark should use for different numbers of people.

	Ingredient	Amount Needed			
		for 4	for 1	for 6	for 2
1.	potato slices	800 mL	200 mL	1,200 mL	
2.	sliced celery	120 mL			
3.	chopped onion	100 mL			
4.	bacon slices	8			
5.	grated cheese	200 mL			
6.	mayonnaise	80 mL			

ON YOUR OWN

Data Search

Find a recipe for some food you like. Adjust the recipe to make enough for everyone in your family. Make a table like the one above.

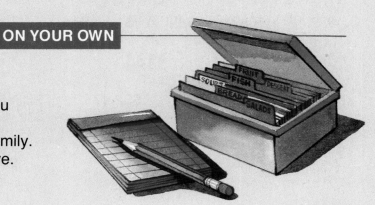

Adding with Decimals

A. Felix made a broad jump of 3.87 meters. His next jump was 4.21 meters. What was the total distance he jumped?

> **Add** to find the total distance.

$$\begin{array}{r} {}^{1} \\ 3.87 \\ +\,4.21 \\ \hline 8.08 \end{array}$$

Estimate:
4 + 4 = 8

Felix jumped a total of 8.08 meters.

B. Always line up the decimal points when adding.

13.4 + 5.77 =

$$\begin{array}{r} {}^{1} \\ 13.4 \\ +\;\;5.77 \\ \hline 19.17 \end{array}$$

Estimate:
13 + 6 = 19

7.328 + 4.59 = ■

$$\begin{array}{r} {}^{1} \\ 7.328 \\ +\,4.59 \\ \hline 11.918 \end{array}$$

Estimate:
7 + 5 = 12

C. $32.47 + $.83 + $5.90 = ■
Line up the decimal points.

Add.

$$\begin{array}{r} \$32.47 \\ .83 \\ +\;\;\;5.90 \\ \hline \end{array}$$

$$\begin{array}{r} {}^{2\;1} \\ \$32.47 \\ .83 \\ +\;\;\;5.90 \\ \hline \$39.20 \end{array}$$

Estimate:
$32 + $1 + $6 = $39

TRY THESE

Estimate. Then add.

1. 25.7
+ 4.6

2. 26.0
+ 8.4

3. 21.4
+ 7.05

4. 26.161
10.871
+ 34.764

5. 517.23
282.87
+ 230.1

6. 5.8 + 6.6 = ■   **7.** 8.70 + 1.384 = ■   **8.** 4.9 + .6 + 2.76 + .81 = ■

SKILLS PRACTICE

Add.

1. 93.5
+ 67.5

2. 260.7
+ 924.5

3. 25.186
+ 6.849

4. 77.8
+ 104.5

5. 2.01
+ 4.9

6. 7.3
+ 8.0

7. .914
+ .603

8. 46.0
+ 29.47

9. $ 4.89
+ 82.53

10. 3.5
+ 9.0

11. $5.70
7.00
+ 6.35

12. 205.62
36.8
+ 24.94

13. $.70
.40
+ .60

★14. $4.01
.89
2.83
+ 3.49

★15. $ 8.60
10.43
2.76
+ 26.84

16. 2.73 + 3.9 = ■   **17.** 21 + .07 = ■   **18.** $12.78 + $4.35 = ■

19. 72.016 + 29.87 = ■   **20.** 5.3 + 4 + 9.6 = ■   **★21.** 150.4 + 60.6 = ■

PROBLEM SOLVING

22. Four runners on a relay team ran their parts of the race in 11.29 seconds, 12.01 seconds, 11.98 seconds, and 11.46 seconds. What was their total time for the race?

★23. Nancy ran the first third of a mile in 1.68 minutes, the second third in 1.99 minutes, and the last third in the same time as the first third. What was her time for the mile?

THINK!

Estimate and Calculate

 Estimate the answer to every odd-numbered exercise in SKILLS PRACTICE.
Use your calculator to find the sum in exercises 5, 11, 17, and 21.

Subtracting with Decimals

A. Beth ran part of a relay race in 24.16 seconds. Kim ran her part of the race in 19.62 seconds. How much more time did Beth take to run her part of the race?

Subtract to find how much more time Beth took.

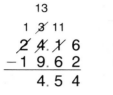

$$\begin{array}{r} {}^{13}\\ {}^{1\ \cancel{3}\ 11}\\ \cancel{2}\ \cancel{4}.\cancel{1}\ 6\\ -1\ 9.6\ 2\\ \hline 4.5\ 4 \end{array}$$

Estimate:
24 − 20 = 4

Beth took 4.54 seconds more than Kim.

B. Always line up the decimal points when subtracting.

25.72 − 16.3 = ■

$$\begin{array}{r} {}^{1\ 15}\\ \cancel{2}\ \cancel{5}.7\ 2\\ -1\ 6.3\\ \hline 9.4\ 2 \end{array}$$

Estimate:
26 − 16 = 10

16.172 − 3.448 = ■

$$\begin{array}{r} {}^{5\ 11\ 6\ 12}\\ 1\ \cancel{6}.\cancel{1}\ \cancel{7}\ \cancel{2}\\ -\ \ \ 3.4\ 4\ 8\\ \hline 1\ 2.7\ 2\ 4 \end{array}$$

Estimate:
16 − 3 = 13

C. $9 − $3.42 = ■

Write $9.00 for $9. Then line up the decimal points.

$$\begin{array}{r} {}^{9}\\ {}^{8\ \cancel{10}\ 10}\\ \$\cancel{9}.\cancel{0}\ \cancel{0}\\ -\ \ 3.4\ 2\\ \hline \$5.5\ 8 \end{array}$$

TRY THESE

Subtract.

1.	**2.**	**3.**	**4.**	**5.**
.64	71.46	104.8	26.435	20.0
− .58	− 65.72	− 104.7	− 6.502	− .7

6. $100 − $40.63 = ■

7. 23 − .9 = ■

8. .37 − .37 = ■

SKILLS PRACTICE

Subtract.

1.	**2.**	**3.**	**4.**	**5.**
6.2	8.1	60.0	6.273	.97
− .7	− 4.8	− 27.3	− 5.78	− .42

6.	**7.**	**8.**	**9.**	**10.**
1.08	16.0	78	$60.13	22.4
− .13	− 9.7	− 30.86	− 59.45	− .86

11.	**12.**	**13.**	**14.**	**15.**
4.61	8.0	45.3	30.4	63.49
− 4.4	− .8	− 8.7	− 6.5	− 6.7

16.	**17.**	**18.**	**19.**	**20.**
$19.08	12.6	.835	7.9	30.01
− 9.25	− 4.8	− .766	− 4.60	− 3.10

21. 5.6 − 4.0 = ■

22. 24.5 − 9.2 = ■

23. 20 − 6.3 = ■

24. 16.822 − 14.501 = ■

25. 2.6 − .48 = ■

★26. 21.0 − (.1 + .2) = ■

PROBLEM SOLVING

27. The track should be 100.00 m long. The coach found that it was only 98.84 m long. How much longer should it be?

★28. Jim and Mary each ran 2.5 km one day. Then, Jim ran 4.3 km and Mary ran 2.9 km. How far did each run? Who ran farther? How much farther?

MIXED REVIEW

Divide.

1. 2)1,411　　**2.** 6)1,875　　**3.** 22)4,100　　**4.** 60)$979.80　　**5.** 57)48,288

Complete.

6. $\frac{2}{3}$ of 15 = ■　　**7.** $\frac{9}{10}$ of 20 = ■　　**8.** $\frac{3}{2}$ of 18 = ■　　**9.** $\frac{4}{9}$ of 36 = ■

Problem Solving

Estimating with Decimals

A. When you solve a problem with decimals, sometimes an exact answer is not needed. Some problems require only an **estimate.**

The Ferri family went swimming in a rectangular pool 46.25 meters long and 28.65 meters wide. About how long is the total distance around the pool?

To find *about* how long, **round** to the nearest one.
Then **add.**

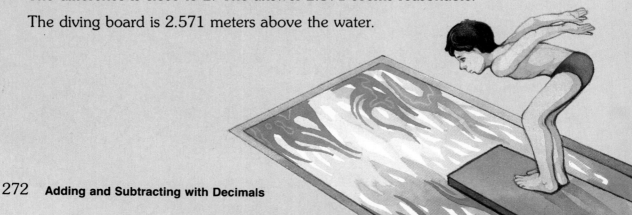

$$
\begin{array}{ll}
46.25 \longrightarrow & 46 \\
28.65 \longrightarrow & 29 \\
46.25 \longrightarrow & 46 \\
+28.65 \longrightarrow & +29 \\
\hline
& 150
\end{array}
$$

46.25 meters

28.65 meters

28.65 meters

46.25 meters

The total distance around the pool is about 150 meters.

B. When an exact answer is needed, estimating first helps you see whether your answer is reasonable.

The water is 4.781 meters deep under the diving board.
The diving board is 7.352 meters above the bottom of the pool.
How far above the water surface is the diving board?

Subtract to find the distance from the diving board to the water.

Estimate: $7 - 5 = 2$ meters

$$
\begin{array}{r}
7.352 \\
-4.781 \\
\hline
2.571
\end{array}
$$

The difference is close to 2. The answer 2.571 seems reasonable.

The diving board is 2.571 meters above the water.

Tell whether an estimate or an exact answer is needed. Solve.

1. How much longer is the pool than it is wide? (Use the diagram on page 272.)

2. Tonio spent $16.19 for goggles and $8.39 for a towel. Was $30 enough to pay for his purchases?

PROBLEM SOLVING PRACTICE

Solve.

1. The swimming pool is 4.781 meters deep at one end and 1.236 meters deep at the other end. How much deeper is it at the deep end?

2. Tonio's mass is 37.896 kg. His sister Gina's mass is 40.317 kg. About how much greater is Gina's mass?

3. Every morning, George swims 1,218.75 meters and Mary swims 2,312.50 meters. About how much farther does Mary swim?

4. Cary swam 114.60 meters underwater and Sally swam 57.30 meters. Exactly how much farther did Cary swim?

5. Mrs. Ferri can swim at 11.3 km/h. Tonio can swim 2.8 km/h faster. About how fast can Tonio swim?

6. Gina bought a bathing cap for $4.75 and flippers for $18.92. How much did she spend in all?

7. Three people, with masses of 37.89 kg, 60.32 kg, and 40.31 kg, stand on the diving board. What is the total mass on the diving board?

★8. Mr. Ferri swam around the edge of the pool 4 times. About how far did he swim? Did he swim at least 1 kilometer?

ON YOUR OWN

Form groups of 3 or 4 students in your class. Estimate the length and width of your classroom. Then measure with a meter stick. How close were your estimates? Whose estimates were the closest?

ESTIMATE!

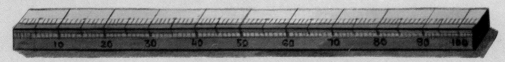

Problem Solving

Using Decimals

A. Jim won the swimming race with a time of 51.82 seconds. Paul came in second with a time of 53.76 seconds. How much less was Jim's time than Paul's?

First estimate. Round to the nearest one.

$$
\begin{array}{r}
53.76 \longrightarrow 54 \\
-51.82 \longrightarrow -52 \\
\hline
2
\end{array}
$$

The difference is about 2.

Subtract to find the exact difference.

Check.

$$
\begin{array}{r}
2\ 17 \\
5\cancel{3}.\cancel{7}6 \\
-51.82 \\
\hline
1.94
\end{array}
\qquad
\begin{array}{r}
1 \\
51.82 \\
+\ 1.94 \\
\hline
53.76 \checkmark
\end{array}
$$

Jim's time was 1.94 seconds less than Paul's.

B. The four swimmers on the relay team swam their parts of the relay race in 43.15 seconds, 48.8 seconds, 50 seconds, and 44.06 seconds. What was the team's time for the race?

Estimate.

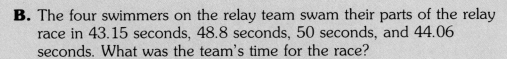

$$
\begin{array}{r}
43.15 \longrightarrow 43 \\
48.8 \longrightarrow 49 \\
50 \longrightarrow 50 \\
+44.06 \longrightarrow +44
\end{array}
$$

about 100   87   The sum is about 187.

Add to find the exact sum.

$$
\begin{array}{r}
11\ 1 \\
43.15 \\
48.80 \\
50.00 \\
+44.06 \\
\hline
186.01
\end{array}
$$

Write 0's to help line up the decimal points.

The team's time was 186.01 seconds.

TRY THESE

Solve.

1. Bill lifted 155.25 kg. Gary lifted 182.5 kg. Who lifted more? How much more?

2. Willie swam 23.85 meters. Marie swam 25.09 meters. How much farther did Marie swim?

3. The four swimmers in the relay swam their parts in 57.616 seconds, 59.15 seconds, 60 seconds, and 58.329 seconds. What was the team's time?

4. A track star ran a 200-meter race. He ran the first 100 meters in 11.3 seconds and the second 100 meters in 10.87 seconds. What was his total time?

PROBLEM SOLVING PRACTICE

Use the table to solve the problems. The table shows the times for the first and second places in three races.

Event	Time: Winner	Time: Second place
100-meter dash	11.88 seconds	12 seconds
200-meter dash	25.03 seconds	25.78 seconds
400-meter dash	54.4 seconds	56.25 seconds

1. What was the difference between the winner's time for the 400-meter dash and the winner's time for the 200-meter dash?

2. How much longer did it take the winner of the 200-meter dash to finish than the winner of the 100-meter dash?

3. What was the total time for the winners of the three races?

4. The winner of the 400-meter dash broke the school record of 55.42 seconds. By how much did she break the record?

★5. By how much time did the second-place finisher of the 400-meter dash lose?

★6. If the winner and second-place finisher of the 100-meter dash could run a 200-meter relay at the same rate, how long would the race take?

ON YOUR OWN

Four horses finished a jumping contest without knocking down any fences. The winner was the horse that jumped in the fastest time. Make up two problems about the jumping times.

Horse	Time
Trinket	34.71 seconds
Jolly Roger	29.43 seconds
Snowflake	31.32 seconds
Gray Lady	36.03 seconds

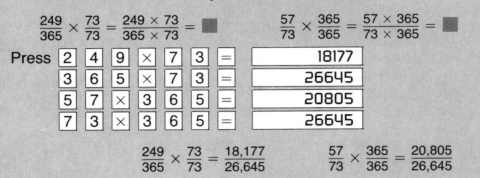

TECHNOLOGY

Fractions and Decimals with a Calculator

Carl and Carol both worked at the supermarket. Carl said he worked $\frac{249}{365}$ of the days of the year. Carol said she worked $\frac{57}{73}$ of the days of the year. Who worked more days? How many more?

If you remember that 365 is a multiple of 73, you can use fractions. You can also use your calculator like this:

$$\frac{249}{365} \times \frac{73}{73} = \frac{249 \times 73}{365 \times 73} = \blacksquare \qquad \frac{57}{73} \times \frac{365}{365} = \frac{57 \times 365}{73 \times 365} = \blacksquare$$

Press
2	4	9	×	7	3	=	18177
3	6	5	×	7	3	=	26645
5	7	×	3	6	5	=	20805
7	3	×	3	6	5	=	26645

$$\frac{249}{365} \times \frac{73}{73} = \frac{18{,}177}{26{,}645} \qquad \frac{57}{73} \times \frac{365}{365} = \frac{20{,}805}{26{,}645}$$

Carol worked more days. To find out how many more:

Press | 2 | 0 | 8 | 0 | 5 | − | 1 | 8 | 1 | 7 | 7 | ÷ | 7 | 3 | = | 36 |

She worked 36 more days.

Calculators are especially easy to use with decimals. If you accept a decimal answer (sometimes an approximation) to a fraction problem, this method will work.

$$\frac{249}{365} = \blacksquare \qquad\qquad \frac{57}{73} = \blacksquare$$

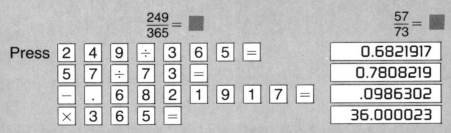

Press
2	4	9	÷	3	6	5	=	0.6821917
5	7	÷	7	3	=	0.7808219
−	.	6	8	2	1	9	1	7	=	.0986302
×	3	6	5	=	36.000023

Solve, first using fractions and then decimals.

1. Karl worked $\frac{182}{365}$ of the days of the year and Kim worked $\frac{38}{73}$ of the days of the year. Who worked more days? How many more?

2. Jan worked $\frac{284}{366}$ of the days of a leap year and Jon worked $\frac{43}{61}$ of the days of the same leap year. Who worked more days? How many more?

Unit Review

Write in words. *(pages 256–261)*

1. 3.7   **2.** 6.93   **3.** 2.518

Write the standard decimal. *(pages 256–261)*

4. 2 ones 4 tenths   **5.** 7 tenths

6. five and nine thousandths   **7.** fourteen and thirty-five hundredths

Write >, <, or = for ●. *(pages 262–263)*

8. 7.62 ● 7.63   **9.** .730 ● .703   **10.** 9.5 ● .95   **11.** .02 ● .003

12. 21.4 ● .21.40   **13.** 6.8 ● 8.6   **14.** 3.14 ● 3.141   **15.** 2.3 ● 2.35

Add. *(pages 268–269)*

16.
$$\begin{array}{r} 47.5 \\ + \ 3.8 \\ \hline \end{array}$$

17.
$$\begin{array}{r} 19.47 \\ +26.95 \\ \hline \end{array}$$

18.
$$\begin{array}{r} 83.95 \\ +37.686 \\ \hline \end{array}$$

19.
$$\begin{array}{r} 83.994 \\ 17.637 \\ + \ 3.802 \\ \hline \end{array}$$

20.
$$\begin{array}{r} \$ \ \ .58 \\ 11.63 \\ + \ \ 4.95 \\ \hline \end{array}$$

21. 163 + 52.7 = ■   **22.** 34.9 + 28.4 = ■   **23.** 2.95 + 6.83 + 4.875 = ■

Subtract. *(pages 270–271)*

24.
$$\begin{array}{r} 8.5 \\ -3.7 \\ \hline \end{array}$$

25.
$$\begin{array}{r} 20.15 \\ - \ 6.89 \\ \hline \end{array}$$

26.
$$\begin{array}{r} 82.5 \\ - \ .86 \\ \hline \end{array}$$

27.
$$\begin{array}{r} 5.432 \\ - \ .684 \\ \hline \end{array}$$

28.
$$\begin{array}{r} 4 \\ - \ .832 \\ \hline \end{array}$$

29. 3.952 − 1.485 = ■   **30.** .864 − .59 = ■   **31.** 31.2 − 29.5 = ■

Estimate. Then solve the problems. *(pages 274–275)*

32. In high diving, Erik got 93.94 points. Klaus got 124.18 points. How many more points did Klaus get than Erik?

33. In gymnastics, Jodi got these scores: 19.865, 19.725, and 19.85. How many points did Jodi get in all?

Reinforcement

More Help with Adding with Decimals

```
  1 1
 14.5
+ 6.8
 21.3

 1  1 1
 3.485
+1.947
 5.432

 65.9
+47.68
```

Write 65.90
for 65.9.

```
  1 1
 65.90
+47.68
113.58
```

Add.

1.   3.7
    +5.9

2.   8.4
    +7.8

3.   6.14
    +3.97

4. $8.73
    + 5.87

5.   2.147
    +3.684

6.   1.383
    +7.869

7. $8.02
    + 6.79

8.   14.9
    +36.4

9.   8.9
    + .5

10.   14.9
    + 8.3

11.   5.238
    +2.795

12.   1.849
    +4.675

13.   25.4
    +16.83

14.   17.9
    +24.28

15.   1.39
    +2.684

16. $3.92
    +7

More Help with Subtracting with Decimals

```
    13
  1 3 13
 24.3
-16.8
  7.5

    11 14
  5 X X 17
 6.257
-3.589
 2.668

 4
-  .673
```

Write 4.000
for 4.

```
  9 9
3 10 10 10
4.000
-  .673
 3.327
```

Subtract.

17.   8.4
    −2.6

18.   5.3
    −1.7

19.   2.15
    −1.68

20.   9.28
    −3.69

21.   9.325
    −4.638

22.   2.458
    −1.683

23.   9.02
    −5.38

24.   38.7
    −26.9

25.   8.635
    − .437

26.   17.63
    − 8.85

27.   .084
    − .067

28.   68.23
    − 7.59

29.   800
    −642.7

30.   41.2
    −28.73

31. $43.20
    − 18.99

32. $42
    − 36.95

Distance Between Integers

This thermometer shows temperatures from ⁻30°C or 30 degrees **below** 0°C to ⁺30°C or 30 degrees **above** 0°C.

Water freezes.

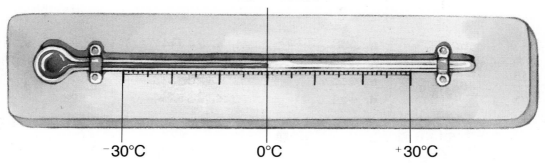

⁻30°C   0°C   ⁺30°C

Use this thermometer to do exercises 1–8. Tell whether the temperature is rising or falling. Then tell by how many degrees. You may want to draw pictures.

1. from 0°C to ⁺23°C   **2.** from ⁺10°C to ⁺21°C   **3.** from ⁺22°C to ⁺9°C

4. from 0°C to ⁻6°C   **5.** from ⁻10°C to ⁻12°C   **6.** from ⁻7°C to ⁻5°C

Use two steps or drawings to do these:

7. from ⁺6°C to ⁻3°C   **8.** from ⁻4°C to ⁺12°C

The set of positive and negative whole numbers and zero are called *integers.*

Use this number line to find the distance between each pair of integers.

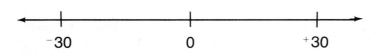

⁻30   0   ⁺30

1. 0 and ⁺23   **2.** ⁺10 and ⁺21   **3.** ⁺22 and ⁺9

4. 0 and ⁻6   **5.** ⁻10 and ⁻12   **6.** ⁻7 and ⁻5

7. ⁺6 and ⁻3   **8.** ⁻4 and ⁺12

Cumulative Review

Choose the correct answer.

1. $\frac{5}{8} + \frac{3}{4} = \blacksquare$

a. $\frac{2}{3}$ **b.** $\frac{1}{2}$

c. $\frac{15}{32}$ **d.** $1\frac{3}{8}$

2. $504 - 96 = \blacksquare$

a. 408
b. 414
c. 418
d. 464

3. $26\overline{)5,308}$

a. 24 R4
b. 204 R4
c. 265 R3
d. 231 R4

4. Find the lowest terms fraction for $\frac{6}{15}$.

a. $\frac{2}{15}$ **b.** $\frac{6}{5}$

c. $\frac{3}{5}$ **d.** $\frac{2}{5}$

5. $78.3 + 3.94 = \blacksquare$

a. 117.7
b. 11.77
c. 82.24
d. 107.7

6. $\frac{5}{6} \times \frac{1}{4} = \blacksquare$

a. 2   **b.** $\frac{5}{24}$

c. $\frac{3}{5}$ **d.** $1\frac{1}{4}$

7. $\begin{array}{r} 12 \\ -\ 9.624 \end{array}$

a. 2.376
b. 3.624
c. 2.486
d. 2.375

8. $\boxed{\begin{array}{l} 1 \text{ hour} \\ = 60 \text{ minutes} \end{array}}$

3 hours
40 minutes
$= \blacksquare$ minutes

a. 340 minutes
b. 180 minutes
c. 220 minutes
d. 160 minutes

9. $\begin{array}{r} 64 \\ \times 35 \end{array}$

a. 512
b. 19,520
c. 482
d. 2,240

10. Find the decimal for 63 thousandths.

a. 63,000
b. .063
c. .0063
d. .63

11. Complete.
   $4.2 \bullet 4.16$

a. <
b. =
c. >

12. Find the standard numeral for sixty million, eight.

a. 60,8
b. 60,008
c. 60,000,8
d. 60,000,008

13. Timothy ran 100 m in 14.8 seconds. Steven ran the same distance in 16 seconds. How much less time did Timothy run?

a. 1.2 seconds   **b.** 1.19 seconds
c. 2.8 seconds   **d.** 30.8 seconds

14. Earl painted $\frac{2}{5}$ of the wall. Tammy painted $\frac{1}{3}$ of it. What part did they paint all together?

a. $\frac{3}{8}$ of the wall   **b.** $\frac{11}{15}$ of the wall

c. $\frac{2}{15}$ of the wall   **d.** $\frac{1}{2}$ of the wall

10 Geometry and Measurement

Helicopter Facts

- The first manned helicopter flight took place in France in 1907. This helicopter reached an altitude of 2 feet for 1 minute. That same year another model reached the altitude of 6 feet for 1 minute.

- In 1937 Heinrich Focke built a helicopter that could remain aloft for 80 minutes, reach a speed of 75 miles per hour, and attain an altitude of 11,243 feet.

- Today the world's largest helicopter is the Soviet Union's MI-12. It is 121 feet long and can lift 68,000 pounds to a height of 9,500 feet.

- The smallest helicopter now available can be strapped to an individual's back.

Points, Lines, and Planes

A. The front cover of this book is a flat surface. Think of the cover "going on forever" in all directions. Such an unending, flat surface is a *plane.*

B. *Line segment* AB (or line segment BA) is the straight path joining *points* A and B. A point is an exact location. A and B are the *endpoints.*

Write: $\overline{AB}$ or $\overline{BA}$.

Read: line segment AB or line segment BA.

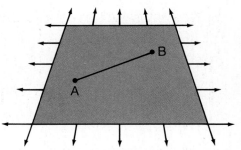

The arrows mean that the plane "goes on forever."

C. If a line segment goes on forever in both directions a *line* is formed. Names for the line shown are:

$\overleftrightarrow{AB}$ $\overleftrightarrow{BA}$ $\overleftrightarrow{AC}$ $\overleftrightarrow{CA}$
$\overleftrightarrow{BC}$ $\overleftrightarrow{CB}$

Use any two points of a line to name it.

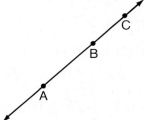

Write: $\overleftrightarrow{AB}$.   Read: line AB.

D. $\overleftrightarrow{EF}$ and $\overleftrightarrow{GH}$ are *intersecting lines.* They *intersect* at point P.

$\overleftrightarrow{IJ}$ and $\overleftrightarrow{KL}$ will intersect at a point that is beyond this diagram.

$\overleftrightarrow{MN}$ and $\overleftrightarrow{RS}$ are *parallel lines.* Parallel lines are lines in a plane that will never intersect.

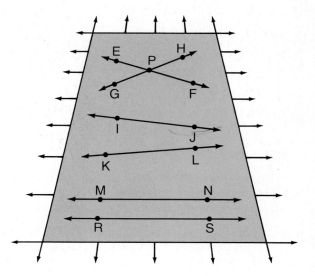

TRY THESE

1. Give six names for this line.

2. Name three different line segments that are part of the line above.

SKILLS PRACTICE

1. Give two names for each line segment in this figure.

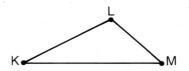

2. Give six names for this line.

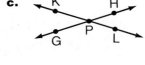

Match.

3. point

4. line segment

5. line

6. parallel lines

7. plane

8. intersecting lines

a.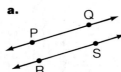

b.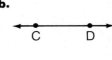

c.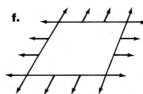

d.

e.

f.

★**9.** How many names can you give for a line that has 2 of its points named? 3 points named? 4 points named?

THINK!

Looking for a Pattern
How many different line segments can you draw using 2 points?

3 points?   4 points?

Complete this table. Look for a pattern. No more than 2 points are on the same line.

Number of points	2	3	4	5	6	7	8	9	11	15
Number of segments	1	3	6	■	■	■	■	■	■	■

Rays and Angles

A. A *ray* is part of a line. It has one endpoint and goes on forever in one direction.

A   B

Write: $\overrightarrow{AB}$.
Read: ray AB.

A   B

Write: $\overrightarrow{BA}$.
Read: ray BA.

B. An *angle* is formed by two rays with the same endpoint. An angle has a *vertex* and two *sides.*

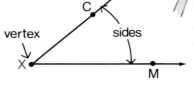
vertex   sides

Write ∠X or ∠CXM or ∠MXC.

∠X has sides $\overrightarrow{XC}$ and $\overrightarrow{XM}$, and vertex X.

C. To measure an angle, select a small angle as a unit of measure. Find how many units fill the inside of the angle.

Unit of measure   Measure of ∠KRT: 5 units

The *degree* (°) is a common unit for measuring angles. 180 one-degree angles fill one side of a line.

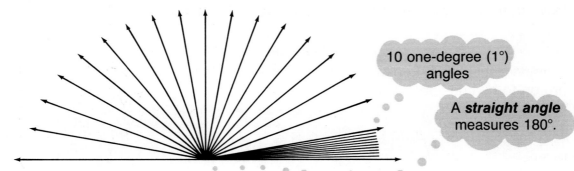

10 one-degree (1°) angles

A *straight angle* measures 180°.

TRY THESE

1. Which picture shows $\overrightarrow{DE}$? $\overrightarrow{ED}$?

a.

b.

2. Name the angle. Then name its sides and vertex.

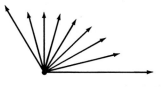

How many units fill the inside of each angle?

3. 
unit

4.
unit

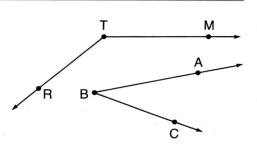

SKILLS PRACTICE

Use the pictures.

1. Name each ray.

2. Name each angle.

3. Name the sides of each angle.

4. Name the vertex of each angle.

Draw three points that are not on a line. Label them P, Q, and L. Then draw:

5. $\overrightarrow{PQ}$ **6.** $\overrightarrow{QP}$ **7.** $\overline{QL}$ **8.** $\angle PLQ$ **9.** $\overline{PL}$

How many units fill the inside of each angle?

10. 
unit

11.
unit

12. 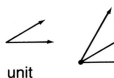
unit

★13. How many 1° angles will fill both sides of a line?

THINK!

On and On

Can you find the length of a line? a ray? a line segment? the side of an angle?

Measuring Angles

A. You can use a *protractor* to measure angles. To measure ∠ABC, place the protractor as shown.

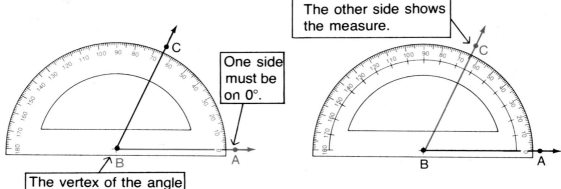

The other side shows the measure.

One side must be on 0°.

The vertex of the angle must be here.

The measure of ∠ABC is 65°.
Write: m∠ABC = 65°.

B. Some protractors list the numbers of degrees in both directions around the protractor.

$\overrightarrow{SR}$ is on 0°.
Use the blue numerals for ∠RSU and ∠RST.

m∠RSU = 55°
m∠RST = 140°

C. Sometimes you need to turn your protractor to measure an angle.

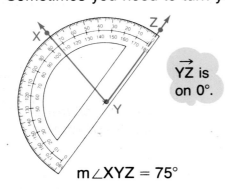

$\overrightarrow{YZ}$ is on 0°.

m∠XYZ = 75°

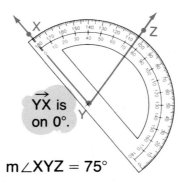

$\overrightarrow{YX}$ is on 0°.

m∠XYZ = 75°

Use this protractor for exercises 1–3.

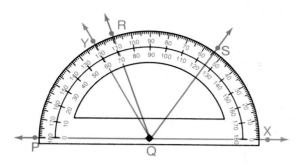

1. m∠PQR = ■

2. m∠PQS = ■

3. m∠XQY = ■

Use this protractor for exercises 1–4.

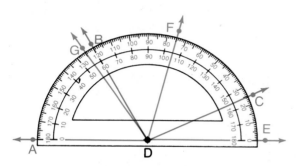

1. m∠ADC = ■

2. m∠EDG = ■

3. m∠EDF = ■

4. m∠ADB = ■

Use your protractor to measure these angles.

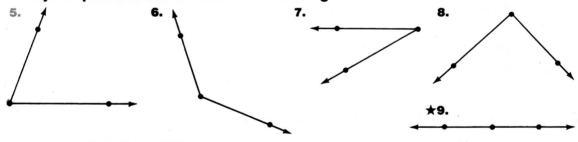

5.   6.   7.   8.

★9.

THINK!

Add or Subtract

Place addition signs and subtraction signs in this row of digits to make the result equal to 100. You can close up the digits to make 2-digit numbers.

9   8   7   6   5   4   3   2   1

Polygons

A. A *polygon* is a plane figure. Its sides are line segments.
Each pair of sides meets at a vertex.
Names of types of polygons tell the numbers of sides,
vertices, and angles they have.

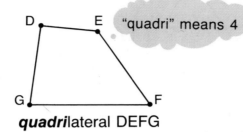
"tri" means 3

triangle ABC

"quadri" means 4

quadrilateral DEFG

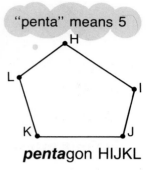
"penta" means 5

pentagon HIJKL

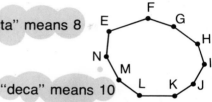
"hexa" means 6

hexagon MNOPQR

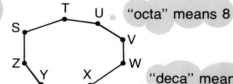
"octa" means 8

octagon STUVWXYZ

"deca" means 10

decagon EFGHIJKLMN

B. A *diagonal* of a polygon is a line segment that has two vertices
as endpoints but is *not* a side. The diagonals of pentagon
ABCDE are:

$$\overline{AC}, \overline{AD}, \overline{BD}, \overline{BE}, \overline{CE}$$

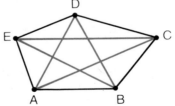

C. A *regular polygon* has all of its sides of equal length and
all of its angles of equal measure.

*Regular
Polygons*

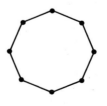

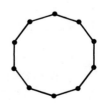

pentagon   hexagon   octagon   decagon

TRY THESE

Give the number of sides of each.

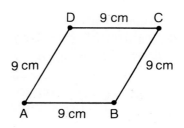

D   9 cm   C

9 cm   9 cm

A   9 cm   B

1. hexagon   **2.** decagon   **3.** pentagon

4. Why is ABCD *not* a regular quadrilateral?

5. Name all of the diagonals of ABCD that could be drawn.

SKILLS PRACTICE

Match.

1. hexagon   **2.** triangle

3. quadrilateral   **4.** octagon

5. pentagon   **6.** decagon

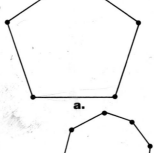

a.

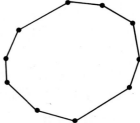

b.

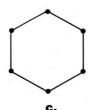

c.

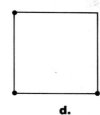

d.

e.

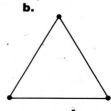

f.

7. Which polygons above are regular polygons?

8. Copy this figure. Draw and name all of its diagonals.

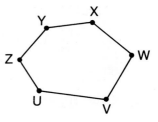

Y   X

Z   W

U   V

★**9.** What is another name for a regular quadrilateral?

★**10.** How many diagonals can be drawn for an octagon?

THINK!

Roman Numeral Sentence

This number sentence, made with toothpicks, is false. By moving only one toothpick, make the sentence true.

Kinds of Angles and Triangles

A. Angles with measures of 90° are *right angles.*
Angles with measures less than 90° are *acute angles.*
Angles with measures greater than 90° are *obtuse angles.*

Right Angles		**Acute Angles**	**Obtuse Angles**	**Straight Angles**

"⌐" means right angle.

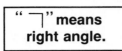

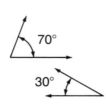

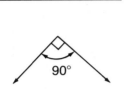

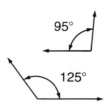

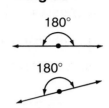

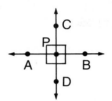

B. Lines that form four right angles at their point of intersection are *perpendicular lines.*

∠APD, ∠DPB, ∠BPC, and ∠CPA are right angles.
↔   ↔
AB and CD are perpendicular lines.

C. Triangles can be described by the kinds of angles they have or by the number of sides of equal length they have.

Acute Triangle	**Right Triangle**	**Obtuse Triangle**

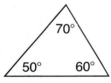

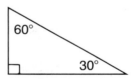

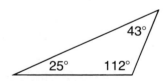

3 acute angles   1 right angle   1 obtuse angle

Isosceles Triangle	**Equilateral Triangle**	**Scalene Triangle**

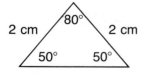

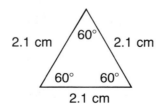

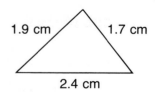

at least
2 sides of equal length
2 angles of equal measure

3 sides of equal length
3 angles of equal measure

3 sides of
different lengths

TRY THESE

1. Which angle is an acute angle?

2. Which angle is a right angle?

3. Which angle is an obtuse angle?

4. Select one word from each list to describe this triangle.

   a. acute, right, obtuse

   b. isosceles (*not* equilateral), equilateral, scalene

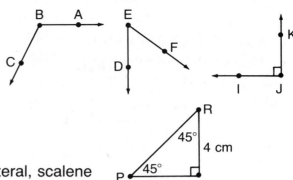

SKILLS PRACTICE

Select one word from list a. and one from list b. to describe each triangle in exercises 1–4.

a. acute, right, obtuse   b. isosceles (*not* equilateral), equilateral, scalene

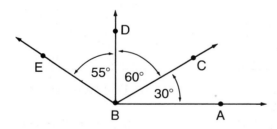

Use this picture.

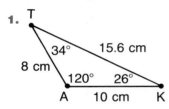

Use this picture.

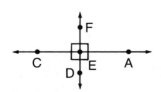

5. Name an acute angle.

6. Name a right angle.

7. Name an obtuse angle.

★8. If ∠ABF is a straight angle, what is the measure of ∠EBF?

9. Name two perpendicular lines.

10. Name four right angles.

11. Name one point of intersection.

★12. Name two straight angles.

Special Quadrilaterals

A. A *quadrilateral* is a closed plane figure with 4 sides.
Adjacent sides of a quadrilateral intersect.
Opposite sides do not intersect.

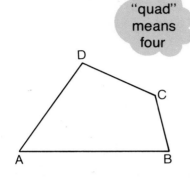

quadrilateral ABCD

Adjacent sides
$\overline{AB}$ and $\overline{BC}$
$\overline{BC}$ and $\overline{CD}$
$\overline{CD}$ and $\overline{DA}$
$\overline{DA}$ and $\overline{AB}$

Opposite sides
$\overline{AB}$ and $\overline{CD}$
$\overline{BC}$ and $\overline{DA}$

"quad" means four

B. A *parallelogram* is a quadrilateral with both pairs of opposite sides parallel. The opposite sides of a parallelogram have equal lengths.

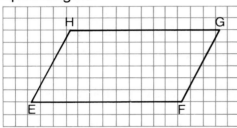

parallelogram EFGH

$\overline{EF}$ and $\overline{HG}$ are parallel and have equal lengths.

$\overline{FG}$ and $\overline{EH}$ are parallel and have equal lengths.

C. A *rectangle* is a parallelogram with 4 right angles.
A *square* is a rectangle with 4 sides of equal lengths.

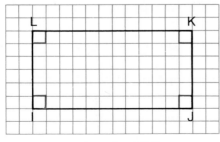

rectangle IJKL

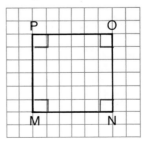

square MNOP

TRY THESE

Use parallelogram PTUV.

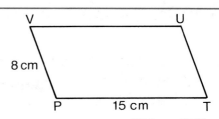

1. Name the sides adjacent to $\overline{PV}$.

2. Name the side opposite $\overline{UV}$.

3. Name the angles of this parallelogram.

4. Give the length of $\overline{TU}$; of $\overline{UV}$.

SKILLS PRACTICE

Use these figures in exercises 1–8.

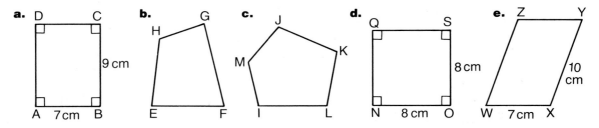

Which of these figures are:

1. quadrilaterals?   **2.** parallelograms?   **3.** rectangles?   **4.** squares?

Give:

5. the sides adjacent to $\overline{EF}$.

6. the side opposite $\overline{XY}$.

7. 6 pairs of parallel sides.

8. the length of $\overline{AD}$; $\overline{NQ}$; $\overline{YZ}$.

★9. Use two different words from the list below to make true statements.

quadrilateral, parallelogram, rectangle, square

Every ▓▓▓▓ is also a ▓▓▓▓.

THINK!

Visual Perception

How many rectangles of any size are in this figure?

Circles

A. All points on a **circle** are the same
distance from the **center** of the circle.
You name a circle by naming its center.

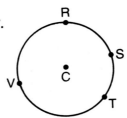

Point C is the center of circle C.
Points R, S, T, and V are
points of the circle.

B. A **chord** is a line segment whose
endpoints are points of the circle.

A **diameter** is a chord that passes
through the center of the circle.

A **radius** is a line segment whose
endpoints are the center of the circle
and a point on the circle.

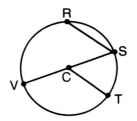

$\overline{RS}$ and $\overline{SV}$
are chords.

$\overline{SV}$ is a diameter.

$\overline{CS}$, $\overline{CV}$, and $\overline{CT}$
are radii (plural
of "radius").

The **circumference** is the distance around the circle.

C. You can make, or construct, a circle using a compass. The
sharp point of a compass marks the center of the circle.
Cover the circumference of the circle with a piece of string.
The length of the string is the circumference of the circle.

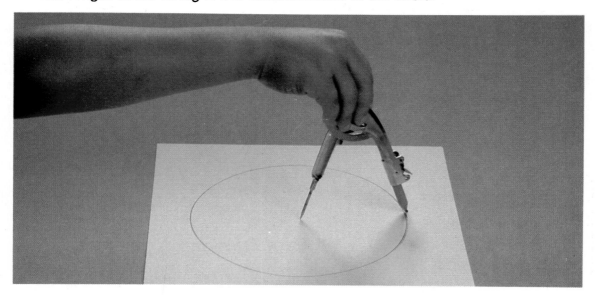

TRY THESE

1. Name the circle. 2. Name a diameter.

3. Name three chords. 4. Name three radii.

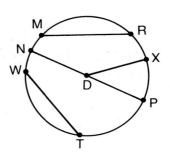

5. Construct several circles using a compass.
   Cover the circumference of each circle
   with a piece of string. Compare the
   circumference of each circle to its
   diameter. What do you notice?

SKILLS PRACTICE

1. Name the center of this circle.

2. Name the diameters shown.

3. Name the chords shown.

4. Name the radii shown.

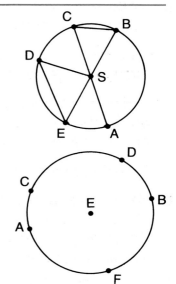

Copy circle E. Use your copy.

5. Draw and name a diameter.

6. Draw and name a chord that is not a diameter.

7. Name a radius that is part of a diameter.

8. Draw and name a radius that is not part
   of the diameter you have drawn.

9. Use string to find the circumference of the circle. Compare the
   circumference to the diameter.

★10. Measure the length of the radius you drew in exercise 7 to the
   nearest millimeter. Write the length of the diameter you drew
   in exercise 6 without measuring.

Checkered Chords

Suppose you have 13 checkers. How can you arrange
them all in 6 rows with 3 checkers in each row?

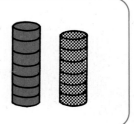

Similarity and Congruence

A. Figures that have the same shape are *similar.*

Triangle ABC is similar to triangle DEF.

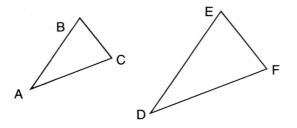

Quadrilateral MNOP is similar to quadrilateral WXYZ.

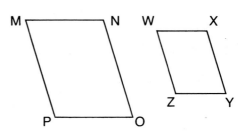

B. Any two squares have the same shape. Square HIJK is similar to square QRST.

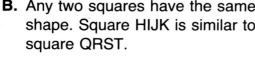

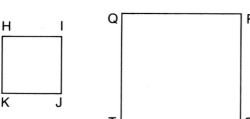

C. Any two circles have the same shape. Circle G is similar to circle L.

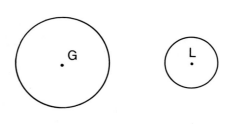

D. Figures that have the same size and shape are *congruent.*

Triangle EFG is congruent to triangle KLM. Triangle EFG is not congruent to triangle RST.

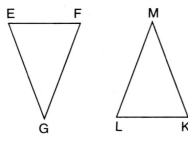

not same shape

Pentagon ABCDE is congruent to pentagon TUVWX but is not congruent to pentagon JKLMN.

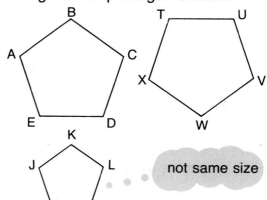

not same size

TRY THESE

1. Which figures are similar to quadrilateral DEFG?
2. Which figures are congruent to quadrilateral DEFG?

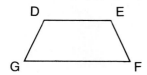

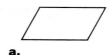

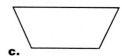

a.   b.   c.

SKILLS PRACTICE

Are the figures similar?

1.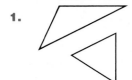
2.
3.
4.

Are the figures congruent?

5.
6.
7.
8.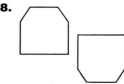

9. On grid paper draw a rectangle 7 units long and 3 units wide. Draw another rectangle similar to the first. Make each side twice as long.

★10. On the same grid paper you used in exercise 9, draw another rectangle congruent to the first. How long is the new rectangle? How wide?

★11. Is it possible to draw a circle that is not congruent to circle T? a circle that is not similar to circle T?

THINK!

Logical Reasoning

What is the smallest number that satisfies *both* conditions?

I. If the number is divided by 2, 3, 4, 5, or 6, the remainder is always 1.

II. If the number is divided by 11, the remainder is 0.

Symmetry

A. The red line is a *line of symmetry* for this figure. If you fold along the line of symmetry, one piece of the figure will fit exactly on the other.

Pieces of a figure that fit exactly on each other are *congruent.* A line of symmetry separates a figure into two congruent pieces.

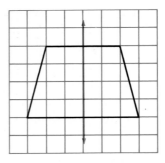

B. Some figures have more than one line of symmetry. Some figures have no lines of symmetry.

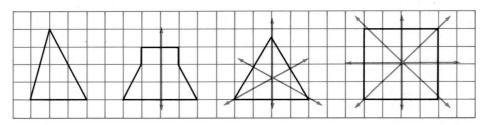

Number of lines of symmetry:　　0　　　　　　1　　　　　　3　　　　　　4

C. You can copy and complete this figure so that the red line is a line of symmetry.

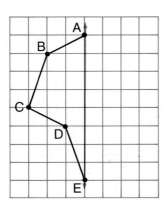

Think about folding along the red line. You can mark the point each vertex would touch, then join these points to complete the figure.

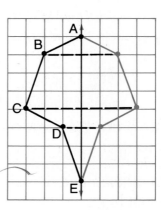

298　**Geometry and Measurement**

TRY THESE

Is the red line a line of symmetry?

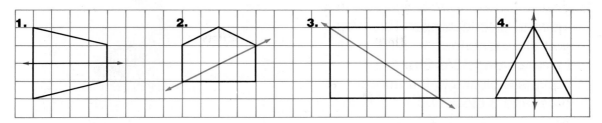

1.　　　　**2.**　　　　**3.**　　　　**4.**

SKILLS PRACTICE

How many lines of symmetry does each figure have?

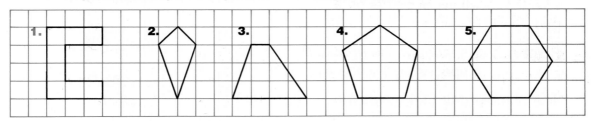

1.　　**2.**　　**3.**　　**4.**　　**5.**

Copy and complete each figure so that the red line is a line of symmetry.

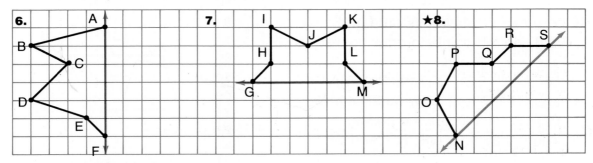

6.　　　　**7.**　　　　**★8.**

★**9.** How many lines of symmetry does a circle have?

★**10.** Complete: For a circle, any line through ▨▨▨▨ is a line of symmetry.

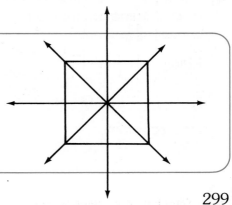

THINK!

Preserving Symmetry

This figure has 4 lines of symmetry.
Add 4 line segments to the figure to make
2 squares and 4 triangles. The new figure
must have the same lines of symmetry.

Locating Points on a Grid

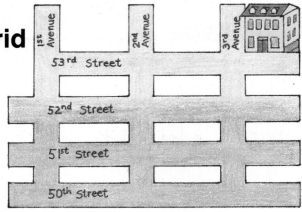

City streets often form a grid that can be used to give locations. This map of part of a city shows a building at 3rd Avenue and 53rd Street. The building is 2 blocks to the *right* of 1st Avenue and 3 blocks *up* from 50th Street.

A. You can use **number pairs** to give the locations of points on a grid.

Point A is: 3 spaces to the *right of 0*
        4 spaces *up from 0*

The number pair (3,4) gives the location of point A. (5,2) gives the location of point B.

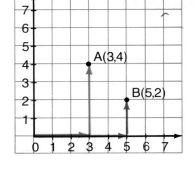

B. You can locate points on a grid and join the points to draw figures.

Locate P (2,3), Q (7,3), R (8,6), and S (3,6) and draw quadrilateral PQRS. First locate the points. Then, draw $\overline{PQ}$, $\overline{QR}$, $\overline{RS}$, and $\overline{SP}$.

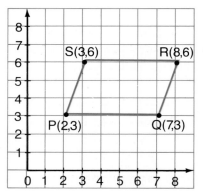

C. You can locate these points and draw the line segments to complete a figure.

Points:
A (2,1), B (6,1), C (6,2), D (3,2), E (1,2), F (3,3), G (3,6), H (5,3)

Line segments:
$\overline{AB}$, $\overline{BC}$, $\overline{CE}$, $\overline{EA}$, $\overline{DG}$, $\overline{GH}$, $\overline{HF}$

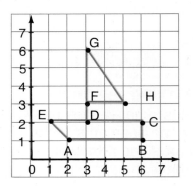

TRY THESE

Give the letter for each number pair.

1. (3,4)   **2.** (4,3)   **3.** (5,1)

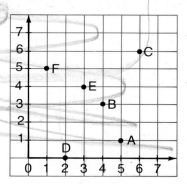

Give the number pair for each point.

4. F   **5.** C   **6.** D

SKILLS PRACTICE

Give the letter for each number pair.

1. (6,4)   **2.** (4,6)   **3.** (2,2)

4. (0,8)   **5.** (5,7)   **6.** (3,1)

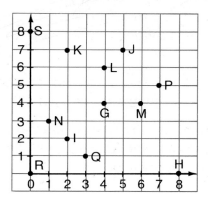

Give the number pair for each point.

7. P   **8.** N   **9.** H

10. G   **11.** K   **12.** R

Copy this grid. Locate the points and draw the line segments.

13. A (3,0), B (7,0), C (9,2), D (7,3),
E (5,4), F (3,3), G (1,2);
$\overline{AB}$, $\overline{BD}$, $\overline{CD}$, $\overline{DE}$, $\overline{EF}$, $\overline{FG}$, $\overline{FA}$

14. H (1,5), I (1,8), J (6,8), K (6,5),
L (7,5), M (7,7), N (9,9), P (9,7)
Q (9,5); $\overline{HI}$, $\overline{IJ}$, $\overline{JK}$, $\overline{LM}$, $\overline{MP}$, $\overline{PN}$, $\overline{PQ}$

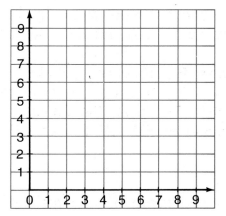

THINK!

Logical Reasoning

A clock strikes all the hours and also chimes once at each half-hour. Sandy has been counting the chimes. She heard the 34th chime at 3:30 P.M. When did she begin counting?

Problem Solving Strategy

Make a Model

Roger and Rosa are building stair-steps to their clubhouse. They have some 1-foot cubic boxes to use. Can you tell how many boxes they need to build stairs 4 feet high?

You can make a model with small cubes to see how many boxes they need.

Roger and Rosa need 10 boxes.

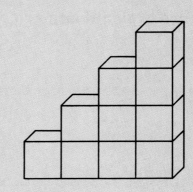

Make models or draw pictures to solve these problems.

1. If Roger and Rosa wanted to paint *all* the outside faces of their stairs, how many squares would they paint?

2. How many boxes would be needed to build stairs 5 feet high? How many outside faces are there?

3. How many boxes are needed to build 4-way stairs like these? How many outside faces are there?

4. How many boxes are needed to build 2-way stairs like these? How many boxes would be needed to make stairs 1 foot higher? How many outside faces are there for each?

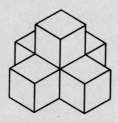

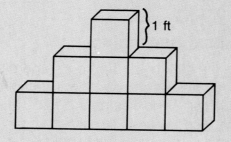

1 ft

Problem Solving Project

Slides, Turns, Flips

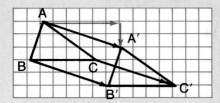

This picture shows a **slide.** By sliding triangle ABC 6 units to the right and 2 units down, you obtain the *image* triangle A'B'C'. The image triangle is the same size and shape as triangle ABC.

This picture shows a **turn.** Rectangle DEFG is turned 90° clockwise about the point G. The image, rectangle D'E'F'G, is the same size and shape as DEFG.

This picture shows a **flip.** Triangle PQR is flipped over line ST. The image, triangle P'Q'R', is the same size and shape as PQR.

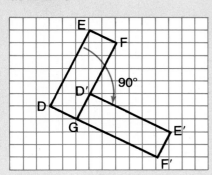

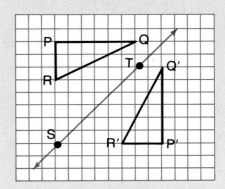

When you slide, turn, or flip a figure, the image is the same size and shape or **congruent** to the original figure.

Copy this triangle. Use 1-centimeter grid paper.

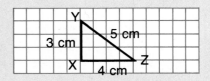

1. Trace the triangle onto your grid paper so that each vertex is at a grid corner. Then slide your triangle 4 units to the right and 3 units down. Draw its image.

2. Turn your triangle 180° clockwise about point Z and draw its image.

3. Draw a line that does not meet your triangle. Flip your triangle over the line and draw its image.

ON YOUR OWN

Draw a figure on grid paper. Do a series of slides, turns, and flips in any order you choose. Then try to find a series of slides, turns, and flips that will return the image figure to its original position.

Perimeter

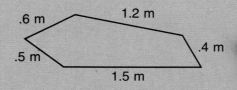

A. The **perimeter** of a polygon is the distance around the polygon. Add the lengths of the sides to find the perimeter.

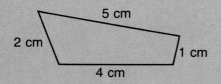

Perimeter = 4 + 1 + 5 + 2
= 12 cm

Perimeter = 1.5 + .4 + 1.2 + .6 + .5
= 4.2 m

B. Mrs. Adams runs once around a field that is shaped like a rectangle. The field is 700 m long and 400 m wide. How far does Mrs. Adams run?

Perimeter = 700 + 400 + ? + ?

Opposite sides of a rectangle have equal lengths.

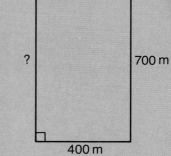

= 700 + 400 + 700 + 400
= 2,200 m

Mrs. Adams runs 2,200 m.

C. For a rectangle:

Perimeter = length + width + length + width

A **formula** is a short way of writing this:

$$P = l + w + l + w$$

TRY THESE

Find the perimeter of each polygon.

1.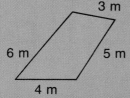

2.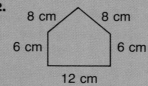

3.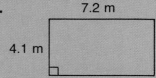

SKILLS PRACTICE

Find the perimeter of each polygon.

1.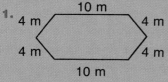

2.

20 cm

25 cm

3.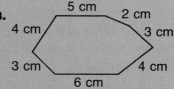

4.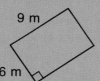

5.

50.7 cm   60.3 cm

40.2 cm

6.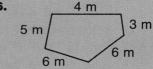

7. a rectangle with
   length: 18 m
   width: 7 m .

8. a rectangle with
   length: 23 cm
   width: 11 cm

★9. a square with
   length of one side:
   5 cm

PROBLEM SOLVING

10. A playground is 55.6 m long and 28.2 m wide. It is shaped like a rectangle. How many meters of fencing are needed to put a fence around this playground?

★11. A garden is shaped like a regular pentagon. Each of its sides is 4 m long. How far must you walk to walk around the outside of this garden one time? six times?

THINK!

Equal Payments

This bar of gold is 7 cm long. Cut the bar in only two places. After it is cut, you must be able to pay someone 1 cm of the bar each day for 7 days.

|←——————— 7 cm ———————→|

Area

A. The **area** of a figure is the size of the inside of the figure.

The **square centimeter** (cm²) and the **square meter** (m²) are metric units used to measure area.

Length of each side of a square	Area of the square
1 cm	1 cm²
1 m	1 m²

The area of this page is about 500 cm².
The area of a door is about 2 m².

B. To find the area of a figure, you can count the square units that fill the inside of the figure.

    By counting: Area = 15 cm²

C. For a rectangle, you can also multiply to find the area.

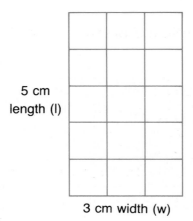

5 cm
length (l)

3 cm width (w)

    5 columns of square centimeters
    3 square centimeters in each column

    5 × 3 = 15 square centimeters in all.
      Area = 15 cm²

D. You can write a formula for the area of a rectangle.

    Area = length × width
      A = l × w

TRY THESE

Find the area of each figure.

1.

10 cm

6 cm

2.

8 m

14 m

3.

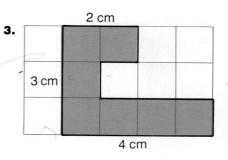

2 cm

3 cm

4 cm

SKILLS PRACTICE

Find the area of each figure.

1.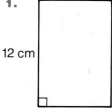
12 cm
8 cm

2.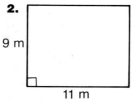
9 m
11 m

3.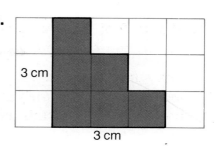
3 cm
3 cm

4. a rectangle with
length: 20 cm
width: 7 cm

5. a rectangle with
length: 15 m
width: 10 m

★**6.** a square with
one side of
length: 12 cm

Complete this table. Each figure is a rectangle.

		7.	8.	9.	★10.	★11.
length (cm)	5	6	25	200	8	■
width (cm)	4	3	10	50	■	3
area (cm²)	20	■	■	■	40	21
perimeter (cm)	18	■	■	■	■	■

PROBLEM SOLVING

12. One wall of a room is 12 m long
and 3 m high. What is the area of
this wall?

★**13.** Each picture is 50 cm long and
35 cm wide. What is the area of
each picture? of 6 pictures?

MIXED REVIEW

Write a decimal for each.

1. nineteen and thirty-five hundredths   **2.** five and forty-six thousandths

Add, subtract, or multiply.

3. 317
× 58

4. 57.13
− 27.56

5. 47.96
+ 354.2

6. 37
+ .027

7. 3.742
− 2.8

8. 7 × 43 = ■   **9.** 84 − 3.087 = ■   **10.** 62 × 96 = ■

Solids

A. The picture shows six different *solids.*

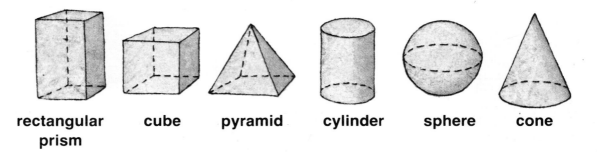

rectangular prism   cube   pyramid   cylinder   sphere   cone

B. The *faces* of solids may be flat or curved.
The *edges* of solids may be straight or curved.
The straight edges meet at corners.
These corners are called *vertices.*

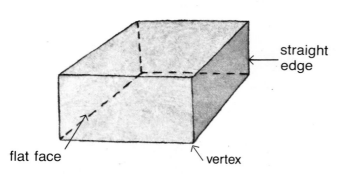

straight edge

flat face

vertex

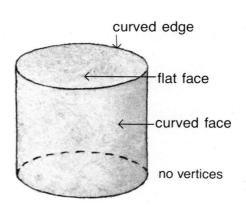

curved edge

flat face

curved face

no vertices

Figure						
Flat faces	6	6	5	2	0	1
Curved faces	0	0	0	1	1	1
Straight edges	12	12	8	0	0	0
Curved edges	0	0	0	2	0	1
Vertices	8	8	5	0	0	0

TRY THESE

Name some objects that have the same shape as each of these solids.

1. **2.** **3.** **4.** **5.** **6.**

SKILLS PRACTICE

Name the solid each of these objects is the most like.

1. **2.** **3.** **4.**

What plane figures would you get by tracing the flat faces of a:

5. rectangular prism?   **6.** cube?   **7.** pyramid?   **8.** cone?

PROBLEM SOLVING

9. What is the area of the bottom of this chest? of the top?

★10. Find the total area of the 6 faces of this chest.

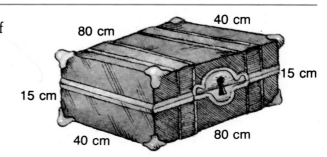

80 cm 40 cm 15 cm 15 cm 40 cm 80 cm

THINK!

Finding Surface Area

You can find the surface area of a solid by finding the area of each of its faces and adding these areas. Find the surface area of each of these solids.

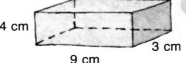

4 cm 3 cm 9 cm 6 faces

3 cm cube

Volume

A. The **volume** or **capacity** of a container is the size of the inside of the container. The **cubic centimeter** (cm^3) and the **cubic meter** (m^3) are metric units used to measure volume.

Length of each edge of a cube	Volume of the cube
1 cm	1 cm³
1 m	1 m³

A glass holds about 240 cm³ of milk.

About 1,000 books like this one have a total volume of 1 m³.

B. To find the volume of a container you can count the cubic units that fill it. For a rectangular prism you can also multiply to find the volume.

In the bottom layer:

5 × 3 = 15 cubic centimeters

In 2 layers:

2 × 15 = 30 cubic centimeters

Volume = 30 cm³

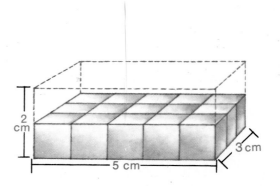

C. For a rectangular prism:

Volume = length × width × height

$$V = l \times w \times h$$

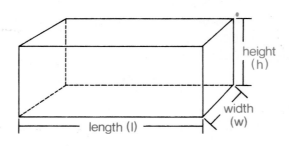

TRY THESE

Find the volume of each rectangular prism.

1.
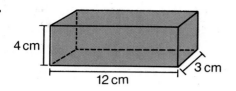
4 cm
12 cm
3 cm

2. length: 16 m
   width: 5 m
   height: 4 m

3. length: 25 cm
   width: 10 cm
   height: 20 cm

SKILLS PRACTICE

Find the volume of each rectangular prism to complete this table.

	1.	2.	3.	4.	5.	6.	7.
length	10 cm	15 m	80 cm	10 m	200 cm	30 m	500 cm
width	8 cm	12 m	60 cm	10 m	150 cm	18 m	400 cm
height	12 cm	6 m	50 cm	10 m	80 cm	9 m	1 cm
volume	■	■	■	■	■	■	■

PROBLEM SOLVING

8. A tool box is 50 cm long and 25 cm wide. Its height is 20 cm. What is the volume of this box?

9. The trailer of a large truck is 9 m long, 3 m wide, and 3 m high. What is the volume of this trailer?

★10. A grain bin is 5 m long, 4 m wide, and 6 m high. What is the volume of this bin? There are 65.4 m³ of grain already in the bin. How much more will it hold?

★11. Each box is 3 m long, 2 m wide, and 2 m high. What is the volume of each box? How many boxes must be used to pack 150 m³ of flour?

THINK!

Using Given Information

∠AFC and ∠BFD are right angles.

m∠CFD = 35°

Find: m∠AFB and m∠DFE.

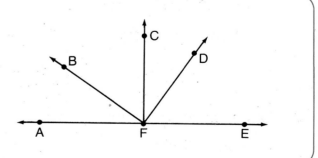

Problem Solving

Using Customary Units

A. The *inch* (in.), *foot* (ft), and *yard* (yd) are customary units used to measure perimeter.

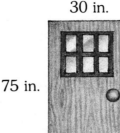

30 in.

The perimeter of this door is
P = l + w + l + w
P = 75 + 30 + 75 + 30 = 210
The perimeter is 210 inches.

75 in.   75 in.

30 in.

B. The *square inch* (in.^{2}), the *square foot* (ft^2), and the *square yard* (yd^2) are customary units used to measure area.

The area of this page is about 78 in.^{2}
The area of a door is about 21 ft^2.
The area of a basketball court is about 560 yd^2.

C. The *cubic inch* (in.^{3}), the *cubic foot* (ft^3), and the *cubic yard* (yd^3) are customary units used to measure volume.

The volume of a shoe box is about 400 in.^{3}
The volume of the inside of a large refrigerator is about 18 ft^3.
About 750 books like this one have a total volume of 1 yd^3.

D. Find the perimeter and area of a rug that is 12 ft long and 9 ft wide.

P = l + w + l + w   A = l × w
  = 12 + 9 + 12 + 9   = 12 × 9
  = 42   = 108
The perimeter is 42 ft.   The area is
                           108 ft^2.

E. Find the volume of a box that is 8 in. long, 5 in. wide, and 3 in. high.

V = l × w × h
  = 8 × 5 × 3
  = 120
The volume is 120 in.^{3}

TRY THESE

Find the perimeter and area of each rectangle.

length	9 in.	12 ft	17 in.	80 yd	50 ft	200 yd	20 in.
width	4 in.	10 ft	9 in.	50 yd	35 ft	60 yd	▩ in.
perimeter	▩	▩	▩	▩	▩	▩	▩
area	▩	▩	▩	▩	▩	▩	180 in.²

Find the volume of each rectangular prism.

length	4 yd	18 yd	12 in.	10 ft	20 ft	40 ft	6 in.
width	3 yd	10 yd	8 in.	10 ft	20 ft	40 ft	5 in.
height	7 yd	3 yd	5 in.	10 ft	20 ft	40 ft	▩ in.
volume	▩	▩	▩	▩	▩	▩	90 in.³

PROBLEM SOLVING PRACTICE

1. A floor is 20 ft long and 14 ft wide. What is its area?

2. A room is 5 yd long, 4 yd wide, and 4 yd high. What is its volume?

3. A rectangular garden is 52 ft long and 31 ft wide. How long is a fence that goes around the edge of it?

4. A towel is 3 ft long and 2 ft wide. What are its perimeter and area?

5. Tiles, each 1 ft² in area, are used to cover a rectangular floor. The floor is 13 ft long and 8 ft wide. How many tiles are needed?

6. A trailer's inside dimensions are 19 ft long, 11 ft wide, and 5 ft high. How many boxes, each 1 ft on each side, can the trailer hold?

7. June wants to sew a ribbon border around all edges of a rectangular blanket. The blanket is 88 in. long and 62 in. wide. How much ribbon does June need?

★8. A tank is shaped like a rectangular prism. The area of its floor is 15 ft². If there is 60 ft³ of water in the tank, what is the depth of the water?

ON YOUR OWN

Find the length, width, and height of a room in your home.

Make up two area problems involving floor or walls, and one volume problem. Solve the problems.

Computer Graphics

When you use a computer game or many educational computer programs, you often see pictures on the screen. The computer screen is made up of a grid of rows and columns. Each location is a square of light called a picture element, or a *pixel* for short.

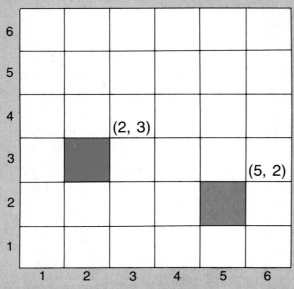

To create a picture, the computer instructs the machine to light up certain pixels and to leave others dark. If the screen is a color one, like a color TV set, then the lighted pixels have colors, too. All numbers, letters, and shapes are drawn by lighting up the correct pixels.

High resolution, or hi-res, graphics are achieved by using grids that have 60,000 or more individual pixels. *Low resolution*, or low-res, graphics use far fewer pixels.

1. What is a pixel? Why is it important in computer graphics?

2. Use graph paper. Label 30 rows and 30 columns. Follow the directions to draw a clown.

Red pixels: (9, 7), (10, 7), (11, 7), (12, 7), (9, 8), (10, 8), (11, 8), (12, 8), (13, 8), (17, 8), (18, 8), (19, 8), (18, 7), (19, 7), (20, 7), (19, 6), (20, 6), (21, 6), (20, 5), (13, 9), (14, 9), (15, 9), (16, 9), (17, 9), (18, 9), (14, 10), (15, 10), (16, 10), (17, 10), (18, 10), (14, 11), (15, 11), (16, 11), (17, 11), (18, 11), (14, 12), (15, 12), (16, 12), (17, 12), (18, 12), (14, 13), (15, 13), (16, 13), (17, 13), (18, 13)

Blue pixels: (15, 14), (16, 14), (17, 14), (14, 15), (15, 15), (16, 15), (17, 15), (18, 15), (12, 16), (13, 16), (14, 16), (15, 16), (16, 16), (17, 16), (18, 16), (19, 16), (20, 16), (11, 17), (12, 17), (13, 17), (14, 17), (15, 17), (16, 17), (17, 17), (18, 17), (19, 17), (20, 17), (21, 17), (10, 18), (11, 18), (13, 18), (14, 18), (15, 18), (16, 18), (17, 18), (18, 18), (19, 18), (21, 18), (22, 18), (9, 19), (10, 19), (22, 19), (23, 19), (9, 20), (10, 20), (22, 20), (23, 20), (9, 21), (10, 21), (22, 21), (23, 21), (14, 23), (15, 23), (16, 23), (17, 23), (18, 23), (15, 24), (16, 24), (17, 24), (16, 25), (17, 26)

Green pixels: (21, 4), (22, 4), (23, 4), (21, 5), (22, 5), (23, 5), (7, 7), (8, 7), (7, 8), (8, 8), (7, 9), (8, 9), (16, 19), (15, 20), (16, 20), (17, 20), (14, 21), (15, 21), (16, 21), (17, 21), (18, 21), (14, 22), (15, 22), (16, 22), (17, 22), (18, 22), (9, 22), (10, 22), (22, 22), (23, 22), (9, 23), (23, 23)

3. Give instructions for a 4 × 4 square that includes (7, 9).

314   **Geometry and Measurement**

Unit Review

Use these pictures to answer the questions below. *(pages 282–299, 308–309)*

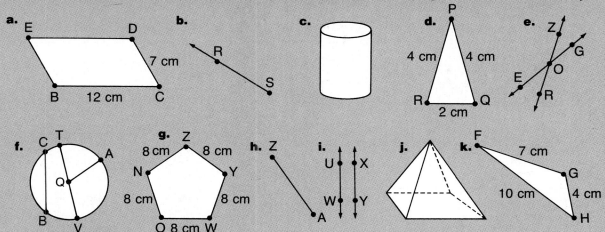

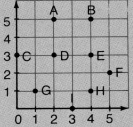

1. Name the parallel lines.
2. Name 2 radii of the circle.
3. Which figure is a cylinder?
4. Name the ray. Name its endpoint.
5. Find the length of ED in **a.**
6. Which figure is a regular polygon?
7. Which figure is an isosceles triangle?
8. How many lines of symmetry does the pentagon have?

Use the grid. *(pages 300–301)*

9. Give the letter for each number pair:
   (3,0)   (2,5)   (4,1)   (2,3)

10. Give the number pair for each point:
    E   B   C   G

Find the perimeter and area of each rectangle. *(pages 304–307)*

11. length: 8 cm; width: 5 cm
12. length: 12 m; width: 10 m

Solve the problems using metric units. *(pages 304–307, 310–311)*

13. A room is 7 m long and 3 m wide. How much molding is needed to go around the ceiling?

14. A jewelry box is 20 cm long, 12 cm wide, and 10 cm high. What is the volume of the box?

Solve the problems using customary units. *(pages 312–313)*

15. The loft of a barn is 45 ft long, 30 ft wide, and 7 ft high. What volume of hay will it hold?

16. How many square yards of carpet are needed to cover the floor of a room 8 yd long and 4 yd wide?

Reinforcement

More Help with Perimeter, Area, and Volume

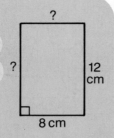

Opposite sides of a rectangle have equal lengths.

Perimeter = l+w+l+w
= **12 + 8 + ? + ?**
= 12 + 8 + 12 + 8
= 40 cm

Find the perimeter of each polygon.

1.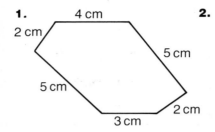

4 cm
2 cm
5 cm
5 cm
2 cm
3 cm

2.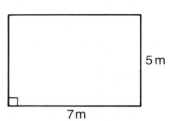

5 m
7 m

3. a rectangle with
   length: 20 cm
   width: 10 cm

4. a square with one
   side of length: 9 m

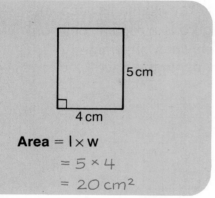

5 cm
4 cm

Area = l × w
= 5 × 4
= 20 cm²

Find the area of each rectangle.

5.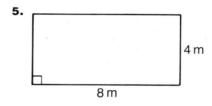

4 m
8 m

6.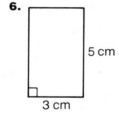

5 cm
3 cm

7. length: 30 cm
   width: 20 cm

8. length: 16 m
   width: 12 m

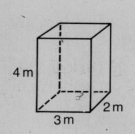

4 m
3 m
2 m

Volume = l × w × h
= 3 × 2 × 4
= 24 m³

Find the volume of each rectangular prism.

9.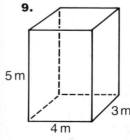

5 m
3 m
4 m

10.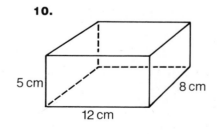

5 cm
12 cm
8 cm

11. length: 11 m
   width: 8 m
   height: 14 m

12. length: 45 cm
   width: 20 cm
   height: 6 cm

Constructions

You can use a compass and ruler to construct a line segment congruent to a given line segment, an angle congruent to a given angle, or a triangle congruent to a given triangle.

A. Construct a line segment congruent to $\overline{AB}$.

Step 1 Measure $\overline{AB}$ with the compass.

Step 2 With the same compass opening, mark off $\overline{CD}$ with the same length as $\overline{AB}$.

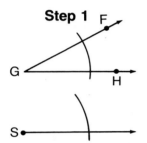

$\overline{CD}$ is congruent to $\overline{AB}$.

B. Construct an angle congruent to $\angle FGH$.

Step 1
Step 2
Step 3

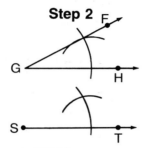
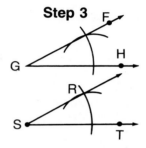

$\angle RST$ is congruent to $\angle FGH$.

C. Construct a triangle congruent to triangle XYZ.

Step 1 Construct $\overline{DE}$ congruent to $\overline{XZ}$.

Step 2 Construct $\angle FDE$ congruent to $\angle YXZ$ and $\angle FED$ congruent to $\angle YZX$.

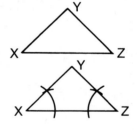

Triangle DFE is congruent to triangle XYZ.

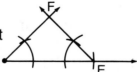

D. You can use a compass and ruler to draw a regular hexagon.

Step 1 Draw a circle.

Step 2 Use the same setting.

Step 3 Repeat 5 more times.

Step 4 Join the 6 points.

any point of the circle

point where mark crosses circle

Use the compass and a ruler to draw a line segment, an angle, a triangle, and a regular hexagon.

Choose the correct answer.

1. Find the total value.

a. $6.36
b. $12
c. $322.23
d. not given

2. $\frac{4}{5} - \frac{3}{4} = \blacksquare$

a. 1

b. $\frac{3}{5}$

c. $\frac{1}{20}$

d. not given

3. 193,467
+ 8,903

a. 191,360
b. 202,370
c. 202,470
d. not given

4. Find the area.

4 cm
7 cm

a. 28 cm²
b. 22 cm²
c. 11 cm²
d. not given

5. 32 − 2.6 = ■

a. 6
b. .6
c. 29.4
d. not given

6. 9)81,477

a. 953
b. 9,053
c. 905R2
d. not given

7. Which fraction is equivalent to $\frac{5}{8}$?

a. $\frac{15}{24}$ b. $\frac{15}{8}$

c. $\frac{3}{24}$ d. not given

8. Find the perimeter.

10 m
5 m
6 m

a. 42 m
b. 30 m
c. 21 m
d. not given

9.   7
  6.3
+19.47

a. 22.77
b. 20.17
c. 27.10
d. not given

10.   592
  ×216

a. 127,872
b. 21,312
c. 5,328
d. not given

11. Complete.
29,416 ● 29,461

a. >
b. <
c. =
d. not given

12. $\frac{2}{3} \times \frac{3}{4} = \blacksquare$

a. $\frac{5}{9}$ b. $\frac{1}{2}$

c. $\frac{23}{34}$ d. not given

13. A tank is shaped like a rectangular prism. It is 4 m long, 3 m wide, and its height is 2 m. What is its volume?

a. 9 m³   b. 12 m³
c. 14 m³   d. not given

14. A store spent a total of $64.75 for 5 lamps. What was the average amount the store spent for a lamp?

a. $323.75   b. $69.75
c. $12.95   d. not given

Multiplying and Dividing with Decimals

NUMBER OF SHIPS IN WORLD'S LARGEST MERCHANT FLEETS (IN THOUSANDS)

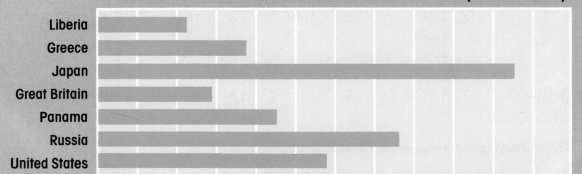

Liberia
Greece
Japan
Great Britain
Panama
Russia
United States

0　1　2　3　4　5　6　7　8　9　10　11　12

Estimating Decimal Products and Quotients

A. Rita has a rug that measures
3.1 meters by 3.9 meters.
About what area does the rug cover?

$3.1 \times 3.9 = $ ■

↓   ↓

$3 \times 4 = 12$

Round each decimal to
the nearest whole
number. Then multiply.

The rug covers about 12 square
meters. You can use your calculator
to find an exact answer.

B. There is a wall hanging in
Jack's room that covers 6.4
square meters. It is 3.1 meters
long. About how wide is it?

$6.4 \div 3.1 = $ ■

↓   ↓

$6 \div 3 = 2$

Round each decimal to
the nearest whole
number. Then divide.

The wall hanging is about 2
meters wide. You can use your
calculator to find an exact answer.

TRY THESE

Estimate the product or quotient.

1. $\begin{array}{r} 5.9 \\ \times 2.2 \\ \hline \end{array}$

2. $\begin{array}{r} 4.1 \\ \times 3.8 \\ \hline \end{array}$

3. $\begin{array}{r} 1.6 \\ \times\ .7 \\ \hline \end{array}$

4. $\begin{array}{r} 15.3 \\ \times\ 1.9 \\ \hline \end{array}$

5. $\begin{array}{r} 20.2 \\ \times\ 9.7 \\ \hline \end{array}$

6. $2.3\overline{)12.1}$

7. $9.9\overline{)30.4}$

8. $5.7\overline{)59.8}$

9. $10.6\overline{)121}$

10. $39.8\overline{)160.1}$

SKILLS PRACTICE

Estimate the product or quotient.

1. 9.3
   × 2.7

2. 1.88
   × 3.6

3. 7.95
   × 4.1

4. 5.2
   × .96

5. 14.77
   × 5.2

6. 11.1
   × .85

7. 35.0
   × 4.0

8. 10.01
   × 6.8

9. 24.93
   × 5.31

10. 36.2
    × 5.05

11. 7.2)48.7

12. 14)279.6

13. 25)750.2

14. 9.04)36.1

15. 8)639.8

16. 72.3 ÷ 8.9 = ■

17. 260.2 ÷ 13 = ■

18. 74.6 ÷ 14.99 = ■

19. 4.6 ÷ 1.3 = ■

20. 48.4 ÷ 15.7 = ■

21. 231.2 ÷ 77.3 = ■

PROBLEM SOLVING

22. Marcia's rectangular garden measures 5.7 meters by 8.2 meters. What is the approximate area of her garden?

23. A sack of flower bulbs has a mass of 116.75 grams. Each bulb has a mass of about 8.5 grams. About how many bulbs are in the sack?

24. Each flowerpot costs $2.89. About how many flowerpots can Marcia buy for $72.25?

25. Each seed pack has a mass of 2.8 grams. Estimate the mass of 12 seed packs.

26. Marcia has 37 seeds in a seed pack. If she plants 3 seeds in each pot, how many pots can she plant?

★27. Marcia bought a 2.85-kg bag of fertilizer. She used 1.37 kg in her garden. Was that more or less than .5 of the total amount?

THINK!

Mental Multiplication

Estimate the area of each.

Town:

Greenville 1.9 km

3.2 km

House:

4.3 m

3.2 m

2.4 m

2.8 m

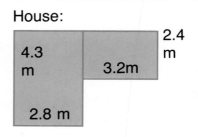

Paper:

27.9 cm

21.6 cm

Multiplying with Decimals

A. José's house has three bedrooms of equal size. He and his mother waxed 2.4 of the bedroom floors. José did .3 of the job. How many floors did he wax?

.3 × 2.4 =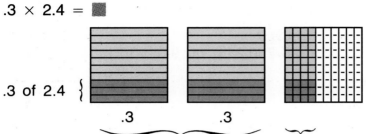

.3 of 2.4 {

.3   .3

.6   .12

.3 × 2.4 = .6 + .12 = .72

To multiply with decimals, you multiply as with whole numbers and then place the decimal point.

Step 1

①

$\begin{array}{r} 2.4 \\ \times\ .3 \\ \hline 72 \end{array}$

24
×3

Step 2

①

$\begin{array}{r} 2.4 \\ \times\ .3 \\ \hline .72 \end{array}$

1 place after the decimal point

+1 place after the decimal point

2 places after the decimal point

José waxed .72 floors.

B. Find 1.4 × 4.28 = 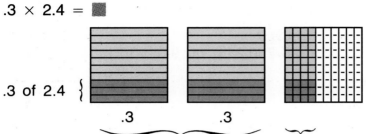.

Step 1

Multiply 14 × 428.

$\begin{array}{r} 4.28 \\ \times\ 1.4 \\ \hline 1712 \\ 4280 \\ \hline 5992 \end{array}$

Step 2

Place the decimal point.

$\begin{array}{r} 4.28 \\ \times\ 1.4 \\ \hline 1712 \\ 4280 \\ \hline 5.992 \end{array}$

2 places

+1 place

3 places

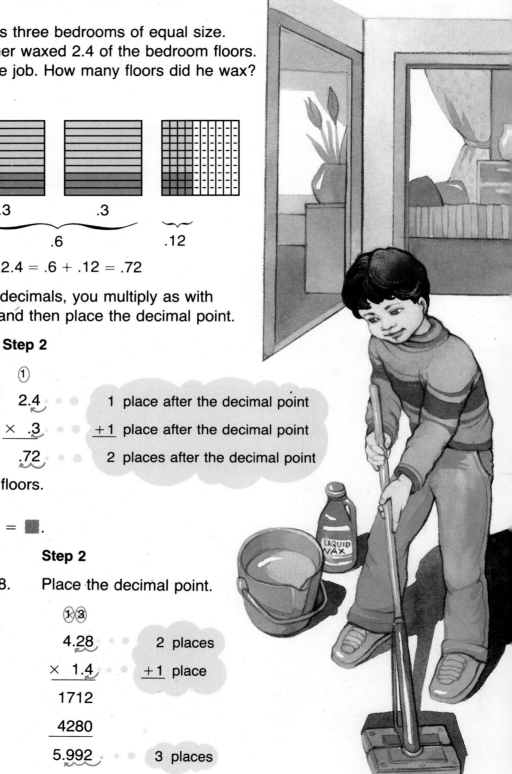

TRY THESE

Multiply.

1. $\begin{array}{r} 1.6 \\ \times\ .4 \\ \hline \end{array}$
2. $\begin{array}{r} 7.3 \\ \times .17 \\ \hline \end{array}$
3. $\begin{array}{r} 1.34 \\ \times\ \ 23 \\ \hline \end{array}$
4. $\begin{array}{r} 9.15 \\ \times\ 1.4 \\ \hline \end{array}$
5. $\begin{array}{r} 342 \\ \times\ .17 \\ \hline \end{array}$

First estimate, then find the product.

6. $7.8 \times 5.3 =$ ■   7. $9.2 \times 3.96 =$ ■   8. $12.7 \times 8.1 =$ ■

SKILLS PRACTICE

Multiply. Estimate to check.

1. $\begin{array}{r} 5.9 \\ \times\ .3 \\ \hline \end{array}$
2. $\begin{array}{r} \$1.80 \\ \times\ \ \ 5 \\ \hline \end{array}$
3. $\begin{array}{r} 17.1 \\ \times\ \ 2 \\ \hline \end{array}$
4. $\begin{array}{r} 1.45 \\ \times\ .6 \\ \hline \end{array}$
5. $\begin{array}{r} 3.15 \\ \times\ .8 \\ \hline \end{array}$

6. $\begin{array}{r} 31 \\ \times 2.7 \\ \hline \end{array}$
7. $\begin{array}{r} 1.46 \\ \times\ .9 \\ \hline \end{array}$
8. $\begin{array}{r} 20.1 \\ \times\ .13 \\ \hline \end{array}$
9. $\begin{array}{r} \$54.60 \\ \times\ \ \ 35 \\ \hline \end{array}$
10. $\begin{array}{r} 67.2 \\ \times\ .24 \\ \hline \end{array}$

11. $\begin{array}{r} 39.2 \\ \times\ 24 \\ \hline \end{array}$
12. $\begin{array}{r} 2.18 \\ \times\ 4.7 \\ \hline \end{array}$
13. $\begin{array}{r} 7.04 \\ \times\ 7.5 \\ \hline \end{array}$
14. $\begin{array}{r} 15.6 \\ \times\ 6.1 \\ \hline \end{array}$
15. $\begin{array}{r} 24.3 \\ \times\ .94 \\ \hline \end{array}$

16. $.5 \times .65 =$ ■   17. $.15 \times \$720 =$ ■   18. $8.2 \times 3.7 =$ ■

19. $.44 \times 3.6 =$ ■   20. $2.3 \times .14 =$ ■   21. $6 \times \$1.58 =$ ■

PROBLEM SOLVING

22. Mr. Evans bought 3 bottles of milk. Each bottle contained 1.5 L of milk. How much milk did he buy?

★23. Mr. Evans bought 2.74 kg of cheese. He used 1.23 kg of the cheese. Was that more or less than .5 of the amount he bought?

THINK!

Decimal Patterns

Choose two decimals between 0 and 1. Multiply. Use your calculator if you wish. Try three or four more pairs of decimals. Follow the same rules. What do you notice about the size of the product in relation to the two factors?

.35   .74

$.35 \times .74 = .259$

More Multiplying with Decimals

A. Mr. Sand's truck has a mass of about 4.5 metric tons. Mr. Sand's own mass is .02 times that of his truck. What is his mass?

Find .02 × 4.5 = ■

Step 1

Multiply 2 × 45.

①

```
   45
 ×  2
   90
```

There are not enough digits for 3 places. Write a 0 on the left to place the decimal point.

Step 2

Place the decimal point.

①

```
  4.5   ←    1 place
×.02   ←   +2 places
.090   ←    3 places
```

Mr. Sand's mass is .090 metric tons.

B. Sometimes you have to write more than one 0 on the left before you can place the decimal point.

Find .3 × .02 = ■

Step 1

Multiply 3 × 2.

```
    2
 ×  3
    6
```

Step 2

Place the decimal point.

```
 .02      2 places
× .3     +1 place
.006      3 places
```

TRY THESE

Find the product.

1.
```
 .12
× .5
```

2.
```
 .53
× .7
```

3.
```
 .162
×    9
```

4.
```
  .38
×2.5
```

5.
```
 .03
× .3
```

SKILLS PRACTICE

Multiply.

1.   1.2
      ×.06

2.   .04
      × .3

3. $1.38
     ×   8

4.   .24
     × .4

5.   20.4
     × .05

6.   34.8
     × .51

7.   1.05
     × 37

8.   35.2
     × 42

9.   .003
     × 23

10.   .05
     × .5

11. 90.5
    ×12.4

12. 16.2
    ×5.05

13.   .03
     × .4

14.   .08
     × .7

15.   .005
     × 8

16.   .01
     × .5

17.   2.3
     ×.04

18.   .17
     × .5

19.   .3
     ×.16

20.   .1
     ×.09

21. .252
    × 500

22. $6.36
    × 250

23.   .031
     × 415

24.   3.5
     ×.02

25.   .2
     ×.05

Estimate, then find the product.

26. 15.9 × 6.82 = ▣   27. 9.2 × 1.92 = ▣   ★28. 1.06 × .03 = ▣

PROBLEM SOLVING

29. Ms. Nash sold her wheat for $20,460. She used .03 of this money to rent farm machinery. How much did she spend on machinery?

★30. Mr. Brown used .02 of his income for seed and .14 of it for fuel. What part of his $18,250 income did he use? How much did he spend in all?

Mental Multiplication

When you want to find a product such as 1.5 × 1.5, you can use a shortcut.

To multiply 1.5 × 1.5, round one factor down and one factor up and then multiply: 1 × 2 = 2. Add .25 to the product for the answer: 2.25.

Multiply using the shortcut method.

1. 2.5 × 2.5   2. 3.5 × 3.5   3. 5.5 × 5.5

4. 7.5 × 7.5   5. 10.5 × 10.5   6. 20.5 × 20.5

Problem Solving Strategy

Use Logical Reasoning

Mark, Sue, Ellen, and Ted each own a different pet.
The pets are a cat, a dog, a bird, and a turtle.
Use the clues below to decide who owns each pet.

Clue 1   Ted's pet does not have feathers or fur.

Clue 2   Sue's pet does not bark or meow.

Clue 3   One of the girls owns a cat.

Make a table. Fill in the facts you know.
Use × for no and √ for yes.

From Clue 3,
Ellen must
own the cat.

From Clue 1,
Ted's pet is
the turtle.

	Ted	Sue	Ellen	Mark
cat	×	×	√	×
dog	×	×	×	√
bird	×	√	×	×
turtle	√	×	×	×

From Clue 2,
Sue's pet is
the bird.

The only pet
left is the dog,
which must belong
to Mark.

Ted owns the turtle, Sue owns the bird,
Ellen owns the cat, and Mark owns the dog.

Solve.

1. Pam, Ed, Dan, and Faye each like a different sport. Their sports are tennis, swimming, football, and baseball.

   Clue 1   Faye's sport does not have a ball.

   Clue 2   One of the girls is on the tennis team.

   Clue 3   Dan uses a bat.

2. Greg, Lois, Bob, and Vera each play an instrument. Their instruments are piano, guitar, drums, and saxophone.

   Clue 1   The saxophone player is a male.

   Clue 2   Neither Bob nor Vera plays piano.

   Clue 3   Someone's instrument begins with the same letter as his or her first name.

Problem Solving Project

Time Cards

Many workers have **time cards.** When they put a time card into a special clock, it stamps the time they started working. When they leave work, the clock stamps the time they finished working. The time card is used to determine their **gross pay.**

This is Mrs. Taylor's time card. It shows that she is paid $7.50 per hour.

On Monday, Mrs. Taylor started working at 6:57 A.M. She finished working at 2:57 P.M.

From 6:57 A.M. to 2:57 P.M. is 8 hours. She is paid for 8 hours at $7.50 per hour. On Monday, Mrs. Taylor earned $60.00.

Copy and complete each time card.

Name __Mrs. Taylor__

Week Ended __May 18__, 19__86__

Hourly Pay $7.50

Day	In	Out	Hours Worked	Pay
Mon.	6:57AM	2:57PM	8	$60.00
Tues.	7:02AM	3:08PM	8.1	$60.75
Wed.	—			—
Thurs.	2:01PM	9:55PM	7.9	$59.25
Fri.	1:59PM	9:59PM	8	$60.00
Sat.	2:03PM	10:15PM	8.2	$61.50
Total ▶			40.2	$301.50

Name __Mr. W. Bellows__

Week Ended __May 18__, 19__86__

Hourly Pay $8.00

Day	In	Out	Hours Worked	Pay
Mon.	12:01AM	8:01AM	8	
Tues.	12:05AM	8:11AM	8.1	
Wed.	12:07AM	8:19AM	8.2	
Thurs.	12:03AM	8:03AM	8	
Fri.	12:10AM	8:04AM	7.9	
Sat.			—	—
Total ▶				

Name __Mrs. A. Clark__

Week Ended __May 18__, 19__86__

Hourly Pay $9.40

Day	In	Out	Hours Worked	Pay
Mon.	7:59AM	3:59PM	8	
Tues.			—	
Wed.	8:05AM	4:23PM	8.3	
Thurs.	7:39AM	3:51PM	8.2	
Fri.	8:22AM	4:10PM	7.8	
Sat.	8:30AM	4:36PM	8.1	
Total ▶				

ON YOUR OWN

Data Search

What is the difference between **gross pay** and **net pay**? Find out about deductions for taxes and Social Security (FICA). What are some other deductions?

Dividing with Decimals

A. The weight of 3 baseball bats is 6.75 lb all together.
Each bat weighs the same amount.
How much does 1 bat weigh?

6.75 ÷ 3 = ■

> Estimate.
> 7 ÷ 3 = ■
> a little
> more than 2

Step 1
Divide the **6 ones.**

```
  2
3)6.75
  6
  0
```

Step 2
Place the decimal point.
Divide the **7 tenths.**

```
  2.2
3)6.75
  6
  0 7
    6
    1
```

The weight of 1 bat is 2.25 lb.

Step 3
Divide the
15 hundredths.

```
  2.25      Sensible
3)6.75
  6
  0 7
    6
    15
    15
     0
```

B. Find: 54)22.734

> Estimate.
> 23 ÷ 54 = ■
> less than .5

Step 1
Place the decimal point.
Divide the **227 tenths.**

```
    .4
54)22.734
   21 6
    1 1
```

Step 2
Divide the
113 hundredths.

```
    .42
54)22.734
   21 6
    1 13
    1 08
       5
```

Step 3
Divide the
54 thousandths.

```
    .421     Sensible
54)22.734
   21 6
    1 13
    1 08
       54
       54
        0
```

TRY THESE

Estimate. Then divide.

1. $4\overline{)8.56}$ **2.** $3\overline{).936}$ **3.** $5\overline{)25.65}$ **4.** $47\overline{)4.935}$ **5.** $2\overline{)\$800.64}$

6. $469.2 \div 34 = \blacksquare$ **7.** $147.84 \div 42 = \blacksquare$ **8.** $.468 \div 4 = \blacksquare$

SKILLS PRACTICE

Estimate. Then divide.

1. $12\overline{)3.36}$ **2.** $56\overline{)14.56}$ **3.** $3\overline{)1.725}$ **4.** $4\overline{)7.156}$ **5.** $96\overline{)595.2}$

6. $30\overline{)66.0}$ **7.** $2\overline{)1.538}$ **8.** $75\overline{)112.5}$ **9.** $63\overline{)6.804}$ **10.** $46\overline{)9.476}$

11. $2\overline{)\$15.08}$ **12.** $3\overline{)\$173.49}$ **13.** $8\overline{)659.2}$ **14.** $7\overline{)99.05}$ **15.** $4\overline{)1.384}$

16. $8\overline{)18.016}$ **17.** $5\overline{)2.315}$ **18.** $4\overline{).612}$ **19.** $6\overline{)527.4}$ **20.** $65\overline{)65.195}$

21. $5\overline{).715}$ **22.** $3\overline{)47.049}$ **23.** $2\overline{)12.318}$ **24.** $4\overline{)1.268}$ **25.** $9\overline{)5.301}$

26. $25.8 \div 3 = \blacksquare$ **27.** $5.168 \div 4 = \blacksquare$ **28.** $37.506 \div 6 = \blacksquare$

29. $4.025 \div 7 = \blacksquare$ **30.** $37.125 \div 5 = \blacksquare$ **31.** $156.37 \div 19 = \blacksquare$

32. $18.6 \div 10 = \blacksquare$ **33.** $25.44 \div 10 = \blacksquare$ **★34.** $573.91 \div 100 = \blacksquare$

PROBLEM SOLVING

35. The Pine Company supplied 14 beams. Their total mass was 339.36 kg. If each beam had the same mass, what was its mass?

★36. A box of nails has a mass of 1.38 kg and costs $1.59. How much would 10 boxes of nails cost?

THINK!

Making Logical Choices

All locker keys are red or blue on one side and have an even or an odd number on the other. Which two keys would you turn over to find out if all of these keys with an even number are red on the other side?

Homework   page 452

Zeros in Quotients

A. Maria has .72 meters of ribbon. She wants to cut it into 9 equal pieces. How long should each piece be?

.72 ÷ 9 =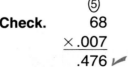

Step 1
Place the decimal point.
Divide the **7 tenths.**

```
  .0
9).72
  0
  7
```

It is **important to write this 0.**

Step 2
Divide the **72 hundredths.**

```
  .08
9).72
  0
  72
  72
   0
```

Each piece should be .08 meters long.

B. .476 ÷ 68 =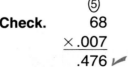

```
   .007
68).476
   0
   47
    0
   476
   476
     0
```

Start with the tenths. Place the decimal point. Record **0 tenths.**

Don't forget to record the **0 hundredths.**

Check.
```
      ⑤
      68
   ×.007
    .476 ✓
```

Do the easier multiplication.

TRY THESE

Divide. Check your answers.

1. 5).405 **2.** 23)1.38 **3.** 6).564 **4.** 20)1.660 **5.** 2).184

6. .348 ÷ 6 = 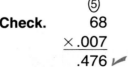 **7.** .364 ÷ 52 =   **8.** $8.32 ÷ 4 =

SKILLS PRACTICE

Divide.

1. $3\overline{)3.12}$ 2. $24\overline{).216}$ 3. $9\overline{)9.81}$ 4. $54\overline{)3.618}$ 5. $2\overline{)4.168}$

6. $5\overline{)5.315}$ 7. $72\overline{)5.688}$ 8. $4\overline{)83.16}$ 9. $9\overline{)91.8}$ 10. $8\overline{).528}$

11. $77\overline{)2.31}$ 12. $6\overline{)30.234}$ 13. $68\overline{)4.896}$ 14. $8\overline{)\$24.08}$ 15. $2\overline{)\$18.16}$

16. $13\overline{).065}$ 17. $3\overline{).417}$ 18. $7\overline{).441}$ 19. $80\overline{)5.680}$ 20. $3\overline{)9.234}$

21. $8\overline{).568}$ 22. $49\overline{).294}$ 23. $6\overline{)18.636}$ 24. $5\overline{)3.525}$ 25. $43\overline{)2.494}$

26. $6.417 \div 3 = \blacksquare$ 27. $36.136 \div 4 = \blacksquare$ 28. $\$25.05 \div 5 = \blacksquare$

29. $1.356 \div 6 = \blacksquare$ 30. $1.275 \div 15 = \blacksquare$ 31. $.056 \div 7 = \blacksquare$

PROBLEM SOLVING

32. Andy used 15.25 L of gasoline. He put the same amount of gasoline into 5 lawn mowers. How much gasoline did he put into each mower?

★33. Andy and 4 helpers collected $23.50 for mowing lawns. Andy kept $8.50 and gave the rest to the others to share equally. How much did each of the others get?

MIXED REVIEW

Find the perimeter of each polygon.

1.
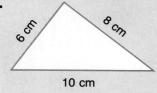

2.
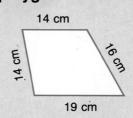

3.

Find the area of each rectangle.

4. length: 50 cm
   width: 35 cm

5. length: 12 cm
   width: 10 cm

6. a square with length of one side: 8 m

Problem Solving Strategy

Choosing the Operation

A. Abbi had two 3.6-liter cans of paint. How much paint did she have all together?

Multiply to find the total amount.

①
3.6
× 2
———
7.2

Estimate.
2 × 4 = ■
about 8

Abbi had 7.2 liters of paint.

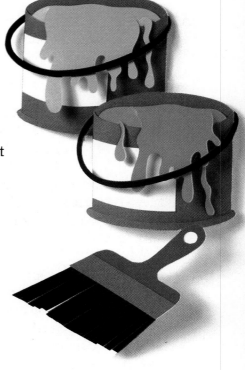

B. Abbi used 6.78 liters of paint to paint 6 tables. What was the average amount she used on each table?

Divide to find the average amount.

```
   1.13
6)6.78
  6
  ———
  0 7
    6
  ———
   18
   18
  ———
    0
```

Estimate.
7 ÷ 6 = ■
a little more than 1 L

Check.
①
1.13
× 6
———
6.78 ✔

Abbi used an average of 1.13 liters of paint on each table.

TRY THESE

Estimate. Then solve.

1. A store bought 8 chairs. Each chair cost $72.45. How much did the store pay for the chairs?

2. The store wants to make a profit of $170.00 on the 8 chairs. How much profit should they make on 1 chair?

3. Ms. Karis worked at the store 7.5 hours each day for 5 days. How many hours did she work in all?

4. Ms. Karis earned $7.20 each hour she worked. How much did she earn for working a 37.5-hour week?

PROBLEM SOLVING PRACTICE _____

Solve each problem.

1. Ms. Loomis worked in the Furniture Market for 15 days one month. She worked 7.5 hours each day. How many hours did she work in all?

2. Ms. Loomis earned $504. The company took out .18 of her earnings for taxes. How much money was taken out?

3. The store ordered a set of 6 chairs for a dining room table. The chairs cost $235.56 in all. What was the cost of each chair?

4. A customer paid $499.90 for a sofa and $359.90 for a matching chair. How much did the customer pay for the two items?

5. Mike drove for 2.75 hours at an average speed of 81.2 kilometers per hour. How far did he drive?

6. Joan drove 285.2 kilometers in 4 hours. What was her average speed in kilometers per hour?

7. The time for each of 4 runners on a relay team was 11.25 seconds. What was the total time for the entire team?

8. The school record for the relay race is 41.84 seconds. What was the average time for each of the 4 runners?

★9. A stereo unit is made up of three sections, one on top of the other. Each section is 11.4 cm high. What is the total height of the three sections? The unit is placed on a table 59.25 cm high. What is the total height of the unit and table?

★10. A sofa 2.68 m long is centered along a wall of a room that is 6 m in length. How much longer is the wall than the sofa? How far beyond the right end of the sofa does the wall extend? How far beyond the left end?

ON YOUR OWN

You are ordering furniture for a new office. Use the information at the right. Make up a problem for each operation: addition, subtraction, multiplication, division. Solve the problems.

Item	Cost
Desk	$149.95
Chair	$ 42.50
Lamp	$ 18.59
Light bulbs (1 dozen)	$ 9.00

Problem Solving

Discounts

A. A store advertises 20% off during a sale.

20% is read 20 **percent.**
20 percent means 20 hundredths or .20.

If you buy during the sale, you save
20% or .20 of the regular price.
The amount you save is called the **discount.**

The regular price of a mirror is $36.
Find the discount.

> Discount = .20 of $36
>
> Multiply.

$$\begin{array}{r} \overset{1}{\$36} \\ \times\,.20 \\ \hline \$7.20 \end{array}$$ The discount is $7.20.

The amount you pay during a sale is the **sale price.**

Sale Price = Regular Price − Discount

For the mirror: Sale Price = $36 − $7.20
= $28.80

The sale price is $28.80.

B. Another store advertises $\frac{1}{3}$ off during its sale.

The regular price of a lamp is $63.
Find the discount and the sale price.

> Discount = $\frac{1}{3}$ of $63
>
> Multiply.

$\frac{1}{3} \times \frac{63}{1} = \frac{63}{3} = \$21$

> Sale price = Regular price − Discount

$\$42 = \$63 − \$21$

The discount is $21. The sale price is $42.

TRY THESE

Complete the table.

	Item	Regular Price	Part Off	Discount	Sale Price
1.	Table	$240	10%	$ ▨	$ ▨
2.	Lamp	$48	50%	▨	▨
3.	Sofa	$465	30%	▨	▨
4.	End table	$72	40%	▨	▨
5.	Painting	$68	$\frac{1}{2}$	▨	▨
6.	Chair	$255	$\frac{2}{5}$	▨	▨

PROBLEM SOLVING PRACTICE

Complete the table.

	Item	Regular Price	Part Off	Discount	Sale Price
1.	Desk	$420	10%	$ ▨	$ ▨
2.	Floor lamp	$87	40%	▨	▨
3.	Rocker	$259	20%	▨	▨
4.	Coffee table	$105	60%	▨	▨
5.	Footstool	$136	$\frac{1}{4}$	▨	▨
6.	Carpet	$504	$\frac{2}{3}$	▨	▨

Solve the problems.

7. During a store's 30%-off sale, Mr. Jonas bought items with a regular price of $1,260. What was the discount? How much did he pay?

★8. Mrs. Jonas bought 2 end tables for $75 each. How much did she pay? Later the same tables were sold for $\frac{3}{5}$ off. What was the price then?

ON YOUR OWN

Look in newspapers for advertised sales. Circle the discounts in red. Bring your material to class. Work in groups to write and solve problems using the information in the advertisements.

Solving Problems with a Calculator

You can use your calculator to solve problems with whole numbers, fractions, and decimals. Estimate first to see if your answer is reasonable.

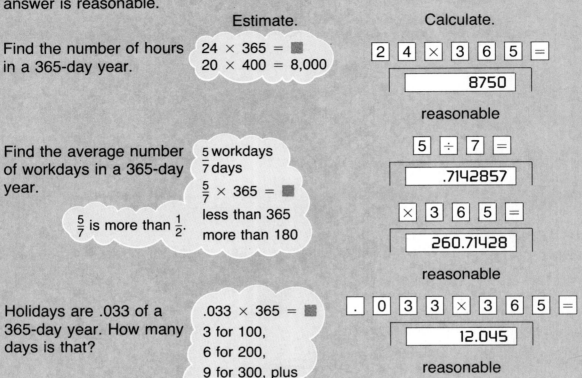

Find the number of hours in a 365-day year.

Estimate.
24 × 365 = ▦
20 × 400 = 8,000

Calculate.
[2] [4] [×] [3] [6] [5] [=]
8750
reasonable

Find the average number of workdays in a 365-day year.

$\frac{5 \text{ workdays}}{7 \text{ days}}$

$\frac{5}{7} \times 365$ = ▦

less than 365
more than 180

$\frac{5}{7}$ is more than $\frac{1}{2}$.

[5] [÷] [7] [=]
.7142857

[×] [3] [6] [5] [=]
260.71428
reasonable

Holidays are .033 of a 365-day year. How many days is that?

.033 × 365 = ▦
3 for 100,
6 for 200,
9 for 300, plus
2 for 65 is
about 11.

[.] [0] [3] [3] [×] [3] [6] [5] [=]
12.045
reasonable

Estimate first to see if your answer is reasonable. Then solve each problem using the calculator.

1. A bus driver works an 8-hour day and a 5-day week. How many hours does she work in 46 weeks?

2. The bus driver collected $366.75, $121.50, and $393.75 in fares on her three Monday trips. How much did she collect for the day?

3. An average of 35,300 riders use the buses each week. It is estimated that .12 of the riders are senior citizens. How many riders is that?

4. The driver collected $586.75 on the morning round trip. If $\frac{4}{5}$ of the money was collected going into the city, how much did she collect on that run?

Unit Review

Estimate. (*pages 320–321*)

1. 3.49 × 26	**2.** 49.83 × 1.4	**3.** .605 × 79	**4.** 52.7 × 2.5	**5.** 95.42 × 5.4

6. 5)9.635 **7.** 1).924 **8.** 6)$35.96 **9.** 37)776.8 **10.** 14)69.92

Multiply. (*pages 322–325*)

11. 3.8 × .4	**12.** .15 × .7	**13.** 4.9 ×3.6	**14.** 7.02 × .4	**15.** 27.3 × .5
16. 30.2 × .14	**17.** .09 × .6	**18.** 2.7 ×.03	**19.** .4 ×.17	**20.** .04 × .3
21. 2.5 ×3.2	**22.** 24.8 × 37	**23.** 6.05 × 2.3	**24.** 24.5 ×3.46	**25.** .68 ×2.7

26. 1.05 × .6 = ■   **27.** .01 × .7 = ■   **28.** 14 × .472 = ■

29. 84.7 × 2.15 = ■   **30.** 7.3 × .04 = ■   **31.** 25.7 × 31.4 = ■

Divide. (*pages 328–331*)

32. 3)9.63   **33.** 2)18.62   **34.** 4)5.648   **35.** 5).825   **36.** 4)$24.76

37. 6).426   **38.** 3).159   **39.** 6).054   **40.** 24)6.72   **41.** 17)22.44

42. 52)192.4   **43.** 95)6.65   **44.** 44)286.44   **45.** 29).986   **46.** 31)11.377

47. 2.052 ÷ 38 = ■   **48.** 102.4 ÷ 64 = ■   **49.** 259.92 ÷ 72 = ■

Solve the problems. (*pages 332–335*)

50. Paul bought 6 guitar strings for $4.50. How much did he pay for each string?

51. Sue worked at a store 8.25 hours each day for 15 days. How many hours did she work in all?

52. Albums are on sale for 30% off. The regular price is $6. What is the discount? What is the sale price?

53. A harmonica costs $24.95. It is on sale for $\frac{1}{5}$ off. What is the discount? What is the sale price?

More Help with Multiplying with Decimals

```
0 0
0 0
3.56  ← 2 places
× 2.3  ← +1 place
1 0 6 8
7 1 2 0
8.188  ← 3 places
```

```
.3   ← 1 place
×.05 ← +2 places
.015 ← 3 places
```

Not enough digits for 3 places! Write a 0 on the left.

Multiply.

1. 41.7
   × .12

2. 6.3
   ×.25

3. 4.38
   ×   2

4. 6.02
   × 3.4

5. 29.3
   × 3.2

6. 25.6
   × 61

7. 1.57
   × 3.2

8. 31.2
   ×7.24

9. .02
   × .4

10. .25
    × .3

11. .4
    ×.14

12. 3.5
    ×.01

13. .13
    × .6

14. 24
    ×.02

15. 35
    ×.05

16. 2.9
    ×.03

More Help with Dividing with Decimals

```
    .124
8).992
    8
   19
   16
    32
    32
     0
```

```
    .07
34)2.38
    0
    238
    238
      0
```

This 0 is important. Don't forget this step.

Divide.

17. 3)63.9
18. 2)74.38
19. 5)2.45
20. 9)2.331

21. 7)32.69
22. 6)412.8
23. 8)89.04
24. 3)1.506

25. 74)5.92
26. 42)1.134
27. 28).168
28. 40)2.520

29. 35).875
30. 61)76.86
31. 30)2.160
32. 75)75.225

Enrichment

Fractions, Decimals, and Percents

A. You can write a fraction, decimal,
or percent to name the same number.

Write 25% as a decimal and as a fraction.

25% = 25 hundredths

25% = .25 ← decimal

$25\% = \dfrac{25}{100} = \dfrac{1}{4}$ ← lowest terms fraction

B. The table shows some useful equivalences.

Fraction	$\dfrac{1}{8}$	$\dfrac{1}{4}$	$\dfrac{3}{8}$	$\dfrac{1}{2}$	$\dfrac{5}{8}$	$\dfrac{3}{4}$	$\dfrac{7}{8}$	1
Decimal	.125	.25	.375	.5	.625	.75	.875	1
Percent	12.5%	25%	37.5%	50%	62.5%	75%	87.5%	100%

Copy and complete the table:

	1.	2.	3.	4.	5.	6.	7.	8.	9.	10.
Fraction	$\dfrac{1}{10}$	$\dfrac{1}{5}$	$\dfrac{3}{10}$	$\dfrac{2}{5}$	$\dfrac{1}{2}$	$\dfrac{3}{5}$	$\dfrac{7}{10}$	$\dfrac{4}{5}$	$\dfrac{9}{10}$	1
Decimal	■	■	■	■	■	■	■	■	■	■
Percent	■	■	■	■	■	■	■	■	■	■

Write the decimal for each percent.

11. 7%   **12.** 26%   **13.** 19%   **14.** 63%   **15.** 85%   **16.** 91%

Write the lowest terms fraction for each percent.

17. 35%   **18.** 58%   **19.** 65%   **20.** 70%   **21.** 72%   **22.** 96%

 23. Which is easier to use when you work with your calculator—
decimals, fractions, or percents? Does your calculator
have a % key? Practice using it.

Cumulative Review

Choose the correct answer.

1. 364,897
$-$ 281,936

a. 123,161
b. 82,961
c. 183,961
d. not above

2. Round 69,976 to the nearest thousand.

a. 60,000
b. 69,000
c. 70,000
d. not above

3. $42\overline{)1,180}$

a. 28 R4
b. 2 R40
c. 29 R20
d. not above

4. Estimate.
$3.1 \times 1.9 = $ ■

a. .06
b. .6
c. 6
d. not above

5. $\frac{11}{12} + \frac{1}{6} = $ ■

a. $\frac{2}{3}$

b. $1\frac{1}{12}$

c. $\frac{11}{12}$

d. not above

6. $26\overline{).052}$

a. 2
b. .02
c. .002
d. not above

7. $2 + .06 = $ ■

a. .12
b. 1.2
c. 12
d. not above

8. Find the time when you might eat lunch.

a. 11:45 P.M.
b. 12:15 A.M.
c. 12:15 P.M.
d. not above

9. Find the decimal for ninety-three hundredths.

a. .93
b. .093
c. 9,300
d. not above

10. Find the lowest terms fraction for $\frac{9}{36}$.

a. $\frac{3}{12}$

b. $\frac{1}{9}$

c. $\frac{1}{4}$

d. not above

11. $9 \times 6 = $ ■

a. 56
b. 15
c. 63
d. not above

12. Complete.
.09 ● .090

a. $>$
b. $=$
c. $<$
d. not above

13. The regular price of a shirt is $12. What is the discount on this shirt during a store's "$\frac{1}{4}$ off" sale?

a. $9   b. $11.75
c. $3   d. not above

14. Each large carton contains 360 light bulbs. How many bulbs are there in 12 large cartons?

a. 4,320 light bulbs   b. 30 light bulbs
c. 372 light bulbs   d. not above

12 Mixed Numerals

DOLLARS SPENT BY TOURISTS ANNUALLY

State	Dollars	$ = 1 billion dollars
California	$ $	
Florida	$ $ $ $ $ $ $ $ $ $ $ $ $ $ $ $	
Illinois	$ $ $ $ $ $ $	
New Jersey	$ $ $ $ $ $ $ $	
New York	$ $ $ $ $ $ $ $ $ $	
Pennsylvania	$ $ $ $ $ $ $	
Wisconsin	$ $ $ $ $ $	

Fractions and Mixed Numerals

Sandy planned a pizza party for the 21 students in the band. She thought each person would eat $\frac{1}{4}$ of a pizza. So she planned to order $21 \times \frac{1}{4}$ or $\frac{21}{4}$ pizzas. Nick said, "That's the same as $5\frac{1}{4}$ pizzas." Is he correct?

A. To find a mixed numeral equivalent to a fraction, you can divide.

$$\frac{21}{4} \longrightarrow 4\overline{)21} \quad \begin{array}{r} 5\frac{1}{4} \\ 20 \\ \hline 1 \end{array}$$

Nick is correct.

B. To find a fraction equivalent to a mixed numeral, you can use addition and multiplication.

$$5\frac{1}{4} = 5 + \frac{1}{4}$$

$$= \frac{5}{1} + \frac{1}{4}$$

$$= \frac{5 \times 4}{1 \times 4} + \frac{1}{4}$$

$$= \frac{20}{4} + \frac{1}{4} = \frac{21}{4}$$

C. You can do this mentally.

Multiply.	Add.	Put answer over denominator.
$5 \times 4 = 20$	$20 + 1 = 21$	$\frac{21}{4}$

TRY THESE

Give a mixed numeral or standard numeral for each.

1. $\dfrac{11}{2}$ 2. $\dfrac{15}{3}$ 3. $\dfrac{17}{3}$ 4. $\dfrac{73}{4}$ 5. $\dfrac{30}{6}$ 6. $\dfrac{123}{8}$

Give a fraction for each. Find the fraction mentally if you can.

7. $5\dfrac{1}{2}$ 8. $4\dfrac{2}{3}$ 9. $2\dfrac{1}{4}$ 10. $5\dfrac{2}{5}$ 11. $4\dfrac{4}{9}$ 12. $6\dfrac{1}{6}$

SKILLS PRACTICE

Give a mixed numeral or standard numeral for each.

1. $\dfrac{15}{4}$ 2. $\dfrac{19}{3}$ 3. $\dfrac{6}{2}$ 4. $\dfrac{11}{5}$ 5. $\dfrac{38}{7}$ 6. $\dfrac{49}{10}$

7. $\dfrac{36}{9}$ 8. $\dfrac{55}{12}$ 9. $\dfrac{35}{8}$ 10. $\dfrac{12}{6}$ 11. $\dfrac{25}{4}$ ★12. $\dfrac{0}{5}$

Give a fraction for each. Find the fraction mentally if you can.

13. $9\dfrac{3}{4}$ 14. $4\dfrac{3}{10}$ 15. $16\dfrac{2}{3}$ 16. $10\dfrac{11}{12}$ 17. $3\dfrac{3}{8}$ 18. $2\dfrac{1}{2}$

19. $3\dfrac{1}{5}$ 20. $5\dfrac{1}{3}$ 21. $3\dfrac{3}{4}$ 22. $2\dfrac{5}{8}$ 23. $12\dfrac{8}{9}$ 24. $3\dfrac{1}{7}$

25. $10\dfrac{1}{2}$ 26. $4\dfrac{7}{8}$ 27. $3\dfrac{1}{3}$ 28. $20\dfrac{1}{4}$ 29. $5\dfrac{7}{12}$ 30. $11\dfrac{2}{3}$

31. $4\dfrac{1}{10}$ 32. $2\dfrac{4}{5}$ 33. $4\dfrac{1}{4}$ 34. $2\dfrac{5}{6}$ 35. $12\dfrac{3}{5}$ ★36. 3

37. $5\dfrac{5}{6}$ baskets of apples 38. $3\dfrac{7}{10}$ jars of pickles 39. $1\dfrac{9}{10}$ cartons of milk

40. $7\dfrac{1}{2}$ hours work

THINK!

Reasoning About Mixed Numerals

1. Suppose each pizza for Sandy's party is cut into 8 slices. How many whole pizzas and how many extra slices should she order?

2. Sandy can order the pizzas from another store, which sells only whole pizzas. How many whole pizzas would she need to be sure of having enough?

Addition and Subtraction with Mixed Numerals

A. Mark sold $1\frac{1}{10}$ yards of corduroy.

Carla sold $2\frac{3}{10}$ yards of denim.

How many yards of material did

they sell in all?

$$1\frac{1}{10} + 2\frac{3}{10} = \blacksquare$$

Add fractions.

$$\begin{array}{r} 1\frac{1}{10} \\ +2\frac{3}{10} \\ \hline \frac{4}{10} \end{array}$$

Add whole numbers.

$$\begin{array}{r} 1\frac{1}{10} \\ +2\frac{3}{10} \\ \hline 3\frac{4}{10} = 3\frac{2}{5} \end{array}$$

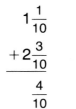

$$\frac{4}{10} = \frac{4 \div 2}{10 \div 2} = \frac{2}{5}$$

They sold $3\frac{2}{5}$ yards of material in all.

B. Use the information above.
How much more material did Carla sell?

$$2\frac{3}{10} - 1\frac{1}{10} = \blacksquare$$

Subtract fractions.

$$\begin{array}{r} 2\frac{3}{10} \\ -1\frac{1}{10} \\ \hline \frac{2}{10} \end{array}$$

Subtract whole numbers.

$$\begin{array}{r} 2\frac{3}{10} \\ 1\frac{1}{10} \\ \hline 1\frac{2}{10} = 1\frac{1}{5} \end{array}$$

Carla sold $1\frac{1}{5}$ yards more.

TRY THESE

Add or subtract.

1. $5\frac{1}{9}$
   $+1\frac{4}{9}$

2. $4\frac{1}{2}$
   -3

3. 5
   $+1\frac{2}{3}$

4. $1\frac{1}{8}$
   $+2\frac{5}{8}$

5. $5\frac{11}{12}$
   $-2\frac{5}{12}$

6. $2\frac{7}{10}$
   $-1\frac{3}{10}$

7. $4\frac{1}{6}$
   $+1\frac{1}{6}$

SKILLS PRACTICE

Add or subtract.

1. $2\frac{1}{5}$
   $+4\frac{3}{5}$

2. $3\frac{9}{10}$
   $-1\frac{3}{10}$

3. $8\frac{4}{5}$
   $-2\frac{1}{5}$

4. $1\frac{2}{5}$
   $+1\frac{2}{5}$

5. $9\frac{2}{3}$
   $-4\frac{1}{3}$

6. $4\frac{2}{15}$
   $+3\frac{4}{15}$

7. $9\frac{7}{11}$
   $+5\frac{3}{11}$

8. $3\frac{11}{20}$
   $-2\frac{3}{20}$

9. $10\frac{15}{16}$
   $-8\frac{11}{16}$

10. $9\frac{3}{20}$
    $+2\frac{7}{20}$

11. $7\frac{8}{15}$
    $+\frac{4}{15}$

12. $1\frac{3}{8}$
    $+6\frac{1}{8}$

13. $2\frac{11}{12}$
    $-2\frac{5}{12}$

14. $8\frac{6}{7}$
    $-3\frac{6}{7}$

15. $1\frac{1}{5} + 4\frac{1}{5} = $ ■

16. $7\frac{5}{6} - 3\frac{1}{6} = $ ■

17. $1\frac{5}{9} + 1\frac{2}{9} = $ ■

18. $14\frac{9}{10} - 11\frac{1}{10} = $ ■

19. $6\frac{3}{4} - 1\frac{1}{4} = $ ■

★20. $2\frac{3}{8} + 8\frac{3}{8} + 1\frac{1}{8} = $ ■

PROBLEM SOLVING

21. Tony bought $3\frac{1}{3}$ yards of wool cloth and $2\frac{1}{3}$ yards of linen. How much did he buy in all?

22. Carla sold $12\frac{5}{6}$ yards of silk cloth and $7\frac{1}{6}$ yards of denim. How much more silk did she sell?

THINK!

Visual Reasoning

A wall has 6 sections. Each section is 1 square yard. Toby painted $2\frac{1}{6}$ square yards. Joy painted $1\frac{5}{6}$ square yards. How many square yards have not been painted?

More Addition and Subtraction with Mixed Numerals

A. Tom painted $1\frac{1}{5}$ square yards of a fence.

Becky painted $2\frac{3}{4}$ square yards of the fence.

How much did they paint all together?

$$1\frac{1}{5} + 2\frac{3}{4} = \blacksquare$$

You need to find a common denominator. Then add.

$$1\frac{1}{5}$$
$$+2\frac{3}{4}$$

Least common denominator is 20.

$$1\frac{1}{5} \rightarrow 1\frac{1 \times 4}{5 \times 4} \rightarrow 1\frac{4}{20}$$
$$+2\frac{3}{4} \rightarrow +2\frac{3 \times 5}{4 \times 5} \rightarrow +2\frac{15}{20}$$
$$3\frac{19}{20}$$

They painted $3\frac{19}{20}$ square yards of the fence.

B. How much more did Becky paint?

$$2\frac{3}{4} - 1\frac{1}{5} = \blacksquare$$

To subtract, use the common denominator you found above.

$$2\frac{3}{4} \rightarrow 2\frac{3 \times 5}{4 \times 5} \rightarrow 2\frac{15}{20}$$
$$-1\frac{1}{5} \rightarrow -1\frac{1 \times 4}{5 \times 4} \rightarrow -1\frac{4}{20}$$
$$1\frac{11}{20}$$

Becky painted $1\frac{11}{20}$ square yards more of the fence than Tom.

C. Find the sum or the difference.

$$5\frac{2}{5} \rightarrow 5\frac{4}{10}$$
$$+3\frac{1}{2} \rightarrow +3\frac{5}{10}$$
$$8\frac{9}{10}$$

Least common denominator is 10.

$$9\frac{2}{3} \rightarrow 9\frac{4}{6}$$
$$-2\frac{1}{6} \rightarrow -2\frac{1}{6}$$
$$7\frac{3}{6} = 7\frac{1}{2}$$

Least common denominator is 6.

TRY THESE

Add or subtract.

1. $2\frac{5}{8}$
$+1\frac{1}{4}$

2. $5\frac{3}{4}$
$-1\frac{2}{3}$

3. $5\frac{7}{10}$
$-2\frac{1}{2}$

4. $3\frac{1}{6}$
$+2\frac{3}{4}$

5. $3\frac{1}{3}$
$-1\frac{1}{6}$

6. $1\frac{1}{2}$
$+4\frac{1}{5}$

7. $3\frac{2}{3}$
$-1\frac{3}{5}$

SKILLS PRACTICE

Find the sum or the difference.

1. $8\frac{5}{6}$
$-2\frac{1}{3}$

2. $1\frac{1}{3}$
$+\ \frac{1}{4}$

3. $6\frac{3}{10}$
$+6\frac{1}{4}$

4. $7\frac{5}{6}$
$-6\frac{1}{2}$

5. $9\frac{2}{3}$
$+4\frac{1}{9}$

6. $8\frac{9}{10}$
$-4\frac{1}{6}$

7. $2\frac{1}{4}$
$+5\frac{1}{6}$

8. $5\frac{7}{8}$
$-2\frac{3}{4}$

9. $5\frac{3}{4}$
$-\ \frac{7}{10}$

10. $3\frac{1}{6}$
$+8\frac{5}{12}$

11. $7\frac{4}{5}$
$-3\frac{7}{15}$

12. $6\frac{2}{5}$
$+3\frac{1}{4}$

13. $4\frac{2}{7}$
$+2\frac{1}{2}$

14. $6\frac{7}{8}$
$-2\frac{1}{2}$

15. $1\frac{3}{10} + 5\frac{1}{5} = \blacksquare$

16. $4\frac{3}{4} - 2\frac{2}{3} = \blacksquare$

17. $5\frac{1}{4} + 3\frac{1}{2} = \blacksquare$

18. $8\frac{4}{5} - 5\frac{2}{3} = \blacksquare$

19. $7\frac{1}{2} - 5\frac{1}{4} = \blacksquare$

★20. $1\frac{1}{4} + 3\frac{1}{3} + 2\frac{1}{4} = \blacksquare$

PROBLEM SOLVING

21. Gene sanded $8\frac{1}{2}$ square yards of a floor. Sal sanded $5\frac{1}{3}$ square yards. How many more square yards did Gene sand?

★22. Tina used $4\frac{1}{8}$ square yards of cloth, Jay used $6\frac{1}{2}$ square yards, and Fran used $6\frac{1}{4}$ square yards. How much cloth was used in all?

THINK!

Making Logical Choices

On 6 tests Maria scored higher than René 4 times. René scored higher than David 4 times. Could David have scored higher than Maria 4 times?

Addition with Mixed Numerals: Renaming

A. One weekend, Inez wrote $2\frac{1}{2}$ pages for her social studies

assignment and $3\frac{7}{8}$ pages for her book report.

How many pages did she write in all?

$$2\frac{1}{2} + 3\frac{7}{8} = \blacksquare$$

Find a common denominator. Then add.
Rename the sum if the fraction part is 1 or greater.

$$
\begin{array}{ll}
2\frac{1}{2} \rightarrow & 2\frac{4}{8} \\
+3\frac{7}{8} \rightarrow & +3\frac{7}{8} \\
\hline
& 5\frac{11}{8} = 5 + 1\frac{3}{8} = 6\frac{3}{8}
\end{array}
$$

$\dfrac{11}{8} > \dfrac{8}{8}$ or 1

Inez wrote $6\frac{3}{8}$ pages in all.

B. Here are some other examples.

$$
\begin{array}{ll}
4\frac{5}{6} \rightarrow & 4\frac{5}{6} \\
+2\frac{2}{3} \rightarrow & +2\frac{4}{6} \\
\hline
& 6\frac{9}{6} = 6 + 1\frac{3}{6} \\
& \quad = 7\frac{3}{6} = 7\frac{1}{2}
\end{array}
$$

$$
\begin{array}{l}
4\frac{3}{5} \\
+ \ \frac{2}{5} \\
\hline
4\frac{5}{5} = 4 + 1 \\
\quad = 5
\end{array}
$$

$\dfrac{5}{5} = 1$

TRY THESE

Add. Rename the sum if the fraction part is 1 or greater.

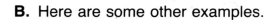

1.	2.	3.	4.	5.	6.	7.
$2\frac{1}{2}$	$5\frac{2}{3}$	$4\frac{3}{4}$	$1\frac{3}{10}$	$7\frac{5}{6}$	$4\frac{5}{8}$	$8\frac{7}{10}$
$+9\frac{1}{2}$	$+3\frac{1}{3}$	$+2\frac{7}{8}$	$+1\frac{4}{5}$	$+3\frac{1}{2}$	$+5\frac{3}{8}$	$+2\frac{1}{2}$

SKILLS PRACTICE

Add.

1. $1\frac{3}{8}$ $+2\frac{7}{8}$

2. $3\frac{1}{2}$ $+4\frac{1}{2}$

3. $3\frac{2}{3}$ $+4\frac{2}{3}$

4. $8\frac{3}{8}$ $+1\frac{3}{4}$

5. $6\frac{5}{8}$ $+1\frac{3}{8}$

6. $4\frac{2}{3}$ $+3\frac{3}{5}$

7. $3\frac{1}{6}$ $+5\frac{9}{10}$

8. $2\frac{1}{2}$ $+3\frac{1}{3}$

9. $1\frac{7}{8}$ $+3\frac{3}{4}$

10. $4\frac{5}{6}$ $+1\frac{1}{2}$

11. $\frac{5}{12}$ $+1\frac{11}{12}$

12. $2\frac{3}{4}$ $+7\frac{9}{10}$

13. $\frac{5}{8}$ $+1\frac{7}{8}$

14. $4\frac{1}{4}$ $+3\frac{4}{5}$

15. $4\frac{1}{2} + \frac{1}{2} = \blacksquare$

16. $6\frac{3}{4} + 1\frac{5}{6} = \blacksquare$

★17. $3\frac{9}{10} + 5\frac{7}{10} + 3\frac{7}{10} = \blacksquare$

PROBLEM SOLVING

18. Roy wrote $2\frac{3}{4}$ pages for the school newspaper and $1\frac{3}{8}$ pages for a science project. How many pages did he write in all?

19. Mindy typed $5\frac{1}{4}$ pages Thursday morning and $6\frac{3}{4}$ pages Thursday afternoon. How many pages did she type in all?

THINK!

Improper Fractions

Fractions that are equal to or greater than 1, such as $\frac{4}{4}$ and $\frac{15}{3}$, are called *improper fractions.* An improper fraction can be written as a mixed numeral or a standard numeral.

1. What is a good test to decide whether you can write a mixed numeral or a standard numeral for an improper fraction?

Write a mixed or a standard numeral for each improper fraction.

2. $\frac{11}{9}$

3. $\frac{8}{4}$

4. $\frac{9}{3}$

5. $\frac{11}{3}$

6. $\frac{3}{11}$

7. $\frac{14}{4}$

Subtraction with Mixed Numerals: Regrouping

A. Jon's recipe for spaghetti uses 3 cups of tomato sauce.
Megan's uses $1\frac{3}{4}$ cups of tomato sauce.
How much more tomato sauce does Jon use?

$3 - 1\frac{3}{4} = $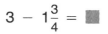

$$\begin{array}{r} 3 \\ -1\frac{3}{4} \\ \hline \end{array}$$

No fourths.
Can't subtract.
Regroup.

Regroup.

$3 = 2 + 1$

$= 2 + \frac{4}{4}$

$= 2\frac{4}{4}$

Subtract.

$$\begin{array}{rcr} 3 & \rightarrow & 2\frac{4}{4} \\ -1\frac{3}{4} & \rightarrow & -1\frac{3}{4} \\ \hline & & 1\frac{1}{4} \end{array}$$

Jon uses $1\frac{1}{4}$ cups more sauce.

B. Jon uses $3\frac{1}{3}$ teaspoons of spice. Megan uses $2\frac{3}{4}$ teaspoons of spice. How much more spice does Jon use?

$3\frac{1}{3} - 2\frac{3}{4} = $ ■

Find a common denominator.

$$\begin{array}{rcr} 3\frac{1}{3} & \rightarrow & 3\frac{4}{12} \\ -2\frac{3}{4} & \rightarrow & -2\frac{9}{12} \\ \hline \end{array}$$

Regroup.

$3\frac{4}{12} = 2 + 1 + \frac{4}{12}$

Not enough twelfths. Regroup.

$= 2 + \frac{12}{12} + \frac{4}{12}$

$= 2\frac{16}{12}$

Subtract.

$$\begin{array}{rcrcr} 3\frac{1}{3} & \rightarrow & 3\frac{4}{12} & \rightarrow & 2\frac{16}{12} \\ -2\frac{3}{4} & & & \rightarrow & -2\frac{9}{12} \\ \hline & & & & \frac{7}{12} \end{array}$$

Jon uses $\frac{7}{12}$ teaspoon more spice than Megan.

C. Always find fractions with a common denominator first. Then decide if you need to regroup.

Regroup.

$$\begin{array}{rcrcr} 6\frac{4}{9} & \rightarrow & 6\frac{8}{18} & \rightarrow & 5\frac{26}{18} \\ -2\frac{1}{2} & \rightarrow & -2\frac{9}{18} & \rightarrow & -2\frac{9}{18} \\ \hline & & & & 3\frac{17}{18} \end{array}$$

No need to regroup.

$$\begin{array}{rcr} 4\frac{5}{6} & \rightarrow & 4\frac{25}{30} \\ -3\frac{7}{10} & \rightarrow & -3\frac{21}{30} \\ \hline & & 1\frac{4}{30} = 1\frac{2}{15} \end{array}$$

TRY THESE

Subtract.

1. $5\frac{1}{10}$
    $-3\frac{3}{10}$

2. 6
    $-1\frac{3}{5}$

3. $5\frac{1}{2}$
    $-2\frac{7}{8}$

4. $6\frac{5}{12}$
    $-1\frac{3}{4}$

5. $2\frac{3}{8}$
    $-\frac{7}{8}$

6. $8\frac{2}{7}$
    $-3\frac{5}{14}$

7. $5\frac{1}{4}$
    $-2\frac{5}{6}$

SKILLS PRACTICE

Add or subtract.

1. $2\frac{1}{5}$
    $-\frac{2}{5}$

2. 3
    $-2\frac{1}{2}$

3. $5\frac{1}{8}$
    $-1\frac{5}{8}$

4. $6\frac{5}{8}$
    $+4\frac{1}{2}$

5. 2
    $-1\frac{7}{10}$

6. $4\frac{3}{4}$
    $+1\frac{1}{4}$

7. $2\frac{5}{12}$
    $-1\frac{5}{6}$

8. $2\frac{1}{8}$
    $-1\frac{1}{3}$

9. $4\frac{3}{4}$
    $-1\frac{1}{4}$

10. $8\frac{1}{6}$
    $+4\frac{5}{6}$

11. $6\frac{3}{10}$
    $-5\frac{9}{10}$

12. $5\frac{2}{9}$
    $-1\frac{5}{9}$

13. $4\frac{5}{6}$
    $-2\frac{1}{4}$

14. 4
    $-3\frac{6}{7}$

15. $5\frac{5}{12} - 2\frac{2}{3} = $ ■

16. $4\frac{5}{6} - 2\frac{3}{10} = $ ■

17. $6 - \frac{5}{6} = $ ■

18. $\frac{5}{6} + 2\frac{1}{2} = $ ■

19. $3\frac{1}{5} - 2\frac{1}{2} = $ ■

20. $4\frac{1}{10} - 2\frac{4}{15} = $ ■

PROBLEM SOLVING

21. Marla had 4 cartons of milk. After making a pot of soup, she had $1\frac{4}{5}$ cartons left. How much milk did she use?

★22. Jamie used $2\frac{1}{2}$ cups of broth to make a stew. Linda used $4\frac{1}{3}$ cups of broth to make sauce. Who used more broth? How much more?

MIXED REVIEW

Add, subtract, multiply, or divide.

1. 4.8
    -2.75

2. 347
    $\times .24$

3. 25.43
    $+37.61$

4. 26.842
    -19.861

5. $9\overline{)86.22}$

6. 85.6
    $\times 7.9$

7. $5.8 + 27.352 = $ ■

8. $28.05 \div 85 = $ ■

9. $.5 \times .07 = $ ■

Problem Solving Strategy

Mixed Strategies

Solve the problems. Use one of the strategies listed or use one of your own strategies.

> Guess and Check
> Work Backwards
> Use Logical Reasoning
> Make a Table

1. There are 23 people on a bus. 13 are wearing hats. 10 are reading. 6 of the people wearing hats are also reading. How many people are neither reading nor wearing hats?

2. Charlene has $7\frac{1}{2}$ quarts of paint in two cans. One can holds $2\frac{1}{2}$ quarts more than the other. How much paint does each can hold?

3. To make vegetable soup, Ken uses 1 pound of potatoes for every $\frac{1}{2}$ pound of carrots. How many pounds of potatoes would he use with $2\frac{1}{2}$ pounds of carrots?

4. Ken also uses $1\frac{1}{2}$ pounds of tomatoes for every pound of potatoes. How many pounds of potatoes would he use with 6 pounds of tomatoes?

5. Rick has $27.60. He wants to buy 2 pillows for $7.50 each and a quilt for $13.50. Does he have enough money?

6. Lisette and her 4 cousins sent each other New Year's cards. How many cards were sent?

7. Pedro went shopping in a supermarket, a hardware store, and a drug store. He bought tissues, sponges, and light bulbs. The hardware store does not sell tissues. Pedro used his supermarket purchase in a new floor lamp. What did he buy in the drugstore?

8. Kevin is 3 years older than Tanya and 5 years younger than Mel. Arif is 10 years older than Tanya. Tanya is as old as the difference between Mel's and Arif's ages. How old is each?

Challenge Problems page 462

Problem Solving **Project**

Estimating Areas

When a figure is drawn on a grid, you can estimate the area.

Estimate the area of the figure shown. First count the whole squares inside the figure. There are 34 whole squares. Then count the part squares. Estimate that each part square is about $\frac{1}{2}$ square unit. There are 6 part squares.

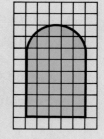

$$\frac{1}{2} \times 6 = \frac{1}{2} \times \frac{6}{1} = \frac{6}{2} = 3 \text{ square units}$$

Add to get an estimate of the area.

The area is about 37 square units.

$$34 + 3 = 37 \text{ square units}$$

green square units

blue square units

Estimate the area of each figure.

1.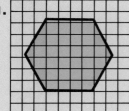

2.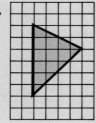

3.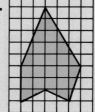

4.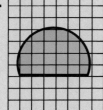

5.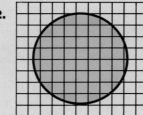

6.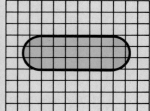

ON YOUR OWN

Data Search

Cut out pictures of 3 objects from a magazine or newspaper. Put each one on a piece of grid paper and estimate its area.

353

Multiplication with Mixed Numerals

A. Danny travels $2\frac{1}{4}$ miles to get to school. He travels $\frac{2}{3}$ of this distance by bus. How far does he travel by bus?

$\frac{2}{3}$ of $2\frac{1}{4}$ is $\frac{2}{3} \times 2\frac{1}{4}$.

$\frac{2}{3} \times 2\frac{1}{4} = \blacksquare$

$\frac{(2 \times 4) + 1}{4}$

Write a fraction for the mixed numeral. Then multiply.

$\frac{2}{3} \times \frac{9}{4} = \blacksquare$

$\frac{2}{3} \times \frac{9}{4} = \frac{18}{12} = 1\frac{6}{12} = 1\frac{1}{2}$

Danny travels $1\frac{1}{2}$ miles by bus.

B. $2\frac{1}{5} \quad \times \quad 1\frac{2}{3} = \blacksquare$

$\frac{(2 \times 5) + 1}{5} \qquad \frac{(1 \times 3) + 2}{3}$

Write a fraction for each mixed numeral. Then multiply.

$\frac{11}{5} \quad \times \quad \frac{5}{3} \quad = \quad \blacksquare$

$\frac{11}{5} \quad \times \quad \frac{5}{3} \quad = \quad \frac{55}{15} = 3\frac{10}{15} = 3\frac{2}{3}$

TRY THESE

Multiply.

1. $\frac{3}{10} \times 1\frac{1}{4} = $ ■ $\frac{3}{8}$

2. $2\frac{1}{2} \times 1\frac{3}{4} = $ ■

3. $1\frac{2}{3} \times 5 = $ ■

4. $3 \times 2\frac{1}{2} = $ ■

5. $1\frac{1}{4} \times 1\frac{1}{3} = $ ■

6. $1\frac{1}{3} \times \frac{5}{6} = $ ■

SKILLS PRACTICE

Multiply.

1. $\frac{4}{5} \times 2\frac{1}{2} = $ ■

2. $\frac{1}{2} \times 1\frac{1}{3} = $ ■

3. $\frac{7}{10} \times 2\frac{1}{2} = $ ■

4. $2\frac{1}{8} \times 1\frac{2}{3} = $ ■

5. $1\frac{3}{4} \times 2\frac{2}{3} = $ ■

6. $8\frac{2}{3} \times 1\frac{1}{2} = $ ■

7. $2\frac{1}{2} \times 1\frac{2}{7} = $ ■

8. $1\frac{1}{2} \times 36 = $ ■

9. $2\frac{3}{4} \times 1\frac{5}{6} = $ ■

10. $1\frac{1}{2} \times 1\frac{4}{5} = $ ■

11. $\frac{3}{8} \times 3\frac{1}{5} = $ ■

12. $11 \times \frac{3}{7} = $ ■

PROBLEM SOLVING

13. Of the 36 students who went to the class party, $\frac{2}{3}$ brought sandwiches. How many students brought sandwiches?

★14. One song on a record lasted $2\frac{1}{4}$ minutes. Another song lasted $2\frac{2}{3}$ times as long. How long did the second song last?

THINK!

Mental Math

You can use this shortcut to multiply some mixed numerals mentally.

$$2 \times 4\frac{3}{5} = ■$$

Multiply the whole number part. $2 \times 4 = \quad 8$

Multiply the fraction part. $2 \times \frac{3}{5} = \frac{6}{5} = +1\frac{1}{5}$

Add.

$$9\frac{1}{5}$$

Use the shortcut to find each product.

1. $3 \times 1\frac{1}{4} = ■$

2. $4 \times 2\frac{1}{3} = ■$

3. $6 \times 1\frac{2}{5} = ■$

When can you use this shortcut?

Problem Solving

Using Mixed Numerals

When solving a problem with mixed numerals, first plan whether to add, subtract, or multiply. Estimate. Then find your answer.

A. A cement truck made two trips on Wednesday. On the first trip, it carried $3\frac{1}{2}$ tons. On the second trip, it carried $2\frac{5}{8}$ tons. How many tons did it carry in all on Wednesday?

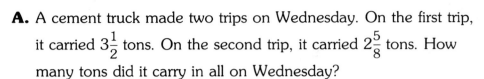

Add to find how many tons in all.

$3\frac{1}{2} + 2\frac{5}{8} = \blacksquare$ Estimate: about $4 + 3 = 7$ tons

$$3\frac{1}{2} \rightarrow \quad 3\frac{4}{8}$$

$$+2\frac{5}{8} \rightarrow \quad +2\frac{5}{8}$$

$$5\frac{9}{8} = 6\frac{1}{8}$$

The truck carried $6\frac{1}{8}$ tons in all.

B. An electrician had $11\frac{1}{4}$ yards of cable. He used $6\frac{3}{4}$ yards of cable for an antenna. How much cable did he have left?

Subtract to find how much he had left.

$11\frac{1}{4} - 6\frac{3}{4} = \blacksquare$ Estimate: about $11 - 7 = 4$ yards

$$11\frac{1}{4} \rightarrow \quad 10\frac{5}{4}$$

$$- \ 6\frac{3}{4} \rightarrow \ - \ 6\frac{3}{4}$$

$$4\frac{2}{4} = 4\frac{1}{2}$$

The electrician had $4\frac{1}{2}$ yards of cable left.

C. Painters used $\frac{7}{8}$ of a can of paint for each of 5 closets. How much paint did they use?

Multiply to find how much paint they used in all.

$5 \times \frac{7}{8} = \blacksquare$ Estimate: about $5 \times 1 = 5$ cans

$$5 \times \frac{7}{8} = \frac{5}{1} \times \frac{7}{8} = \frac{35}{8} = 4\frac{3}{8}$$

The painters used $4\frac{3}{8}$ cans of paint in all.

Solve.

1. Nina had $10\frac{5}{8}$ cans of paint. She used $6\frac{1}{2}$ cans to paint a roof. How many cans did she have left?

2. Joe used $\frac{5}{8}$ of a can of paint on a chair and $1\frac{3}{8}$ cans on a table. How much paint did he use in all?

PROBLEM SOLVING PRACTICE

Solve.

1. An electrician has two cables. One is $7\frac{1}{3}$ yards long. The other is $10\frac{5}{9}$ yards long. How many yards of cable does she have in all?

2. A truck made 4 trips. It carried $1\frac{3}{10}$ tons on each trip. How many tons in all did the truck carry?

3. A painter mixed $2\frac{5}{8}$ gallons of blue paint with $3\frac{1}{2}$ gallons of yellow paint. How many gallons of paint were in the mixture?

4. An electrician used 5 pieces of cable. Each piece was $7\frac{5}{6}$ feet long. How many feet of cable did she use in all?

5. Janet has $7\frac{3}{4}$ boxes of brass hooks, $12\frac{1}{2}$ boxes of steel hooks, and $4\frac{1}{5}$ boxes of plastic hooks. How many boxes of hooks does she have in all?

★6. A construction crew had $95\frac{1}{2}$ bags of cement. At the end of the first day, $47\frac{2}{3}$ bags were left. On the second day $21\frac{1}{6}$ bags were used. How many bags did they use in all?

ON YOUR OWN

Mike, Hanna, and Dan are carpenters. The hours they worked on Monday and Tuesday are shown. They earn $22 an hour. Make up three problems. Use addition, subtraction, and multiplication.

Day	Mike	Hanna	Dan
Monday	$5\frac{3}{4}$ h	$5\frac{3}{4}$ h	$5\frac{3}{4}$ h
Tuesday	$4\frac{1}{2}$ h	7 h	$3\frac{1}{4}$ h

Mixed Numerals with a Calculator

Dora and Don checked the Stock Exchange tables in the daily newspaper for the difference between the high and low prices of Jifco stock during the past 52 weeks. The tables showed Jifco's high at $25\frac{1}{4}$ and low at $10\frac{3}{8}$ ($\$25\frac{1}{4}$ and $\$10\frac{3}{8}$ per share; $\$25\frac{1}{4}$ means \$25.25 and $\$10\frac{3}{8}$ means \$10.375). To find the difference, they subtracted:

$$25\frac{1}{4} - 10\frac{3}{8} = \blacksquare$$

One way to use the calculator is to find decimal equivalents for each fraction.

$25\frac{1}{4}$ $\boxed{1}$ $\boxed{\div}$ $\boxed{4}$ $\boxed{=}$ | 0.25 |

$10\frac{3}{8}$ $\boxed{3}$ $\boxed{\div}$ $\boxed{8}$ $\boxed{=}$ | 0.375 |

Then enter the complete stock prices in decimal form.

$\boxed{2}$ $\boxed{5}$ $\boxed{.}$ $\boxed{2}$ $\boxed{5}$ $\boxed{-}$ $\boxed{1}$ $\boxed{0}$ $\boxed{.}$ $\boxed{3}$ $\boxed{7}$ $\boxed{5}$ $\boxed{=}$ | 14.875 |

To convert 14.875 to a mixed numeral, find the lowest terms fraction equivalent to .875.

$$.875 = \frac{875}{1{,}000} \underset{\div\,5}{\overset{\div\,5}{}} = \frac{175}{200} \underset{\div\,5}{\overset{\div\,5}{}} = \frac{35}{40} \underset{\div\,5}{\overset{\div\,5}{}} = \frac{7}{8}$$

Use your calculator.

The difference between the high and low prices of Jifco stock was $14\frac{7}{8}$ ($\$14\frac{7}{8}$).

Use the calculator to solve each problem.

1. Dora has 473 shares of Jifco stock. If today's opening price is $18\frac{3}{4}$ per share, how much are her shares worth?

2. Don bought 372 shares of Jifco at yesterday's closing price. If he paid $18\frac{1}{4}$ per share, how much did he pay?

3. Dora paid $53\frac{5}{8}$ for Roidco stock. If the company pays a dividend of \$2.34 four times a year, approximately how many years will it take for the dividends to equal her cost?

4. Don noticed that the high and low prices for Roidco stock during the past 52 weeks were $105\frac{1}{4}$ and $47\frac{7}{8}$. What would the price difference be for 279 shares?

Give a mixed numeral or standard numeral for each. (*pages 342–343*)

1. $\dfrac{11}{4}$ 2. $\dfrac{17}{5}$ 3. $\dfrac{21}{3}$ 4. $\dfrac{13}{2}$ 5. $\dfrac{29}{6}$ 6. $\dfrac{10}{10}$ 7. $\dfrac{15}{8}$

Give a fraction for each. (*pages 342–343*)

8. $1\dfrac{6}{7}$ 9. $2\dfrac{3}{5}$ 10. $5\dfrac{1}{4}$ 11. $4\dfrac{5}{8}$ 12. $3\dfrac{2}{3}$ 13. $6\dfrac{5}{9}$ 14. $7\dfrac{3}{10}$

Add or subtract. (*pages 344–345*)

15. $\begin{array}{r} 2\frac{4}{9} \\ +3\frac{1}{9} \\ \hline \end{array}$ 16. $\begin{array}{r} 4\frac{6}{7} \\ -3\frac{2}{7} \\ \hline \end{array}$ 17. $\begin{array}{r} 2\frac{1}{4} \\ +2\frac{3}{8} \\ \hline \end{array}$ 18. $\begin{array}{r} 4\frac{1}{10} \\ +1\frac{3}{10} \\ \hline \end{array}$ 19. $\begin{array}{r} 5\frac{2}{3} \\ -1\frac{1}{4} \\ \hline \end{array}$ 20. $\begin{array}{r} 2\frac{11}{12} \\ -\frac{5}{6} \\ \hline \end{array}$ 21. $\begin{array}{r} 4\frac{1}{2} \\ +2\frac{2}{5} \\ \hline \end{array}$

Add or subtract. (*pages 348–351*)

22. $\begin{array}{r} 5\frac{3}{10} \\ -1\frac{7}{10} \\ \hline \end{array}$ 23. $\begin{array}{r} 2\frac{5}{8} \\ +5\frac{7}{8} \\ \hline \end{array}$ 24. $\begin{array}{r} 6\frac{1}{8} \\ -3\frac{1}{2} \\ \hline \end{array}$ 25. $\begin{array}{r} 4\frac{1}{2} \\ +6\frac{1}{10} \\ \hline \end{array}$ 26. $\begin{array}{r} 3\frac{2}{5} \\ -1\frac{4}{5} \\ \hline \end{array}$ 27. $\begin{array}{r} 5\frac{3}{4} \\ +3\frac{1}{4} \\ \hline \end{array}$ 28. $\begin{array}{r} 3\frac{1}{6} \\ -2\frac{3}{4} \\ \hline \end{array}$

29. $3\dfrac{5}{12} - 2\dfrac{3}{4} = \blacksquare$ 30. $5\dfrac{5}{6} + \dfrac{5}{6} = \blacksquare$ 31. $4\dfrac{1}{6} + 3\dfrac{3}{10} = \blacksquare$

Multiply. (*pages 354–355*)

32. $3 \times 1\dfrac{1}{4} = \blacksquare$ 33. $\dfrac{4}{5} \times 2\dfrac{2}{3} = \blacksquare$ 34. $2\dfrac{3}{4} \times 2\dfrac{1}{2} = \blacksquare$

35. $1\dfrac{3}{5} \times 10 = \blacksquare$ 36. $2\dfrac{1}{5} \times \dfrac{5}{6} = \blacksquare$ 37. $4\dfrac{1}{2} \times 1\dfrac{1}{3} = \blacksquare$

Solve the problems. (*pages 356–357*)

38. It took the cooks $3\dfrac{2}{3}$ hours to prepare Monday's lunch. Tuesday's lunch took $2\dfrac{3}{4}$ hours to prepare. How much longer did it take to prepare Monday's lunch?

39. A produce stand sold $6\dfrac{1}{3}$ boxes of peaches one day. Each box of peaches weighed $9\dfrac{1}{2}$ lb. How many pounds of peaches were sold in all?

Reinforcement

More Help with Mixed Numerals

$$3\frac{1}{4} \rightarrow 3\frac{3}{12}$$
$$+2\frac{1}{3} \rightarrow +2\frac{4}{12}$$
$$5\frac{7}{12}$$

$$2\frac{5}{8} \rightarrow 2\frac{5}{8}$$
$$+4\frac{1}{2} \rightarrow +4\frac{4}{8}$$
$$6\frac{9}{8} = 7\frac{1}{8}$$

$$\frac{9}{8} = 1\frac{1}{8}$$

Add.

1. $3\frac{2}{7}$
$+5\frac{4}{7}$

2. $4\frac{1}{10}$
$+6\frac{1}{2}$

3. $3\frac{1}{2}$
$+4\frac{1}{3}$

4. $4\frac{7}{10}$
$+5\frac{9}{10}$

5. $2\frac{5}{6}$
$+3\frac{3}{8}$

6. $1\frac{2}{3}$
$+6\frac{5}{9}$

$$7\frac{9}{10} \rightarrow 7\frac{9}{10}$$
$$-2\frac{1}{2} \rightarrow -2\frac{5}{10}$$
$$5\frac{4}{10} = 5\frac{2}{5}$$

$$6\frac{2}{9} \rightarrow 5\frac{11}{9}$$
$$-4\frac{7}{9} \rightarrow -4\frac{7}{9}$$
$$1\frac{4}{9}$$

$$6\frac{2}{9}$$
$$= 5 + 1\frac{2}{9}$$
$$= 5 + \frac{11}{9}$$

Subtract.

7. $8\frac{7}{9}$
$-3\frac{5}{9}$

8. $6\frac{2}{3}$
$-4\frac{1}{4}$

9. $7\frac{5}{6}$
$-5\frac{1}{3}$

10. $5\frac{3}{8}$
$-4\frac{7}{8}$

11. $6\frac{3}{8}$
$-3\frac{3}{4}$

12. $5\frac{1}{4}$
$-2\frac{5}{6}$

$$4\frac{1}{3} \times 2\frac{1}{2} = \frac{13}{3} \times \frac{5}{2}$$
$$= \frac{13 \times 5}{3 \times 2}$$
$$= \frac{65}{6}$$
$$= 10\frac{5}{6}$$

$$10\frac{5}{6}$$
$$6\overline{)65}$$

Multiply.

13. $\frac{3}{4} \times 2\frac{1}{5} = \blacksquare$

14. $1\frac{2}{3} \times 7 = \blacksquare$

15. $3\frac{1}{2} \times 2\frac{1}{4} = \blacksquare$

16. $6\frac{1}{4} \times \frac{3}{5} = \blacksquare$

17. $5\frac{1}{2} \times 1\frac{1}{3} = \blacksquare$

18. $10 \times 1\frac{4}{7} = \blacksquare$

19. $3\frac{2}{3} \times 1\frac{1}{5} = \blacksquare$

20. $4\frac{3}{4} \times 2\frac{2}{3} = \blacksquare$

Dial Arithmetic

This dial is like a clock face in some ways. But it has only the numbers 0, 1, and 2 and only one hand. The hand starts at 0 and moves clockwise.

3-number dial

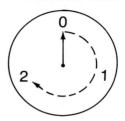

To add 2 + 2 on the dial, move the hand from zero to 2. Then move it 2 more. The hand stops at 1.

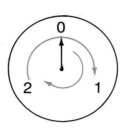

Add on the 3-number dial.

1. 1 + 1 = ▨   **2.** 1 + 2 = ▨   **3.** 2 + 0 = ▨   **4.** 1 + 2 + 1 = ▨

This dial has the numbers 0, 1, 2, 3, 4, and 5.

6-number dial

To add 4 + 3, move the hand from 0 to 4. Then move it 3 more.

$$4 + 3 = 1$$

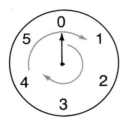

You can also multiply on the dial.

$$2 \times 5 = ▩$$
$$2 \times 5 = 4$$

Add on the 6-number dial.

5. 3 + 3 = ▨   **6.** 1 + 5 = ▨   **7.** 4 + 4 = ▨   **8.** 5 + 3 = ▨

9. 0 + 4 = ▨   **10.** 5 + 4 = ▨   **11.** 3 + 4 = ▨   **12.** 4 + 2 + 5 = ▨

Multiply on the 6-number dial.

13. 2 × 3 = ▨   **14.** 4 × 1 = ▨   **15.** 3 × 5 = ▨   **16.** 4 × 2 = ▨

Cumulative Review

Choose the correct answer. Choose NG if the correct answer is *not given*.

1. | 1 minute = 60 seconds |

5 minutes
12 seconds
= ▨ seconds

a. 512 seconds
b. 500 seconds
c. 312 seconds
d. NG

2. Find the standard numeral for five million, eighty-six.

a. 5,86
b. 5,086
c. 5,086,000
d. NG

3. $4\frac{5}{7}$
$+2\frac{3}{7}$

a. $7\frac{1}{7}$ b. $2\frac{2}{7}$
c. $6\frac{1}{7}$ d. NG

4. Find the area of this rectangle:
length: 12 m
width: 9 m

a. 21 m²
b. 42 m²
c. 108 m²
d. NG

5. $8 - 2.163 = $ ▨

a. 6.163
b. 5.836
c. 5.947
d. NG

6. $3\overline{).273}$

a. .91
b. .091
c. 91
d. NG

7.   561
   $\times 308$

a. 172,788
b. 21,318
c. 6,171
d. NG

8.   4
   $-2\frac{5}{6}$

a. $2\frac{5}{6}$ b. $2\frac{1}{6}$
c. $1\frac{1}{6}$ d. NG

9. $26.75
   $\times$ .2

a. $5.35
b. $53.50
c. $535.0
d. NG

10. $\frac{9}{10} - \frac{3}{4} = $ ▨

a. 1   b. $\frac{3}{20}$
c. $\frac{27}{40}$ d. NG

11. $76\overline{)3,590}$

a. 51 R20
b. 47 R18
c. 461 R18
d. NG

12. What does the digit 7 mean in 9.073?

a. 7 tens
b. 7 tenths
c. 7 hundredths
d. NG

13. Nina was downtown for $2\frac{1}{4}$ hours. She spent $\frac{1}{2}$ of this time shopping. How long did she shop?

a. $\frac{3}{4}$ hour   b. $1\frac{1}{8}$ hours
c. $\frac{7}{8}$ hour   d. NG

14. Gina pasted 256 stamps into her stamp book. Each page will hold 12 stamps. How many pages did she paste stamps on?

a.   22 pages   b.   21 pages
c.   21 R4 pages   d.   NG

Problem Solving Situations

Buying on Credit

You want to buy a bike and a helmet. You can pay cash or buy on credit. What will you choose to do?

Your Notes

Prices (Cash only)
Bike $195
Bike helmet . . . . $ 50

Buy on Credit
Bike: $60 down and 12 weekly
payments of $15 each
Helmet: $15 down and 6 weekly
payments of $8 each

Other Conditions
- You must use a helmet for safety.
- You have only saved $163.
- You can borrow only $29 from your brother and $48 from your sister.
- You don't like to borrow money from your family.
- You want to enter a bike race in 3 months.

Work in small groups to find answers and make decisions.

1. Suppose you borrow money from your brother and sister. You also use all the money you have saved. How much more money do you need to buy the bike and helmet for cash?

2. How much extra do you pay if you buy the bike on credit?

3. How much extra do you pay if you buy the helmet on credit?

4. Suppose you buy both items on credit. How much money in all will you have paid after 8 weeks?

5. Suppose you have bought both items on credit. Your records show that you have already paid, in total, $144. How many weekly payments have you made?

6. If you can save $6 a week, will you be able to buy the items for cash in time for the race?

7. What other things should you think about?

8. Will you buy for cash or for credit?

Problem Solving Situations

Weekday or Weekend?

You and your friends want to see a play. You have a choice of 3 plays. Each play is performed on weekdays and weekends. Which play will you and your friends see? When will you see the play?

Your Notes

Play	Mon.–Thurs.	Weekends
Romeo and Juliet	$8.75	$10.50
Oz (a musical)	$6.50	$ 7.80
The Mousetrap (a mystery)	$7.50	$ 9.00

Other Conditions

- No discounts on weekends.
- You have homework on weekdays.
- The most you can spend for a ticket is $9.00.

Student Discounts (Weekdays Only)

Take $\frac{1}{5}$ off each ticket for *Romeo and Juliet*.

Take $\frac{3}{10}$ off each ticket for *Oz*.

Take $\frac{1}{3}$ off each ticket for *The Mousetrap*.

Work in small groups to find answers and make decisions.

1. Suppose you and your friends bought tickets to see *Oz* on Tuesday. The total cost of the tickets, including the discount, was $18.20. How many tickets did you buy?

2. What fraction of the weekend price is the weekday price for each play?

3. Suppose you and 3 friends buy tickets to see a play on Sunday. You pay for the tickets with a $50 bill. Your change is $18.80. What is the name of the play?

4. Suppose you and 5 friends buy tickets to see *The Mousetrap* on Wednesday. What is the total cost? (Hint: Remember the discount.)

5. What other things should you think about?

6. What play will you see? When?

Problem Solving Situations

Organizing a Raffle

Your school wants to raise $2,000 for a local charity. You have two choices for organizing a raffle. Which choice will you make?

Your Notes

Plan A—Raffle	**Plan B**—Raffle
First Prize: $1,000	First Prize: $800
Second Prize: $500	3 Second Prizes: $400 each
9 Third Prizes: $100 each	5 Third Prizes: $100 each
Other Conditions	**Other Conditions**
• Tickets cost $2.00.	• Tickets cost $1.25.
• It costs you $2.00 to print every 100 tickets.	• It costs you $2.50 to print every 100 tickets.

Work in small groups to find answers and make decisions.

1. How many more prizes do you offer with Plan A than Plan B?

2. How much prize money do you raffle off in Plan A? Plan B?

3. How many raffle tickets must you sell to pay for the prizes in Plan A? Plan B?

4. How much more money would it cost you to print 3,000 raffle tickets for Plan B than Plan A?

5. About how many raffle tickets must you sell using Plan B to raise $2,000 for your charity? using Plan A?

6. What other things should you think about?

7. Which plan will you choose?

Buying Lunch

You buy lunch in school *every* school day. You can order lunch from a menu or choose the "flat-rate" student lunch plan. What will you choose?

Your Notes

Menu	
Sandwiches	
Chicken	$1.35
Cheese	$1.05
Tuna	$1.15
Egg	$ .90
Beverages	
Juice	$ .65
Milk	$ .50

"Flat-Rate" Student Lunch Plan

1 sandwich and 1 beverage $1.50
No choice: A different sandwich and beverage each day.

Other Conditions

- You do not like to take lunch.
- You like chicken the best.
- You do not like egg very much.

Work in small groups to find answers and make decisions.

1. You buy a sandwich and a beverage from the menu. You spend $1.65. What did you buy?

2. Suppose you buy a sandwich and a beverage from the menu. You give the cashier $2 and get back $.45. What did you buy? (Hint: There is more than 1 answer.)

3. Suppose you choose the "flat-rate" plan. How many different kinds of lunches are there? List each kind.

4. Suppose you order the most expensive lunch on the menu. Suppose the next day you order the least expensive. What is the average price of these 2 lunches?

5. What other things should you think about?

6. What will you choose?

Problem Solving Situations

Hexagon Tiles

You want to tile the floor in your
room with a design using hexagons.
You can make each hexagonal
shape from either tiles shaped
like equilateral triangles or
parallelograms. You need 3 rows
of 10 hexagonal shapes and 2 rows
of 9 hexagonal shapes.
Will you choose the triangles
or the parallelograms?

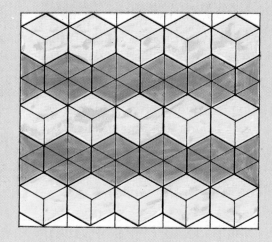

Your Notes

Costs	Other Conditions
Costs	**Other Conditions**

Costs
Equilateral triangle = $.39 each
Parallelogram = $.65 each

Other Conditions
- You can make a hexagon using equilateral triangles in 3 minutes.
- You can make a hexagon using parallelograms in 2 minutes.
- You think a design with triangles looks better.

Work in small groups to find answers and make decisions.

1. If you use only equilateral triangles, how many will you need? If you use only parallelograms, how many will you need?

2. How much more money would it cost you to use triangles?

3. How much less time would it take you to use parallelograms?

4. Suppose you use triangles for the rows having 10 hexagonal shapes. Also, suppose you use parallelograms for the rest of the rows. What is your total cost?

5. What other things should you think about?

6. What type of tile will you choose? Explain.

367

Problem Solving Situations

Choosing Advertising Space

Your parents want to place advertisements in a magazine for their business. They have asked you to help. You can place a full page ad, a one-half page ad, or a one-quarter page ad. Each page is 8 inches by 11 inches. What types of ads will you suggest?

Your Notes

Prices (Black and white)

full page ad	$1,200
one-half page ad	$ 750
one-quarter page ad	$ 600

For a color ad, multiply the above price by $2\frac{1}{2}$.

Other Conditions

- There are 32 lines on each page.
- You cannot spend more than $3,000.
- Your ad space can be less than or equal to 88 in.^{2}
- You prefer ads in color.
- You do not want to buy more than 4 ads.

Work in small groups to find answers and make decisions.

1. Suppose you buy a full page ad in color. What is the cost for 1 square inch?

2. Suppose you bought 1 full page ad, 1 one-half page ad, and 1 one-quarter page ad? How many ad lines in total did you buy?

3. Suppose you buy ads in black and white. The total ad space is three-quarters of a page. What is the smallest amount of money that you could spend? What is the greatest amount of money that you could spend?

4. What would the amounts be for the ads in question 3 if they were color?

5. Suppose you bought 4 ads in black and white that total one and three-quarter pages. How many square inches of ad space did you buy? How much did you spend?

6. What other things should you think about?

7. What type of ads will you choose?

Probability: Simple Probability

A. In this box of counters, $\frac{1}{6}$ of the counters are red. Write a fraction for the part that is:

1. green

2. blue

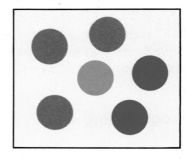

To select a counter **at random** from this box means that the selection is made without looking, so that each counter is equally likely to be chosen.

3. If one counter is selected at random, which color is most likely to be selected? least likely?

B. There are 3 chances in 6 that a green counter will be selected, since $\frac{3}{6}$ of the counters are green.

Another way of saying this is:

> The **probability** that a random selection will give a green counter is $\frac{3}{6}$.

Write: Probability of getting a green counter $= \frac{3}{6}$
  or: P(green) $= \frac{3}{6}$

4. Probability of getting a red counter $= \frac{}{6}$
  or P(red) $=$ ▩

5. P (blue) $=$ ▩

6. $\frac{5}{6}$ of the counters are blue or green.
  P(blue or green) $=$ ▩

7. P(red or green) $=$ ▩

8. P(blue or red) $=$ ▩

9. Use 6 counters, 6 pieces of colored paper (same size and shape), or 6 pieces of paper with names of colors written on them— 3 green, 2 blue, 1 red. Select a piece of paper at random, record its color, replace it, stir, and select again until you have completed 120 selections. Write fractions for the parts of your selections that are green, blue, red. Compare with the fractions for P(green), P(blue), and P(red).

B. $\frac{6}{6}$ of the counters are red, or blue, or green. If you select a counter at random, it is certain to be red, or blue, or green.

$$P(\text{red, or blue, or green}) = \frac{6}{6}, \text{ or } 1$$

> If something is certain to happen as the result of a random selection, the probability that that will happen is 1.
> P(something certain) = 1

$\frac{0}{6}$ of the counters are yellow.

$$P(\text{yellow}) = \frac{0}{6}, \text{ or } 0$$

> If something is impossible as the result of a random selection, the probability that it will happen is 0.
> P(something impossible) = 0

C. Use this box of counters. Find:

10. P(blue)
11. P(orange)
12. P(red)
13. P(brown)
14. P(green)
15. P(black)
16. P(blue or green)
17. P(not red)
18. P(not yellow)
19. P(red, or blue, or brown)

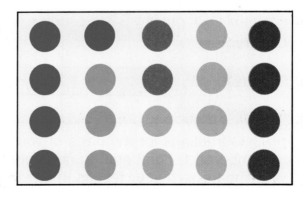

371

Probability: More on Finding Probability

A. The counters in this box have both a color and a number. Give the number of counters that are:

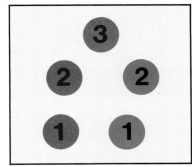

1. red   **2.** blue   **3.** numbered 1

4. numbered 2   **5.** numbered 3

Write a fraction for the part of the counters that are:

6. red   **7.** blue   **8.** numbered 1

9. numbered 2   **10.** numbered 3   **11.** red and numbered 1

Probability (blue and numbered 1) = P(blue and 1) = $\frac{1}{5}$
Find:

12. P(red)   **13.** P(1)   **14.** P(blue)

15. P(2)   **16.** P(3)   **17.** P(red and 1)

18. P(blue and 2)   **19.** P(blue and 3)   **20.** P(less than 4)

21. P(less than 3)   **22.** P(greater than 1)   **23.** P(odd number)

24. P(even number)   **25.** P(red and odd number)

26. Make a set of counters like those shown above. Make 100 random selections. Use tally marks to record your results in a table.

	1	2	3	Total
Red and				
Blue and				
Total				

Write fractions for the parts of your selections that are red; blue; numbered 1; numbered 2; numbered 3; red and numbered 1. Compare with your results in exercises **12–17**.

B.

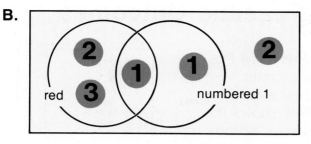

3 counters are red. 2 counters are numbered 1.

1 counter is red *and* numbered 1. ———⟶

4 counters are red *or* numbered 1. ———⟶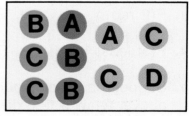

Count this one only once.

$\frac{4}{5}$ of the counters are red or numbered 1.

P(red or 1) $= \frac{4}{5}$

Find:

27. P(red or 2) **28.** P(red or 3)

29. P(blue or 3) **30.** P(blue or 2)

31. P(blue or odd number) **32.** P(white or yellow)

Use this box of counters. Find:

33. P(A) **34.** P(B) **35.** P(C) **36.** P(D)

37. P(blue) **38.** P(green)

39. P(orange) **40.** P(brown) **41.** P(A or green)

42. P(B or green) **43.** P(C or green) **44.** P(D or green)

45. P(C or orange) **46.** P(D or orange) **47.** P(B or orange)

48. P(A or brown) **49.** P(B or brown) **50.** P(C or brown)

Probability: Listing Possible Outcomes

A. One counter is selected at random from this box. The result is recorded, the counter is replaced, and a second random selection is made. The **tree diagram** below shows the 9 possible outcomes of these two selections.

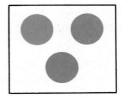

First Selection	Second Selection	Outcome
red	red	red and red
	blue	red and blue
	green	red and green
blue	red	blue and red
	blue	blue and blue
	green	blue and green
green	red	green and red
	blue	green and blue
	green	green and green

$P(1 \text{ red}, 1 \text{ green}) = \frac{2}{9}$ ← red and green *and* green and red

$P(2 \text{ green}) = \frac{1}{9}$

Find:

1. P(2 red)　　**2.** P(1 blue, 1 green)　　**3.** P(1 red, 1 blue)

4. P(at least 1 red)　**5.** P(0 red)　　**6.** P(at most 1 red)

7. Suppose a yellow counter is added to the box of counters above. Draw a tree diagram to list the 16 possible outcomes of two selections with replacement from this new box of counters.

Use your tree diagram to find:

8. P(0 red)　　**9.** P(exactly 1 red)　　**10.** P(2 red)

11. P(yellow on the first selection)　**12.** P(blue on the second selection)

B. Suppose two random selections are made from the box of counters shown on page 374. However, the first is *not* replaced before the second is selected. There are only 6 possible outcomes of these two selections.

13. Copy and complete the tree diagram below to list the 6 outcomes of the two selections without replacement.

First Selection	Second Selection	Outcome
red	blue	red and blue
	green	■
blue	■	■
	■	■
green	■	■
	■	■

Use your tree diagram and list of outcomes to find:

14. P(2 red)   **15.** P(1 blue, 1 green)   **16.** P(1 red, 1 blue)

17. P(at least 1 red)   **18.** P(0 red)   **19.** P(at most 1 blue)

20. Suppose an orange counter is added to the box of counters shown on page 374. Draw a tree diagram to list the outcomes of two selections *without* replacement from this set of four counters. How many outcomes do you find?

Use your tree diagram in exercise 20 to find:

21. P(1 orange)   **22.** P(2 orange)

23. P(0 orange)   **24.** P(1 orange, 1 red)

25. P(at least 1 blue)   **26.** P(at most 1 green)

27. P(2 of the same color)

Statistics: Some Important Statistics

This table shows the total score in each of 17 professional football games.

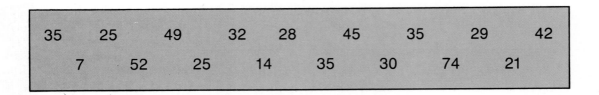

| 35 | 25 | 49 | 32 | 28 | 45 | 35 | 29 | 42 |
| | 7 | 52 | 25 | 14 | 35 | 30 | 74 | 21 |

A. Statisticians have invented a number of **statistics** to use in describing sets of numerical information, or **data.** The **mean,** or average, of these scores is one such statistic.

Mean = Sum of the Scores ÷ Number of Scores

1. Find the sum of these 17 scores.

2. Find the mean of this set of 17 scores.

B. Another statistic, the **median,** or middle score, of a set of data is found by listing the numbers in order from largest to smallest. The median is the middle number of this list.

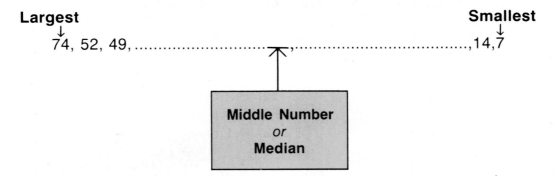

Largest

Smallest

74, 52, 49,..,.................................,14,7

Middle Number
or
Median

3. Complete the list above. Find the median of these scores.

If another score of 30 were added to this list, there would be 18 numbers. Then there would be two "middle numbers."

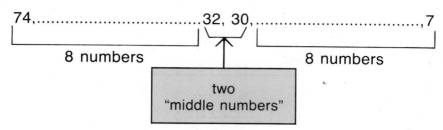

When there are two middle numbers, their mean is the median of the set of data.

4. Find the median of a set of data with the two "middle numbers" 32 and 30.

C. The **mode,** still another statistic, of a set of data is the number that appears the most times in the set.

5. Find the mode of the set of scores on page 376. Your list from exercise **3** should help you.

If you find that two or more numbers appear the "most times" in a set of data, each of these numbers is a mode of the data.

D. The **range** of a set of data is another interesting statistic.

Range = Largest Number − Smallest Number

6. Find the range of the set of scores on page 376. Your list from exercise **3** should help you.

Use the data set in the box.

| 350 | 420 | 320 | 370 | 430 | 350 | 400 | 320 |

7. Find the mean, median, mode, and range of these numbers.

Statistics: Using Data from Graphs

A. This graph shows the 1980 populations, rounded to the nearest ten-thousand, of six cities.

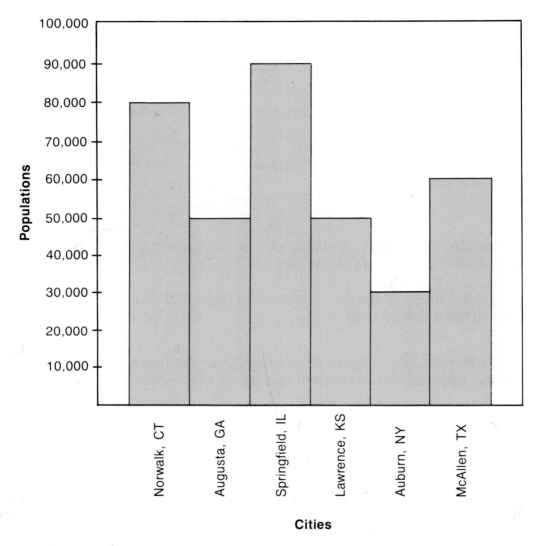

Cities

1. Find the mean, or average, of the populations of these cities.

2. Find the median of these populations. Note that there are two middle numbers.

3. Find the mode of these populations.

4. Find the range of these data.

B. Suppose the names of these cities were written on identical pieces of paper, placed in a box, and one was selected at random. Find these probabilities.

5. P(population is 50,000) **6.** P(city is in Texas)

7. P(population > mean) **8.** P(population < median)

9. P(population = mode) **10.** P(city name has **A** as first letter)

11. P(city is east of the Mississippi River)

12. Use the set of data below. Draw a graph like the one on page 378.

Cities	Populations (nearest 10,000)
Fort Myers, FL	40,000
Gloucester, MA	30,000
Chapel Hill, NC	30,000
Euclid, OH	60,000
Jefferson, PA	50,000

13. Find the mean of these populations.

14. Find the median of these data.

15. Find the mode of this set of data.

16. Find the range of these populations.

Suppose that from these cities you selected the name of one city at random. Find:

17. P(population = mean) **18.** P(population < mean)

19. P(population < median) **20.** P(population < mode)

379

Statistics: Using Statistics in Marketing

A. A marketing analyst collected information, or data, about the number of passengers per flight on his airline's planes between Chicago and Dallas. He rounded the numbers to the nearest ten and made this table. Copy and complete the table.

Passengers per Flight	Number of Flights	Number of Passengers on These Flights (Number of Flights × Number of Passengers per Flight)
90	20	1,800 (20 × 90)
100	19	1,900 (19 × 100)
110	14	1. ▨
120	6	2. ▨
130	4	3. ▨
140	2	4. ▨
Totals	5. ▨	6. ▨

B. The analyst used the mean, median, and mode to describe the center of these data. To find the mean he used:

Mean = $\dfrac{\text{Total Number of Passengers on These Flights (Column 3)}}{\text{Total Number of Flights (Column 2)}}$

7. Find the mean, or average, of the number of passengers per flight.

8. Find the median, or middle number, of the number of passengers per flight.

9. Find the mode, or number appearing most often, of the number of passengers per flight.

10. Find the range of the number of passengers per flight.

C. To show the data for these flights the marketing analyst used a line graph.

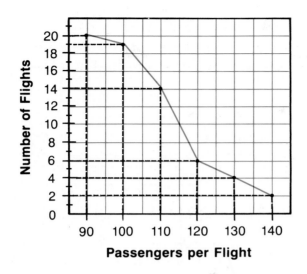

Passengers per Flight

The mode and range of these data are easy to read directly from this graph:

The mode, 90, has the highest point of the graph.
The range, 50, is the difference of the largest and the smallest number of passengers per flight.

To find the median and mean from the graph, use the points of the graph to find the numbers in the first two columns of the table on page 380:

Passengers per Flight	Number of Flights
90	20
100	19
110	14
120	6
130	4
140	2

Numbers on the bottom

Corresponding numbers at the side

Then, find the mean and median as you did in exercises **7** and **8.**

D. The marketing analyst decided to advertise on radio and television to increase the number of passengers per flight. The graph below shows data he collected for flights on the same route after the advertising campaign. These numbers of passengers per flight are rounded to the nearest ten.

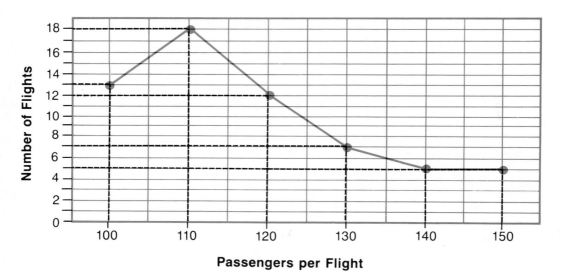

Passengers per Flight

11. Find the mode and range of these new data.
Use this graph to complete the table below.

Passengers per Flight	Number of Flights	Number of Passengers on These Flights (Number of Flights × Number of Passengers per Flight)
100	13	**12.** ▧
110	**13.** ▧	**14.** ▧
120	**15.** ▧	**16.** ▧
130	**17.** ▧	**18.** ▧
140	**19.** ▧	**20.** ▧
150	**21.** ▧	**22.** ▧
Totals	**23.** ▧	**24.** ▧

25. Find the mean and median for these data.

26. By how much did the advertising campaign increase the mean? the median? the mode?

Ratio

A. You can use **ratio** to compare numbers.

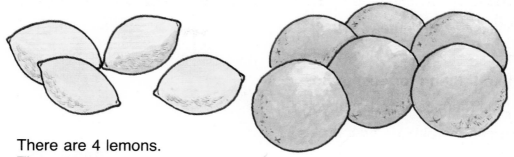

There are 4 lemons.
There are 6 oranges.
There are 10 pieces of fruit in all.

The ratio of lemons to pieces of fruit is 4 to 10.

The ratio of oranges to pieces of fruit is 6 to 10.

The ratio of lemons to oranges is 4 to 6.

The ratio of oranges to lemons is 6 to 4.

B. You can name a ratio in three different ways.

4 to 10   4 : 10 $\frac{4}{10}$

Read each of these names for the ratio as 4 to 10.

In the ratio $\frac{4}{10}$, 4 is the first term of the ratio. 10 is the second.

C. You can write many ratios from this picture.

Tomatoes to baskets: 8 to 1 or 8 : 1 or $\frac{8}{1}$

Baskets to tomatoes: 1 to 8 or 1 : 8 or $\frac{1}{8}$

Dollars to tomatoes: 2 to 8 or 2 : 8 or $\frac{2}{8}$

Tomatoes to dollars: 8 to 2 or 8 : 2 or $\frac{8}{2}$

Baskets to dollars: 1 to 2 or 1 : 2 or $\frac{1}{2}$

Dollars to baskets: 2 to 1 or 2 : 1 or $\frac{2}{1}$

Write each ratio three ways.

1. circles to triangles

2. triangles to circles

3. circles to all figures

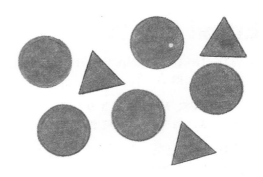

Write a fraction for each ratio.

4. blue marbles to red marbles

5. green marbles to red marbles

6. blue marbles to all marbles

7. all marbles to green marbles

8. red marbles to blue marbles

9. jars to all marbles

10. red marbles *and* blue marbles to all marbles

Give the ratio of:

11. pink flowers to yellow flowers

12. pink flowers to all flowers

13. yellow flowers to pink flowers

14. all flowers to yellow flowers

15. flowers to dollars

16. bunches to dollars

Equal Ratios

A. The ratio of bicycles to wheels is 3 : 6.

You can also say the ratio. of bicycles to wheels is 1 : 2.

The ratios 3 : 6 and 1 : 2 are **equal ratios.** Write a fraction for each ratio.

$$\frac{3}{6}, \frac{1}{2} \longleftarrow \text{equivalent fractions}$$

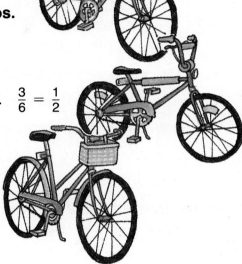

Equivalent fractions name equal ratios. $\frac{3}{6} = \frac{1}{2}$

The ratio $\frac{1}{2}$ is in **lowest terms.**

B. Multiply to find equal ratios.

Erasers are sold 3 for 20¢.
Senta bought 9 erasers.
How much did she pay for them?

erasers
cents
$$\frac{3}{20} = \frac{9}{\blacksquare}$$ Think: $9 = 3 \times 3$

$$\frac{3}{20} = \frac{3 \times 3}{20 \times 3} = \frac{9}{60}$$

Senta paid 60¢.

C. Divide to find equal ratios.

4 notebooks cost $10.
How many notebooks
can Victor buy for $5?

notebooks
dollars
$$\frac{4}{10} = \frac{\blacksquare}{5}$$ Think: $5 = 10 \div 2$

$$\frac{4}{10} = \frac{4 \div 2}{10 \div 2} = \frac{2}{5}$$

Victor can buy 2 notebooks.

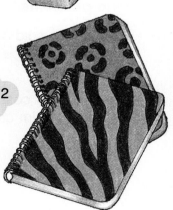

Give an equal ratio in lowest terms.

1. $\dfrac{4}{8}$　　2. $\dfrac{6}{10}$　　3. $\dfrac{7}{14}$　　4. $\dfrac{9}{12}$

Multiply to give equal ratios.

5. $\dfrac{1}{3} = \dfrac{2}{6} = \dfrac{\blacksquare}{9} = \dfrac{\blacksquare}{12} = \dfrac{\blacksquare}{15} = \dfrac{\blacksquare}{18}$

6. $\dfrac{1}{4} = \dfrac{2}{8} = \dfrac{\blacksquare}{12} = \dfrac{\blacksquare}{16} = \dfrac{\blacksquare}{20} = \dfrac{\blacksquare}{24}$

7. $\dfrac{3}{4} = \dfrac{6}{8} = \dfrac{\blacksquare}{12} = \dfrac{\blacksquare}{16} = \dfrac{\blacksquare}{20} = \dfrac{\blacksquare}{24}$

8. $\dfrac{2}{5} = \dfrac{\blacksquare}{10} = \dfrac{\blacksquare}{15} = \dfrac{\blacksquare}{20} = \dfrac{\blacksquare}{25} = \dfrac{\blacksquare}{\blacksquare}$

Divide to give equal ratios.

9. $\dfrac{24}{48} = \dfrac{12}{24} = \dfrac{\blacksquare}{12} = \dfrac{\blacksquare}{6} = \dfrac{\blacksquare}{2}$

10. $\dfrac{36}{72} = \dfrac{18}{\blacksquare} = \dfrac{9}{\blacksquare} = \dfrac{3}{\blacksquare} = \dfrac{1}{\blacksquare}$

11. $\dfrac{40}{60} = \dfrac{20}{\blacksquare} = \dfrac{10}{\blacksquare} = \dfrac{2}{\blacksquare}$

12. $\dfrac{80}{100} = \dfrac{\blacksquare}{50} = \dfrac{\blacksquare}{25} = \dfrac{\blacksquare}{5}$

Solve the problems.

13. Batteries are sold 3 for $2. How many can you buy for $6?

14. The store sold 8 blank tapes for $20. How much would 2 tapes cost?

15. Six rolls of film cost $15. How many rolls of film can you buy for $5?

16. Karyn earns $9 a week baby-sitting. She saves $1 a week. She uses $8 for her weekly expenses. What is the ratio of Karyn's weekly savings to her earnings?

Ratio and Proportion

Each package contains 4 batteries.
The ratio is 1 to 4.
No matter how many packs you buy,
the ratio will be the same.

Packs		1	2	3	4
Batteries		4	8	12	16
Ratio of packs to batteries		$\frac{1}{4}$	$\frac{2}{8}$	$\frac{3}{12}$	$\frac{4}{16}$

A **proportion** is a statement that two ratios are equal.

packs $\qquad \dfrac{2}{8} = \dfrac{3}{12}$ ⟵——— packs
batteries $\qquad\qquad\qquad$ ⟵——— batteries

Look at the proportion again.

$$\frac{2}{8} \times \frac{3}{12}$$

2×12 and 3×8 are the **cross products** of this proportion.

$2 \times 12 = 24$ Cross products
$3 \times 8 = 24$ of equal ratios are equal.

If the cross products are equal, then the proportion is true.

Is the proportion $\frac{3}{5} = \frac{12}{20}$ true?

$$\frac{3}{5} \overset{?}{\times} \frac{12}{20}$$

Does $3 \times 20 = 12 \times 5$?

$60 = 60$

The cross products are equal.
The proportion is true.
The ratios are equal.

Is the proportion $\frac{5}{12} = \frac{8}{15}$ true?

$$\frac{5}{12} \overset{?}{\times} \frac{8}{15}$$

Does $5 \times 15 = 8 \times 12$?

$75 \neq 96$

The cross products are not equal.
The proportion is not true.
The ratios are not equal.

For each proportion, show that the cross products are equal.

1. $\dfrac{2}{5} = \dfrac{6}{15}$

2. $\dfrac{3}{4} = \dfrac{12}{16}$

3. $\dfrac{3}{8} = \dfrac{9}{24}$

4. $\dfrac{2}{6} = \dfrac{7}{21}$

Do the ratios form a proportion? Compare cross products. Write yes or no.

5. $\dfrac{4}{8}, \dfrac{5}{10}$

6. $\dfrac{2}{3}, \dfrac{8}{12}$

7. $\dfrac{6}{9}, \dfrac{12}{16}$

8. $\dfrac{4}{10}, \dfrac{8}{25}$

9. $\dfrac{12}{16}, \dfrac{15}{20}$

10. $\dfrac{3}{4}, \dfrac{18}{24}$

Write = or ≠ for ●.

11. $\dfrac{2}{5}$ ● $\dfrac{10}{25}$

12. $\dfrac{5}{6}$ ● $\dfrac{3}{4}$

13. $\dfrac{10}{4}$ ● $\dfrac{5}{2}$

14. $\dfrac{6}{20}$ ● $\dfrac{3}{10}$

15. $\dfrac{35}{40}$ ● $\dfrac{7}{8}$

16. $\dfrac{8}{11}$ ● $\dfrac{20}{33}$

17. $\dfrac{1}{4}$ ● $\dfrac{12}{48}$

18. $\dfrac{6}{9}$ ● $\dfrac{30}{50}$

19. $\dfrac{3}{6}$ ● $\dfrac{15}{30}$

Are the prices the same?

20. 2 for 25¢
8 for $1.00

21. 3 for 69¢
10 for $2.50

22. 6 for 99¢
24 for $3.96

23. 4 for $1.50
12 for $5.00

Write yes or no.

24. The ratio of hamburger rolls to packages is 6 to 1. Will 8 packages contain 40 rolls?

25. The ratio of packages to paper plates is 1 to 12. Will 5 packages contain 60 plates?

Programming with Logo

A. To communicate with a computer, you must use a **language** that a computer can understand. There are many such languages. Each has its own rules. **Logo** is a language used to tell a "turtle" how to draw shapes. There are several different versions of Logo. These rules work for most.

DRAW means: Erase the screen, then put the turtle in the middle of the screen, pointing toward the top of the screen.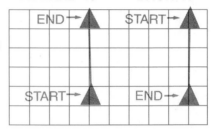

FORWARD and BACK mean: Move forward or move back. You use a number with these words, to tell the turtle how many "turtle steps" to take. Because turtle steps are very small, multiples of 10 steps are usually used.

RIGHT 90 and LEFT 90 mean: Turn right 90° or turn left 90°.

FORWARD 40 **BACK 40**

To make a right angle, place the turtle in the middle of the screen, go forward 40 steps, turn right 90°, and go forward 40 more steps. The distance between grid lines is 10 turtle steps.

Program

```
DRAW
FORWARD 40
RIGHT 90
FORWARD 40
```

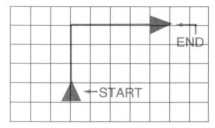

1. How would you instruct the turtle to make a right angle facing left?

2. How would you instruct the turtle to make a right angle facing left with sides of 70 steps showing?

3. Draw the output.

```
DRAW
FORWARD 40
RIGHT 90
FORWARD 40
LEFT 90
FORWARD 40
RIGHT 90
FORWARD 40
```

4. Write the program.

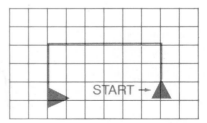

389

B. You can write algorithms and programs for geometric shapes.

Suppose that you wanted to teach the LOGO turtle to draw a rectangle. You could use three steps.

1. **Plan your work.** For LOGO a good plan is a *sketch.*

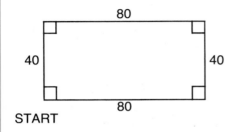

2. **Write an algorithm** for the rectangle in your sketch.

Step 1 Go forward 40 steps.
Step 2 Turn right 90°.
Step 3 Go forward 80 steps.
Step 4 Turn right 90°.
Step 5 Go forward 40 steps.
Step 6 Turn right 90°.
Step 7 Go forward 80 steps.
Step 8 Turn right 90°.

3. **Translate your algorithm into LOGO,** so that the computer will understand it. You will need two new instructions:

`TO RECTANGLE` means: This program is called RECTANGLE.

`END` means: The program is finished.

```
TO RECTANGLE
FORWARD 40
RIGHT 90
FORWARD 80
RIGHT 90
FORWARD 40
RIGHT 90
FORWARD 80
RIGHT 90
END
```

As soon as you type `END`, the computer will print: `RECTANGLE DEFINED`. That means that it knows the program. To see the shape, just type `RECTANGLE`, the program's name.

4. Draw the output on graph paper: `DRAW RECTANGLE`

5. Write a new LOGO program for this rectangle. Call the program `OBLONG`.

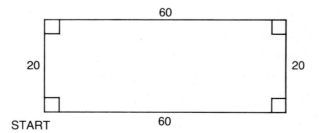

More Programming with Logo

A. You can create bigger programs using small programs that the computer already knows. This new program uses the RECTANGLE program from page 390.

```
TO WHIRLIGIG
RECTANGLE RIGHT 90 ◄─────
RECTANGLE RIGHT 90
RECTANGLE RIGHT 90
RECTANGLE RIGHT 90
END
```

> You can put more than 1 instruction on a line.

1. Draw the output: DRAW
  WHIRLIGIG

B. REPEAT, used with a number, tells the turtle to do the same thing that many times. Use brackets to show the steps to be repeated:

```
TO SQUARE
REPEAT 4 [FORWARD 20 LEFT 90] ◄─────
END
```

> Go FORWARD 20 and LEFT 90 4 times.

2. Draw the output: DRAW
  SQUARE

3. Rewrite the WHIRLIGIG program using REPEAT 4.

4. Create a new "whirligig" program using OBLONG. First draw a sketch. Then write an algorithm. Then write the Logo program. Use REPEAT whenever you can.

C. Sometimes you do not want the turtle to draw a line. In Logo, you use the instruction PENUP to tell the computer not to draw. To instruct the turtle to draw lines again, you use the instruction PENDOWN.

5. Draw the output for this Logo program:
```
DRAW
TO LETTERU
PENDOWN FORWARD 40 RIGHT 90
PENUP FORWARD 30 RIGHT 90
PENDOWN FORWARD 40 RIGHT 90
FORWARD 30 RIGHT 90
END
```

D. You can instruct the turtle to draw triangles too. Be sure you instruct the turtle to draw angles correctly.

Example

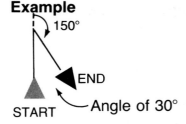

START

Angle of 30° $180° - 30° = 150°$

Algorithm

Step 1 Go forward 40 steps.

Step 2 Turn right 150°.

Step 3 Go forward 20 steps.

E. Here is a three-part plan to draw a right triangle using Logo.

   i. Plan your work. For Logo a good plan is a sketch.

   ii. Write an algorithm for the triangle in your sketch.

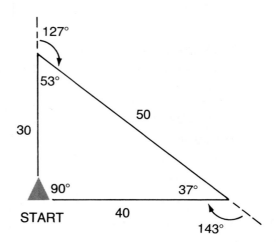

     Step 1 Go forward 30 steps.

     Step 2 Turn right 127°.

     Step 3 Go forward 50 steps.

     Step 4 Turn right 143°.

     Step 5 Go forward 40 steps.

     Step 6 Turn right 90°.

     Step 7 Stop.

   iii. Translate your algorithm into Logo.

```
TO  TRIANGLE
FORWARD  30  RIGHT  127
FORWARD  50  RIGHT  143
FORWARD  40  RIGHT  90
END
```

⟵ This is the name of the program.

⟵ You can put more than one direction on a line.

⟵ The program stops.

Look at this drawing of an equilateral triangle carefully.

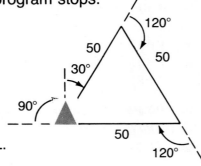

6. Write an algorithm for the triangle in the sketch.

7. Translate your algorithm into a Logo program called TO EQUILATERAL.

Programming with BASIC

Another frequently used computer programming language is **BASIC.**
You can use BASIC to write programs that tell the computer what to do.

A. Computers are especially valuable for work
with large numbers. Suppose, for example, that you
wanted to subtract 30,478 from 730,523.

Program

```
10  PRINT  "THE DIFFERENCE OF"
20  PRINT  "730523 AND 30478 IS"
30  PRINT  730523 - 30478
40  END
```

Output

```
THE DIFFERENCE OF
730523 AND 30478 IS
700045
```

BASIC does not use commas in numerals.

Each line of a BASIC program is numbered, usually by tens.
Notice that the command PRINT appears in lines 10, 20, and 30.
In lines 10 and 20, PRINT is followed by words in
quotes, and the computer prints only the words between
the quotes. In line 30, there are no quotes, so the
computer does the calculation. It subtracts 30,478 from
730,523 and the screen shows the difference of 700,045.

B. You can write a general subtraction program in BASIC.
You must allow different numbers to be input.

Program

```
10  PRINT "WHAT IS THE"
20  PRINT "LARGER NUMBER?"
30  INPUT A1
```
Value is needed for A1.
```
40  PRINT "WHAT IS THE"
50  PRINT "SMALLER NUMBER?"
60  INPUT A2
```
Value is needed for A2.
```
70  PRINT "THE DIFFERENCE IS"
80  PRINT A1 - A2
90  END
```

Output

```
WHAT IS THE
LARGER NUMBER?
? 21467
```
The computer shows ? The user inputs a number.
```
WHAT IS THE
SMALLER NUMBER?
? 2579

THE DIFFERENCE IS
18888
```

There are some special symbols in BASIC that you must learn.

Here is a BASIC program for multiplying 237 by 78. The asterisk * is a special symbol used for multiplication.

```
10  PRINT "THE PRODUCT";        THE PRODUCT OF 237 AND 78
20  PRINT "OF 237 AND 78"       IS 18486
30  PRINT "IS "; 237 * 78
40  END
```

The semicolon prints the next display on the same line.

Here is a BASIC program that can be used to divide 12,765 by 5. Notice the special symbol / that is used for division.

```
10  PRINT "THE QUOTIENT"        THE QUOTIENT
20  PRINT "OF 12765 AND 5"      OF 12765 AND 5
30  PRINT "IS "; 12765 / 5      IS 2553
40  END
```

The / means divide.

1. Use the BASIC program for subtracting any two numbers. Write what the computer screen would show as output at each step for 175,466 − 26,587.

In 2 and 3 below, write the output for each BASIC program. Tell what the program does.

2.
```
10  PRINT "WHAT IS THE SUM ";
20  PRINT "OF 3989 AND 72333?"
30  PRINT "THE SUM IS"
40  PRINT 3989 + 72333
50  END
```

3.
```
10  PRINT "WHAT IS THE DIVIDEND ?"
20  INPUT A
30  PRINT "WHAT IS THE DIVISOR ?"
40  INPUT B
50  PRINT "THE QUOTIENT IS"
60  PRINT A / B
70  END
```

4. Write a BASIC program to add any two numbers.

5. Write a BASIC program to multiply any two numbers.

More Programming with BASIC

A. BASIC can be used to solve many general mathematical problems. For example, the area of a square is the length of one side times itself. You can use a letter such as S to stand for the length of a side. The value of S may change, but the area of the square is still S × S.

On the left is a BASIC program for finding the area of a square. On the right is the computer's output.

Program

```
10  PRINT "WHAT IS THE LENGTH"
20  PRINT "OF A SIDE?"
30  INPUT S ←── Value for S is needed.

40  PRINT "THE AREA IS ";
50  PRINT  S * S
60  END
```

Output

```
WHAT IS THE LENGTH
OF A SIDE?
? 5      The computer shows ?
         The user inputs a value.

THE AREA IS 25
```

1. Tell what this BASIC program does. Write the output if the value of S is 12.

```
10  PRINT "LENGTH"
20  PRINT "OF A SIDE ?"
30  INPUT S
40  PRINT "PERIMETER IS"
50  PRINT 4 * S
60  END
```

2. Tell what this BASIC program does. Write the output if S1 is 5 and S2 is 10.

```
10  PRINT "LENGTH"
20  PRINT "OF SIDE 1?"
30  INPUT S1
40  PRINT "LENGTH"
50  PRINT "OF SIDE 2?"
60  INPUT S2
70  PRINT "PERIMETER IS"
80  PRINT 2 * (S1 + S2)
90  END
```

B. Many BASIC programs require the computer to repeat steps. To do this the program uses **loops.** The command GOTO tells the computer to go back to the line mentioned. Then the computer repeats the steps. Here is a BASIC program for counting by fives. Notice the way the loop works.

```
10 LET A = 0        LET stores the value 0 in the computer.

20 LET A = A + 5    The computer adds 5 to the number A.

30 PRINT A          The computer prints the new value of A.

40 GOTO 20          The computer is sent back to line 20.
                    It adds 5 to the new value of A.
                    Then it goes on to line 30 and prints
                    the new number.
```

This counting program has an endless loop. The computer will count by fives until someone presses the RUN/STOP key or turns off the computer.

C. If you want the computer to stop counting after a particular number is reached (for example, 100) you can introduce an IF . . . THEN statement. In BASIC, IF . . . THEN statements introduce a condition: Stop counting if the number reached is greater than 100. Here is the same program from above with an IF . . . THEN condition.

```
10 LET A = 0            The value 0 is stored.

20 LET A = A + 5        The computer adds 5 to A.

30 IF A > 100 THEN 60   If A > 100, the program ends.
                        If A < 100, the computer goes
                        to line 40.

40 PRINT A              The computer prints the new A.

50 GOTO 20              The computer is sent back to
                        line 20, adds 5 to the new
60 END                  A, and then goes on to line 30.
```

3. Write a BASIC program to count by tens.

4. Write a BASIC program to count by tens to 1,000.

396   **Computer Programming**

UNIT 1 Reviewing Basic Facts

Addition Facts *(pages 2–3)*

```
  7 ←
+ 3 ← ──addends
─────
 10 ← ──sum
```

1. 9 +6	**2.** 8 +4	**3.** 3 +6	**4.** 6 +6	**5.** 5 +8
6. 1 +3	**7.** 4 +2	**8.** 7 +7	**9.** 2 +9	**10.** 6 +3	**11.** 8 +0	**12.** 5 +4
13. 8 +9	**14.** 3 +4	**15.** 0 +5	**16.** 6 +1	**17.** 7 +8	**18.** 2 +7	**19.** 6 +9

20. 5 + 9 = ■   **21.** 9 + 1 = ■   **22.** 6 + 0 = ■   **23.** 8 + 2 = ■

24. 4 + 8 = ■   **25.** 2 + 2 = ■   **26.** 9 + 7 = ■   **27.** 6 + 8 = ■

Count the dogs in your neighborhood. Count the cats.
Add to find the sum of dogs and cats.

Subtraction Facts *(pages 4–5)*

```
 11
−  6
────
  5 ← ── difference
```

1. 13 − 8	**2.** 11 − 5	**3.** 8 −3	**4.** 17 − 9	**5.** 12 − 7
6. 10 − 9	**7.** 7 −3	**8.** 10 − 4	**9.** 6 −5	**10.** 17 − 8	**11.** 10 − 8	**12.** 13 − 9
13. 8 −5	**14.** 9 −2	**15.** 11 − 8	**16.** 13 − 4	**17.** 10 − 7	**18.** 15 − 7	**19.** 12 − 5

20. 9 − 5 = ■   **21.** 6 − 4 = ■   **22.** 5 − 2 = ■   **23.** 7 − 7 = ■

Count the windows in your home. Count the doors.
What is the difference between the two totals?

Addition and Subtraction Properties: Mental Math *(pages 6–7)*

Add or subtract.

Zero Property
8   0   5   5
+0   +8   −0   −5
8   8   5   0

Order		Inverse	
6	3	14	6
+3	+6	−8	+8
9	9	6	14

Grouping

$9\!<\!\genfrac{}{}{0pt}{}{2}{7}$ 2
1 +1 8
10 10 10

1. 9
   +6

2. 6
   +9

3. 7
   +0

4. 6
   +2

5. 2
   +6

6. 16
   − 9

7. 8
   −7

8. 2
   −0

9. 8
   +5

10. 13
   − 5

11. 4
    2
   +7

12. 6
    3
   +4

13. 5
    3
   +6

14. 3
    2
   +5

15. 5
    1
   +6

 At dinner, count the forks, knives, and spoons on the table. What is the sum?

Problem Solving: A 5-Step Plan *(pages 8–9)*

Use the five steps to solve each problem.

1. **Read**	2. **Plan**	4. **Answer**

Mary hiked 7 kilometers before lunch and 9 kilometers after lunch. How far did she hike in all?	Add.
	 7 + 9 = ▣
	
	 3. **Do** 7
	      + 9
	      16
		Mary hiked 16 kilometers in all.
		
		 5. **Check** 9
		      + 7
		      16 ✔

1. Wendy scored 15 points in the basketball game. Alice scored 8 points. How many more points did Wendy score?

2. Julie had 5 T-shirts in her locker. Jan had 7 T-shirts in her locker. How many T-shirts did they have all together?

3. Terry spent $7 for running shorts and $4 for socks. How much money did he spend in all?

4. Ray had 8 golf balls. He lost 3 of them. How many golf balls did he have left?

 Use the steps to find the number of hours of television you have watched in the last two days.

Problem Solving: Uses of Subtraction (pages 10–11)

1. The distance across the lake is 9 kilometers. Jill has rowed 4 kilometers. How much farther must she row to cross the lake?

2. Subtract to find how much farther.

3.
$$\begin{array}{r} 9 \\ -4 \\ \hline 5 \end{array}$$

5.
$$\begin{array}{r} 5 \\ +4 \\ \hline 9 \end{array}\checkmark$$

4. Jill must row 5 kilometers farther.

---

1. Mike spent $6 to rent a boat. He spent an additional $2 to rent oars. How much more was the boat?

2. It costs $6 to rent a rowboat. It costs $11 for a motorboat. How much less does the rowboat cost?

3. It cost $14 to rent a sailboat. Sally paid $5 before using the boat. How much more does she owe?

4. Joe rented a canoe for 9 hours. He paddled for 5 hours. How many hours were left before he had to return the canoe?

5. A group rented a fishing boat. They caught 8 perch and 7 bonito. How many fish did they catch in all?

6. There were 9 members in a fishing party. Only 5 of them caught fish. How many of them did not catch fish?

 How many more chairs than tables do you have in your home?

Multiplication Facts (pages 14–15)

Multiply.

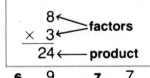
$$\begin{array}{r} 8 \\ \times\ 3 \\ \hline 24 \end{array}$$
8 ← factors
3 ← factors
24 ← product

1.
$$\begin{array}{r} 8 \\ \times 6 \\ \hline \end{array}$$

2.
$$\begin{array}{r} 4 \\ \times 3 \\ \hline \end{array}$$

3.
$$\begin{array}{r} 2 \\ \times 5 \\ \hline \end{array}$$

4.
$$\begin{array}{r} 8 \\ \times 8 \\ \hline \end{array}$$

5.
$$\begin{array}{r} 6 \\ \times 5 \\ \hline \end{array}$$

6.
$$\begin{array}{r} 9 \\ \times 2 \\ \hline \end{array}$$

7.
$$\begin{array}{r} 7 \\ \times 3 \\ \hline \end{array}$$

8.
$$\begin{array}{r} 3 \\ \times 6 \\ \hline \end{array}$$

9.
$$\begin{array}{r} 6 \\ \times 9 \\ \hline \end{array}$$

10.
$$\begin{array}{r} 6 \\ \times 2 \\ \hline \end{array}$$

11.
$$\begin{array}{r} 9 \\ \times 7 \\ \hline \end{array}$$

12.
$$\begin{array}{r} 2 \\ \times 3 \\ \hline \end{array}$$

13. $4 \times 8 =$ ■

14. $9 \times 9 =$ ■

15. $5 \times 4 =$ ■

16. $7 \times 8 =$ ■

17. $6 \times 7 =$ ■

18. $4 \times 5 =$ ■

19. $9 \times 8 =$ ■

20. $8 \times 4 =$ ■

 What is the product of the number of windows and the number of doors in your room?

Multiplication Properties: Mental Math *(pages 16–17)*

Order Property	
6	4
× 4	× 6
24	24
Property of:	
Zero	One
5	6
×0	×1
0	6

Multiply.

1. 3
×9

2. 9
×3

3. 5
×8

4. 8
×5

5. 3
×0

6. 0
×6

7. 9
×1

8. 1
×9

9. 4
×7

10. 7
×4

11. 7
×0

12. 1
×4

Complete the number sentences.

13. $9 \times$ ▆ $= 45$ 14. ▆ $\times 7 = 56$ 15. $3 \times 3 \times 2 =$ ▆   16. $1 \times 5 \times 0 =$ ▆

Multiply your age by 2. Multiply 2 by your age.
Then multiply your age by 0 and 1.

Problem Solving Strategy: Choosing the Operation
(pages 18–19)

Baseballs sell for $5 each. How much will 7 baseballs cost?

7 sets of $5
Multiply.

$ 5
×7
$35

7 baseballs cost $35 in all.

1. Each baseball team has 9 players. How many players do 6 teams have?

2. It costs $3 for each ticket to the ice show. How much would it cost to buy 8 tickets?

3. 7 tennis courts are being used. There are 2 players on each court. How many people are playing tennis?

4. 7 people were skating. There were also 2 guards and 6 people watching. How many people in all were at the pond?

5. The health club gave 7 of its members 3 free passes each. How many free passes were given?

6. The baseball team won 16 games and lost 9. How many more games did they win than lose?

If everyone in your family wanted 2 hamburgers, how many would you have to make?

Division Facts (pages 20–21)

Divide.

$$24 \div 8 = \blacksquare$$
$$\blacksquare \times 8 = 24$$
$$3 \times 8 = 24$$
$$8\overline{)24}^{\,3}$$

1. $2\overline{)10}$ **2.** $3\overline{)24}$ **3.** $8\overline{)32}$ **4.** $5\overline{)20}$ **5.** $6\overline{)30}$

6. $7\overline{)56}$ **7.** $4\overline{)24}$ **8.** $3\overline{)27}$ **9.** $6\overline{)48}$ **10.** $3\overline{)21}$

11. $42 \div 6 = \blacksquare$ **12.** $63 \div 7 = \blacksquare$ **13.** $14 \div 2 = \blacksquare$

 Add the digits for the year you were born.
Divide by the sum of the digits in your age.

Division Properties: Mental Math (pages 22–23)

Divide.

$$2\overline{)0}^{\,0}$$
$$0 \div 2 = 0$$
$$1\overline{)2}^{\,2}$$
$$2 \div 1 = 2$$

1. $1\overline{)7}$ **2.** $8\overline{)0}$ **3.** $3\overline{)3}$ **4.** $8\overline{)56}$ **5.** $7\overline{)7}$

6. $3\overline{)0}$ **7.** $1\overline{)8}$ **8.** $4\overline{)4}$ **9.** $1\overline{)0}$ **10.** $7\overline{)0}$

11. $6 \div 1 = \blacksquare$ **12.** $0 \div 9 = \blacksquare$ **13.** $28 \div 4 = \blacksquare$

 Divide 0 by your age. Then divide your age by 1.

Problem Solving: Uses of Division (pages 24–25)

These are 35 students in gym class.
Each basketball team has 5 players.
How many teams are there?

$$5\overline{)35}^{\,7} \quad \begin{array}{l} \leftarrow \text{sets} \\ \leftarrow \text{in all} \end{array}$$

7 teams

1. There are 28 students in a class. There are 4 rows of seats. How many students are in each row?

2. There are 45 classrooms in the school. There are 9 on each floor. How many floors are in the school?

3. There are 6 bookshelves with 54 books. How many books are on each shelf if there are the same number on each?

4. The 4 stairways have a total of 32 steps. Each stairway has the same number of steps. How many steps are in each stairway?

 Count the number of windowpanes in your home.
Divide by the number of windows.

401

UNIT 2 Place Value

Hundreds, Tens, and Ones *(pages 32–33)*

Write the standard numerals. Then tell what each digit means.

> eight hundred fifty-nine: 859 $\longrightarrow$ 8 hundreds, 5 tens, 9 ones

1. two hundred sixteen

2. six hundred seventy-five

3. five hundred forty

4. one hundred thirty-two

In each numeral name the digit in the hundreds place.

5. 378 **6.** 506 **7.** 924 **8.** 600 **9.** 710 **10.** 423

 Find a container whose weight is a 3-digit number.
What does each digit mean?

Thousands *(pages 34–35)*

In each numeral name the place of the digit 5.
Then tell what the digit 5 means.

> 752,490   5 is in the ten-thousands place.
> The digit 5 means 5 ten-thousands.

1. 135,629

2. 537,000

Write the numerals. Name the digit in the thousands place.

3. forty-six thousand, five hundred twenty

4. three thousand, seventy-two

5. Tell what each digit means in the numeral 743,985.

 Tell what each digit means in the year a parent or relative was born.

Comparing and Ordering Numbers
Write >, <, or = for ●. *(pages 36–37)*

> 62 < 69   2 is less than 9.
> 62 is less than 69.

1. 75 ● 78

2. 186 ● 176

3. 3,649 ● 3,649

4. 46,768 ● 46,539

5. 263,174 ● 263,175

6. 99,894 ● 101,021

Write the numbers in order from least to greatest.

7. 6,789; 6,876; 5,438

8. 70,309; 700,309; 77,309

 Write the following in order from least to greatest: year of your birth,
pages in any 3 books, your house or apartment number times 3.

Rounding Numbers *(pages 38–39)*

Round to the nearest ten. Use the number line if needed.

447 is nearer 450 than 440.	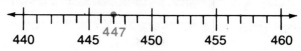
Round 447 up to 450.	

1. 442 **2.** 455 **3.** 457 **4.** 451 **5.** 456

Round to the nearest hundred.

6. 430 **7.** 568 **8.** 850 **9.** 453 **10.** 749 **11.** 300

Round to the nearest dollar.

12. $7.55 **13.** $7.45 **14.** $7.75 **15.** $7.50 **16.** $1.60 **17.** $9.49

Round each number to the nearest ten and to the nearest hundred.

18. 850 **19.** 741 **20.** 236 **21.** 464 **22.** 694 **23.** 395

 Add the weights of 3 people in your family. Round to the nearest ten and then to the nearest hundred.

Millions *(pages 42–43)*

Name the place of the digit 7. Then tell what 7 means.

725,483,109	7 is in the hundred-millions place.	**1.** 374,592,610
	The digit 7 means 7 hundred-millions.	**2.** 17,295,000

Write the numerals. Name the digit in the millions place.

3. four hundred thirty-five million, six hundred eighty thousand

4. five million, two hundred twelve thousand, three hundred seventy-six

5. thirty million, four hundred thousand, five hundred

Compare. Write >, <, or = for ●.

6. 526,394,010 ● 526,394,001   **7.** 130,213,800 ● 130,212,900

8. 100,000,001 ● 99,999,998   **9.** 439,000,110 ● 439,000,111

 Put your zip code and the last 4 digits of your telephone number together. What does each digit mean?

403

Billions *(pages 44–45)*

Name the place of the digit 2. Then tell what 2 means.

2 is in the ten-billions place.
125,634,000,000
The digit 2 means 2 ten-billions.

1. 42,635,000,000

2. 273,500,000,000

Write the numerals. Tell what digit is in the billions place.

3. sixteen billion, three hundred forty million, seven hundred thousand

4. five hundred sixty billion, seventy million

5. four billion, two hundred eleven million, sixty thousand, twenty-seven

Write in order from least to greatest.

6. 6,340,763,825; 10,086,395,217; 5,938,694,825

7. 210,300,000,000; 210,290,000,000; 210,295,000,000

 Put the house or apartment numbers of 4 friends together.
Tell what digit is in the billions place.

Problem Solving: Data from Tables and Graphs *(pages 46–47)*

Use the table to solve these problems.

Were the expenses greater for Justice or Agriculture?	$20,368,000 > $2,397,000 So, greater for Agriculture.

1. Which department had the least expenses?

2. Which department had the greatest expenses?

3. Were the expenses greater for Agriculture or Labor?

4. Write the expenses in order from least to greatest.

United States Government Expenses (1978)	
Department	**Expenses (in thousands)**
Justice	$ 2,397
Agriculture	$ 20,368
Labor	$ 22,902
Defense	$106,667
Health, Education, Welfare	$162,809

5. The President's expenses were $4,475,000. Which departments listed in the table had expenses greater?

6. The Treasury Department's expenses were $56,309,000. Which departments in the table had less expenses?

 Find the price of 4 cars advertised in the newspaper. What is the difference between the least and most expensive cars?

UNIT 3 Addition and Subtraction

Addition *(pages 54–55)*

Add.

	742
1	+ 596
	1,338

1. 65
+ 32

2. 82
+ 76

3. 29
+ 49

4. 642
+ 743

5. 439
+ 932

6. 193
+ 659

7. 97
+ 997

8. 686
+ 72

9. 308
+ 238

10. 314
+ 397

11. 779
+ 689

12. 935
+ 698

13. 46
+ 38

14. 153
+ 86

15. 429
+ 754

16. 534
+ 676

17. 249 + 35 = ▓

18. 546 + 317 = ▓

19. 496 + 685 = ▓

 Add the last three numbers of your telephone number to the top degree on your oven dial.

Adding More Than Two Numbers *(pages 56–57)*

Add.

	3 2
	493
	86
	275
	+ 548
	1,402

1. 84
93
+ 65

2. 37
28
+ 45

3. 71
92
+ 46

4. 89
76
+ 45

5. 237
492
+ 516

6. 584
76
+ 219

7. 417
256
+ 327

8. 623
827
+ 46

9. 259
27
+ 864

10. 480
547
+ 675

11. 371
53
42
+ 227

12. 341
856
291
+ 804

13. 380
290
570
+ 680

14. 825
315
9
+ 293

15. 73
816
877
+ 914

16. 285
349
67
+ 361

17. 53 + 435 + 78 = ▓

18. 400 + 850 + 600 + 700 = ▓

 Add the ages of all the members of your family.

405

Adding Larger Numbers *(pages 58–59)*

Add.

1 1   1
83,526
+ 17,948
101,474

1. $16.32
+ 55.42

2. 6,695
+ 1,731

3. 35,379
+ 36,722

4. 817,892
+ 758,736

5. $66.06
+ 97.40

6. 56,465
+ 67,847

7. $2,858.30
+   773.00

8. 956,839
+ 547,213

 Add the prices of two expensive items in a catalog.

Estimating Sums: Mental Math *(pages 60–61)*

Add. Use estimation to check.

1 1 1 1		
214,837	210,000	312,045 is near 310,000.
+ 97,208	+ 100,000	The total is reasonable.
312,045	310,000	

1. 35,400
29,050
+ 6,007

2. $ 432.71
1,896.14
+   751.98

3. 47,386
72,581
+ 61,257

4. 429,630
564,850
+ 137,260

5. $1,724.79
847.43
+ 1,254.36

 Add three different zip codes. Estimate to check.

Problem Solving: Estimates and Answers *(pages 62–63)*

Use the table. Estimate to solve each problem.

Immigration to the United States

Years	1881–1900	1901–1920	1921–1940	1941–1960
Number of Immigrants	8,934,177	14,531,197	4,635,640	3,550,518

How many people moved to the U.S. between 1921–1960?	5,000,000 + 4,000,000 9,000,000	4,635,640 + 3,550,518 8,186,158	8,186,158 people Reasonable!

1. How many more people moved to the U.S. between 1901–1920 than between 1921–1940?

2. About how many people in all moved to the U.S. between 1881–1920?

3. How many fewer people moved to the U.S. between 1941–1960 than between 1881–1900?

4. About how many people in all moved to the U.S. between 1901–1960?

Estimate the difference between any 2 seven-digit telephone numbers.

Subtraction *(pages 66–67)*

Subtract.

```
      13        Check.
   2 ⁄3 12       1 1
    3⁄ 4⁄ 2⁄       175
   - 1 6 7      + 167
    1 7 5        342 ✓
```

1. 967
  − 32

2. 976
  −755

3. 62
  − 7

4. 691
  −476

5. 746
  − 89

6. 933
  −286

7. 62
  − 56

8. 824
  −755

9. 821
  −687

10. 816
  −187

11. 620
  −147

12. 411
  −353

13. 132
  − 94

14. 508
  −145

15. $214 - 121 =$ ▪

16. $135 - 76 =$ ▪

17. $500 - 240 =$ ▪

18. $750 - 200 =$ ▪

19. $456 - 448 =$ ▪

20. $714 - 309 =$ ▪

 Write down your home address and area code.
What is the difference between the two?

Subtracting Larger Numbers *(pages 68–69)*

Subtract.

```
       12          Check.
    6 ⁄7 14 5 12     1 1   1
    7⁄ 3⁄, 4⁄ 6⁄ 2⁄     33,727
   - 3 9, 7 3 5    + 39,735
    3 3, 7 2 7      73,462 ✓
```

1. 4,567
  − 334

2. $83.90
  − 36.77

3. 42,167
  − 4,666

4. 490,641
  −218,387

5. $660.80
  − 89.26

6. 98,099
  − 1,556

7. $7,631.84
  − 843.85

8. 947,499
  −842,848

9. $429.60
  − 62.21

10. 94,324
  −27,639

11. 527,600
  −419,450

12. $24{,}347 - 9{,}615 =$ ▪

13. $70{,}425 - 51{,}263 =$ ▪

14. $\$2{,}460.00 - \$915.00 =$ ▪

15. $614{,}374 - 613{,}531 =$ ▪

 Find the difference between the populations
of two large cities.

407

Subtracting Across Zeros *(pages 70–71)*

Subtract.

9 12 9 4 1̸0 2̸ 1̸0 11 5̸0̸,3̸0̸1̸ −16,725 33,576	**1.** 5,000 − 3,527	**2.** $100.48 − 41.47	**3.** 400 − 19	**4.** 48,006 −38,744

5. $93.55   **6.** $80.08   **7.**   13,221   **8.**   80,032
     − 89.77   − 22.99   − 7,945   −79,568

9.   60,236   **10.**   90,000   **11.**   104,300   **12.**   840,250   **13.**   502,340
    −17,357   −45,247   − 95,160   −173,185   −495,613

14. $100,000 - 20,406 = $ ■   **15.** $\$5,000.00 - \$680.75 = $ ■

Find the price of something under $100 that you would like to buy. Subtract the price from $100.

Estimating Differences: Mental Math *(pages 72–73)*

Subtract. Use estimation to check.

16 15 1 6̸ 5̸ 18 2̸7,6̸8̸4 − 8,792 1 8,8 9 2	27,684 ⟶ 28,000 − 8,792 ⟶ − 9,000 19,000	18,892 is near 19,000. The answer is reasonable.

1.   8,427   **2.**   46,302   **3.**   19,783   **4.**   536,284   **5.** $4,320.00
   − 5,389   −27,516   − 6,109   −247,316   −   740.80

Add or subtract. Use estimation to check.

6.   62,743   **7.**   8,342   **8.**   39,842   **9.** $145.63   **10.** $236.74
   −28,690   + 3,675   +57,318   − 34.40   − 28.43

11.   26,712   **12.**   19,576   **13.**   678,321   **14.**   72,136   **15.**   314,027
   −15,483   − 7,845   +284,974   + 8,571   − 59,843

Subtract the year of your birth from a year in the distant future. Estimate to check your answer.

Problem Solving: Working with Larger Numbers (pages 74–75)

Solve the problems.

A city collected $84 million in taxes.	$84 million
The total amount spent was $75 million.	− 75 million
How much money was left over?	$ 9 million

1. A city issued bonds worth $160 million in March and another $110 million in April. What was the total value of the bonds?

2. The city's budget included $8,752,648 for police and $2,225,250 for sanitation. About how much was included for both?

3. The state expects to collect $185,000,000 in taxes. So far, $65,128,079 has been collected. About how much more does the state expect to collect?

4. Last year, the city's budget was $84 million. This year, $27 million must be cut. What will the new budget be?

Look in a newspaper for examples of large numbers that are written in standard form and in rounded form.

Problem Solving: Too Much Information (pages 76–77)

Solve. Use the data in the paragraph on page 76.

How many more people speak Mandarin than English?	755 million ← Mandarin
	− 409 million ← English
	346 million

1. How many more people speak Hindustani than Russian?

2. How many people in all speak Swahili or Hausa?

3. Are there more speakers of Russian or Japanese?

4. How many people in all speak Spanish or Swahili?

5. Which language is spoken by more people than any other language?

6. Name two languages that are spoken by fewer than 40 million people.

Estimate the difference between any 8-digit number and the seven digits in your telephone number.

UNIT 4 Multiplication

Multiplying 2-digit Numbers (pages 84–85)

Multiply.

④			
36			
× 8			
288			

1. 43
        × 2

2. 61
        × 5

3. 38
        × 2

4. 45
        × 9

5. 81
        × 6

6. 97
        × 3

7. 80
        × 7

8. 85
        × 4

9. 21
        × 8

10. 52
         × 4

11. 25
         × 6

12. 54
         × 7

13. 73
         × 3

14. 96
         × 5

15. 29
         × 9

16. 26
         × 4

17. 5 × 45 = ■   **18.** 2 × 57 = ■   **19.** 3 × 48 = ■

 Multiply by 8 the number of cups, saucers, bowls, and plates in your kitchen.

Multiplying Larger Numbers (pages 86–87)

Multiply.

③ ③	
2,918	
× 4	
11,672	

1. 701
        × 2

2. 692
        × 6

3. $9.13
        × 7

4. 1,467
        × 3

5. 6,138
        × 7

6. $5.28
        × 3

7. 77,517
        × 5

8. 428
        × 9

9. $50.17
        × 4

10. 28,309
         × 2

11. 2,714
         × 5

12. 35,182
         × 7

13. 16,500
         × 4

14. 583 × 8 = ■   **15.** 3 × 13,642 = ■   **16.** 9 × $25.63 = ■

 Find the total Calorie content of a product in your kitchen. Multiply it by the number of people in your family.

Estimating Products: Mental Math (pages 88–89)

Find each product. Then estimate to check your product.

```
    ②
   ⑧⑧
  ⑦18           700
  × ③8  ──→   × 40
  5 744  ──→  28,000
  21 540       27,284 is near
  27,284          28,000.
```

1. 9,221
    × 44

2. $73.24
    × 52

3. $21.23
    × 38

4. $61.39
    × 46

5. 6,153
    × 85

6. 68
    × 1,010

7. 986
    × 64

8. $36.59
    × 80

9. $82.11
    × 97

10. 369
    × 25

11. 5,916
    × 73

 Multiply the pages in the telephone directory by the number of books in your room. Estimate to check the product.

Problem Solving: Labeling Answers (pages 90–91)

Solve the problems.

A freight train traveled for 3 hours at a speed of 72 km/h. How far did the train travel?

3 sets
72 km in each set
Multiply.

```
   72
  × 3
  216
```

The train traveled 216 km.

1. A pickup truck is carrying 27 cement blocks. Each block has a mass of 9 kg. What is the total mass of the blocks?

2. A truck driver traveled 385 km before stopping for lunch. He traveled 403 km after lunch. How far did he drive that day?

3. A dealer bought 5 campers. Each cost $2,365. What was the total cost of the campers?

4. A moving van traveled for 4 hours at a speed of 85 km/h. How far did it travel in all?

5. An airliner flew for 6 hours at a speed of 775 km/h. How far did the plane fly?

6. One boxcar had 1,946 kg of grain. A second had 2,170 kg. How much more was in the second boxcar?

 Approximately how far is it from your home to your school? How far do you travel in a week?

Multiplying by Multiples of 10 (pages 94–95)

Multiply 276 by 10, then by 30, then by 70.

$$\begin{array}{r} 276 \\ \times\ 10 \\ \hline 2,760 \end{array} \qquad \overset{②①}{\begin{array}{r} 276 \\ \times\ 30 \\ \hline 8,280 \end{array}} \qquad \overset{⑤④}{\begin{array}{r} 276 \\ \times\ 70 \\ \hline 19,320 \end{array}}$$

1. Multiply 65 by 10, then by 20, then by 60.
2. Multiply 730 by 10, then by 40, then by 90.
3. Multiply 2,183 by 10, then by 30, then by 50.

Multiply.

4. $\begin{array}{r} 54 \\ \times 10 \\ \hline \end{array}$
5. $\begin{array}{r} 798 \\ \times\ 10 \\ \hline \end{array}$
6. $\begin{array}{r} 506 \\ \times\ 40 \\ \hline \end{array}$
7. $\begin{array}{r} 4,132 \\ \times\quad 10 \\ \hline \end{array}$
8. $\begin{array}{r} 369 \\ \times\ 60 \\ \hline \end{array}$

9. $\begin{array}{r} 2,387 \\ \times\quad 20 \\ \hline \end{array}$
10. $\begin{array}{r} 765 \\ \times\ 50 \\ \hline \end{array}$
11. $\begin{array}{r} 30 \\ \times 6,500 \\ \hline \end{array}$
12. $\begin{array}{r} 9,830 \\ \times\quad 90 \\ \hline \end{array}$
13. $\begin{array}{r} 80 \\ \times 5,675 \\ \hline \end{array}$

Multiply the number of days until your next birthday by multiples of 10 through 90.

Multiplying by 2-digit Numbers (pages 96–97)
Multiply.

$$\begin{array}{r} 732 \\ \times\ 23 \\ \hline 2\ 196 \\ 14\ 640 \\ \hline 16,836 \end{array}$$

1. $\begin{array}{r} \$6.10 \\ \times\quad 15 \\ \hline \end{array}$
2. $\begin{array}{r} 6,232 \\ \times\quad 23 \\ \hline \end{array}$
3. $\begin{array}{r} 911 \\ \times\ 47 \\ \hline \end{array}$
4. $\begin{array}{r} 91 \\ \times 51 \\ \hline \end{array}$

5. $\begin{array}{r} 8,400 \\ \times\quad 20 \\ \hline \end{array}$
6. $\begin{array}{r} 3,110 \\ \times\quad 28 \\ \hline \end{array}$
7. $\begin{array}{r} 7,001 \\ \times\quad 17 \\ \hline \end{array}$
8. $\begin{array}{r} 32 \\ \times 2,302 \\ \hline \end{array}$

Multiply the number of steps it takes to walk through all the rooms of your home by the number of inches in 2 feet.

More Multiplication (pages 98–99)
Multiply.

$$\begin{array}{r} \overset{③\ ②}{\cancel{2\ 8\ 1\ 5}} \\ 2,815 \\ \times\quad 47 \\ \hline 19\ 705 \\ 112\ 600 \\ \hline 132,305 \end{array}$$

1. $\begin{array}{r} 7,549 \\ \times\quad 16 \\ \hline \end{array}$
2. $\begin{array}{r} 5,361 \\ \times\quad 21 \\ \hline \end{array}$
3. $\begin{array}{r} 4,312 \\ \times\quad 72 \\ \hline \end{array}$
4. $\begin{array}{r} 3,006 \\ \times\quad 17 \\ \hline \end{array}$

5. $\begin{array}{r} 707 \\ \times\ 79 \\ \hline \end{array}$
6. $\begin{array}{r} \$63.41 \\ \times\quad 18 \\ \hline \end{array}$
7. $\begin{array}{r} \$46.13 \\ \times\quad 51 \\ \hline \end{array}$
8. $\begin{array}{r} 2,165 \\ \times\quad 59 \\ \hline \end{array}$

Multiply the price of something in the newspaper by the number of pages in that newspaper.

Multiplying by Multiples of 100 *(pages 100–101)*

Multiply 538 by 100, by 300, by 700.

538	①② 538	②⑤ 538
× 100	× 300	× 700
53,800	161,400	376,600

1. Multiply 49 by 100, by 200, by 600.

2. Multiply 850 by 100, by 400, by 900.

3. Multiply 3,625 by 100, by 300, by 500.

Multiply.

4.   51
   × 100

5.   534
   × 100

6.   3,182
   ×   100

7.   785
   × 200

8.   94
   × 600

9.   7,369
   ×   400

10.   263
   × 300

11.   800
   × 9,640

12.   1,369
   ×   500

13.   781
   × 700

14. 900 × 306 = ■   15. 700 × 900 = ■   16. 600 × 575 = ■

 Multiply your weight plus that of three friends by 100, 300, 500, 700, and 900.

Multiplying by 3-digit Numbers *(pages 102–103)*

Multiply. Use estimation to check.

⑤ ⨯ ⨯	
	Check.
891 ⟶	900
× 624 ⟶	× 600
3564	540,000
17820	
534600	555,984 is
555,984	near 540,000.

1.   584
   × 273

2.   626
   × 418

3.   216
   × 346

4.   1,428
   ×   631

5.   3,017
   ×   513

6.   1,136
   ×   825

7.   936
   × 457

8.   2,471
   ×   934

9.   1,814
   ×   792

 Choose any book. Multiply the number of words on one page by the total number of pages in the book.

Multiplying with Zeros *(pages 104–105)*

① ⊗⊗⊗ 624 ×350 31 200 ⟵—— 50 × 624 187 200 ⟵—— 300 × 624 218,400 ⟵—— 350 × 624	① ⊗⊗⊗ 536 ×208 4 288 ⟵—— 8 × 536 107 200 ⟵—— 200 × 536 111,488 ⟵—— 208 × 536

1. 457 ×240	2. 982 ×604	3. 863 ×720	4. 2,506 × 207	5. 3,124 × 806

6. 120 × 5,030 = ■   7. 250 × 3,400 = ■   8. 903 × 1,450 = ■

  Add a 0 to the last four digits of your home number. Multiply by 1,001.

Problem Solving: Order Forms *(pages 106–107)*

Using the catalog page on page 106, complete order forms for 1 and 2.

Name of Item	Catalog Number	Quantity	Price Each	Total Price
Sleeping bag	39A73	2	$42.35	$ 84.70
Canteen	36B19	1	$ 8.50	$ 8.50
Cooking Fuel	27X51	2	$ .89	$ 1.78
	Total for Merchandise			$ 94.98
	5% Sales Tax			$ 4.75
	Handling Charge			$ 1.50
	Total Amount Enclosed			$101.23

1. 2 canteens, 1 lantern, 4 cans of fuel, and 1 stove. Handling: $1.00

2. 1 tent, 3 sleeping bags, and 2 backpacks. Handling: $1.50

5% Sales Tax	Price	Tax	Price	Tax
	$94.90 – $95.09	$4.75	$260.10 – $260.29	$13.01
	$95.10 – $95.29	$4.76	$260.30 – $260.49	$13.02

Choose 3 items from the catalog on page 106 and find the total price. Add 7% sales tax and $4.50 for handling.

Reviewing Division Facts *(pages 114–115)*

Divide.

$$24 \div 8 =$$

$$\blacksquare \times 8 = 24$$

$$2 \times 8 = 16$$
$$3 \times 8 = 24$$

$$\overset{3}{8\overline{)24}}$$

1. $6\overline{)42}$
2. $8\overline{)72}$
3. $5\overline{)40}$
4. $9\overline{)36}$
5. $8\overline{)40}$

6. $8\overline{)64}$
7. $9\overline{)45}$
8. $6\overline{)54}$
9. $5\overline{)45}$
10. $4\overline{)36}$

11. $7\overline{)35}$
12. $4\overline{)32}$
13. $5\overline{)30}$
14. $7\overline{)63}$
15. $9\overline{)81}$

16. $4\overline{)16}$
17. $9\overline{)72}$
18. $6\overline{)48}$
19. $8\overline{)56}$
20. $7\overline{)56}$

21. $42 \div 7 = \blacksquare$
22. $64 \div 8 = \blacksquare$
23. $27 \div 3 = \blacksquare$
24. $72 \div 8 = \blacksquare$

 Divide the number of students in your class by the number of students in each row.

Using Division Facts *(pages 116–117)*

Use mental math to find the answer.

$$3{,}500 \div 70 = \blacksquare$$
Think:
$$35 \div 7 = 5$$
$$3{,}500 \div 70 = 50$$

1. $480 \div 6 = \blacksquare$
2. $5{,}600 \div 7 = \blacksquare$
3. $6{,}300 \div 90 = \blacksquare$
4. $18{,}000 \div 30 = \blacksquare$
5. $28{,}000 \div 400 = \blacksquare$
6. $16{,}000 \div 8 = \blacksquare$
7. $1{,}000 \div 50 = \blacksquare$
8. $40{,}000 \div 80 = \blacksquare$
9. $560{,}000 \div 800 = \blacksquare$

Tell if each answer is reasonable.

10. $795 \div 43 = 184.88$
11. $608 \div 51 = 11.922$
12. $5{,}287 \div 15 = 352.47$

 Divide the number of pages in another textbook by the number of units or chapters.

415

Dividing 2-digit Numbers   *(pages 118–119)*

Divide. Check your answers.

```
   32 R1
2)65    Think:
   6        3 × 2 = 6
  05     Use 3.
   4        2 × 2 = 5
   1     Use 2.
```

1. 2)86   **2.** 5)59   **3.** 4)87   **4.** 8)89

5. 3)68   **6.** 7)85   **7.** 6)68   **8.** 8)96

9. 2)48   **10.** 4)89   **11.** 9)99   **12.** 3)75

13. 4)86   **14.** 2)27   **15.** 4)47   **16.** 3)97   **17.** 5)95   **18.** 2)82

19. $92 \div 2 =$ **20.** $77 \div 7 =$ ▨   **21.** $88 \div 4 =$ ▨   **22.** $72 \div 6 =$ ▨

Count the number of books in your home. How many times can you divide the total by 2, 3, 4, and 5? How many have remainders?

Placing Digits in the Quotient   *(pages 120–121)*

Divide. Check your answers.

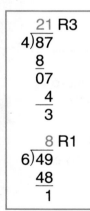

```
   21 R3
4)87
  8
  07
   4
   3


   8 R1
6)49
  48
   1
```

1. 5)68   **2.** 9)75   **3.** 2)87   **4.** 6)79   **5.** 4)86

6. 3)58   **7.** 8)67   **8.** 5)48   **9.** 7)88   **10.** 4)53

11. 6)55   **12.** 8)73   **13.** 9)89   **14.** 5)75   **15.** 7)94

16. 2)86   **17.** 6)54   **18.** 9)57   **19.** 5)85   **20.** 3)83

21. $48 \div 3 =$ ▧   **22.** $81 \div 9 =$ ▧   **23.** $27 \div 3 =$ ▧   **24.** $86 \div 2 =$ ▧

Count all the cans, containers, and boxes in your kitchen.
Divide by the number of shelves.

416   **Homework**

Zeros in Division *(pages 122–123)*

Divide. Check your answers.

```
  12 R2
4)50
  4
  10
   8
   2
```

Check:
4 × 12 = 48
48 + 2 = 50

1. 3)30
2. 4)80
3. 2)60
4. 5)53
5. 4)60

6. 7)75
7. 5)50
8. 4)42
9. 3)62
10. 6)30

11. 9)95
12. 3)70
13. 7)80
14. 5)72
15. 8)90

16. 4)81
17. 6)65
18. 3)50
19. 8)87
20. 5)43

 Multiply the number of people in your family by 10.
Divide by a number less than 10.

Problem Solving: Too Much Information *(pages 124–125)*

Tell which information you do not need. Then solve the problems.

Mr. Dalk drove 32 kilometers to work. He worked 8 hours and earned $96. How much did he earn per hour?

$96 in all. 8 hours. How much per hour?

```
  12
8)96
  8
  16
  16
   0
```

You do not need the distance.

He earned $12 per hour.

8 × 12 = 96 ✓

1. Joni earned $52 at her job. She worked on 5 different days and is paid $4 per hour. How many hours did she work?

2. A plumber charged $78 for repairing the bathroom. He fixed 4 leaks in 3 hours. How much did he charge per hour?

3. A club had $96 to spend for trophies for 2 races. The trophies cost $9 each. How many trophies could it buy?

4. A restaurant bill of $72 was divided equally among 6 people. How much did each person have to pay?

5. Each book costs $8. A bookcase costs $64. How much do 16 books cost?

6. Ms. Cook spent $42 in all for 6 books. She gave the clerk $50. How much did she get back?

 You have $35. A pen costs $2. A notebook costs $3. How much would you spend to buy each of your friends a notebook?

417

Dividing 3-digit Numbers   *(pages 128–129)*

Divide.

```
  231 R1
4)925
  8
  12
  12
  05
   4
   1
```

1. 3)504
2. 9)756
3. 7)850
4. 6)745
5. 4)472

6. 8)937
7. 5)707
8. 2)843
9. 4)847
10. 9)572

11. 7)903
12. 6)942
13. 4)638
14. 7)600
15. 2)729

16. 5)826
17. 3)950
18. 8)909
19. 9)427
20. 2)670
21. 6)465

22. 732 ÷ 3 = ■
23. 584 ÷ 2 = ■
24. 395 ÷ 5 = ■
25. 584 ÷ 8 = ■

 Divide the number of days in two years by the month in which you were born.

Zeros in the Quotient   *(pages 130–131)*

Divide.

```
  308 R1
2)617
  6
  01
  0
  17
  16
   1
```
2 × 0 = 0

1. 5)543
2. 6)663
3. 3)851
4. 9)542
5. 8)973

6. 3)512
7. 4)162
8. 4)647
9. 7)842
10. 5)352

11. 6)703
12. 7)952
13. 9)918
14. 8)870
15. 9)277

16. 5)679
17. 8)847
18. 6)654
19. 2)735
20. 2)500

21. 9)987
22. 3)617
23. 4)833
24. 3)900
25. 7)705

26. 800 ÷ 5 = ■
27. 800 ÷ 2 = ■
28. 420 ÷ 6 = ■
29. 496 ÷ 8 = ■

 Multiply the number of people in your family by that number. Add zero to the end. Divide by the number of people in your family.

Mental Math: Short Division and Estimation *(pages 132–133)*

Estimate the quotient. Then use short division to find the exact answer.

```
  1 4 6 R3
4)5¹8²7

600 ÷ 4 = 150
560 ÷ 4 = 140

500 ÷ 4 is about
          120.
87 ÷ 4 is about
          20.
120 + 20 = 140
```

1. 6)595   **2.** 8)816   **3.** 5)468   **4.** 7)850   **5.** 4)879

6. 3)739   **7.** 5)755   **8.** 4)791   **9.** 6)809   **10.** 7)676

11. 8)952   **12.** 6)374   **13.** 2)648   **14.** 5)286   **15.** 4)263

16. 3)875   **17.** 5)148   **18.** 7)847   **19.** 8)572   **20.** 6)548

21. 535 ÷ 5 = ▨   **22.** 158 ÷ 2 = ▨   **23.** 665 ÷ 7 = ▨

Divide the first three digits in your phone number by the fourth digit.

Dividing Larger Numbers *(pages 134–135)*

Divide.

```
     8 4 0 3 R3
4)33,615
  32
  16
  16
   01
    0 ←
   15
   12
    3
```

| Don't forget to write 0 in the quotient. |

1. 4)6,329   **2.** 2)5,413   **3.** 6)13,824   **4.** 8)3,808

5. 9)6,880   **6.** 7)35,000   **7.** 5)7,396   **8.** 3)24,042

9. 9)76,788   **10.** 6)30,024   **11.** 3)8,124   **12.** 5)42,180

13. 4)2,653   **14.** 7)8,347   **15.** 9)10,368   **16.** 6)9,078

17. 37,210 ÷ 2 = ▨   **18.** 15,000 ÷ 8 = ▨

19. 14,000 ÷ 5 = ▨   **20.** 61,500 ÷ 3 = ▨

Multiply the year you were born by 5, 6, 7, 8, or 9. Then divide the product by the number of people in your family.

Problem Solving: Answers in Division   *(pages 136–137)*

In a section of the theater each row has 8 seats. How many rows in this section are needed to seat 125 people?

$$
\begin{array}{r}
15 \\
8)\overline{125} \\
\underline{8} \\
45 \\
\underline{40} \\
5
\end{array}
$$

1 more row is needed for 5 people.

16 rows are needed.

1. Copies of a play cost $7 each. The drama club has $68. How many copies can it buy?

2. The drama club has 68 wigs. It can store 7 wigs in each box. How many boxes will it need?

3. Tom had a 50-foot coil of rope. He cut it into 3 pieces of equal length. How long was each?

4. Tickets for the play cost $4 each. How many tickets can Max buy with $51?

5. The manager has $68 to buy new softballs. Each softball costs $5. How many softballs can the manager buy?

6. Pam worked the same amount of time each day for 4 days. She worked 27 hours in all. How many hours did she work each day?

 How many apples would you and each of your friends get if you divided 2 dozen apples equally?

Problem Solving: Finding Averages   *(pages 138–139)*

Ms. Ross rode her bicycle 18 km on Monday, 24 km on Tuesday, and 27 km on Wednesday. What was the average number of km she traveled each day?

$$
\begin{array}{r}
1 \\
18 \\
24 \\
+27 \\
\hline
69
\end{array}
$$

3 days

$$
\begin{array}{r}
23 \\
3)\overline{69} \\
\underline{6} \\
09 \\
\underline{9} \\
0
\end{array}
$$

She rode an average of 23 kilometers.

1. On 4 tests Bob had scores of 78, 82, 85, and 91. What was his average score?

2. Mr. Burton drove 5,877 km on a 9-day trip. How many km did he average each day?

3. In 6 basketball games, the Tigers scored 79, 95, 83, 102, 97, and 84 points. What was the average score?

4. In 5 basketball games, Lisa scored 16, 25, 18, 22, and 14 points. What was Lisa's average number of points per game?

 What is the average age of any four people in your family?

Telling Time   *(pages 146–147)*
Read each clock.

3 : 25
25 minutes past 3

1.

■ : ■
■ minutes to ■

2.

■:■
■ minutes past ■
■ minutes to ■

Match the times.

3. 10:10   **a.** 14 minutes to 4
4. 12:35   **b.** 10 minutes past 10
5. 3:46   **c.** 15 minutes to 9
6. 8:45   **d.** 25 minutes to 1

Is it light or dark outside at:

7. 3:05 A.M.?
8. 3:05 P.M.?
9. 10:20 A.M.?
10. 10:20 P.M.?

 Look at a clock. Write the time in three ways.

Elapsed Time   *(pages 148–149)*

Carl's lunch period is from 11:40 A.M. to 12:25 P.M. How long is his lunch period?

Find the time between 11:40 A.M. and 12:25 P.M.

  20 minutes to 12 noon
+ 25 minutes after 12 noon
―――――――――――
  45

His lunch period is 45 minutes long.

1. Karen leaves for school at 8:20 A.M. She gets home at 3:20 P.M. How long is she gone?

2. Mike watched television for 45 minutes. He quit at 8:25 P.M. At what time did he start?

3. Mr. Albano left for work at 7:40 A.M. He was gone for 10 hours. At what time did he return?

4. Alice started writing a letter at 7:15 P.M. She finished at 8:10 P.M. How long did it take her?

5. Jan was on a bus for 4 hours. She got off the bus at 2:15 P.M. When did she get on the bus?

6. Bill started his piano lesson at 3:50 P.M. It lasted 40 minutes. When did his lesson end?

 What time do you leave for school? If it takes you 27 minutes to walk, what time do you get to school?

421

More Elapsed Time (pages 150–151)

Solve the problems.

An electrician started a job at 8:30 A.M. and finished at 11:15 A.M. How long did the job take?	**Step 1** 8:30 AM. to 10:30 A.M.
	      2 hours
	 Step 2 10:30 A.M. to 11:15 A.M.
	      30 + 15 = 45 minutes

Find the time between 8:30 A.M. and 11:15 A.M.	The job took 2 hours 45 minutes.

1. Tom was supposed to come home at 4:25 P.M. He came home at 6:40 P.M. How late was he?

2. The Wylies stopped driving at 4:30 P.M. They had driven for 10 hours 20 minutes. When did they start?

3. The trip from home to camp takes 4 hours and 30 minutes. At what time should Janice leave if she wants to be there at 2:15 P.M.?

4. José's train left Chicago at 3:25 P.M. It arrived in St. Louis 5 hours 40 minutes later. At what time did the train arrive in St. Louis?

 What time did you go to bed last night? What time did you get up this morning? How many hours did you sleep?

Units of Time (pages 152–153)

Find the missing numbers.

5 years 9 months = ▓ months	

5 years = 5 × 1 year
      = 5 × 12 months
      = 60 months
	5 years 9 months = 60 months + 9 months
	      = 69 months

1. 12 minutes = ▓ seconds

2. 12 days = ▓ hours

3. 3 hours 25 minutes = ▓ minutes

4. 8 weeks = ▓ days

5. 12 hours = ▓ minutes

6. 7 weeks 2 days = ▓ days

7. 14 years = ▓ months

8. 5 centuries = ▓ years

 Find the number of months, weeks, days, hours, and minutes until the end of the school year.

Money *(pages 154–155)*
Count the money.

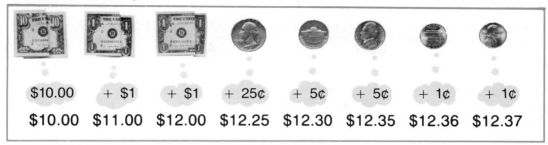

$10.00	+ $1	+ $1	+ 25¢	+ 5¢	+ 5¢	+ 1¢	+ 1¢
$10.00	$11.00	$12.00	$12.25	$12.30	$12.35	$12.36	$12.37

1.    **2.**

3.    **4.**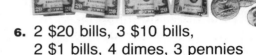

5. 1 $10 bill, 1 $5 bill, 3 $1 bills,
3 quarters, 5 dimes, 2 nickels

6. 2 $20 bills, 3 $10 bills,
2 $1 bills, 4 dimes, 3 pennies

 Find the price of something in a newspaper ad.
What coins and bills could you use to buy it?

Problem Solving: Making Change *(pages 156–157)*
Use the least number of coins and bills to make change.

	Change	🏦$10	💵$5	💵$1	half dollar	quarter	dime	nickel	penny
	$ 8.09	0	1	3	0	0	0	1	4
1.	$17.26								
2.	$ 4.77								
3.	$14.63								

4. Mr. Chambers bought lunch for
$3.47 and paid with a $10 bill.
What change should he receive?

5. Ms. Hollis bought a souvenir for
$1.26 and paid with a $5 bill.
What change should she receive?

6. George bought a tablet for 29¢
and paid with a $1 bill. What
change should he receive?

7. Mrs. Roberts bought a book for
$6.89 and paid with a $20 bill.
What should her change be?

 Use the price on a package in your kitchen. What change would
you get back from $10 using the fewest coins and bills?

Centimeter and Millimeter *(pages 160–161)*

Measure to the nearest centimeter. Then measure to the nearest millimeter.

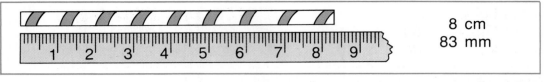

8 cm
83 mm

1. **2.** **3.**

4. The distance across a record is: **a.** 17 mm   **b.** 17 cm   **c.** 170 cm

5. The thickness of a pencil is: **a.** 6 cm   **b.** 60 cm   **c.** 6 mm

6. The width of a paper clip is: **a.** 7 cm   **b.** 7 mm   **c.** 70 mm

 Measure something in your room to the nearest centimeter.
Then measure it again to the nearest millimeter.

Meter and Kilometer *(pages 162-163)*

| The doorway is about 2 m high. |

1. A sheet of paper is about 30 ▪ long.

2. A desk is about 2 ▪ long.

3. A book is about 17 ▪ wide.

4. A person can walk about 6 ▪ in an hour.

5. A school hallway is about 3 ▪ wide.

 Give examples of things in your room that can be
measured in meters, centimeters, and millimeters.

Other Metric Units *(pages 164–165)*

| A box of breakfast food holds about 500 g of dry cereal. |

1. A tall drinking glass holds about 300 ▪ of water.

2. The mass of a bag of flour is about 5 ▪.

3. The temperature of a hot bath is about 40 ▪.

4. A perfume bottle holds 5 ▪.

5. The mass of a greeting card is about 20 ▪.

 Find the metric weight or measure of a tube of toothpaste,
a box of cereal, a can, and a container of juice or milk.

Changing Metric Units Mentally (pages 166–167)

Complete.

4 km = ■ m	5,000 kg = ■ metric tons
1 km = 1,000 m	1,000 kg = 1 metric ton
so 4 km = 4,000 m	so 5,000 kg = 5 metric tons

1. 5 m = ■ cm   **2.** 7,000 g = ■ kg   **3.** 8 L = ■ mL

4. 6,000 m = ■ km   **5.** 8 cm = ■ mm   **6.** 6,000 mm = ■ m

7. 900 cm = ■ m   **8.** 40 mm = ■ cm   **9.** 2 m = ■ mm

10. 8 kg = ■ g   **11.** 3,000 mL = ■ L   **12.** 7 metric tons = ■ kg

Find examples of items measured in metric units. Then convert
each to another metric unit. For example, change km to m.

Problem Solving: Finding Needed Facts (pages 168–169)

**What fact must you know to solve each problem?
Solve the problem if you can.**

The bottom of a trunk is 2 m long and 120 cm wide. How much greater is the length than the width?	Need the fact 1 m = 100 cm so 2 m = 200 cm	200 cm − 120 cm 80 cm
	The length is 80 cm greater than the width.	

1. Alice ran 3 km on Wednesday. She ran 2,645 m on Thursday. How many meters farther did she run on Wednesday?

2. Max used 2 m of string to wrap one package, 138 cm of string for another, and 76 cm for a third. How many centimeters of string did he use?

3. Mr. Jones's car has a mass of 1,348 kg; Mrs. Jones's car has a mass of 1,593 kg; Paul's compact has a mass of 1 metric ton. What is the total mass of the three cars in kilograms?

4. Sue should drink 1 L of milk each day. She drank 250 mL of milk at breakfast, 350 mL at lunch, and 275 mL at dinner. How much has she drunk so far? How many more milliliters should she drink?

You have a bag that holds 3 kg. Fill the bag with products
from your kitchen. List the items and the weight of each item.

425

Inch, Half-Inch, Quarter-Inch, Eighth-Inch (pages 170–171)
Measure to the nearest quarter-inch. To the nearest eighth-inch.

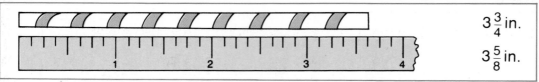

$3\frac{3}{4}$ in.

$3\frac{5}{8}$ in.

1. **2.**

3. **4.**

5. **6.**

7. the width of this book

8. the length of your pencil

9. the thickness of this book

10. the length of your shoe

 Find examples of items in your house that measure to the nearest inch, half-inch, quarter-inch, and eighth-inch.

Foot, Yard, and Mile (pages 172–173)
Complete.

5 yd 2 ft = ■ ft	Change 5 yards to feet. 5 yd = 5 × 1 yd = 5 × 3 ft = 15 ft	Add the feet. 5 yd 2 ft = 15 ft + 2 ft = 17 ft

1. 6 ft = ■ in.

2. 5 yd = ■ ft

3. 6 ft 3 in. = ■ in.

4. 4 mi = ■ yd

5. 4 ft = ■ in.

6. 6 yd 2 ft = ■ ft

7. 3 mi 440 yd = ■ yd

8. 30 ft = ■ in.

9. 6 mi 880 yd = ■ yd

Solve the problem.

10. Bill's height is 77 in. Joe's height is 5 ft 11 in. Who is taller? How much taller?

11. A marathon race has a length of 26 miles and 385 yards. What is this length in yards?

 Measure the height of two people in your family. Who is taller? How much taller?

Units of Liquid Volume *(pages 174–175)*

Complete.

3 gal 2 qt = ■ qt	Change 3 gallons to quarts.	Add the quarts.
	3 gal = 3 × 1 gal = 3 × 4 qt = 12 qt	3 gal 2 qt = 12 qt + 2 qt = 14 qt

1. 3 cups = ■ fl oz

2. 4 gal = ■ qt

3. 5 pt 1 cup = ■ cups

4. 6 qt = ■ pt

5. 16 gal = ■ qt

6. 2 cups 5 fl oz = ■ fl oz

7. 3 cups 7 fl oz = ■ fl oz

8. 2 qt 1 pt = ■ pt

9. 8 pt 1 cup = ■ cups

Solve the problem.

10. A jar contained 7 cups of water. How many fluid ounces was this?

11. The milk dispenser holds 2 gal 2 qt. How many quarts of milk will the dispenser hold?

 Estimate the total volume of all liquids in your refrigerator. Express the total in gallons, quarts, cups, and fluid ounces.

Other Customary Units *(pages 176–177)*

Complete.

7 lb 11 oz = ■ oz	Change 7 pounds to ounces.	Add the ounces.
	7 lb = 7 × 1 lb = 7 × 16 oz = 112 oz	7 lb 11 oz = 112 oz + 11 oz = 123 oz

1. 5 lb = ■ oz

2. 5 tons = ■ lb

3. 2 lb 5 oz = ■ oz

4. 3 lb = ■ oz

5. 3 tons 453 lb = ■ lb

6. 8 tons = ■ lb

7. 2 tons 1,000 lb = ■ lb

8. 4 lb 10 oz = ■ oz

9. 3 lb 7 oz = ■ oz

10. 9 tons = ■ lb

11. 8 lb = ■ oz

12. 4 tons 650 lb = ■ lb

 Find several items in your kitchen that are measured in pounds. Change each to ounces.

427

UNIT 7 Dividing by Tens and Ones

Divisors Less Than 10 (pages 190–191)

Divide.

```
    703 R5
6)4,223
  4 2
  ‾‾‾‾
    02
     0
    ‾‾
    23
    18
    ‾‾
     5
```

1. 2)43,625 2. 7)8,529 3. 9)63,548 4. 3)3,600

5. 4)12,359 6. 8)5,872 7. 5)37,689 8. 7)626

9. 6)55,236 10. 9)3,782 11. 3)81,555 12. 8)76,000

 Divide the population of your town, city, or state by the number of people in your family.

Dividing by Multiples of 10 (pages 192–193)

Divide.

```
      83 R20    Think:
50)4,170      ■ × 50 = 417
   4 00       Use 8.
   ‾‾‾‾
    170       ■ × 50 = 170
    150       Use 3.
    ‾‾‾
     20
```

1. 70)5,265 2. 50)6,436 3. 90)72,657

4. 60)57,432 5. 30)82,605 6. 80)58,436

7. 40)5,600 8. 20)96,020 9. 90)65,784

 Divide the last 4 digits of your telephone number by all 2-digit multiples of 10.

2-digit Divisors (pages 194–195)

Divide.

```
      628 R13
84)52,765
   50 4   ←— 6 × 84
   ‾‾‾‾
    2 36
    1 68   ←— 2 × 84
    ‾‾‾‾
     685
     672   ←— 8 × 84
     ‾‾‾
      13
```

1. 62)4,153 2. 21)3,024 3. 48)6,064

4. 67)15,610 5. 55)47,880 6. 39)41,707

7. 68)1,735 8. 41)3,295 9. 82)6,324

10. 24)45,700 11. 51)59,113 12. 73)90,000

 Add your zip code, your telephone number, and your house or apartment number. Divide by any 2-digit divisor.

Revising Overestimates *(pages 196–197)*

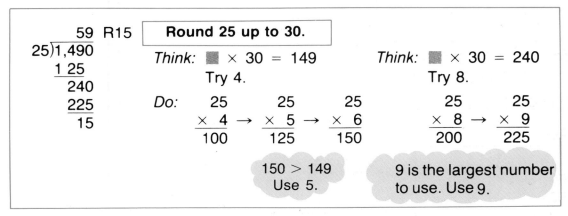

```
      57
24)1,368
   1 20     Think: ■ × 20 = 136        Think: ■ × 20 = 168
    168            Try 6.                      8 is the largest number
    168                                        to try. Try 8.
      0     Do:  24        24          24         24
                ×6   →    × 5         × 8        × 7
                144       120         192        168

        Too big!    120 < 136 ✓    Too big!    168 = 168 ✓
                      Use 5.                      Use 7.
```

1. 54)3,534 **2.** 74)2,847 **3.** 94)6,479 **4.** 83)6,081 **5.** 61)3,690

6. 44)1,260 **7.** 33)2,553 **8.** 82)4,071 **9.** 93)4,614 **10.** 54)4,644

11. 24)1,290 **12.** 44)1,230 **13.** 12)584 **14.** 34)1,675 **15.** 13)9,580

 Divide the sum of pages in any 7 books by 53, 74, 83, and 64.

Revising Underestimates *(pages 198–199)*

```
      59 R15     Round 25 up to 30.
25)1,490
   1 25          Think: ■ × 30 = 149        Think: ■ × 30 = 240
    240                 Try 4.                      Try 8.
    225          Do:   25     25     25         25       25
     15               × 4  →  × 5  →  × 6        × 8   →  × 9
                      100    125    150         200      225

                           150 > 149        9 is the largest number
                             Use 5.          to use. Use 9.
```

1. 57)3,534 **2.** 68)6,132 **3.** 95)6,479 **4.** 77)4,709 **5.** 68)3,890

6. 48)1,400 **7.** 38)2,695 **8.** 87)4,263 **9.** 97)5,290 **10.** 66)4,691

11. 27)1,290 **12.** 56)2,988 **13.** 15)584 **14.** 35)1,675 **15.** 58)5,243

Write the year of birth for each member of your family.
Add. Then divide the total by 46, 58, and 67.

Estimating Quotients *(pages 202–203)*
Estimate each quotient.

	Step 1 Find the first digit of the quotient.	
$\begin{array}{r} 6{,}000 \\ 7)\overline{44{,}440} \\ \underline{42} \phantom{{,}000} \\ 2 \phantom{{,}0000} \end{array}$		$\begin{array}{r} 700 \\ 25)\overline{19{,}087} \\ \underline{17\,5} \\ 1\,5 \end{array}$
6,000 is an estimate of 7)44,440.	Step 2 Write 0's for the other digits.	700 is an estimate of 25)19,087.

1. 4)7,632

2. 3)7,906

3. 5)23,856

4. 8)57,952

5. 2)91,746

6. 9)40,325

7. 12)745

8. 76)6,550

9. 73)56,924

10. 94)81,256

11. 52)52,301

12. 39)79,351

Add the house or apartment numbers of 10 friends. Divide the sum by 12, 27, and 33. Estimate each quotient.

Dividing Larger Numbers *(pages 204–205)*

21,016 ÷ 74 = ▪️ | **Round 74 down to 70.** |

Step 1
Divide the 210 hundreds.

$\begin{array}{r} 2 \\ 74)\overline{21{,}016} \\ \underline{14\,8} \\ 6\,21 \end{array}$

Step 2
Divide the 621 tens.

$\begin{array}{r} 28 \\ 74)\overline{21{,}016} \\ \underline{14\,8} \\ 6\,21 \\ \underline{5\,92} \\ 296 \end{array}$

Step 3
Divide the 296 ones.

$\begin{array}{r} 284 \\ 74)\overline{21{,}016} \\ \underline{14\,8} \\ 6\,21 \\ \underline{5\,92} \\ 296 \\ \underline{296} \end{array}$

1. 65)27,500

2. 52)5,097

3. 78)8,034

4. 95)28,130

5. 83)6,330

6. 38)38,114

7. 44)11,279

8. 29)27,750

9. 35)14,115

10. 23)72,930

11. 56)33,208

12. 14)86,879

Find the total net weight of all the food items on a shelf in your kitchen. Divide by 75.

Changing Units *(pages 206–207)*
Use the tables on page 206.

1,000 seconds = ■ minutes ■ seconds

1 minute = 60 seconds
How many sets of 60 seconds?

1,000 seconds = 16 minutes 40 seconds

```
        16  ← minutes
60)1,000
    60
   400
   360
    40  ← seconds
```

1. 4 ft 3 in. = ■ in.

2. 1,302 seconds = ■ minutes ■ seconds

3. 65 ft = ■ yd ■ ft

4. 2 hours 16 minutes = ■ minutes

5. 7 lb 9 oz = ■ oz

6. 120 hours = ■ days

7. 35 qt = ■ gal ■ qt

8. 5 years 8 months = ■ months

Change the width of your room from feet to inches.
Change the hours you slept last night to minutes.

Problem Solving: Two-Step Problems *(pages 208–209)*

Mr. Wall bought 2 heads of lettuce at $.94 each. He gave the clerk a $5 bill. How much change should he receive?	Change = Gave − Cost
	          = $5 − 2 at $.94 each
	
	  $.94 $5.00 He should
	  × 2 − 1.88 receive $3.12
	  $1.88 $3.12 in change.

1. Mrs. Baker bought 8 oranges for 14¢ each and a carton of milk for $1.96. How much did she spend?

2. John had $4.50. He bought 2 loaves of bread for 89¢ each. How much money did he have left?

3. Mr. Cole bought a ham for $13.65 and bread for $1.29. If he gave the clerk $20, how much should he get back?

4. Ruth spent $1.45 for bananas, $1.06 for apples, and $1.29 for oranges. How much did she spend in all?

Which is the better buy?

5. Oranges: 12 for $2.00 or 1 for 16¢

6. Jam: 1 jar for 69¢ or 3 jars for $2.00

Choose 3 or 4 items in your kitchen with prices on them. How much change would you get from $10 if you bought them?

UNIT 8 Fractions

Fractions *(pages 216–217)* **Give a fraction for the shaded part.**

Shaded → 3
In all → 7

1.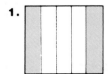

2.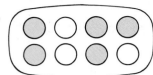

Use the fraction rulers. Write >, <, or = for ●.

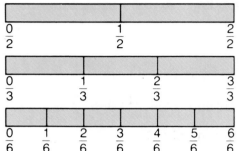

$\dfrac{2}{3}$ ● $\dfrac{4}{6}$ $\dfrac{2}{3} = \dfrac{4}{6}$

3. $\dfrac{5}{6}$ ● $\dfrac{1}{6}$ **4.** $\dfrac{2}{3}$ ● $\dfrac{3}{3}$

5. $\dfrac{2}{6}$ ● $\dfrac{1}{3}$ **6.** $\dfrac{1}{2}$ ● 0

7. $\dfrac{0}{6}$ ● $\dfrac{0}{2}$ **8.** $\dfrac{3}{3}$ ● 1

9. $\dfrac{6}{6}$ ● $\dfrac{2}{2}$ **10.** $\dfrac{1}{2}$ ● $\dfrac{3}{6}$

 What fraction of a dozen eggs is left in your refrigerator?

Multiplying to Find Equivalent Fractions *(pages 218–219)* **Complete.**

$\dfrac{3}{4} = \dfrac{\blacksquare}{20}$ Denominator 20 is 4 × 5.
So, numerator must be 3 × 5. $\dfrac{3}{4} = \dfrac{3 \times 5}{4 \times 5} = \dfrac{15}{20}$

1. $\dfrac{2}{3} = \dfrac{\blacksquare}{9}$ **2.** $\dfrac{4}{7} = \dfrac{\blacksquare}{21}$ **3.** $\dfrac{3}{8} = \dfrac{\blacksquare}{32}$ **4.** $\dfrac{5}{6} = \dfrac{\blacksquare}{12}$ **5.** $\dfrac{5}{8} = \dfrac{\blacksquare}{16}$

6. $\dfrac{3}{4} = \dfrac{\blacksquare}{16}$ **7.** $\dfrac{7}{8} = \dfrac{\blacksquare}{24}$ **8.** $\dfrac{2}{5} = \dfrac{\blacksquare}{20}$ **9.** $\dfrac{9}{10} = \dfrac{\blacksquare}{40}$ **10.** $\dfrac{4}{5} = \dfrac{\blacksquare}{10}$

Write >, <, or = for ●.

$\dfrac{2}{3}$ ● $\dfrac{5}{12}$ $\dfrac{2}{3} = \dfrac{2 \times 4}{3 \times 4} = \dfrac{8}{12}$ $\dfrac{8}{12} > \dfrac{5}{12}$ so $\dfrac{2}{3} > \dfrac{5}{12}$

11. $\dfrac{3}{5}$ ● $\dfrac{7}{10}$ **12.** $\dfrac{7}{4}$ ● $\dfrac{9}{8}$ **13.** $\dfrac{17}{10}$ ● $\dfrac{19}{10}$ **14.** $\dfrac{2}{3}$ ● $\dfrac{4}{6}$ **15.** $\dfrac{7}{10}$ ● $\dfrac{4}{5}$

Compare $\dfrac{\text{area code}}{\text{zip code}}$ with $\dfrac{\text{home address}}{\text{last 4 digits of telephone number}}$.

Comparing and Ordering Fractions *(pages 220–221)*

Write >, <, or = in the ●.

Compare $\frac{5}{6}$ and $\frac{7}{9}$.

$\frac{5}{6} = \frac{15}{18}$ 15 > 14   so $\frac{15}{18} > \frac{14}{18}$ and $\frac{5}{6} > \frac{7}{9}$

$\frac{7}{9} = \frac{14}{18}$

1. $\frac{2}{3}$ ● $\frac{7}{8}$ **2.** $\frac{3}{8}$ ● $\frac{3}{5}$ **3.** $\frac{7}{9}$ ● $\frac{7}{12}$ **4.** $\frac{1}{6}$ ● $\frac{1}{3}$ **5.** $\frac{9}{10}$ ● $\frac{2}{9}$

6. $\frac{5}{12}$ ● $\frac{1}{3}$ **7.** $\frac{2}{3}$ ● $\frac{6}{9}$ **8.** $\frac{15}{16}$ ● $\frac{5}{16}$ **9.** $\frac{2}{5}$ ● $\frac{3}{10}$ **10.** $\frac{7}{12}$ ● $\frac{3}{4}$

Put in order from least to greatest.

11. $\frac{2}{5}, \frac{3}{4}, \frac{2}{7}$ **12.** $\frac{1}{6}, \frac{1}{2}, \frac{1}{3}$ **13.** $\frac{8}{9}, \frac{5}{7}, \frac{5}{6}$

 Write fractions for the parts of a day you spend in school, playing, and sleeping.

Lowest Terms Fractions *(pages 222–223)*

Find the greatest common factor.

30 and 48	30 = 1 × 30 Factors of 30:	48 = 1 × 48 Factors of 48:	
	= 2 × 15 1,2,3,5,6,10,15,30	= 2 × 24 1,2,3,4,6,8,12,16,24,48	
	= 3 × 10	= 3 × 16	
	= 5 × 6	= 4 × 12	
		= 6 × 8	

Common factors of 30 and 48: 1,2,3,6   Greatest common factor of 30 and 48: 6

1. 15 and 25   **2.** 12 and 27   **3.** 18 and 27   **4.** 16 and 36

Give the lowest terms fraction for each.

$\frac{30}{48} = \blacksquare$ Greatest common factor: 6 $\frac{30 \div 6}{48 \div 6} = \frac{5}{8}$ **5.** $\frac{15}{25}$ **6.** $\frac{12}{27}$

7. $\frac{18}{27}$ **8.** $\frac{16}{36}$ **9.** $\frac{6}{8}$ **10.** $\frac{8}{24}$ **11.** $\frac{8}{16}$ **12.** $\frac{8}{22}$

13. $\frac{20}{32}$ **14.** $\frac{18}{60}$ **15.** $\frac{12}{28}$ **16.** $\frac{30}{50}$ **17.** $\frac{24}{42}$ **18.** $\frac{30}{45}$

 Find the lowest terms fraction for $\frac{\text{ounces in a pound}}{\text{your weight in ounces}}$.

Mixed and Standard Numerals *(pages 224–225)*

Write a lowest terms mixed numeral or a standard numeral.

$$\frac{50}{8} \qquad \begin{array}{r} 6\frac{2}{8} \\ 8\overline{)50} \\ \underline{48} \\ 2 \end{array} \qquad \begin{array}{l} \frac{2 \div 2}{8 \div 2} = \frac{1}{4} \\[4pt] \text{so } 6\frac{2}{8} = 6\frac{1}{4} \end{array} \qquad\qquad \frac{51}{17} \qquad \begin{array}{r} 3 \\ 17\overline{)51} \\ \underline{51} \\ 0 \end{array} \qquad \frac{51}{17} = 3$$

1. $\frac{7}{3}$ **2.** $\frac{17}{6}$ **3.** $\frac{21}{7}$ **4.** $\frac{0}{8}$ **5.** $\frac{24}{11}$ **6.** $\frac{12}{8}$

7. $\frac{37}{10}$ **8.** $\frac{48}{16}$ **9.** $\frac{30}{9}$ **10.** $\frac{40}{12}$ **11.** $\frac{55}{5}$ **12.** $\frac{67}{1}$

13. $\frac{73}{2}$ **14.** $\frac{72}{5}$ **15.** $\frac{60}{7}$ **16.** $\frac{120}{9}$ **17.** $\frac{50}{3}$ **18.** $\frac{72}{6}$

 Write a lowest terms mixed numeral for $\dfrac{\text{your weight in ounces}}{\text{ounces in a pound}}$.

Addition: Common Denominators *(pages 226–227)*

Add.

$$\frac{5}{16} + \frac{7}{16} = \frac{12}{16} \qquad \frac{12}{16} = \frac{12 \div 4}{16 \div 4} = \frac{3}{4} \qquad \frac{4}{5} + \frac{3}{5} = \frac{7}{5} \qquad \begin{array}{r} 1\frac{2}{5} \\ 5\overline{)7} \\ \underline{5} \\ 2 \end{array}$$
$$= \frac{3}{4} \qquad\qquad\qquad\qquad\qquad\qquad = 1\frac{2}{5}$$

1. $\frac{2}{3} + \frac{4}{3} = \blacksquare$ **2.** $\frac{4}{9} + \frac{3}{9} = \blacksquare$ **3.** $\frac{8}{7} + \frac{9}{7} = \blacksquare$ **4.** $\frac{1}{3} + \frac{1}{3} = \blacksquare$

5. $\frac{3}{2} + \frac{5}{2} = \blacksquare$ **6.** $\frac{8}{15} + \frac{4}{15} = \blacksquare$ **7.** $\frac{2}{5} + \frac{3}{5} = \blacksquare$ **8.** $\frac{1}{2} + \frac{3}{2} = \blacksquare$

9. $\frac{5}{8} + \frac{3}{8} = \blacksquare$ **10.** $\frac{2}{3} + \frac{1}{3} = \blacksquare$ **11.** $\frac{4}{9} + \frac{8}{9} = \blacksquare$ **12.** $\frac{7}{16} + \frac{9}{16} = \blacksquare$

13. $\begin{array}{r} \frac{2}{7} \\ +\frac{4}{7} \\ \hline \end{array}$ **14.** $\begin{array}{r} \frac{4}{5} \\ +\frac{4}{5} \\ \hline \end{array}$ **15.** $\begin{array}{r} \frac{3}{10} \\ +\frac{9}{10} \\ \hline \end{array}$ **16.** $\begin{array}{r} \frac{5}{6} \\ +\frac{1}{6} \\ \hline \end{array}$ **17.** $\begin{array}{r} \frac{7}{8} \\ +\frac{5}{8} \\ \hline \end{array}$ **18.** $\begin{array}{r} \frac{11}{16} \\ +\frac{15}{16} \\ \hline \end{array}$

 Add $\dfrac{\text{letters in first name}}{\text{number of letters in alphabet}} + \dfrac{\text{letters in last name}}{\text{number of letters in alphabet}}$.

Subtraction: Common Denominators *(pages 228–229)*

Subtract.

$$\frac{11}{12} - \frac{5}{12} = \frac{6}{12} \qquad \frac{6}{12} = \frac{6 \div 6}{12 \div 6} = \frac{1}{2} \qquad \frac{19}{8} - \frac{3}{8} = \frac{16}{8} \qquad \begin{array}{r} 2 \\ 8\overline{)16} \\ \underline{16} \\ 0 \end{array}$$

$$= \frac{1}{2} \qquad\qquad\qquad\qquad\qquad\qquad = 2$$

1. $\frac{7}{5} - \frac{3}{5} = $ ▧

2. $\frac{6}{7} - \frac{2}{7} = $ ▧

3. $\frac{5}{2} - \frac{3}{2} = $ ▧

4. $\frac{11}{3} - \frac{7}{3} = $ ▧

5. $\frac{18}{10} - \frac{3}{10} = $ ▧

6. $\frac{18}{9} - \frac{3}{9} = $ ▧

7. $\frac{7}{4} - \frac{1}{4} = $ ▧

8. $\frac{9}{5} - \frac{4}{5} = $ ▧

9. $\begin{array}{r} \frac{9}{2} \\ -\frac{7}{2} \\ \hline \end{array}$

10. $\begin{array}{r} \frac{11}{6} \\ -\frac{7}{6} \\ \hline \end{array}$

11. $\begin{array}{r} \frac{3}{4} \\ -\frac{3}{4} \\ \hline \end{array}$

12. $\begin{array}{r} \frac{10}{9} \\ -\frac{4}{9} \\ \hline \end{array}$

13. $\begin{array}{r} \frac{4}{5} \\ -\frac{3}{5} \\ \hline \end{array}$

14. $\begin{array}{r} \frac{25}{12} \\ -\frac{5}{12} \\ \hline \end{array}$

 Subtract $\dfrac{\text{number of eggs eaten this week}}{12}$ from $\dfrac{\text{eggs in a dozen}}{12}$.

Problem Solving: Using Fractions *(pages 230–231)*

Paul can change a bicycle tire in $\frac{1}{4}$ hour.

He needs $\frac{1}{6}$ hour to adjust a bicycle seat.

Which takes him longer to do?

It takes Paul longer to change a tire.

$$\frac{1}{4} \; ● \; \frac{1}{6}$$
$$\downarrow \qquad \downarrow$$
$$\frac{3}{12} > \frac{2}{12}$$
$$\text{so } \frac{1}{4} > \frac{1}{6}$$

1. Baylor's bike shop rented $\frac{1}{3}$ of its bikes on Saturday. On Sunday it rented $\frac{2}{7}$ of its bikes. When did the shop rent more bikes?

2. Of the bikes in Baylor's shop, $\frac{2}{9}$ are red and $\frac{1}{4}$ are blue. Are there more red bikes or blue bikes?

3. Fred rode his bike from home to the park in $\frac{4}{10}$ of an hour. He rode in the park for $\frac{1}{2}$ of an hour. Which part of his ride was longer?

4. The Penville bike club sent $\frac{3}{8}$ of its members to a cross-country race. Did more than $\frac{1}{2}$ of the members go to the race?

 Write a fraction for $\dfrac{\text{minutes spent doing homework}}{\text{minutes spent in class}}$.

Least Common Denominator *(pages 232–233)*

Find the least common multiple of each pair of numbers.

4 and 10	$4 \times 1 = 4$	$10 \times 1 = 10$	20 is the least common
	$4 \times 2 = 8$	$10 \times 2 = 20$	multiple of 4 and 10.
	$4 \times 3 = 12$		
	$4 \times 4 = 16$		
	$4 \times 5 = 20$		

1. 3 and 5 **2.** 2 and 3 **3.** 9 and 12 **4.** 8 and 10

Find equivalent fractions with the least common denominator for:

$\frac{7}{10}$ and $\frac{3}{4}$	20 is the least common denominator.	$\frac{7}{10} = \frac{14}{20}$	$\frac{3}{4} = \frac{15}{20}$

5. $\frac{3}{5}$ and $\frac{2}{3}$ **6.** $\frac{1}{2}$ and $\frac{1}{3}$ **7.** $\frac{7}{12}$ and $\frac{5}{9}$ **8.** $\frac{1}{2}$ and $\frac{5}{6}$ **9.** $\frac{3}{8}$ and $\frac{3}{10}$

10. $\frac{3}{4}$ and $\frac{4}{5}$ **11.** $\frac{1}{2}$ and $\frac{3}{5}$ **12.** $\frac{2}{3}$ and $\frac{7}{8}$ **13.** $\frac{1}{3}$ and $\frac{3}{10}$ **14.** $\frac{5}{6}$ and $\frac{9}{10}$

Write >, <, or = for ●.

15. $\frac{3}{5} ● \frac{2}{3}$ **16.** $\frac{1}{2} ● \frac{1}{3}$ **17.** $\frac{7}{12} ● \frac{5}{9}$ **18.** $\frac{1}{2} ● \frac{5}{6}$ **19.** $\frac{3}{8} ● \frac{3}{10}$

 Find the least common multiple for the number of people in your family and the number of children in your class. Find the least common denominator for $\frac{2}{3}$ and $\frac{\text{your family members}}{\text{family and relatives}}$.

Addition: Different Denominators *(pages 234–235)*

Add.

$\frac{3}{10} + \frac{2}{5} = ■$
$\frac{3}{10} + \frac{4}{10} = \frac{7}{10}$

1. $\frac{5}{7} + \frac{1}{7} = ■$ **2.** $\frac{1}{4} + \frac{5}{8} = ■$ **3.** $\frac{1}{6} + \frac{5}{12} = ■$

4. $\frac{3}{5} + \frac{4}{15} = ■$ **5.** $\frac{2}{3} + \frac{11}{12} = ■$ **6.** $\frac{1}{2} + \frac{5}{10} = ■$

7. $\begin{array}{r} \frac{5}{12} \\ + \frac{3}{4} \\ \hline \end{array}$ **8.** $\begin{array}{r} \frac{3}{2} \\ + \frac{1}{4} \\ \hline \end{array}$ **9.** $\begin{array}{r} \frac{5}{6} \\ + \frac{7}{24} \\ \hline \end{array}$ **10.** $\begin{array}{r} \frac{1}{6} \\ + \frac{2}{3} \\ \hline \end{array}$ **11.** $\begin{array}{r} \frac{5}{16} \\ + \frac{3}{8} \\ \hline \end{array}$ **12.** $\begin{array}{r} \frac{3}{10} \\ + \frac{13}{20} \\ \hline \end{array}$

 Add $\frac{\text{glasses of milk this week}}{\text{glasses of milk last week}} + \frac{\text{glasses of juice this week}}{\text{glasses of juice last week}}$.

Subtraction: Different Denominators *(pages 236–237)*

Subtract.

$$\frac{9}{10} - \frac{4}{5} = \blacksquare$$
$$\downarrow \qquad \downarrow$$
$$\frac{9}{10} - \frac{8}{10} = \frac{1}{10}$$

1. $\frac{5}{7} - \frac{3}{7} = \blacksquare$

2. $\frac{7}{12} - \frac{1}{6} = \blacksquare$

3. $\frac{3}{4} - \frac{5}{12} = \blacksquare$

4. $\frac{9}{14} - \frac{2}{7} = \blacksquare$

5. $\frac{3}{6} - \frac{1}{2} = \blacksquare$

6. $\frac{11}{15} - \frac{3}{5} = \blacksquare$

7. $\frac{7}{8} - \frac{1}{2} = \blacksquare$

8. $\frac{5}{6} - \frac{13}{24} = \blacksquare$

9. $\frac{2}{3} - \frac{5}{12} = \blacksquare$

10. $\frac{11}{20} - \frac{2}{5} = \blacksquare$

11. $\begin{array}{r} \frac{15}{16} \\ -\frac{3}{4} \\ \hline \end{array}$

12. $\begin{array}{r} \frac{3}{2} \\ -\frac{7}{10} \\ \hline \end{array}$

13. $\begin{array}{r} \frac{7}{16} \\ -\frac{3}{8} \\ \hline \end{array}$

14. $\begin{array}{r} \frac{4}{3} \\ -\frac{2}{9} \\ \hline \end{array}$

15. $\begin{array}{r} \frac{7}{8} \\ -\frac{1}{2} \\ \hline \end{array}$

16. $\begin{array}{r} \frac{7}{10} \\ -\frac{13}{40} \\ \hline \end{array}$

 Subtract using $\dfrac{\text{eggs eaten this week}}{12}$ and $\dfrac{\text{glasses of milk this week}}{16}$.

Multiplication *(pages 240–241)*

Multiply.

$$\frac{4}{5} \times \frac{7}{8} \;=\; \frac{4 \times 7}{5 \times 8} \;=\; \frac{28}{40} \;=\; \frac{28 \div 4}{40 \div 4} \;=\; \frac{7}{10}$$

1. $\frac{1}{3} \times \frac{2}{5} = \blacksquare$

2. $5 \times \frac{2}{3} = \blacksquare$

3. $\frac{1}{4} \times \frac{5}{6} = \blacksquare$

4. $\frac{5}{6} \times \frac{2}{3} = \blacksquare$

5. $\frac{3}{5} \times \frac{7}{8} = \blacksquare$

6. $\frac{5}{6} \times \frac{6}{5} = \blacksquare$

7. $4 \times \frac{2}{9} = \blacksquare$

8. $\frac{1}{2} \times \frac{1}{3} = \blacksquare$

9. $\frac{5}{2} \times \frac{4}{3} = \blacksquare$

10. $\frac{2}{5} \times \frac{4}{5} = \blacksquare$

11. $\frac{1}{4} \times 10 = \blacksquare$

12. $\frac{1}{5} \times \frac{3}{8} = \blacksquare$

13. $\frac{2}{5} \times \frac{3}{4} = \blacksquare$

14. $\frac{5}{12} \times 3 = \blacksquare$

15. $\frac{3}{8} \times \frac{5}{9} = \blacksquare$

16. $\frac{2}{3} \times \frac{2}{3} = \blacksquare$

17. $\frac{5}{8} \times \frac{7}{10} = \blacksquare$

18. $\frac{2}{3} \times \frac{3}{2} = \blacksquare$

19. $6 \times \frac{3}{2} = \blacksquare$

20. $\frac{7}{12} \times \frac{9}{10} = \blacksquare$

 Multiply $\dfrac{\text{number of boxes on a shelf}}{\text{number of cans on a shelf}}$ by $\dfrac{2}{3}$.

Finding Parts of Numbers *(pages 242–243)*

Find.

$$\frac{3}{4} \text{ of } 17 \text{ is } \frac{3}{4} \times 17$$

$$\frac{3}{4} \times 17 = \frac{3}{4} \times \frac{17}{1} \quad\cdots\cdots\quad 17 = \frac{17}{1}$$

$$= \frac{3 \times 17}{4 \times 1} = \frac{51}{4} = 12\frac{3}{4} \quad\cdots\cdots$$

$$4\overline{)51}^{\ 12\frac{3}{4}}$$
$$\frac{4}{11}$$
$$\frac{8}{3}$$

1. $\frac{1}{2}$ of 6 **2.** $\frac{2}{3}$ of 12 **3.** $\frac{3}{5}$ of 10 **4.** $\frac{5}{6}$ of 9 **5.** $\frac{2}{7}$ of 14

6. $\frac{3}{8}$ of 11 **7.** $\frac{3}{4}$ of $\frac{2}{3}$ **8.** $\frac{5}{3}$ of $\frac{3}{10}$ **9.** $\frac{1}{2}$ of 25 **10.** $\frac{3}{4}$ of 52

11. $\frac{2}{3}$ of 24 **12.** $\frac{1}{2}$ of $\frac{5}{8}$ **13.** $\frac{5}{8}$ of $\frac{9}{5}$ **14.** $\frac{4}{5}$ of 16 **15.** $\frac{2}{3}$ of 17

 Find $\frac{1}{2}, \frac{1}{4}, \frac{3}{4}, \frac{1}{3}, \frac{2}{3}$ of all the books in your house.

Division *(pages 244–245)*

Divide. Write the answer in lowest terms.

$$\frac{2}{5} \div \frac{1}{2} = \frac{2}{5} \times \frac{2}{1} = \frac{4}{5}$$

$$7 \div \frac{1}{4} = \frac{7}{1} \times \frac{4}{1} = 28$$

1. $\frac{7}{8} \div \frac{2}{3} = \blacksquare$ **2.** $\frac{2}{4} \div \frac{6}{7} = \blacksquare$ **3.** $\frac{9}{2} \div \frac{7}{5} = \blacksquare$

4. $4 \div \frac{3}{5} = \blacksquare$ **5.** $\frac{4}{3} \div \frac{1}{2} = \blacksquare$ **6.** $\frac{1}{8} \div \frac{11}{4} = \blacksquare$

7. $\frac{8}{5} \div \frac{1}{5} = \blacksquare$ **8.** $\frac{7}{2} \div \frac{1}{3} = \blacksquare$ **9.** $\frac{12}{3} \div \frac{1}{2} = \blacksquare$ **10.** $\frac{5}{6} \div \frac{1}{7} = \blacksquare$ **11.** $3 \div \frac{4}{5} = \blacksquare$

12. $\frac{13}{4} \div \frac{1}{4} = \blacksquare$ **13.** $\frac{3}{4} \div \frac{1}{12} = \blacksquare$ **14.** $\frac{10}{2} \div \frac{2}{3} = \blacksquare$ **15.** $\frac{6}{5} \div \frac{9}{2} = \blacksquare$ **16.** $5 \div \frac{1}{2} = \blacksquare$

17. $2 \div \frac{8}{10} = \blacksquare$ **18.** $\frac{1}{11} \div \frac{3}{4} = \blacksquare$ **19.** $\frac{7}{2} \div \frac{1}{2} = \blacksquare$ **20.** $\frac{6}{4} \div \frac{3}{8} = \blacksquare$ **21.** $9 \div \frac{2}{5} = \blacksquare$

 Divide your age by $\frac{5}{3}, \frac{2}{4}, \frac{1}{10}$, and $\frac{12}{8}$.

Problem Solving Strategy: Choosing the Operation *(pages 246–247)*

Shirley painted $\frac{3}{8}$ of the fence and Stan painted $\frac{1}{5}$ of the fence. Together, what part had they painted?

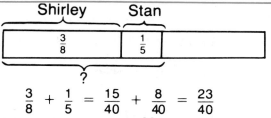

$$\frac{3}{8} + \frac{1}{5} = \frac{15}{40} + \frac{8}{40} = \frac{23}{40}$$

Together they had painted $\frac{23}{40}$ of the fence.

1. Bill must read $\frac{1}{3}$ of a book for homework this weekend. He has already read $\frac{1}{5}$ of the book. How much more does he have to read?

2. Ann is going to plant tomatoes in $\frac{1}{5}$ of her garden. She has already planted $\frac{2}{3}$ of the tomatoes. What part of the garden has she planted?

3. Frank had $\frac{4}{5}$ box of crayons. He gave Mark $\frac{1}{3}$ box of crayons. What part of a box of crayons did Frank have left?

4. Harold's book contains 438 pages. Harold has already read $\frac{2}{3}$ of the book. How many pages has he read?

 Choose a school book other than this one. If you have finished $\frac{2}{3}$ of it, how many pages are left?

Problem Solving: Data from Circle Graphs *(pages 248–249)*
Use the circle graphs on pages 248-249.

Ms. Mallory's income each month is $1,500. How much does she plan to spend for food?

$$\frac{1}{4} \text{ of } \$1500 = \frac{1}{4} \times \frac{1500}{1} = \frac{1500}{4}$$
$$= 375$$

She plans to spend $375 for food.

1. What part more of her income does Ms. Mallory plan to spend for food than for transportation?

2. Ms. Mallory's salary was raised to $400 weekly. How much should she save each week?

3. How much of his $1,440 monthly income does Mr. Cooper plan to spend on clothing?

4. What part of his income does Mr. Cooper spend on food and travel?

 Think of a weekly allowance that you would like. If you spent $\frac{3}{5}$ of your allowance for the month, how much is left?

UNIT 9 Adding and Subtracting with Decimals

Tenths *(pages 256–257)*

Write a standard decimal to tell how much is shaded. Then name the place of each digit.

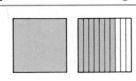
1.7
1 is in the ones place.
7 is in the tenths place.

1.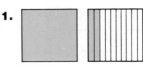

2. **3.** 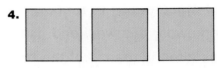 **4.**

Write the standard decimal.

5. 6 ones 7 tenths   **6.** 3 tenths   **7.** 2 tens 5 ones 9 tenths

8. forty and two tenths   **9.** sixteen point zero   **10.** zero point eight

 Divide the number of pages in a book into tenths. Write a decimal to show how many tenths you have read.

Hundredths *(pages 258–259)*

Write a standard decimal to tell how much is shaded. Then name the place of each digit.

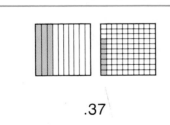
.37
3 is in the tenths place.
7 is in the hundredths place.

1.   **2.**

3. 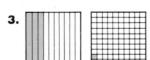 **4.**

Write the standard decimal.

5. 6 ones 3 tenths 8 hundredths   **6.** 2 tens 8 ones 9 tenths 7 hundredths

7. five and ninety-six hundredths   **8.** three hundredths

 Divide a square into hundredths. Shade one hundredth for each relative. Write a decimal to show the total.

Thousandths *(pages 260–261)*

In each decimal name the place of the digit 3.
Then tell what the digit 3 means.

> 2.134 3 is in the hundredths place.
> The digit 3 means 3 hundredths.

1. 0.423

2. 5.367

3. 1.023

4. 4.937

Write the standard decimal. Name the digit in the thousandths place.

5. two and four hundred seventy-two thousandths

6. three hundred forty-seven thousandths

7. one and two thousandths

8. seventy-five thousandths

9. four thousandths

10. six and ninety thousandths

11. Tell what each digit means in the decimal 0.817.

Write the standard decimal.

12. 2 ones 6 tenths 7 hundredths 4 thousandths

13. 0 tenths 5 hundredths 9 thousandths

Make a decimal to the thousandths place using your telephone number.
Tell what each digit means.

Comparing and Ordering with Decimals *(pages 262–263)*

Write >, <, or = for ●.

> 6.02 ● 6.1
> 6.02
> 6.1
> 0 < 1 so
> 6.02 < 6.1

1. .8 ● .78

2. 241.7 ● 214.7

3. 1.00 ● 9.9

4. 7.2 ● 6.7

5. 5.62 ● 5.6

6. .04 ● .4

7. 3.02 ● 3.0

8. .6 ● .60

9. 4.7 ● 4.07

Write in order from least to greatest.

10. 3; 1.4; .08

11. 6; 4.18; 5.7

12. .11; .10; .01; 1.0

Find 3 containers whose contents are marked to tenths and hundredths.
Write the decimals in order from least to greatest.

Rounding Decimals *(pages 264–265)*
Round to the nearest tenth. To the nearest one.

25.47	$\begin{array}{r} 25.\textcircled{4}\,7 \\ +\quad 1 \\ \hline 25.\;5 \end{array}$	$7 > 5$ Round up.	$\begin{array}{r} 2\,\textcircled{5}.\,4\,7 \\ \downarrow \\ 2\;5 \end{array}$	$4 < 5$ Round down.	

1. 6.82   **2.** 4.37   **3.** 9.23   **4.** 6.95   **5.** 8.03   **6.** 12.05

7. 12.73   **8.** 9.36   **9.** 7.92   **10.** 3.25   **11.** 0.45   **12.** 29.97

 Find the sum and difference between two containers marked to tenths and hundredths. Estimate to check.

Adding with Decimals *(pages 268–269)*
Add.

$$2.5 + .78 = \blacksquare$$
$$\begin{array}{r} 2.50 \\ +\ .78 \\ \hline 3.28 \end{array}$$

1. $\begin{array}{r} 5.38 \\ +1.92 \end{array}$ **2.** $\begin{array}{r} 16.35 \\ +\ 9.72 \end{array}$ **3.** $\begin{array}{r} \$12 \\ +\quad 4.35 \end{array}$ **4.** $\begin{array}{r} 36.5 \\ +21.64 \end{array}$

5. $\begin{array}{r} \$19.49 \\ +\quad 8.68 \end{array}$ **6.** $\begin{array}{r} 24.6 \\ +17.29 \end{array}$ **7.** $\begin{array}{r} 132.8 \\ +\ 69 \end{array}$ **8.** $\begin{array}{r} 27.67 \\ +84.4 \end{array}$

9. $18 + $.49 = $\blacksquare$ **10.** 17 + 3.2 + 5.61 = $\blacksquare$ **11.** 25 + 6.7 + .09 = $\blacksquare$

 Find the cost of two items in your refrigerator. Add that total to $15.

Subtracting with Decimals *(pages 270–271)*
Subtract.

$$\$20 - \$6.07 = \blacksquare$$
$$\begin{array}{r} \overset{9\ \ 9}{\underset{}{1\ \cancel{10}\,\cancel{10}\,10}} \\ \$\cancel{2}\,\cancel{0}.\,\cancel{0}\,\cancel{0} \\ -\ 6.07 \\ \hline \$13.93 \end{array}$$

1. $\begin{array}{r} \$62.07 \\ -\ 15.29 \end{array}$ **2.** $\begin{array}{r} 18.7 \\ -\ 9.2 \end{array}$ **3.** $\begin{array}{r} 65 \\ -18.3 \end{array}$ **4.** $\begin{array}{r} \$14 \\ -\ 9.36 \end{array}$

5. $\begin{array}{r} 12.3 \\ -\ 2.53 \end{array}$ **6.** $\begin{array}{r} 61 \\ -\ 6.7 \end{array}$ **7.** $\begin{array}{r} \$400 \\ -\ 84.65 \end{array}$ **8.** $\begin{array}{r} 14.2 \\ -14.16 \end{array}$

9. 20.4 − 19.6 = $\blacksquare$ **10.** $137.25 − $82.75 = $\blacksquare$

 Find the difference between two containers whose contents are marked to tenths and hundredths.

Problem Solving: Estimating with Decimals *(pages 272–273)*

Nancy ran 2.73 kilometers. She walked
another 1.45 kilometers. About how far did
Nancy travel in all?

about 4 kilometers

$$2.73 \longrightarrow 3$$
$$+1.45 \longrightarrow +1$$
$$4$$

1. Dale rode his bicycle 6.85 km.
   He walked another 2.04 km.
   About how far did Dale travel in
   all?

2. Peter spent $17.59 for a shirt and
   $8.29 for a tie. Was $25 enough to
   pay for his purchases?

2. Amy has a mass of 38.625 kg.
   Kim has a mass of 41.195 kg.
   About how much greater is
   Kim's mass?

4. A horse can run at 76.48 km/h.
   A human can run at 44.9 km/h.
   About how much faster can a
   horse run?

 Make a list of the distances you walk during one day.
Then, estimate the total distance.

Problem Solving: Using Decimals *(pages 274–275)*

The class high jump
record is 1.85 meters.
Rhonda jumped 1.805
meters. How close was
she to the record?

Subtract to find
how much more.

$$\overset{4\ 10}{1.8\,\cancel{5}\,\cancel{0}}$$
$$-1.805$$
$$0.045$$

She was
0.045 meters
close to
the record.

1. Anne bought a radio for $38, a
   record for $5.98, and a tape for
   $7.27. How much did she spend
   all together?

2. Joe high-jumped 1.752 m.
   Willie high-jumped 1.847 m.
   Who jumped higher? How much
   higher?

3. At the beginning of a speed-
   reading course, Marilyn could
   read 500 words in 3.34 minutes.
   After a week, she could read
   500 words in 2.16 minutes. How
   much faster can she read?

4. Bob bought a shirt for $7.49, a
   pair of jeans for $15, and a pair
   of boots for $22.50. How much
   did the clothes cost all together?
   How much more did the boots
   cost than the shirt?

 Find the total cost of the most expensive item and the least expensive item
you can find in the newspaper.

443

UNIT 10 Geometry and Measurement

Points, Lines, and Planes *(pages 282–283)*

Give two names for each line segment in this figure.

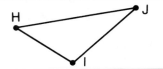

$\overline{HJ}$ and $\overline{JH}$
$\overline{HI}$ and $\overline{IH}$
$\overline{IJ}$ and $\overline{JI}$

Name:

1. two parallel lines

2. four line segments

3. two intersecting lines

4. two other names for $\overleftrightarrow{CD}$

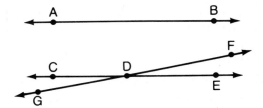

 Draw four intersecting lines. Label each point of intersection and each line segment.

Rays and Angles *(pages 284–285)*

Use the pictures. Name:

each angle	∠XYZ, ∠PRQ

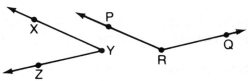

1. each ray   2. the sides of each angle   3. the vertex of each angle

Draw points S, T, and U that are not on a line. Then draw:

4. $\overrightarrow{SU}$ 5. $\overrightarrow{US}$ 6. $\overline{TS}$ 7. ∠STU   8. ∠SUT

 Draw three intersecting lines. Label each point and each line segment. Then name each angle.

Measuring Angles *(pages 286–287)*

Use the protractors and angles on page 287.

m ∠RQX = 110°

1. m∠SQX = ▓   2. m∠ADF = ▓

3. m∠ADG = ▓   4. m∠EDC = ▓   5. m∠EDB = ▓

Use your protractor to measure these angles.

6.
7.
8.

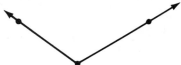

 Draw four angles. Measure each angle with your protractor.

Polygons   *(pages 288–289)*

Match.

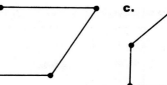

Triangle **f**

1. Pentagon

2. Decagon

3. Hexagon

4. Quadrilateral

5. Octagon

6. Which of the polygons drawn are regular polygons?

7. Copy VWXYZ. Draw and name all of its diagonals.

 Design your own polygon. Label each vertex. Then draw and name all of its diagonals.

Kinds of Angles and Triangles   *(pages 290–291)*

Use this picture. Name:

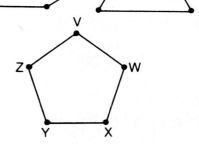

an acute angle ∠UXV or ∠TXU or ∠SXT or ∠TXV

1. a right angle

2. an obtuse angle

Select one word from a. and one from b. to describe each triangle.

a. acute, right, obtuse

b. isosceles (but not equilateral), equilateral, scalene

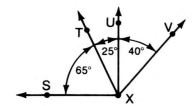

right, scalene

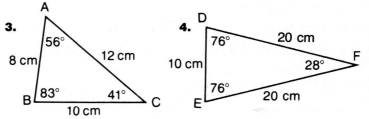

 Draw four triangles. Tell what kind of triangle each one is. Measure each angle.

445

Special Quadrilaterals   *(pages 292–293)*

Use these figures.

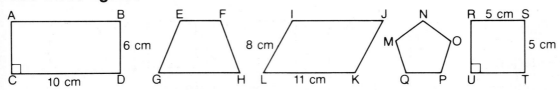

Which are:

squares?
RSTU

1. quadrilaterals?   **2.** rectangles?   **3.** parallelograms?

Give: **4.** the side opposite $\overline{IJ}$ **5.** the sides adjacent to $\overline{EF}$

6. the length of $\overline{JK}$ **7.** the length of $\overline{AB}$

8. the length of $\overline{UT}$ **9.** the length of $\overline{IJ}$

 Find examples of the above figures in and around your home and neighborhood. Tell what each example is.

Circles   *(pages 294–295)*

Use this circle to name the following:

circle   circle 0

1. center   **2.** three radii   **3.** three chords   **4.** diameter

5. a radius that is not part of the diameter drawn

6. a radius that is part of the diameter shown

Copy circle M. Use your copy.

7. Draw and name a diameter.

8. Draw and name a chord that is not a diameter.

9. Name a radius that is part of the diameter you have drawn.

10. Draw and name a radius that is not part of the diameter you have drawn.

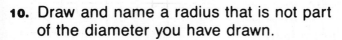 Trace something circular in your home. Draw and name a diameter, a chord, and a radius.

Similarity and Congruence   *(pages 296–297)*

Are the figures similar?

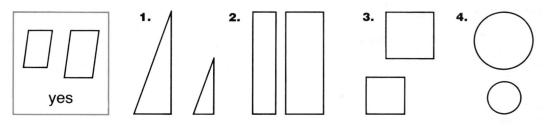

yes

Are the figures congruent?

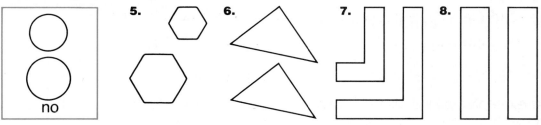

no

 Look for figures around your home that are similar or congruent. Make a list for each.

Symmetry   *(pages 298–299)*

How many lines of symmetry does each figure have?

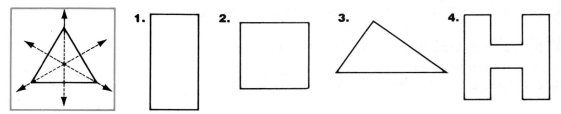

Copy and complete each figure so that the heavy line is a line of symmetry.

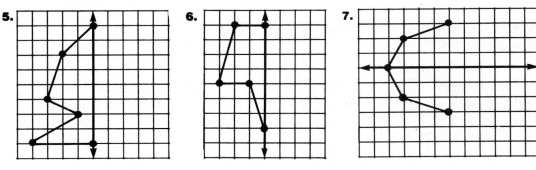

 Design your own shape. Draw each line of symmetry.

447

Locating Points on a Grid *(pages 300–301)*

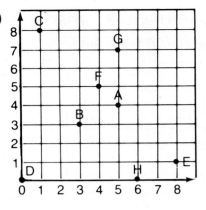

(5,7) G
5 spaces right
7 spaces up

Give the letter for each number pair.

1. (1,8) **2.** (4,5)

3. (5,4)

Give the number pair for each point.

4. D **5.** B **6.** E **7.** H

Copy this grid. Locate the points and draw the line segments.

8. I (1,1), J (3,1), K (7,1), L (9,1)

9. M (7,5), N (6,7), O (5,6), P (4,7), Q (3,5)

10. $\overline{IL}$, $\overline{KM}$, $\overline{MN}$, $\overline{NO}$, $\overline{OP}$, $\overline{PQ}$, $\overline{QJ}$

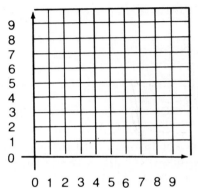

 Draw a grid. Place 6 points anywhere. Write the number pair that gives the location for each point.

Perimeter   *(pages 304–305)*

Find the perimeter of each polygon.

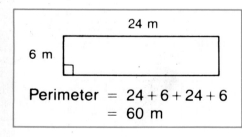

Perimeter = 24 + 6 + 24 + 6
= 60 m

1.

11 cm
11 cm   11 cm
11 cm   11 cm
11 cm

2.

12 cm
15 cm

3. a rectangle with
length: 38 m
width: 15 m

4. a rectangle with
length: 86 cm
width: 52 cm

5. a square with length
of one side: 14 m

 Find the perimeter of as many objects in your room as you can.

448   **Homework**

Area *(pages 306–307)*
Find the area of each figure.

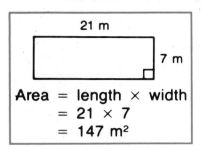

21 m

7 m

Area = length × width
= 21 × 7
= 147 m²

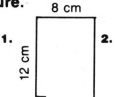

1. 8 cm / 12 cm

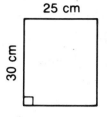

2. 25 cm / 30 cm

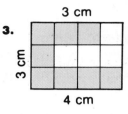

3. 3 cm / 3 cm / 4 cm

Complete this table. Each figure is a rectangle.

	4.	**5.**	**6.**	**7.**	**8.**	**9.**
length (m)	6	10	5	15	1	9
width (m)	2	9	5	1	1	■
perimeter (m)	■	■	■	■	■	■
area (m²)	■	■	■	■	■	36

 Measure the length and width of your bed, bureau top, rug, window. Find the area of each.

Solids *(pages 308–309)*
Name the object that each of these objects is the most like.

rectangular prism

1.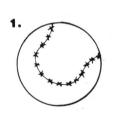

2.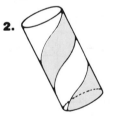

3.

4.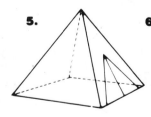

5.

6.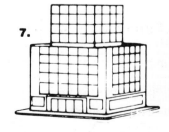

7.

 Find examples in and around your home of rectangular prisms, cubes, cylinders, spheres, cones, and pyramids.

449

Volume *(pages 310–311)*

Find the volume of each rectangular prism.

length: 16 cm	volume = length × width × height	16	④ 160
width: 10 cm	= 16 × 10 × 7	×10	× 7
height: 7 cm	= 1,120 cm³	160	1,120

	1.	2.	3.	4.	5.	6.	7.
length	5 cm	13 cm	70 m	11 m	100 cm	20 m	400 cm
width	4 cm	6 cm	50 m	11 m	50 cm	10 m	1 cm
height	3 cm	12 cm	40 m	11 m	30 cm	5 m	1 cm
volume	■	■	■	■	■	■	■

 Measure a box in your kitchen. Then find the volume.

Problem Solving: Using Customary Units *(pages 312–313)*

Find the perimeter and area of each rectangle.

6 ft ▭ 16 ft	Perimeter = 6+16+6+16 = 44 ft	Area = length × width = 16 × 6 = 96 ft²

	1.	2.	3.	4.	5.	6.	7.
length	12 yd	20 ft	14 in.	20 yd	25 ft	56 in.	■
width	9 yd	6 ft	14 in.	15 yd	12 ft	27 in.	3 in.
perimeter	■	■	■	■	■	■	■
area	■	■	■	■	■	■	45 in²

Find the volume of each rectangular prism.

	8.	9.	10.	11.	12.	13.	14.
length	7 ft	15 in.	13 yd	250 ft	8 in.	14 yd	50 ft
width	6 ft	10 in.	13 yd	30 ft	6 in.	7 yd	24 ft
height	5 ft	10 in.	13 yd	50 ft	5 in.	3 yd	16 ft
volume	■	■	■	■	■	■	■

 Find the perimeter of the front panel of a box or package.
Then find the volume of the same box or package.

UNIT 11 Multiplying and Dividing with Decimals

Estimating Decimal Products and Quotients *(pages 320–321)*
Estimate the product or quotient.

```
634 →   600
×.057 →×  .06
        36.00


    .07
53) 3.816
     0
    3 81      Stop.
    3 71
      10
```

1. 3.2   **2.** .12   **3.** 9.4   **4.** 196.4
      ×4.6   ×2.6   ×6.1   × .82

5. .89   **6.** 7.214   **7.** .11   **8.** 37
      ×7.3   ×   58   × .3   ×.012

9. 6)4.986   **10.** 3).219   **11.** 8)36.256   **12.** 4)170.8

13. 25)13.25   **14.** 57)3.648   **15.** 13)811.07   **16.** 34)80.852

 Multiply and divide using the prices of any two items.
Estimate the product and the quotient.

Multiplying with Decimals *(pages 322–323)*

Multiply.

```
  ⊗⊗
 8.47      2 places
× 1.6    + 1 place
 5082
 8470
13.552     3 places
```

1. 2.7   **2.** 2.43   **3.** 2.4
      × .9   × 7.6   ×.53

4. 4.76   **5.** 4.76   **6.** .65
      × 39   × 3.9   ×6.5

7. 3.7   **8.** 94.2   **9.** 1.352   **10.** .79   **11.** $36.75
      ×9.4   × .46   ×   78   ×1.9   ×   24

12. .6 × .74 = ▆   **13.** .25 × $124 = ▆   **14.** 9.3 × 2.6 = ▆

15. .35 × 4.8 = ▆   **16.** 3.4 × .27 = ▆   **17.** .15 × $61 = ▆

 Find the cost of an item in the newspaper. Multiply it by 204.

More Multiplying with Decimals *(pages 324–325)*

Multiply.

```
 ③
.16      2 places
×.06   + 2 places
.0096    4 places
```

1. .36
× .4

2. 2.36
× 7.1

3. 1.3
×.08

4. 1.4
×.61

5. 27.8
× .09

6. .06
× .1

7. .04 × 3.6 = ■

8. .002 × 48 = ■

9. .7 × .9 = ■

10. .2 × .03 = ■

11. .05 × $14 = ■

12. .2 × $7.25 = ■

 Put a decimal point after the second digit of your address.
Multiply by 2.8.

Dividing with Decimals *(pages 328–329)*

Divide.

```
   .584        Check
7)4.088         ⑤②
  35           .584
  58         ×     7
  56         4.088 ✓
  28
  28
   0
```

1. 3)73.95

2. 5)4.915

3. 2)569.8

4. 6)25.434

5. 9)7.911

6. 7)342.72

7. 8)6.128

8. 6)210.72

9. 5)3.895

10. 36)12.24

11. 84)291.48

12. 45)787.5

 Add a decimal point to any 4-digit number you can find in the
newspaper. Add 0 at the end. Then divide it by 25.

Zeros in Quotients *(pages 330–331)*

Divide.

```
  .083
6).498     Place the
  0        decimal point
  49       and write
  48       this 0!
  18
  18
   0
```

1. 2)2.086

2. 7).413

3. 4)129.84

4. 8)32.184

5. 6).522

6. 9)18.972

7. 5)10.165

8. 3)3.024

9. 7).056

10. 62)5.58

11. 93).744

12. 27)2.403

 Add a decimal point and a 0 to the beginning of your address.
Divide the number by your age.

Problem Solving Strategy: Choosing the Operation *(pages 332–333)*

Solve the problems.

Angelo bought 2.9 kg of celery. He used .35 of it for a salad. How much celery did he use?	Multiply to find part. .35 of 2.9 = .35 × 2.9	2.9 × .35 145 870 1.015	Angelo used 1.015 kg.

1. Ted bought a bottle of milk containing 2.4 L. He drank .45 of it. How much milk did he drink?

2. Sue had 2.4 L of juice. She put the same amount into 2 pitchers. How much was in each pitcher?

3. Mr. Thomas's salary is $1,574 per month. He pays .24 of this for rent. How much is his rent?

4. The coach bought 12 shirts for $82.08. How much did each shirt cost?

 Find the cost of something you would like to buy. Then calculate your state's sales tax and find the total price.

Problem Solving: Discounts *(pages 334–335)*

Ms. Hanson bought a desk at "25% off." The regular price was $275. What was the sale price?	Sale Price = Regular Price − Discount Discount = .25 of $275 = .25 × $275 = $68.75 *sale price*	$275.00 − 68.75 $206.25

Complete the table.

	Item	Regular Price	Part Off	Discount	Sale Price
1.	Jeans	$18	10%	■	■
2.	Jacket	$24	30%	■	■
3.	Sneakers	$16	$\frac{1}{4}$	■	■
4.	Shirt	$15	$\frac{2}{5}$	■	■
5.	Cap	$ 8	15%	■	■
6.	Raincoat	$12	$\frac{1}{3}$	■	■
7.	Sweater	$14	20%	■	■

 Find the cost of something you would like. What would it cost at 10%, 15%, 25%, and 33% off?

UNIT 12 Mixed Numerals

Fractions and Mixed Numerals *(pages 342–343)*

Give a mixed numeral or standard numeral for each.

$$\frac{47}{6} \qquad 7\frac{5}{6} \\ 6\overline{)47} \\ \underline{42} \\ 5$$

1. $\frac{9}{2}$ 2. $\frac{24}{3}$ 3. $\frac{29}{7}$ 4. $\frac{32}{5}$ 5. $\frac{59}{4}$

6. $\frac{108}{9}$ 7. $\frac{51}{8}$ 8. $\frac{72}{6}$ 9. $\frac{47}{10}$ 10. $\frac{65}{12}$

Give a fraction for each.

$$2\frac{7}{8} = \frac{(2\times 8)+7}{8} \\ = \frac{23}{8}$$

11. $1\frac{5}{6}$ 12. $4\frac{3}{5}$ 13. $8\frac{1}{9}$ 14. $6\frac{2}{3}$ 15. $5\frac{3}{7}$

16. $7\frac{4}{9}$ 17. $10\frac{1}{2}$ 18. $14\frac{3}{4}$ 19. $4\frac{3}{8}$ 20. $2\frac{3}{10}$

 Give a mixed numeral or standard numeral for
$\dfrac{\text{sum of ages for your family}}{\text{number of people in your family}}$.

Addition and Subtraction with Mixed Numerals *(pages 344–345)*
Add or subtract.

$$4\frac{1}{5} \qquad 6\frac{4}{7} \\ +3\frac{2}{5} \qquad -2\frac{2}{7} \\ \overline{} \qquad \overline{} \\ 7\frac{3}{5} \qquad 4\frac{2}{7}$$

1. $5\frac{3}{9}$ $+3\frac{2}{9}$ 2. $7\frac{3}{10}$ $-4\frac{2}{10}$ 3. $3\frac{2}{5}$ $+2\frac{1}{5}$ 4. $3\frac{5}{8}$ $-1\frac{2}{8}$ 5. $6\frac{1}{6}$ $+6\frac{3}{6}$

6. $5\frac{1}{12} + 4\frac{1}{12} = \blacksquare$ 7. $14\frac{8}{10} - 11\frac{2}{10} = \blacksquare$ 8. $3\frac{2}{9} + 4\frac{4}{9} = \blacksquare$

 Subtract your age from an adult's age. Express in fractions.

More Addition and Subtraction with Mixed Numerals *(pages 346–347)*
Add or subtract.

$$4\frac{1}{5} + 3\frac{3}{4} \rightarrow 4\frac{4}{20} + 3\frac{15}{20} = 7\frac{19}{20}$$

$$8\frac{4}{5} - 2\frac{1}{10} \rightarrow 8\frac{8}{10} - 2\frac{1}{10} = 6\frac{7}{10}$$

1. $4\frac{1}{6}$ $+7\frac{3}{4}$ 2. $4\frac{9}{10}$ $-1\frac{3}{4}$ 3. $7\frac{2}{9}$ $+6\frac{1}{18}$ 4. $8\frac{7}{12}$ $-4\frac{1}{6}$

5. $5\frac{1}{2}$ $+4\frac{2}{7}$ 6. $9\frac{7}{8}$ $-6\frac{1}{16}$ 7. $8\frac{1}{5}$ $+5\frac{3}{4}$ 8. $6\frac{4}{7}$ $-3\frac{2}{21}$

 What fraction of a gallon of milk or juice have you
had this week? Add to find the total.

Addition with Mixed Numerals: Renaming *(pages 348–349)*

Add.

$$5\frac{3}{4} \rightarrow 5\frac{9}{12}$$
$$+2\frac{5}{6} \rightarrow +2\frac{10}{12}$$
$$7\frac{19}{12} = 7 + 1\frac{7}{12}$$
$$= 8\frac{7}{12}$$

1. $7\frac{9}{10}$ $+3\frac{3}{10}$

2. $5\frac{5}{8}$ $+5\frac{2}{3}$

3. $8\frac{5}{6}$ $+\frac{2}{3}$

4. $6\frac{5}{6}$ $+5\frac{7}{9}$

5. $8\frac{7}{8}$ $+8\frac{5}{8}$

6. $4\frac{3}{4}$ $+2\frac{3}{5}$

7. $1\frac{5}{7}$ $+1\frac{1}{3}$

8. $8\frac{1}{2}$ $+6\frac{3}{5}$

9. $5\frac{2}{3} + 2\frac{1}{2} = \blacksquare$

10. $7\frac{3}{4} + 2\frac{3}{10} = \blacksquare$

11. $6\frac{5}{6} + 1\frac{1}{4} = \blacksquare$

12. $7\frac{9}{10} + 3\frac{4}{5} = \blacksquare$

13. $4\frac{7}{10} + 4\frac{1}{2} = \blacksquare$

14. $9\frac{5}{12} + 1\frac{7}{8} = \blacksquare$

Give a mixed numeral or standard numeral for:

$$\frac{\text{your mom's or dad's height in inches}}{\text{your height in inches}} + \frac{\text{your height in inches}}{\text{12 inches}}$$

Subtraction with Mixed Numerals: Regrouping *(pages 350–351)*

Subtract.

$$7\frac{1}{4} \rightarrow 7\frac{3}{12} \rightarrow 6\frac{15}{12}$$
$$-2\frac{5}{6} \rightarrow -2\frac{10}{12} \rightarrow 2\frac{10}{12}$$
$$4\frac{5}{12}$$

1. $7\frac{1}{6}$ $-5\frac{5}{6}$

2. 6 $-5\frac{4}{7}$

3. $9\frac{1}{6}$ $-3\frac{2}{3}$

4. $4\frac{1}{4}$ $-3\frac{3}{5}$

5. $5\frac{3}{4}$ $-1\frac{5}{6}$

6. $7\frac{5}{12}$ $-6\frac{11}{12}$

7. $4\frac{3}{10}$ $-1\frac{1}{2}$

8. $14\frac{1}{2}$ $-9\frac{3}{4}$

9. $12 - 4\frac{2}{5} = \blacksquare$

10. $14\frac{3}{4} - 12 = \blacksquare$

11. $5\frac{3}{8} - 2\frac{3}{10} = \blacksquare$

12. $6\frac{1}{4} - 3\frac{1}{3} = \blacksquare$

13. $7\frac{3}{5} - 4\frac{7}{10} = \blacksquare$

14. $2\frac{9}{10} - 1\frac{3}{4} = \blacksquare$

15. $7\frac{1}{3} - 2\frac{4}{5} = \blacksquare$

16. $2\frac{1}{5} - \frac{1}{2} = \blacksquare$

Suppose you had $4\frac{5}{8}$ cartons of juice last week. How many cartons have you had this week? Find the difference.

Multiplication with Mixed Numerals *(pages 354–355)*

Multiply.

$$2\tfrac{3}{4} \times 2\tfrac{2}{3} \quad = \tfrac{11}{4} \times \tfrac{8}{3}$$

$$7\tfrac{4}{12}$$
$$12\overline{)88}$$
$$\underline{84}$$
$$4$$

$$\tfrac{4}{12} = \tfrac{1}{3}$$

$$= \tfrac{11 \times 8}{4 \times 3}$$
$$= \tfrac{88}{12}$$
$$= 7\tfrac{4}{12}$$
$$= 7\tfrac{1}{3}$$

1. $\tfrac{2}{3} \times 4\tfrac{3}{4} = $ ■

2. $6 \times \tfrac{5}{6} = $ ■

3. $4\tfrac{2}{3} \times 1\tfrac{2}{7} = $ ■

4. $3\tfrac{4}{5} \times 2\tfrac{1}{2} = $ ■

5. $\tfrac{5}{9} \times 3\tfrac{3}{5} = $ ■

6. $8\tfrac{1}{3} \times 2\tfrac{2}{5} = $ ■

7. $\tfrac{3}{4} \times 4\tfrac{4}{5} = $ ■

8. $3\tfrac{1}{2} \times 1\tfrac{5}{7} = $ ■

9. $3\tfrac{2}{3} \times 2\tfrac{1}{2} = $ ■ **10.** $\tfrac{7}{8} \times 6\tfrac{2}{5} = $ ■ **11.** $2\tfrac{2}{5} \times 5\tfrac{5}{6} = $ ■ **12.** $3\tfrac{3}{4} \times 24 = $ ■

 Multiply $\tfrac{1}{8}$ of your age by $\tfrac{1}{9}$ of your age.

Problem Solving: Using Mixed Numerals *(pages 356–357)*

Solve.

Janet had $3\tfrac{1}{3}$ rows of green beans in her garden. She planted $2\tfrac{5}{6}$ more rows. How many rows did she have in all?

Had 3 rows. Planted 3 more rows. Add to find how many in all.

$3 + 3 = 6$

She had $6\tfrac{1}{6}$ rows in all.

Do: $3\tfrac{1}{3} + 2\tfrac{5}{6} =$

$$3\tfrac{1}{3} \rightarrow 3\tfrac{2}{6}$$
$$+2\tfrac{5}{6} \rightarrow +2\tfrac{5}{6}$$
$$5\tfrac{7}{6} = 6\tfrac{1}{6}$$

1. What is the total cost of 17.6 bags of cement? Each bag costs $4.70.

2. Ms. Hall had $35\tfrac{2}{3}$ cans of paint. How much paint was used, if she has $16\tfrac{5}{6}$ cans of paint left?

3. Marie worked $2\tfrac{1}{2}$ hours at her part-time job on Thursday. She worked $3\tfrac{3}{4}$ hours Friday and $9\tfrac{1}{6}$ hours Saturday. How many hours did she work in all?

4. A hardware store has $9\tfrac{3}{5}$ boxes of electrical switches. Each box weighs $8\tfrac{3}{4}$ lb. What is the total weight of the switches?

 Find a recipe that uses fractions to measure the ingredients. How much would you need of each ingredient if you tripled the recipe?

Unit 1 Draw a Picture *(page 12)*

1. Dave's geography text is longer than his science text but shorter than his math text. His English text is not the shortest of his books, but it is shorter than his geography text. Dave's longest book is his history text. List the books in order from shortest to longest.

2. Maria read 6 books. She started her reading with a biography on July 1, and also read a book on diving and a mystery in July. In August she read books on astronomy, skiing, and carpentry. She read the carpentry book right after the diving book. She read one book after the astronomy book. In what order did she read the books?

3. Five books are on a shelf. The authors are Scott, Lorca, Austen, Tolstoy, and Dumas. The book by Scott is just to the left of the book by Dumas. The book by Dumas is not in the middle. If exactly one book were moved, the authors' names would be in alphabetical order from left to right. In what order are the books on the shelf, from left to right?

4. A library has books on archery, baseball, basketball, hockey, skating, and soccer. The number of baseball books is greater than the number of basketball books but less than the number of skating books. Only one sport has more books than hockey. There are more basketball books than soccer books. There are two sports with fewer books than archery. List the sports books from most to least numerous.

Unit 2 Guess and Check *(page 40)*

1. Lin has some nickels. Hal has 1 more than 3 times as many nickels as Lin. In all, the value of their nickels is $.85. How many nickels does each have?

2. Stan's age is 5 more than 2 times Amy's age. Last year, Stan was 3 times as old as Amy was then. What are Stan's and Amy's ages?

3. A record plays songs A, B, and C. Songs A and C together last a total of 23 minutes. Song B is 1 minute longer than Song C. Together, songs A, B, and C last 38 minutes. Find how long each song is.

4. Evan has some dimes. The number of dimes Joel has is 2 less than twice as many as Evan has. Yuri has one more dime than Joel has. The total value of their dimes is $2.20. How many dimes does each have?

Unit 3 Solve a Simpler Problem *(page 64)*

1. Suppose you cut a pizza and all the cuts go through the center. What is the greatest number of pieces you could have by making 5 cuts?

2. If all the cuts go through the center, what is the greatest number of pieces you could have by making 8 cuts in a pizza?

3. Suppose you cut a pizza but the cuts do not have to go through the center. What is the greatest number of pieces you could have by making 5 cuts?

4. If the cuts do not have to go through the center, what is the greatest number of pieces you could have by making 8 cuts in a pizza?

Unit 4 Find a Pattern *(page 92)*

1. A train starts out empty. It picks up 1 passenger at the first stop, 3 at the second stop, 5 at the third stop, and so on. If no passengers get off, how many will there be after the fifth stop?

2. If the train continues to pick up passengers in the same pattern and makes 12 stops in all, how many passengers will there be after the twelfth stop?

3. A store uses one rule to set the sale price of all items. During the sale, a $10 sweater sells for $8 and a $30 jacket sells for $24. What would be the sale price of a $60 suit?

4. During the same sale, Steve wanted to buy a coat that regularly sells for $80. What would the sale price of the coat be?

Unit 5 **Make an Organized List** *(page 126)*

1. Ricardo is buying a shirt. He can choose a shirt made from cotton, flannel, or polyester. Each material comes in 5 solid colors: beige, rose, yellow, white, and blue. In addition, flannel comes in a tan check or green check pattern. From how many different shirts can Ricardo choose?

2. Evelyn is buying a sweater. She can buy a pullover or a cardigan made of wool, acrylic, or cashmere. The color can be rust, green, gray, blue, camel, or heather. In how many ways can Evelyn choose a sweater?

3. Janet is choosing a robe to give her sister. A robe can have either buttons or a zipper. The colors available are blue, pink, beige, green, and yellow. Any robe is available with or without pockets. From how many different robes can Janet choose?

4. Bill is buying shoes to wear to a dance. He can buy bone, gray, black, or blue shoes of suede, kid, or patent leather. He can choose either leather or composition soles. In how many ways can Bill choose a pair of shoes?

Unit 6 **Working Backwards** *(page 158)*

1. Tim plans to buy a pair of headphones and some 8-track tapes. If he has $20, what is the greatest number of 8-track tapes he can buy?

Special Prices This Week Only!	
Headphones	$9.50
90-minute cassettes	$3.50
60-minute cassettes	$2.75
8-track tapes	$4.80

2. Phil needs 4 90-minute cassettes and 2 8-track tapes. He has $35. What is the greatest number of 60-minute cassettes he can also buy?

3. Elaine has $27. She plans to buy headphones for herself and her brother. She also needs either 2 90-minute cassettes or 3 60-minute cassettes. Which can she buy along with the headphones?

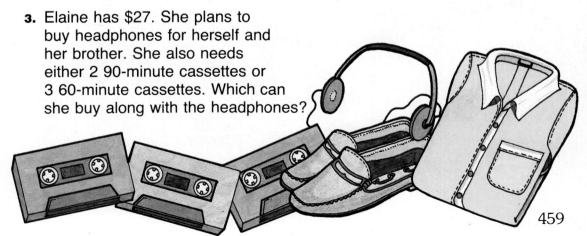

Unit 7 **Make a Table** *(page 200)*

1. A plane leaves Dallas at 3:00 P.M. and flies north at 320 km/h. A jet leaves Dallas at the same time and flies north at 500 km/h. How far apart will the plane and the jet be at 6:00 P.M.?

2. If the plane and the jet keep flying at the same speeds, at what time will the jet be 1,080 km ahead of the plane?

3. Bus A leaves Chicago at 10:00 A.M. and travels south at 50 km/h. Bus B leaves Chicago at noon and travels south at 70 km/h. At what time will bus B overtake bus A?

4. Bus C leaves Chicago at 1:00 P.M., following buses A and B south at 60 km/h. How far apart are buses B and C at 6:00 P.M.?

Unit 8 **Find a Pattern** *(page 238)*

1. A travel club has 6 members. Last month, each member spoke to every other member on the telephone exactly once. How many phone calls were made?

2. Suppose each of the 6 members sends every other member a postcard. How many postcards will be sent?

3. Suppose there were 9 members of the travel club and each sends every other member a postcard. How many postcards will be sent?

4. In June, each member of a chess club spoke to every other member on the telephone exactly once. In all, 45 phone calls were made. How many members does the club have?

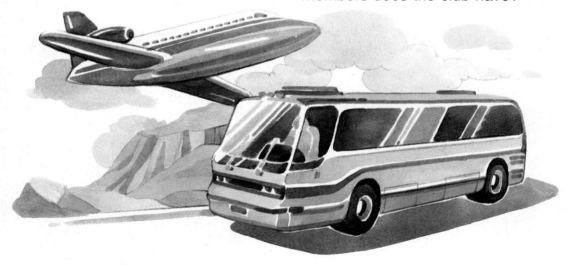

460

Unit 9 **Mixed Strategies** *(page 266)*

1. Arif drove 10 kilometers east, then 5 kilometers north, then 3 kilometers east, then 11 kilometers south, then 13 kilometers west. How far was he from his starting place?

2. Manny wants to buy a $7.50 clock. He also plans to buy 2 mugs for each of his 2 sisters. He has $22. The mugs cost $3.30 each. Can he afford all of these?

3. A piece of wire is 45 cm long. Ginny cuts a 21-cm piece off the wire. Then she cuts the 21-cm piece into two parts, so that one part is 3 cm longer than the other. How long is each piece of wire now?

4. On Monday, the Olympia Theater sold 523 adults' tickets, 241 children's tickets, and 360 senior citizens' tickets. On Tuesday, the theater sold 487 adults' tickets, 262 children's tickets, and 355 senior citizens' tickets. On which day did the theater sell more tickets?

Unit 10 **Make a Model** *(page 302)*

1. Ken made a large cube from 27 smaller cubes. He painted the top and bottom faces of the large cube green, as shown. He painted the other faces of the large cube red. Then he took the cube apart. How many of the small cubes had 1 green face?

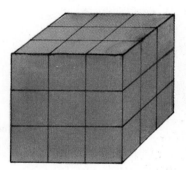

2. How many of the small cubes had only 1 red face?

3. How many of the small cubes had 2 red faces?

4. How many of the small cubes had 3 red faces?

5. How many of the small cubes had 2 red faces and 1 green face?

6. How many of the small cubes had 1 red face and 1 green face?

7. How many of the small cubes had no colored faces?

461

Unit 11 Use Logical Reasoning (page 326)

1. Mr. Lincoln, Mr. Peron, Miss Yee, Mr. Moll, and Mrs. Moll are a typist, an electrician, a zookeeper, a lawyer, and an aviator.

   Clue 1 The aviator often uses his plane to take Mr. Lincoln flying.

   Clue 2 The zookeeper is married to the lawyer.

   Clue 3 Neither Miss Yee nor Mrs. Moll has ever been to court.

   Clue 4 The electrician recently wired Mr. Lincoln's home.

   Give each person's occupation.

2. For a pot-luck party, Jo, Mick, Flora, Brad, and Regina each brought a different kind of food. The foods were bread, meatballs, salad, shrimp, and cheese.

   Clue 1 The person whose name comes last in the alphabet brought the food that comes first in the alphabet.

   Clue 2 Neither Mick nor Flora brought the cheese, and neither Brad nor Flora brought the salad.

   Clue 3 Jo did not bring salad, meatballs, or shrimp.

   Clue 4 Everyone liked the meatballs, but Jo didn't like the foods that Mick and Brad brought.

   Which food did each person bring?

Unit 12 Mixed Strategies (page 352)

1. A computer console has a row of 8 switches. Each switch can be either on or off. In how many different ways can all switches be positioned?

2. A large cube is made from 27 smaller cubes. The top, bottom, and front of the large cube are painted blue. How many of the small cubes have no blue paint?

3. A store has scarves in black, brown, tan, gray, and blue. There are more blue than tan scarves but not as many blue as gray scarves. There are 40 brown scarves. The only color of which there are more than 40 scarves is the manager's favorite color. There are more tan than black scarves. What is the manager's favorite color?

4. Rosalie has $40. She wants to buy 3 wallets for $8 each and some key rings. What is the largest number of key rings she can buy if each key ring costs $3.75?

Tables of Measure

TIME

1 minute = 60 seconds
1 hour = 60 minutes
1 day = 24 hours
1 week = 7 days
1 year = 12 months = 52 weeks
1 century = 100 years

METRIC UNITS

Length

1 centimeter (cm) = 10 millimeters (mm)
1 meter (m) = 100 centimeters
1 kilometer (km) = 1,000 meters

Mass

1 kilogram (kg) = 1,000 grams (g)

Liquid volume

1 liter (L) = 1,000 milliliters (mL)

Temperature

At 0 degrees Celsius (°C), water freezes.
At 100 degrees Celsius (°C), water boils.

CUSTOMARY UNITS

Length

1 foot (ft) = 12 inches (in.)
1 yard (yd) = 3 feet = 36 inches
1 mile (mi) = 1,760 yards = 5,280 feet

Weight

1 pound (lb) = 16 ounces (oz)
1 ton (tn) = 2,000 pounds

Liquid volume

1 cup (c) = 8 fluid ounces
1 pint (pt) = 2 cups
1 quart (qt) = 2 pints = 4 cups
1 gallon (gal) = 4 quarts

Temperature

At 32 degrees Fahrenheit (°F), water freezes.
At 212 degrees Fahrenheit (°F), water boils.

Estimation Strategies

Strategy	Examples
1. Rounding	$59.77 ··· about $60 ··· The difference is about $50. − 11.38 ··· about $10
	$\frac{7}{8}$ ··· about 1 The sum is almost 2. $+\frac{5}{6}$ ··· about 1
2. Comparison	402 ··· more than 400 ··· The sum is more than 600. +213 ··· more than 200
3. Clustering	538 ⎤ 87 ⎤ ··· about 1,000 The sum is about 1,100. 465 ⎦ + 20 ⎦ ··· about 100
4. Compatible Numbers	$13\overline{)2{,}598}$ 2,598 is close to 2,600. It is easier to do: $13\overline{)2{,}600}$ The quotient is a little less than 200.
5. Reasonable in Context	The cost of 12 records at $5.98 each is: **a.** $.50 **b.** $17.98 **c.** $717.60 **d.** $71.76 The records cost about $6 each. $6 \times (10 + 2) = \$72$ Answer **d.** is the most reasonable.

Mental Math Strategies

Strategy	Examples
1. Work from left to right.	$4,608$ $+7,379$ $11,000 + 900 + 70 + 17 = 11,987$ The sum is 11,987.
2. Start with the first number and add or subtract from left to right.	$3,574 + 895 = \blacksquare$ $3,574 + 800 = 4,374$ $\qquad 4,374 + 90 = 4,464$ $\qquad\qquad 4,464 + 5 = 4,469$ The sum is 4,469.
	$4,709 - 3,842 = \blacksquare$ $4,709 - 3,000 = 1,709$ $\quad 1,709 - 800 = 909$ $\qquad 909 - 40 = 869$ $\qquad 869 - 2 = 867$ The difference is 867.
3. Compensate: Add or subtract from the given numbers to work with easier numbers. (In subtraction make the bottom number the easy number.)	$\begin{array}{rl} 8,496 & +4 = 8,500 \\ +4,254 & -4 = +4,250 \\ \hline & 12,750 \end{array}$ The sum is 12,750.
	$\begin{array}{rl} 6,748 & +2 = 6,750 \\ -398 & +2 = -400 \\ \hline & 6,350 \end{array}$ The difference is 6,350.
4. Use the distributive property.	$13 \times 435 = \blacksquare$ 13 is 10 + 3. $\begin{array}{rl} 10 \times 435 = & 4,350 \\ 3 \times 435 = & +1,305 \\ \hline & 5,655 \end{array}$ The product is 5,655.
	$4 \times 307 = \blacksquare$ 307 is 300 + 7. $\begin{array}{rl} 4 \times 300 = & 1,200 \\ 4 \times 7 = & +28 \\ \hline & 1,228 \end{array}$ The product is 1,228.

Glossary

A

Addition An operation on two or more numbers that tells how many in all or how much in all. Addition exercises are written in vertical or horizontal form.

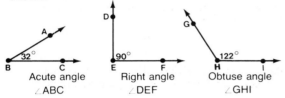

Angle A figure formed by two rays with the same endpoint. The *degree measures* of these angles are shown.

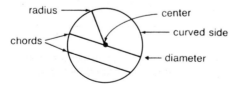

Acute angle   Right angle   Obtuse angle
∠ABC   ∠DEF   ∠GHI

Area The number of square units it takes to cover the inside of a figure.

For a rectangle: Area = length × width

B

Basic Facts Additions, subtractions, multiplications, or divisions where two of the three numbers are 9 or less:

$$\begin{array}{cccc} 9 & 14 & 8 & 7 \\ +6 & -8 & \times 7 & 9\overline{)63} \\ \hline 15 & 6 & 56 & \end{array}$$

C

Circle A plane figure shaped like this.

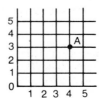

radius —   — center
                — curved side
chords —
                — diameter

Coordinate Grid A picture of lines that cross at right angles and regular intervals. The lines are numbered so that positions can be located.

The *number pair* (4,3) locates point A.

Common Denominator Two fractions that have the same denominator are said to have a common denominator.

Composite Number A whole number such as 6 that has factors other than 1 and the number itself.

Computer Literacy Knowledge of what computers can and cannot do, how computers operate, how to communicate with computers, and how to use computers to solve problems.

Congruent Figures Figures that have exactly the same size and shape.

Cone An object that looks like this.

curved face
flat face

Counting Numbers Any of the numbers 1, 2, 3, . . . 58, 59, 60, . . . 144, 145, 146, . . . used in counting.

Cube A special kind of rectangular prism. Each face of a cube is a square.

Curve A continuous path. A path that can be drawn without lifting the pencil.

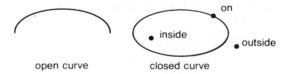

on
inside
outside

open curve   closed curve

Points can be inside, outside, or on a closed curve.

Customary Measurement System The measurement system that uses inches, feet, yards, and miles as units of length; fluid ounces, cups, pints, quarts, and gallons as units of liquid volume; ounces, pounds, and tons as units of weight; degrees Fahrenheit (°F) as units of temperature; and seconds, minutes, weeks, months, years, and centuries as units of time.

Cylinder An object shaped like this. The flat faces of a cylinder are circles.

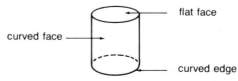

flat face
curved face
curved edge

D

Decimal A place value numeral that includes tenths, or tenths and hundredths, or tenths, hundredths, and thousandths.

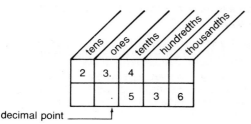

decimal point

Digit Any of the symbols 0, 1, 2, 3, 4, 5, 6, 7, 8, or 9.

Distance The distance between two points is the length of the straight path joining the points.

Division An operation on two numbers that tells how many sets with the same number of objects can be formed from a given number of objects, and how many objects are left over.

$$\text{quotient} \rightarrow \quad 7 \ \text{R1} \leftarrow \text{remainder}$$
$$\text{divisor} \rightarrow 5\overline{)36} \leftarrow \text{dividend}$$

Division also tells how many objects in each set and how many left over when a given number of sets of the same size are formed from a given number of objects.

When 0 objects are left over, a division exercise can be written as:

$$\begin{array}{cc} 5 \ \text{R0} & 5 \\ 7\overline{)35} & 7\overline{)35} \end{array} \qquad 35 \div 7 = 5$$

E

Equal (is, =) Exactly the same.

Even Numbers Any of the whole numbers, 0, 2, 4, 6, 8, . . .

Equivalent Fractions Two or more fractions that name the same part of an object or set.

Expanded Form A form showing the meaning of a standard numeral as a sum.

Standard numeral	Expanded numeral
256	200 + 50 + 6
	or $(2 \times 100) + (5 \times 10) + 6$

F

Flowchart A visual way to show the steps used in carrying out an activity.

Fraction A symbol such as $\frac{1}{2}, \frac{1}{3}, \frac{2}{3}, \frac{1}{4}, \frac{3}{4}$ that names part of an object or set.

$$\text{numerator} \rightarrow \ 1 \ \begin{array}{l} \leftarrow \text{number of equal pieces} \\ \leftarrow \text{in the part named} \end{array}$$
$$\text{denominator} \rightarrow \ 2 \ \begin{array}{l} \leftarrow \text{number of equal pieces in} \\ \text{the whole object or set} \end{array}$$

G

Graph A picture used to show data. Types of graphs are bar graphs, line graphs, pictographs, and circle graphs.

Greater Than (>) One of the two basic relations for comparing numbers that are not the same. *See Also* Less Than (<).

$$7 > 5 \qquad \frac{2}{3} > \frac{1}{3}$$

Greatest Common Factor The largest number that is a common factor of two or more numbers.

I

Intersecting Lines Lines that have a common point.

L

Length The measure of an object from end to end. The inch, foot, yard, mile, and millimeter, centimeter, meter, and kilometer are standard units for measuring length.

Less Than (<) One of the two basic relations for comparing numbers that are not the same. *See Also* Greater Than (>).

$$5 < 7 \qquad \frac{1}{3} < \frac{2}{3}$$

Line (straight) The figure that results from extending a line segment in both directions.

$\overleftrightarrow{AB}$, or $\overleftrightarrow{BA}$, names this line. The arrowheads indicate that it goes on forever in both directions.

Line Segment The straight path from one point to another.

A   B

$\overline{AB}$ and $\overline{BA}$ name the line segments with endpoints A and B.

Line of Symmetry A line that separates a figure into two parts that will fit exactly on each other. The two parts formed by a line of symmetry are *congruent*.

Liquid Capacity The amount of liquid a container will hold.

Liquid Volume The number of unit containers a given amount of liquid will fill. The fluid ounce, cup, pint, quart, gallon, and milliliter and liter are standard units for finding liquid volume.

Lowest Terms Fraction A fraction with numerator and denominator having no common factor greater than 1.

M

Metric Measurement System The measurement system that uses millimeters, centimeters, meters, and kilometers as units of length; milliliters and liters as units of liquid volume; grams, kilograms, and metric tons as units of mass; degrees Celsius (°C) as units of temperature; and seconds, minutes, hours, days, weeks, months, years, and centuries as units of time.

Mixed Numeral A symbol for a number greater than 1, formed using a standard numeral and a fraction.

$$4\frac{2}{3} \qquad 1\frac{5}{6} \qquad 12\frac{1}{2}$$

A *lowest terms mixed numeral* contains a lowest terms fraction for less than 1.

Multiple Multiples of a number are formed by multiplying the number by whole numbers. Some multiples of 3 are 3, 6, 9, 12, 27, and 33.

Multiplication An operation on two numbers that tells how many in all when one number is the number of sets and the other number is the number in each set. Multiplication exercises are written in vertical or horizontal form.

$$
\begin{array}{r}
.4 \leftarrow \text{factor} \\
\text{times} \rightarrow \times\ \underline{.3} \leftarrow \text{factor} \\
.12 \leftarrow \text{product}
\end{array}
\qquad .3 \times .4 = .12
$$

N

Number Line A line showing numbers in order.

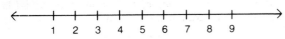

Number Sentence A completed exercise written in horizontal form.

Numeral A symbol for a number.

O

Odd Number Any of the whole numbers 1, 3, 5, 7, 9, . . .

P

Parallel Lines Lines in a plane that never meet.

Parallelogram A quadrilateral with opposite sides parallel and equal in length.

Parentheses ( ) Symbols of grouping. Parentheses tell which operation to perform first.

$$(6 - 4) - 1 = 2 - 1 \qquad 6 - (4 - 1) = 6 - 3$$
$$\uparrow \qquad\qquad\qquad \uparrow$$
$$\text{Do first} \qquad\qquad\quad \text{Do first}$$

Percent Per hundred. 30% = .30

Perimeter The sum of the lengths of the sides of a figure.

Perpendicular Lines Lines that meet to form right angles.

Place Value The value given to the place in which a digit appears in a numeral. The digit 9 is in the thousands place in 9,752.

Plane A flat surface.

Points A point is an exact location. Capital letters are used to name points. The picture shows points A and B.　A ·　　　　· B

Polygon A plane figure with *sides* that are line segments. Each pair of sides meet at a *vertex*. Triangles, quadrilaterals, pentagons, hexagons, octagons, and decagons are polygons.

Prime Number A whole number such as 7 that is divisible only by 1 and the number itself.

Probability A number 0 through 1 that tells how likely it is that something will happen.

Protractor An instrument used to measure angles.

Pyramid (square-based) An object shaped like this.

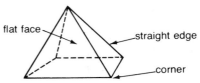

Four of the faces of a pyramid are triangles; one face is a square.

Q

Quadrilateral Any closed figure with four straight sides on the same plane.

R

Ray The figure that results from extending a line segment in one direction. A ray has one endpoint and goes on forever in one direction.

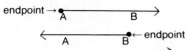

$\overrightarrow{AB}$ names the ray with endpoint A. $\overrightarrow{BA}$ names the ray with endpoint B.

Rectangle A quadrilateral with four right angles. Opposite sides of a rectangle are parallel and equal in length.

Rectangular Prism An object with square corners shaped like a box.

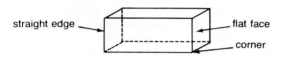

Each face of a rectangular prism is a rectangle.

Regroup Use ones to form 1 set of ten, or use 1 set of ten to form ten ones. You can also regroup tens as hundreds and hundreds as tens, hundreds as thousands and thousands as hundreds, and so on.

Roman Numerals The symbols I, V, X, . . ., that the Romans used to name whole numbers.

I = 1	V = 5	X = 10
IV = 4	VII = 7	XXIX = 29

Rounding Replacing a number by the nearest multiple of ten, one hundred, one thousand, etc.

3,529 rounded to the nearest ten is 3,530.
3,529 rounded to the nearest hundred is 3,500.
3,529 rounded to the nearest thousand is 4,000.

S

Sphere An object shaped like this.

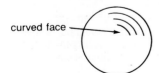

Square A rectangle with all sides the same length.

Standard Numeral A numeral for a whole number formed using the digits 0–9 and a place value system. Any whole number can be expressed by writing a digit 0–9 in the ones place for the number of ones, in the tens place for the number of tens, . . .

Statistics A part of mathematics that includes describing, picturing, and drawing conclusions from sets of information, or data.

Subtraction An operation on two numbers that tells how many are left when some are taken away, or how much is left when some is taken away. Subtraction exercises are written in vertical or horizontal form.

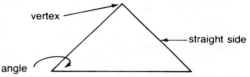

$$7 - 5 = 2$$

Subtraction is used to solve *take away* and *comparison* story problems and to answer the question "How many more are needed?" in story problems.

T

Triangle A plane figure with three straight sides.

An *acute* triangle has three acute angles.
A *right* triangle has one right angle.
An *obtuse* triangle has one obtuse angle.
An *equilateral triangle* has three sides of equal lengths.
An *isosceles* triangle has at least two sides of equal lengths.
A *scalene* triangle has three sides of different lengths.

V

Venn Diagram A graph that uses circles to show relations between and operations on sets.

Vertex Corner point of a figure.

Volume The number of unit cubes that would fit inside an object if it were hollow.

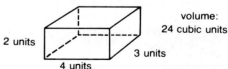

For a rectangular prism: Volume = length × width × height.

W

Whole Number Any of the numbers 0, 1, 2, 3, 4, . . . 47, 48, 49, . . . 170, 171, 172, . . .

Index